When Young People
Break the Law

When Young People Break the Law

Debating Issues on Punishment for Juveniles

Karsten J. Struhl and Kimora, editors

International Debate Education Association

New York, London & Amsterdam

Published by
The International Debate Education Association
P.O. Box 922
New York, NY 10009

This book is published with the generous support of the Open Society Foundations.

Library of Congress Cataloging-in-Publication Data
When young people break the law : debating issues on punishment for juveniles/
Karsten J. Struhl and Kimora, editors.
    pages cm
    ISBN 978-1-61770-097-2
    1. Juvenile justice, Administration of—United States.   2. Juvenile delinquents—
United States.   3. Punishment—United States.   I. Struhl, Karsten J.   II. Kimora,
1956–
    HV9104.W482 2014
    364.360973—dc23   2014031637

Composition by Brad Walrod/Kenoza Type, Inc.
Printed in the USA

IDEBATE Press

Contents

Acknowledgments

We want to express our deepest gratitude to Eleanora von Dehsen who shepherded this book from its inception and whose insightful editorial comments helped shape its final form. Our special thanks to Martin Greenwald for inviting us to do this project and for his endless patience. We also want to thank Jordon Breslow, Glenn Novak, and Maeghan Donohue for their essential help in the preparation of this manuscript. In addition, we want to thank Tziporah Kasachkoff and Jonathan Jacobs for agreeing to write original articles for this book. Many thanks to Olga Bukhina for her continuous support on this project. Kimora also wants to thank Srijan, her soul mate.

Introduction

The degree of civilization in a society can be judged by entering its prisons.

— Fyodor Dostoyevsky, *The House of the Dead,* 1862

History will judge us by the difference we make in the everyday lives of children.

— Nelson Mandela, at a luncheon for a special session of the UN for children, New York City, May 9, 2002

With only 5 percent of the world's population, the United States has almost 25 percent of the world's prisoners. The comparison becomes even more striking when we compare specific countries. The incarceration rate in the United States is about 750 persons per 100,000. Russia, which is the country with the next highest incarceration rate, has a little over 600 persons for every 100,000. Countries like Iran and Mexico each have about 200 persons incarcerated for every 100,000. China has just over 100 persons incarcerated for every 100,000. If we compare the United States to other modern industrialized nations, we find that its incarceration rate is six to ten times higher.

Furthermore, there has been a huge increase in the general incarceration rate since 1972, when the United States had fewer than 350,000 prisoners. Today the figure is between 2 million and 2.5 million prisoners. Many of these new prisoners are juveniles, although, in fact, there has been a decline in juvenile incarceration from a high of 107,637 in 1995 to 70,792 in 2010.[1] Still, the juvenile rate of incarceration per 100,000 is 336, compared to 46.8 in England and Wales, 23.1 in Germany, 11.3 in Italy, 4.1 in Sweden, and 3.6 in Finland.[2] Overall, even with the decline in incarceration, "the United States still incarcerates more young people than does any other industrialized nation—seven times the rate of Great Britain and eighteen times that of France—spending a total of $5 billion a year to keep kids . . . in juvenile institutions. Even our closest competitor, South Africa, incarcerates its children at one-fifth the rate of the voracious United States."[3]

It should not be surprising that the juveniles who are tried, convicted, and incarcerated come disproportionately from communities of color and the poor. Of those juveniles incarcerated, two out of five are African American, and one out of five are Hispanic. According to the U.S. Bureau of Justice Statistics, in 2007, while 820 white juveniles per 100,000 were incarcerated, the number for African Americans incarcerated per 100,000 was 5,126, and for Hispanics the number was 1,907.[4] Is this just a reflection of the difference between white, black, and brown criminality? But African American juveniles are detained 4.5 times more than their white counterparts and have a much higher rate of incarceration *for the same offenses*; for example, they are nine times as likely to be incarcerated for crimes against persons, four times as likely for property crimes, and forty-eight times as likely for drug offenses.[5]

What happens to these young people when they are incarcerated? The basic answer is that they suffer horrible physical and mental abuse. They are beaten and sexually abused. In fact, the rates of sexual abuse by members of the staff are higher in juvenile than in adult prisons. According to a national survey by the U.S. Department of Justice, 35 percent of juveniles in juvenile detention facilities were placed in solitary confinement, which is considered a form of torture by the United Nations.[6] According to the American Academy of Child and Adolescent Psychiatry, juveniles in solitary detention are particularly at risk for depression, anxiety, and psychosis.[7]

The stated goal of the juvenile justice system has been to rehabilitate juvenile offenders. However, there is good reason to believe that far from rehabilitating these young people, juvenile detention centers are more likely to be incubators of future criminal activity. It is estimated that 80 to 90 percent of all teenagers have committed illegal acts that would qualify for some time in prison. However, most eventually grow out of this delinquent stage *if they do not end up in prison*. On the other hand, those who do go to prison are more likely to become criminals as adults. Multiple studies have shown that 70 to 80 percent of youth who are incarcerated return to prison within two or three years.[8] "The single most significant factor in predicting whether youth will offend again is incarceration—more than family difficulties or gang membership."[9] This can be explained in several ways. First, incarcerating a juvenile makes the problems that contributed to the crime even worse, so that it is more likely that he or she will commit more crimes in the future. For example, a juvenile whose criminal behavior stems in part from a sense of isolation will experience more severe isolation in prison. Second, incarceration is fundamentally a dehumanizing and traumatic experience. The young person is removed from his home and community, given a number, wears a drab uniform, is put in a cage, and is the subject of continuous surveillance and often arbitrary physical and mental abuse. For the adolescent "incarceration is *intrinsically* traumatizing.... The years teenagers spend locked away in juvenile prisons are exactly those in which a young person's sense of himself and the world might crystalize, with tremendous implications for who he will become as an adult."[10] Third, the young person is aware that society now regards him as "the other," as someone who is less than human and, therefore, is much less amenable to considering himself or herself a responsible member of the society. "Airlifted out of their homes and communities, hidden away behind bars and high fences, young prisoners experience what sociologists call social death—'the condition of people not accepted as fully human by wider society.'"[11] Fourth, the rigid rules and authoritarian structure of prisons undermine the ability of young people to develop critical-thinking skills and the sense of autonomy needed for taking responsibility. Finally, thrown together with other juveniles who break the law, the young person learns new skills of criminal behavior. In all, the juvenile justice system fails to achieve its goal of rehabilitating young people who break the law and of deterring them from committing future criminal acts. How did this happen? How did we devise a system that is so counter to its stated aims?

THE JUVENILE JUSTICE SYSTEM: HISTORICAL BACKGROUND

The first step in the creation of what was to become the juvenile justice system in the United States was the establishment in New York in 1825 of the House of Refuge by the Society for the Prevention of Juvenile Delinquency. Its stated mission was to rescue young people from adult prisons and provide a "home" environment that would have the result of reducing juvenile crime. Within a few years, almost every major city in the country had a house of refuge. However, there was no clear distinction made between juveniles convicted of crimes and those who were simply considered at risk for criminal behavior. As a result, many young people who were sent to these houses of refuge were "convicted" simply of being "disorderly" or were brought there because they were destitute or were vagrants or had parents who were considered unfit to provide adequate supervision. Furthermore, not all juvenile criminals qualified for admittance to a house of refuge. Those juveniles who committed only minor crimes were judged not yet truly criminal and were seen as individuals who could still be rescued. In contrast, those juveniles who committed more serious crimes were generally assumed to be incapable of being rescued and were sent to adult prison facilities.

There were, however, several problems with these houses of refuge. The first was that they operated under the doctrine of *parens patriae*, which saw the state as the ultimate parent whenever the natural parents were deemed incapable of providing adequate supervision. This doctrine gave the government not only the right but the "duty to intervene in the lives of *all* children who might become a community crime problem."[12] The result was that these houses of refuge had almost unlimited power to commit young people, without any possible legal recourse. The second problem was that while the goal was to establish a "home-like" environment, these houses of refuge took on some of the harsher aspects of adult prisons, with excessive solitary confinement, whippings, and other forms of severe physical punishment. In reaction to this second problem, a group of reformers in Chicago established the Chicago Reform School in 1855. These reformers advocated the creation of state juvenile facilities in place of privately run houses of refuges, facilities that would organize small living groups for the purpose of creating a family life for juveniles.

The latter part of the nineteenth century was an era in which a huge wave of immigrants, especially from Southern and Eastern Europe, entered some of the major cities of the United States, including New York, Boston, Chicago, and Philadelphia. It was also a time when significant internal migration from rural to urban America occurred. These movements presented a number of challenges and raised serious questions about how to assimilate these newcomers. One of the basic questions was what to do with the children of these immigrants, who often acted in ways that were against the standard norms of social behavior in urban America. At the same time, a number of progressive reformers began to redefine adolescence. Adolescents, according to many of these reformers, were not so much small adults as they were developing children who needed care and protection. Thus, when young people broke the law, they were considered less culpable than adults. The emphasis was put not on punishing these juveniles but identifying the social causes behind their behavior and rehabilitating them. They were to be regarded not as criminals but as "delinquents" in need of help and support. The efforts of this progressive reform movement culminated in the Illinois state legislature passing the Juvenile Court Act in 1899. This act was the first comprehensive child legislation and established the first juvenile family court with authority over delinquent youths. By 1917, juvenile court legislation existed in almost every state in the United States.

The Juvenile Court Act also echoed the concerns of the Chicago Reform School, stating as its purpose "that the care, custody, and discipline of a child shall approximate as nearly as may be that which should be given by its parents."[13] However, while there was now judicial oversight, "juvenile court philosophy still made no distinction between criminal and non-criminal behavior, as long as the behavior was deviant or inappropriate to the age of the juvenile."[14] This meant that forms of behavior that would not be criminalized for adults could now be the basis for juvenile court intervention—for example, smoking, sexual activity, running away from home, and truancy. Furthermore, juveniles could be put on probation or incarcerated indefinitely until they were adults. They would be released only when they were certified as "rehabilitated." Finally, trial by jury was not available in most juvenile courts, and there were very few of the procedural protections that existed in adult criminal courts.

The ideology of the juvenile court was stated succinctly by Judge Julian W. Mack in 1909: "The problem for determination by the judge is not, Has this boy or girl committed a specific wrong, but What is he, how has he become what he is, and what had best be done in his interests and in the interest of the state to save him from a downward career."[15] The question, of course, was which interest was to take precedence: the interest of the juvenile or the interest of the state. The answer soon became clear. The real function of juvenile court was social control of the urban poor. Whatever the subjective intentions of the early social reformers, their ability to enact these reforms depended in large part on members of the upper class who understood that such reforms served their interests in maintaining the status quo and defusing challenges from below. In fact, it has been argued that the progressive reforms of the juvenile justice system "tried to do for the criminal justice system what industrialists and corporate leaders were trying to do for the economy—that is, achieve order, stability, and control while preserving the existing class system and distribution of wealth."[16]

THE TRANSFORMATION OF THE JUVENILE COURT SYSTEM AND ITS PROBLEMS

We have now discussed the two landmark reforms that established the juvenile justice system—the establishment of the House of Refuge in 1825 and the establishment of a juvenile court system by the Juvenile Court Act in 1899. The third major landmark reform was the U.S. Supreme Court decision in 1967, officially referred to as *In re Gault*, that established for the first time the constitutional requirement that there be significant due process protections for juveniles within the juvenile court system.

The case brought before the Court was that of Gerald Gault, who in 1964 was arrested in Gila County, Arizona, after a neighbor complained that he had made an obscene telephone call to her, a charge that he denied. He was at this time only fourteen years old. Gault's parents were never notified of the arrest, and his mother, who did not know why he had not returned home, finally found him at the Children's Detention Home. Some days later, a judge ordered him to be incarcerated in a juvenile facility until he was twenty-one years old, on the basis of the charge itself. The neighbor who accused him did not come to the hearing, and so Gault never had an opportunity to confront his accuser. He was not provided with any means to defend himself in the court. In short, Gault did not have any of the procedural protections that would be available to adults in an ordinary criminal court. Furthermore, had he been an adult convicted of the same crime in Arizona, he would have been sentenced to no more than a fifty dollar fine and two months in jail.

Gault's parents filed a writ of habeas corpus, and his case eventually went to the Supreme Court, which in 1967 ruled in his favor. *In re Gault* set an important precedent, insisting that juveniles who faced possible incarceration are entitled to the same procedural rights as adults under the due process clause of the Fourteenth Amendment, especially the right to an attorney. The perhaps unintended result of this decision was to begin the process of transforming the juvenile court, where the accused had almost no procedural rights, into something more like a criminal court with constitutional guarantees of due process protections.

But to what extent did juveniles actually receive due process protections after the *Gault* decision? The answer, although it varied from state to state, is very little. As Barry C. Feld, a professor of law at the University of Minnesota Law School and an eminent scholar of juvenile justice, puts it, "For more than two decades since *Gault*, juvenile courts have defected, co-opted, ignored, or accommodated constitutional and legislative reforms with minimal institutional change. Despite its transformation from a welfare agency into a criminal court, the juvenile court remains essentially unreformed."[17]

To make the *Gault* decision a reality in providing due process protections for juveniles would require, at the very least, affording the accused juvenile the opportunity to have a jury trial, as "the most striking difference between juvenile court adjudications and those in criminal court is the lack of a jury trial for juveniles."[18] However, despite *Gault*, there has been very little move in this direction. At present, juvenile courts in thirty-one states afford no right to jury trial, eleven states provide jury trials for juveniles only under special circumstances, while only nine states provide the right to a jury trial, and even in those states there are a number of exceptions.[19] This presents a number of problems for the accused. First, without a jury trial, the juvenile has no protection against the whims or biases of a judge. Second, while a conviction by a jury is subject to appeal if there is an error in the judge's instruction, no such review is possible when the judge alone makes the decision on the guilt or innocence of the accused. Finally, juries are less likely to convict than judges, and judges, because they have often too many cases to consider, are less likely than jurors to carefully weigh all the evidence.[20]

Overall, the transformation of the juvenile court into a quasi-criminal court has neither advanced the goal of rehabilitation nor provided adequate protections for the accused. One year earlier than the *In re Gault* decision, the U.S. Supreme Court observed that a juvenile who enters the juvenile justice system gets "the worst of both worlds: he gets neither the protections accorded to adults nor the solicitous care and regenerative treatment postulated for children."[21] Although *Gault* did open a constitutional space for reforms, the juvenile court system has not changed very much, and the accused juvenile is still put in the position of "the worst of both worlds."

The recognition that this is still the case has led some liberal reformers to give up the hope of reform and advocate the abolition of the juvenile court. For example, reflecting on the failure of the juvenile court system to implement meaningful reforms since *Gault*, Feld argues that "the fundamental shortcoming of the traditional juvenile court is not a failure of implementation but a failure of conception.... Historical analyses of juvenile justice suggest that when social services and social control are combined in one setting, social welfare considerations quickly are subordinated to custodial ones."[22] Feld proposes that juveniles instead be tried in criminal courts, where they can receive the due process protections that adults are accorded, but that laws be passed to provide "youth discounts" at sentencing so that, depending on their age, juveniles would receive proportionately less punishment than adults who committed the same crime. The problem is that many conservatives also advocate the abolition of the juvenile court, but their reasons are quite different. The juvenile offender, says the conservative, has been too often given a "slap on the wrist" and instead should be given "adult time for adult crimes."

MORAL PANIC AND THE FEAR OF THE SUPER-PREDATOR IN THE 1980S AND 1990S

> What is happening to our young people? They disrespect their elders, they disobey their parents. They ignore the law. They riot in the streets, inflamed with wild notions. Their morals are decaying. What is to become of them?
>
> —Plato, *Laws*

The British psychologist and TV presenter Tanya Byron suggests that adults often suffer from ephebiphobia—the fear of young people. While, as the quotation above indicates, this fear has a long historical reach, it has taken on new dimensions in contemporary society, where "our anxieties are fueled by stories and images of violent and aggressive crimes. And then we label children as troublemakers or failures."[23] In the 1980s and 1990s this fear became especially exaggerated, and the situation became more serious for juveniles in the juvenile justice system.

During these two decades in the United States there was an increase in juvenile crime, partly as the result of the greater availability of crack cocaine and guns. The news media was filled with stories of the most horrific sorts of crimes, and some criminal justice researchers began projecting the rise of a new kind of "super-predator," juveniles who banded together to form temporary gangs who went on wild sprees of robbery and violence and who could do the most terrible things for the most trivial reasons. In fact, these projections were wrong, as between 1995 and 2004, violent juvenile crimes fell by 45 percent. Nonetheless, the exaggerated *fear* of the "super-predator," which some sociologist have termed a "moral panic," had a significant effect on the politicians, who in state after state passed laws that punished juveniles more severely. The age of judicial transfer from juvenile to criminal court was lowered in many states to fourteen and sometimes even younger, and the list of crimes for which they could be transferred was increased. In a number of states, the legislature mandated automatic transfers for certain crimes, so that more and more young people were treated as adult criminals. One result of this was the imposition of "life without parole" for juveniles who committed homicide, or sometimes for juveniles who simply were present at the commission of the homicide.[24]

THE PROBLEM OF PUNISHING YOUNG PEOPLE

This brings us to the general questions: What should we do with young people who break the law? How severely should they be punished? Are there reasonable alternatives to punishing juveniles who break the law? There are no simple answers to these questions, and, in fact, they are the subject of intense debate.

In this book, we begin with two questions about punishment in general. Part 1 asks us to consider the question of what exactly is punishment. The question is not merely a request for a definition, but for criteria by which we can determine when something is punishment and when it is not. The articles in this section raise a number of questions about these criteria. For example, are there any necessary and sufficient conditions for the application of the term, or does the concept vary according to context? Is there a difference between a parent who punishes a child and the criminal justice system punishing a lawbreaker? Is punishing an innocent person still punishment? Is demanding reparations from the offender a form of punishment, or is it a possible alternative to punishment?

Without some clarity on these and other such questions, debates about punishment often speak at cross-purposes. For example, the debate over whether juveniles should receive the same kind of punishment as adults will be unproductive if the opponents mean different things by punishment—if, say, one of debaters thinks that mandating community service is not a form of punishment, while the other debater thinks it is. Again, the debate about whether there are any reasonable alternatives to punishment will be confused if one side of the debate thinks that reparation is a form of punishment, while the other side thinks that it is not.

Part 2 of the book focuses on whether punishment can ever be justified and, if so, how? When debating the issues concerning whether juveniles should or should not receive certain kinds of punishment, it is important to consider what, if anything, might justify punishment. When debating whether the juvenile justice system should be reformed, it is important to consider what theory of punishment makes most sense. When debating whether there are any reasonable alternatives to punishment for juveniles (or for anyone else), it is important to consider whether any of the attempts to justify punishment are reasonable. This section poses a debate between those who would defend a retributive theory of punishment—where punishment is justified as payback for what the offender did, as what the offender deserves simply as a result of the offense—and those who would offer some alternative theory: a deterrence theory, where punishment is justified as a way to deter potential offenders from committing crimes; or a rehabilitative, or moral education, theory, where punishment has as its main goal to change the offender into someone who respects the moral and legal norms of society. Some of the alternatives represented by the selections in this section are, in fact, hybrid theories that combine two or more justifications of punishment. This section also considers the possibility that the motive for punishing has more to do with revenge than most people who advocate punishment would like to admit, a possibility that suggests that at least the retributive justification for punishment is problematic.

After discussing these philosophical questions about punishment in general, we move in parts 3, 4, and 5 of this book to a number of specific debates concerning the punishment of juveniles. Part 3 considers whether or not juveniles who commit a crime should receive a lesser punishment than adults. Specifically, it presents the debate between conservative thinkers, who argue for abolishing the juvenile court system and trying juveniles as adults, and liberal thinkers, who argue that juveniles do not belong in the criminal court system and should not receive the same penalty as an adult who committed the same crime.

Part 4 focuses on a question that has plagued the U.S. Supreme Court and which is fiercely debated today—should juveniles, even if they have done some horrible crime, ever receive a sentence of life without the possibility of parole? The debate in this section pits the families of the victims of these crimes, who argue that to allow the possibility of parole is unjust to the victims, against those who argue that such sentences are fundamentally unfair to the juvenile offender and ignore recent social scientific and neuropsychological research.

Part 5 considers the possibilities and ways that the juvenile justice system can be reformed. While each of the articles in this section is in favor of some kind of change, they offer different assessments and solutions to the problem— respectively, playing down the punitive aspect and returning to the original reha- bilitative intent of the juvenile justice system, developing an intermediate legal category of juvenile offenders who are held responsible for their crimes but whose youth is taken into account as a mitigating factor, and developing a cognitive skills education program as a significant component of the rehabilitative process.

Finally, part 6 asks what is perhaps the most difficult and vexing question: Are there reasonable alternatives to punishment? The first article in this sec- tion argues that social policies that address the economic, social, cultural, and psychological causes of crime in conjunction with institutional forms of symbolic condemnation, victim-offender reconciliation programs, and mandating that the offender pay compensation (reparations) to the victim would be a reasonable alternative to punishment. The second article argues that the standard justifica- tions for punishment—the retributive justification, deterrence, and moral educa- tion (rehabilitation)—would all be better served by a system of legal reparations.

As the reader will soon discover, the articles in this book present a set of arguments on both sides—or sometimes more than two sides—of the issues. We hope that the reader will approach these selections with his or her own critical thinking, engage in the debate, but also be willing to explore the issues more deeply in the spirit of continued dialogue.

NOTES

1. Amanda Paulson, "Why Juvenile Incarceration Reached Its Lowest Rate in 38 Years," *Christian Science Monitor*, February 27, 2013.
2. Anna Aizer and Joseph Doyle, "What Is the Long-Term Impact of Incarcerating Juveniles?," *Vox: Research-Based Policy Analysis and Commentary Analysis from Leading Economists*, July 16, 2013, http://www.voxeu.org/article/what-long-term-impact-incarcerating-juveniles.
3. Nell Bernstein, *Burning Down the House: The End of Juvenile Prison* (New York: New Press, 2014), 12–13.
4. Hanna Holleman, Robert W. McChesney, John Bellamy Foster, and R. Jamil Jonna, "The Penal State in an Age of Crisis," *Monthly Review* 61, no. 2 (June 2009): 15.
5. Bernstein, *Burning Down the House*, 60.
6. Ibid., 132.

7. Ibid., 131.

8. Ibid., 182.

9. Ibid., 7.

10. Ibid., 308.

11. Ibid., 315.

12. Sanford J. Fox, "Juvenile Justice Reform: A Historical Perspective," *Stanford Law Review* 25, no. 6 (June 1970): 1190.

13. Ibid., 1211.

14. Janet E. Ainsworth, "Re-Imagining Childhood and Reconstructing the Legal Order: The Case for Abolishing the Criminal Court," in *Readings in Juvenile Justice Administration*, ed. Barry C. Feld (New York: Oxford University Press, 1999), 12.

15. Julian W. Mack, "The Juvenile Court," ibid., 12.

16. Anthony Platt, "The Triumph of Benevolence: The Origins of the Juvenile Justice System in the United States," in ibid., 24.

17. Barry C. Feld, "Criminalizing the American Juvenile Court," in ibid., 356.

18. Janet E. Ainsworth, "Re-Imagining Childhood and Reconstructing the Legal Order: The Case for Abolishing the Criminal Court," in ibid., 147.

19. Linda A. Syzmanski, "Juvenile Delinquents' Right to a Jury Trial (2007 update)," *NCJJ Snapshot* 13, no. 2 (February 2008), available at the National Center for Juvenile Justice website, www.ncjj.org. Syzmanski is director of legal research at NCJJ.

20. See Janet E. Ainsworth, "The Court's Effectiveness in Protecting the Rights of Juveniles in Delinquency Cases," in "The Future of Children," special issue, *Juvenile Court* 6, no. 3 (Winter 1996): 64–74.

21. *Kent v. the United States*, 383 U.S. 541 (1966).

22. Barry C. Feld, "Criminalizing the American Juvenile Court," in Feld, *Readings in Juvenile Justice Administration*, 358.

23. Tanya Byron, *Guardian*, March 16, 2009, http://www.theguardian.com/education/2009/mar/17/ephebiphobia-young-people-mosquito.

24. See the introduction to part 4 in this book, which gives some additional background to juveniles receiving life sentences without the possibility of parole.

Part 1:
What Is Punishment?

What is punishment? The *Oxford English Dictionary* defines punishment as "the infliction or imposition of a penalty as retribution for an offense." On the surface, that and other such definitions seem straightforward enough. However, with a little reflection, the definition raises a number of questions. Does the penalty imposed require that the offender be harmed? What if the offender is a masochist who enjoys the penalty? If the person on whom the penalty is imposed is innocent, is it still punishment? What if, instead of a jail sentence, the offender is made to pay restitution or forced to do community service or mandated to undergo psychotherapy or committed to an institution for the mentally insane? Is each of these still a form of punishment, or are they alternatives to punishment? If a police officer decides to beat the offender, is that punishment? When a teacher "punishes" an entire class for what she knows is the act of one person, is that really punishment? If a parent "punishes" an unruly child by forcing her hand in scalding water, is that still punishment? If a judge sentences a rape offender to castration and being slowly tortured to death, is that still punishment?

What the questions above suggest is that a simple definition will not tell us what punishment is. To reasonably debate questions of juvenile punishment, we need some clear criteria for the application of the term. Debates over whether punishment is justified will be unproductive if the opponents in the debate have different conceptions of what it means to punish. Similarly, the question of whether juveniles and adults should receive different kinds of punishment, or whether there are reasonable alternatives to punishment, will depend on what we mean by punishment. For us to confront these issues head-on, we need criteria that both capture the way we use the word "punishment" and that can distinguish between punishment and alternative actions we might take against juvenile offenders that are not punishment. In developing such criteria, we must be careful not to build into them a value judgment that would already provide an answer to the debate. For example, if one of our criteria for punishment is that the harm inflicted must be justified, then we cannot meaningfully debate the question of whether punishment is justified. In all, if we are not clear about what we mean by punishment—if, in fact, debate opponents are using the word "punish" in different ways—then we are confusing each other rather than genuinely debating the issues.

Each of the three articles in this section discusses various criteria for the concept of punishment and focuses on certain problems that arise with the use of these criteria. Sidney Gendin argues that there can be no one definition of punishment that fits all cases and that it is best to think of "punishment" as a concept in which several different criteria overlap without one of them being the central criteria. At best, these criteria have a "family resemblance" that unites them. He begins his article, "The Meaning of 'Punishment,'" with a "first approximation" of the meaning—"infliction of suffering upon wrongdoers"—and then proceeds to show several problems with this definition, which require that it be revised. The first problem is that we may be mistaken about the guilt of the person on whom we inflict suffering. A related problem is that not all cases of inflicting suffering on a wrongdoer can count as punishment—for example, suffering inflicted by a lynch mob. For these problems, Gendin argues that we amend the first approximation with two additional criteria—that those inflicting the suffering at least believe that the person made to suffer is guilty and that the punishment needs to be administered by a disinterested party. Another problem with this first approximation is that the person on whom the penalty is inflicted may in fact desire what is done to her—for example, a homeless individual may want to go to jail because she will be sheltered and fed. Gendin suggests that we then need to amend the first approximation further, substituting for the criterion that punishment must inflict suffering the idea that it must bring about an objective deprivation without regard to the subjective responses of the wrongdoer. Still other problems arise from the first approximation—whether excessive punishment is still punishment or whether punishment need always be aimed at the wrongdoer.

Tziporah Kasachkoff, whose essay "Determining What Punishment Is: Some Neglected Considerations" was written especially for this book, agrees with Gendin that no one definition of "punishment" encompasses all cases that we would call punishment. In arguing this claim, she considers six general criteria that are often assumed to be conjointly necessary for an act to be considered punishment and argues that whether they are necessary or not depends on the context. While she agrees with Gendin's general position, she disagrees with him in terms of particulars. For example, in contrast to Gendin, she argues that when someone welcomes the "punishment" imposed, we should not think of it as punishment. She further argues, again in contrast to Gendin, that not all cases of inflicting punishment on someone require that the pain or unpleasantness be for what the punisher considers an offense or that the person on whom it is inflicted is presumed guilty. Her argument for these claims focuses on situations where the concept applies outside the legal or quasi-legal context—for example, when a teacher punishes the whole class knowing that certain members of the class were not involved in the wrongdoing, or when a boxer is said to "punish" the opponent by pummeling him. She uses this last example (as well as others) to make the point that for an act to count as punishment the agent need not be an authority. She concludes that the standard six criteria fit best in a legal or quasi-legal context, but that even within the context of a legal institution, they are not all necessary or jointly sufficient. She also argues that it is a mistake to restrict the concept of punishment to legal or quasi-legal contexts.

In contrast to Kasachkoff's admonition above, the final selection in this section, "What Punishment Is," by David Boonin, does restrict the concept of punishment to the legal context. This is because the focus of Boonin's book *The Problem of Punishment*, from which this selection comes, is whether legal punishment is ever morally permissible. To answer this question, Boonin insists that we need to identify certain essential properties that constitute punishment. In other words, in contrast to both Gendin and Kasachkoff, we need to find certain criteria that are both necessary and conjointly sufficient for the application of the term in the legal context. Boonin then proceeds to offer five such criteria—that it must cause harm, making the offender worse off in some way; that the harm is intended for its own sake; that the intentional harm be in retribution for something the offender did; that the infliction of this harm expresses a disapproval of the offender's action; and that the punishment must be carried out by an authorized agent of the state. Boonin considers possible objections to each of these criteria and argues that the objections are not successful in undermining them. One of the substantive consequences of Boonin's criteria is that it draws a clear distinction between punishment and restitution, or reparations. This distinction makes it possible to consider reparations as an alternative to punishment. This distinction will become important in the last chapter of this book, where Geoffrey Sayre-McCord will use it to argue that the concerns that motivate the main traditional theories that attempt to justify punishment would be more effectively served by a system of reparations.

As you read the excerpts in this section, consider some of the following questions:

- If someone is convicted of a crime but is in fact innocent, is he or she being punished? Why or why not?

- If someone is a masochist and enjoys being punished, is that still punishment? Why or why not?

- Is there a definition of punishment that can apply to all situations, or does the meaning of the term vary with the context?
- Is there a clear distinction between punishment and restitution, or reparations?

The Meaning of "Punishment"

by *Sidney Gendin**

The two principal questions concerning punishment are, "What gives us the moral right to punish anyone?" and "What do we hope to accomplish when we punish someone?" A third question, which so far seems to be of interest only to philosophers and not to persons directly concerned with the administration of punishment is, "What is the proper analysis of the concept of punishment?" This question is much neglected, unfortunately, by some penal reformers who *assume* that to favor punishment in lieu of rehabilitation implies favoring retribution or implies the desiring of revenge. In this essay I wish to deal only with the third question.

For the most part we are reasonably clear as to what a punishment is. We know that someone put into prison is being punished. When a child does something wrong, the spanking it receives is its punishment. As a first approximation it is natural to say "punishment" means "infliction of suffering upon wrongdoers." There are difficulties with this quick approximation. First, while we may hope that punishment will be limited only to wrongdoers, we realize it is possible to punish by mistake persons who are not wrongdoers. Second, the manner in which suffering may be imposed may affect our opinion as to whether the suffering is, or should be called, punishment. Let us concentrate for awhile on the first objection.

The point of that objection is that since it is not self-contradictory to say "he was punished for something he did not do," the proposed definition is too narrow. What we ought to say is that if the person being made to suffer is genuinely believed to be the guilty party then the suffering we inflict upon him is his punishment. Indeed, the most we can say about people in penitentiaries is that we *think* they are guilty of crimes. It is right to say they are being punished although we realize that probably some of them are not guilty of the crimes for which they have been convicted. I do not mean that any time we make persons suffer whom we genuinely believe to be guilty of crimes that that counts as punishment. Consider lynching. My inclination is to say that lynching is not punishment even in the face of such usages as "Let's get the bastard and give him the punishment he deserves," uttered by someone in a mob. I do not know what can be said against this except that there are all sorts of deviant and metaphorical usages with respect to any concept. (Sportswriters wrote of the severe punishment Sonny Liston gave to Floyd Patterson. Babe Ruth could really punish a baseball.) No doubt a family resemblance exists which one might painstakingly trace out between all the usages. But a theory concerning punishment in relation to criminal behavior is· not likely to benefit from such an undertaking.

Let us return to lynching. My reason for saying that lynching is not punishment is that it is not conducted in an impersonal fashion. Punishment is calm and deliberate and therefore requires administration by a disinterested party. A cornered beast which, from fright, kills its attacker is not punishing it. Even under the *lex talionis* theory, which some people take to be the sanctioning of revenge, the wild retaliation of one party on another does not qualify as punishment. The *lex talionis* theory considers retaliation to be punishment when it is fitting, and this implies a *considered* aim in the inflicted suffering (e.g., an eye for an eye). Lynching is angry response to a real or imagined hurt. Striking back in fear or in anger may be a natural response but it is not punishment.

There are certain difficulties in explicating the concept of punishment which arise in a totally different way. Suppose a man is put into jail for a crime. Supposed he is whipped, stretched and beaten. Suppose none of this pains him. Suppose, further, that nothing we could do to him would bother him. Has he been punished? Is he punishable? These suppositions result from consideration of another objection which goes as follows: A says imprisonment, per se, is a punishment. B replies that he can imagine someone wanting to go to prison so that, for that person, prison is not a punishment. Now by extending his argument, B might go on to say that being beaten, stretched, and whipped are not punishments if the person receiving them wants them. The force of B's objection, "He wanted to go to jail, so he really wasn't punished," is that whatever else punishment may be it must at least involve consequences that the one who receives them regards as unpleasant. Thus, if a person wants to go to jail, it becomes self-contradictory to say that going to jail is his punishment. However, I believe this line of reasoning is a mistake. For if that were self-contradictory think how much more obviously would "he wants to be punished" be self-contradictory. Yet we sometimes say just this about some people. We cannot define the activity of punishment in terms of its subjective effects on each and every person who is punished. If we try to, we run the risk of a new "oddball" appearing each time we think we have settled the question of what punishment is. The question is, therefore, not what the person being punished wants but what we want. Again, the question is, "Do we give the prisoner any choice in the matter?" If a person goes into prison of his own choice and can leave when he wants to, he is not being punished. That he wants to stay there becomes irrelevant if we are determined to keep him there. With respect to the claim that the consequences of punishment should be unpleasant, Mabbott has pointed out that even when a person is being deprived of his life the idea is not to make him suffer.[1] The thought of his coming punishment will cause a person some suffering but the punishment will cause him very little. (Unless, of course, it is of a crude form like blood-letting.) In fact, as forms of capital punishment have evolved, one aim has been to make them as painless as possible. We may note that those who regard capital punishment as the primitive rite of barbaric revenge do not make mention of the above point.

We should think of punishment in terms of such objective deprivations as loss of life, limb, property, and liberty rather than in terms of physical suffering. If we run through the normal channels of punishment then we may say a person has been punished irrespective of the subjective effects they have had on him.

The second objection to the first, approximate definition (p. 17) was that the manner of the suffering affects our opinion as to whether that suffering is punishment. Someone might say that for punishment *to be* punishment it must be just—the suffering or deprivation must fit the crime. There are special problems connected with the idea of "fitting the crime" which a retributivist would have to face. Here, only some general points need to be considered. We sometimes use the expression "cruel and unnecessarily harsh punishment." We do not regard this as self-contradictory. Hence we recognize that punishments do not always fit the crimes for which they are imposed. It is possible that some persons who say "punishment to be punishment must be just" are recommending that the label "punishment" be dropped in certain circumstances in which it is now considered acceptable. More likely the objection is a rhetorical way of registering moral disapproval of certain punishments (unjust ones). To disapprove of unjust punishments, however, is to recognize the propriety of the phrase "unjust punishments."

The expression "cruel and unnecessarily harsh punishment" is explained, I think, by the fact that what the party imposing the suffering thinks constitutes a just punishment may be radically at odds with what an observer thinks is just. It would be queer if the one imposing the punishment considered it cruel and unjust. But if the observer believes that the party is not concerning himself with the matter of justice then he will withhold the appellation "punishment" altogether, rather than merely regard what he sees as a cruel and unjust punishment. Thus "cruel and unjust punishment" is not self-contradictory even though it is true that punishment to be punishment involves a consideration of justice. The expression is used by those passing judgment on those doing the punishing. It presupposes that those doing the punishing are trying to do what is right and, in the opinion of the observer, are failing to do so. If a man believes there is no God, he may oppose punishments imposed for alleged offenses against God. He may even cry, "That is not punishment!", but we may reasonably take this to be an exclamation of disapproval at the punishment. On the other hand, if he thinks those inflicting the suffering are insincere, are themselves really atheists secretly furthering private interests then the cry is meant literally.

In quarrelling over whether punishment should be for legal, moral, or religious offenses, philosophers have inquired into the nature of a criminal offense as a general concept. For example, Mill said that for anything to be a punishable offense there must be some injury to someone other than the offender. Mill was attacked by several of his contemporaries.[2] Many of them felt that if the commission of any act was generally regarded as extremely repulsive or was so unnatural as to be an affront to God then that constituted sufficient ground for it to be a punishable offense. Homosexuality is the classic example. It has been condemned by some persons who have insisted it is not necessary to ascertain whether it involves one person's harming another. The subject of what a punishable offense should be is important and needs to be examined in connection with the aims and justification of punishment. But it usually has been included in discussions of definition for persuasive purposes: "Real punishment is for...."; "Punishment can only be for...."; "Nothing is punishment which does not aim at...."; etc. All these are typical instances of persuasive definitions. Their intent is not so much to inform us of correct usages as they are to push pet normative theories about the aims of punishment.

All this time I have viewed punishment as something aimed at wrongdoers. Is this essential? Can we not punish persons who are not suspected of any crimes if our intention is to produce good? The definitional question is easier to answer than the moral question. It is conceivable that sometimes more good will come of imposing suffering on some innocent persons than if we did not impose that suffering. And it may be argued that our obligation is always to produce the maximum amount of goodness we can. But obviously not all good things are acts of punishment. Some people are made to suffer because they are thought to deserve it; perhaps others should also be made to suffer. But we need a word to preserve this difference—and we have it. Thus we do not prejudge any moral issue by insisting that punishment must be for a wrong. Now some utilitarians have made too much of this definitional point. Critics of utilitarianism have said that since utilitarianism is a theory consistent with punishing the innocent it must be rejected as morally objectionable. The peculiar reply to this criticism is that utilitarianism is a theory of punishment, not a theory of suffering and, since by definition punishment refers to imposing suffering upon the guilty, the objection is a non sequitur.[3] Hart has called this way of putting down a challenge the "definitional stop."[4] Those who use the definitional stop misconceive the nature of the challenge put to them. The point the anti-utilitarian is making is that if your interest in making anyone suffer is solely to produce certain desirable consequences then, logically, you must approve of making the innocent suffer if it has those consequences. We are not merely interested in what punishment is but even more in the question of who we should make suffer and under what circumstances. As Hart says, "No account of punishment can afford to dismiss the question with a definition."[5]

The conclusion, then, is necessarily a modest one. I have discussed a few cases which make explication troublesome. The importance of explicating the concept is greater than for most concepts because it is so emotion-laden. Its definition may be used to sway moral opinions. I have not entirely succeeded in adopting a neutral tone. For example, I said that lynching is not a punishment. But my purpose was not to agitate against lynching (which is hardly necessary, anyhow), for I could have accomplished that by insisting that it is always unjust punishment. Rather, for the previously discussed reasons, I claimed it was not punishment at all. A single definition of "punishment" is bound to be too narrow unless one focuses on a very particular aspect of punishment. For like any concept, there is at best a family resemblance uniting the threads; but tracing these threads would not help us to solve the problem of establishing a normative theory of punishment in its most central use. Concerning that central use, I said that "punishment" is a word best restricted to the suffering imposed on suspected wrongdoers. This cannot be construed, as it sometimes is, as an argument affecting the question whether to extend suffering to the innocent if social utility warrants it.

NOTES

1. J. D. Mabbott, "Professor Flew on Punishment," *Philosophy*, 1955, p. 7.
2. For a spirited defense of Mill against his critics see H. L. A. Hart, *Law, Liberty and Morality* (Oxford: Clarendon Press, 1962).
3. S. I. Benn, "An Approach to the Problems of Punishment," *Philosophy* (1958), p. 332.
4. H. L. A. Hart, "Prolegomenon to the Principles of Punishment," *Aristotelian Society Proceedings* (1959–60), p. 5.
5. *Ibid.*

*Sidney Gendin (1934–2013) was professor of philosophy, emeritus, at Eastern Michigan University, where he taught for thirty-five years. He was an associate editor of *The Freud Encyclopedia: Theory, Therapy, and Culture* (Routledge, 2002) and coedited *Ethical Issues in Scientific Research: An Anthology* (Routledge, 1994).

Gendin, Sidney. "The Meaning of 'Punishment.'" *Philosophy and Phenomenological Research* 28, no. 2 (December 1967): 235–240.

Reproduced with permission of Blackwell Publishing Ltd.

Determining What Punishment Is: Some Neglected Considerations

by Tziporah Kasachkoff*

What is meant when we speak of "punishment"? Some have claimed that for an act to qualify as punishment, it must fulfill all of the following criteria:[1]

1. It is the infliction of pain or at least unpleasantness.

2. The pain or unpleasantness that is inflicted must be for an offense that may be either real or imagined.

3. The person punished must be guilty or presumed guilty of the real or imagined offense.

4. The unpleasantness that is inflicted must be inflicted by some agent (and not, say, be the result of an accident or an "act of nature," such as a storm or a flood).

5. The agent who inflicts the unpleasantness must have the authority to uphold the rules against which the offense is taken to be a violation.

6. The pain or unpleasantness involved in punishment is itself intended; it is not an *un*intended side-effect of the punishment.[2]

We will examine the above-listed features to see whether each is necessary for applying the term "punishment." We shall ask whether an act that lacked one or more of these features would still count as punishment. Many who subscribe to the above criteria hold that each of these features is a necessary condition for proper employment of the term "punishment" and also hold that, collectively, these features are sufficient for proper use of the term. The view that definitions generally and the definition of the term "punishment" in particular are to be delineated by a set of necessary and sufficient conditions is not one that I shall take up directly, though my discussion will have implications for the acceptability of this view.

Must Punishment Be the Infliction of Something Unpleasant?

At first glance, criterion 1 seems uncontroversial. At the very least, we associate punishment with some pain or unpleasantness to the person punished. On reflection, however, we might come to think otherwise. For sometimes a person may be punished by being made to do something that she does not find unpleasant at all. Think of a teacher punishing a student by making her stay late, although she had intended to stay late in any case. Or imagine someone living on the streets deliberately committing punishable offenses so that she will be sent to jail and thereby have the security, at least for a while, of a bed and meals. These examples raise the question of whether punishment must always involve pain or unpleasantness, and whether, at least on occasion, it may involve something desired or even experienced as pleasant by the person punished.

To delve more deeply into this question, let us consider the following two cases:

Case 1:

A student who is punished by detention announces that the detention not only does not bother her but, on the contrary, actually provides her with some benefit (perhaps it provides her with the excuse she needs not to come home early).

Case 2:

A student who is punished by detention and who intended to stay late in any case says nothing about her intention to stay late and so gives no indication that the unpleasantness usually associated with detention is not present for her (in this case at least).

As described, in neither of these two cases does the detention cause any *actual* unpleasantness. However, in Case 1, not only is there no actual unpleasantness; there is not even any supposition of unpleasantness. As in the case of a criminal who announces that she deliberately broke the law in order to incur what for her would be a desirable stay in jail, what is done to her is not the infliction of what we would *straightforwardly* call "punishment" because not only is there no actual imposition of unpleasantness, there is not even any supposition of such imposition. In describing what was done to the student, we would most likely (and more accurately) say that she was "punished," the use of scare quotes indicating that although we know that what was done to the student was intended as punishment, it did not succeed as such. What is conventionally understood in saying that someone was punished is in this way called into question.

For Infliction of Unpleasantness to Be Considered "Punishment," Must That Infliction Be for an Offense and of an Offender?

Most contemporary writers on the meaning of the term "punishment" have insisted that for infliction of hardship or suffering to be considered punishment, the hardship must be inflicted *in response to an offense*, and it must be inflicted *on the person who has (or who is believed to have) committed that offense*. (Criteria

2 and 3.) In the view of these writers, any infliction of hardship on persons who are recognized or believed to be innocent of wrongdoing is hardship that cannot count *as* punishment. In their view, "punishment of the known or presumed innocent" makes no sense.

To see if this view is acceptable, let us consider the following: Suppose a teacher punishes an entire class because some of her papers have been stolen, even though it is quite clear (both to her and the students) that the responsibility for the theft lies with only one member of the class. Someone who argues that "punishment of the recognized or presumed innocent" makes no sense, and who nonetheless views what the teacher does as "punishing" the entire class, must insist that every member in the class is to be considered as "an actual or supposed" offender (perhaps on the grounds that although it is known that only one student committed the theft, since the identity of that person is not known, *every* member of the class is suspect).[3]

But what if the teacher *knows* that certain members in the class were not in any way involved in the theft? Would the inclusion of *these* members in the suffering that is inflicted on the entire group count as punishment? If the answer is yes, then "being (known or presumed) guilty of an offense" cannot be part of the meaning of the concept of punishment.

At this point, we might call attention to the fact that we often use the word "punishment" to describe the infliction of suffering when it is clear that the person on whom the suffering is inflicted is not only not guilty of any offense, but no offense has even been committed. For example, it is not unusual to describe as "punishment" the pain inflicted by boxers in the ring, a description that makes no reference, not even an implicit one, either to the guilt of the person on whom the blows are inflicted or to the commission of any offense (either by that person or by anyone else).

Now, someone might reply that the use of the term "punishment" in the boxing example is only a secondary or nonstandard use of the term, so the lack of an offender (known or presumed) or offense (known or presumed) shows nothing about what is necessary for correct but *standard* uses of "punishment" in other contexts. Whether or not this reply is acceptable depends on whether we accept the criteria that are held to distinguish the standard use of a term from its nonstandard use.

We could, of course, decide that the standard use of a term is "that which is the usual, common, or typical use" of that term. But if we accept *this* as the criterion for "standard use," then the use of the term "punishment" to describe a boxing blow does indeed count as a standard use, for there is nothing unusual in describing what takes place in the boxing ring as "punishing blows" and nothing uncommon in describing one boxing contender as "really punishing" the other.

At this point someone might wish to argue that the term "punishment" as used in sports contexts is indeed a standard and common use, but that it is standard and common only for a use that is secondary. As with the suggestion that a particular use of "punishment" may be nonstandard, the suggestion that a particular use is secondary is helpful only if we understand what *makes* the use of a term "secondary."[4] Furthermore, the fact that a particular use of a term is secondary is no reason to dismiss that use as philosophically irrelevant to the analysis of the primary use of the term because the meaning of a concept may well go beyond the cases that have become its primary expression.[5] For this reason, a full explication of a term should take into account not merely its primary use but its secondary use(s) as well.

With the above in mind, let us look at the following two cases: (1) a boxer who pummels his opponent in a professional match, and (2) a courtroom judge who strikes an innocent person—say, a member of the jury or an onlooker to the court proceedings. The first case may be, and often is, expressed by the statement "He is punishing him." But we would not describe what the judge does in the same way, even though the judge's blows are inflicted (as are the boxer's) on someone who is neither guilty nor presumed to be guilty of any offense. What accounts for this difference?

My suggestion is this:[6] We generally view what people say as carrying, in a particular context, the strongest possible implications.[7] In the context of a court of law, the strongest implication of the use of the term "punishment" is that the person punished is made to suffer because of guilt (real or supposed) for some punishable offense. So, if being guilty of some offense is clearly *not* the reason for the judge's blows, then we must refrain from describing the judge's blows as punishment in order to avoid suggesting otherwise. However, given that the notions of guilt and offense have no place in the context of the boxing ring, the pummeling in the ring can be described as "punishment" without suggesting that the victim of the blows is guilty of some offense.

Another example, suggested by John King-Farlow, may reinforce this point:[8] Suppose a boxer inflicts suffering on his opponent far beyond what is permitted by the conventions or rules of the sport—say he engages in eye gouging, kicking in the groin, biting, and kicking his opponent's head after his opponent has been knocked to the canvas. Some would balk at describing the behavior of this vicious fighter as "severely *punishing* his opponent." However, this very same behavior might be acceptably so described were it to occur in the context of an alley fight or in trench combat (where there are no rules regarding the impropriety of certain kinds of pain infliction). King-Farlow has suggested that unwillingness to describe the extraordinary brutality of the boxing-ring case as "punishment" reflects our refusal to suggest that the sorts of brutality engaged in are consistent with the accepted and institutionalized rules of boxing. On the other hand, our use of the term "punishment" to describe what takes place in either an alley fight or trench warfare carries no such implication, and for this reason use of the term "punishment" is not similarly restricted as a description of what takes place in these latter contexts.

Taking the above points seriously should diminish the temptation to view the term "punishment" as used in the boxing case as either nonstandard or secondary. What the above analysis shows is that although one might say that the meaning of "punishment" changes with change of context, it may be more accurate to say that the implications we are entitled to draw from use of the term "punish" change with the different circumstances of its use. We should conclude, then, that use of the term "punishment" as a description of the pain inflicted in the boxing ring should not be judged as either nonstandard or secondary *on grounds* that in the boxing context there is neither an offender nor an offense (actual or supposed). "Offender and offense (actual or supposed)" are not criteria that *all* bona fide cases of "punishment" must fulfill. The general lesson to be learned here is that "punishment" is not to be *defined* by its marks in any one particular context. Though "for an offense" and "of an offender" are indeed implied by the term "punishment" when used in legal or quasi-legal contexts, these features should not be taken as implied by use of the term in other contexts.[9]

Is the Infliction of Pain or Unpleasantness to Be Considered "Punishment" Even If the Person Who Inflicts It Is Not Authorized to Uphold The Rule(S) Against Which the (Actual or Supposed) Offense Was a Violation?

The answer to this question is "No" when it comes to legal and quasi-legal contexts. But outside those contexts it makes perfect sense to say that someone has inflicted punishment while lacking—and perhaps even making no pretense of having—any authority to do so. That is why the parent who complains that her neighbor punished her child without having any right to do so, and the shopkeeper who admits to punishing a shoplifter while explicitly acknowledging her lack of authority to do so, are not misusing the term "punishment." "Infliction by an authority who represents the rules whose violation is the reason for the punishment" is not part of the very *meaning* of the term "punishment"[10] but only an implication of the use of that term in legal and quasi-legal contexts.

Given that the term "punishment" may correctly be used to describe the intentional imposition of hardship on someone without the punisher having the authority to impose that punishment, one might well wonder why it has been thought that the concept of punishment *necessarily* involves reference to infliction by some authority. I suggest that the reason for this is our sense that punishments imposed by those who do *not* have the requisite authority to impose them are wrongfully inflicted punishments. But morally impermissible punishments are not, on account of their moral wrongfulness, to be disqualified as acts of punishment. The defining criteria of a concept do not determine the moral limits of the practice denoted by that concept.[11] (Suppose a policeman sees someone commit a crime, apprehends him, and then beats him up as punishment. In apprehending the suspect, the policeman correctly acts on his authority. But he clearly acts without authority when he assumes the role of judge, jury, sentencer, and punisher. Now, given that, in punishing the suspect, the policeman acts beyond the bounds of his authority, his punishment of the suspect may reasonably be judged as morally wrong. But it remains an act of punishment nonetheless.)

* * * * * *

A Possible Objection to the Arguments Presented Here for Rejecting Criteria 1, 2, and 3 as Definitive of "Punishment"

Of the first five criteria proposed for the analysis of the concept of punishment, at least four have been shown to be problematic. (The exception, criterion 4—that punishment be the work of personal agencies—does not fall prey to objection so long as the "personal agency" is interpreted so that it may include divine as well as human action.) But some writers have claimed that criticisms of the sort I have made of criteria 1, 2, and 3 do not successfully undermine the proposed analysis of the concept of punishment because these criteria are to be understood not merely as an analysis *of the concept* punishment but also as an analysis *of a system* of punishment. These writers argue that bona fide cases of punishments that fail to meet the criteria for a system of punishment are not to be viewed as counter-examples to those criteria because, as is true for all social systems, systems of punishment can, and invariably do, admit of exceptions. A system of punishment remains a system of punishment even given exceptions, so long, that is, that the exceptions do not become too numerous.

In reply, let me start with a minor point: It is true that a system does not cease to be a system because of exceptions to or misapplication of its rules. This is true *even if* the exceptions or misapplications take place in great numbers. All that is necessary for a system to remain a system is that violations of its rules be recognized as such—that is, *as* exceptions or *as* misapplications to the rules that define the system.

More important: the suggestion that the criteria proposed for the analysis of the concept of punishment are to be viewed as criteria that define not only the concept of punishment but also *a system* of punishment[12] wrongly assumes that the concept of punishment has its home conceptually and exclusively within legal or quasi-legal contexts. Of course, once punishment is conceptually tied to a system, the way is paved for the claim that when a system of punishment no longer qualifies as a "system" (because of, say, multiple violations), the *meaning* of "punishment" has undergone change. However, we should reject the view that : (a) there is a *conceptual* tie between punishment and legal systems as well as the allied claim that (b) whatever undermines a system of punishment does injury to the concept of punishment. A teacher who adopts a method of grading in which she adheres to or abandons at will the traditional rules of grade assignment—say, she gives particular students preferential marks according to her whim on that day—may or may not be said to be using a method that qualifies as a "system." But her idiosyncratic way of arriving at the grades that she assigns does not suggest an alteration in the *meaning* of the concept *grading.* Similarly, when under a certain system of (legal or quasi-legal) punishment, many innocent people get punished—say, through judicial error or through malice—it does not follow that the *meaning* of "punishment" has changed. The marks of a system of punishment are not the same as the marks of the concept of punishment, and so the breakdown of a system of punishment need not involve a change in the meaning of that concept.

The criteria we have been looking at and discussing—most especially, the second, third, and fifth criteria—though advanced as features necessary for correct use *of the concept* of punishment and later defended against counterexamples on grounds that they are features of a *system* of punishment—are indeed most reasonably viewed as marks of a legal or quasi-legal system of punishment. The mistake is to conflate the two and take the criteria appropriate to an analysis of legal or quasi-legal punishment as the terms in which we are to understand the concept of punishment per se.

We should, however, note that even if we regard the proposed criteria as the correct elucidation of the concept of punishment when restricted to legal or quasi-legal contexts, these criteria are not to be viewed as features each of which is necessary and all of which are jointly sufficient for an act to be one of (legal or quasi-legal) punishment. The criteria are rightly to be understood, rather, as characteristic "marks" of systems of punishment rather than as necessary features of them. The many examples of punishment presented here serve to demonstrate that acts of punishment are to be identified as such not on the basis of the fulfillment of necessary conditions but on the basis of their (sometimes tight and at other times loose) association with a context-dependent complex of features.[13]

Conclusion

In summary: (1) There is a difference between the concept of punishment and a system of punishment; (2) criteria for the use of the term "punishment" in legal and/or quasi-legal contexts should not be taken as the conditions for correct use of the term in other contexts; and, more generally, (3) appropriate contexts and uses of the term "punishment" are many and varied, and their analysis shows that there is not one or even several necessary conditions for correct use of the term. Rather, acts of punishment are to be identified as such on the basis of a mix of context-dependent features, with different acts of punishment bearing a family resemblance to one another rather than all qualifying as punishment on the basis of a set of common features that are always and necessarily present.

NOTES

1. Antony Flew, "The Justification of Punishment," *Philosophy* 29 (October 1954).

2. The first five are suggested by Antony Flew, ibid. The sixth is suggested by S. I. Benn and R. S. Peters in *Social Principles and the Democratic State* (London: Allen & Unwin, 1959), 174.

3. The suggestion that punishment is tied to acknowledgment or, at the least, presumption of guilt rather than to guilt per se was elaborated by Kurt Baier in "Is Punishment Retributive?" *Analysis* 16, no. 2 (December 1955).

4. But we should be careful not to regard all reasons given for regarding a particular use of "punishment" as secondary—say, that that particular use of the term entered the language long after other uses of the term were common—as relevant to our philosophical understanding of the term. Specifically with respect to our discussion of "punishment," that the sports-context use of the term entered the language chronologically long after its other uses may not be at all relevant to the philosophical analysis of the concept of punishment.

5. See, for example, Robert A. Samek, "Punishment: A Postscript to Two Prolegomena," *Philosophy* 41 (1966): 220.

6. Conversations held with Sidney Morgenbesser were helpful to me in thinking about the cases under discussion.

7. See H. P. Grice, "The Causal Theory of Perception," *Proceedings of the Aristotelian Society*, supplementary vol. 35 (1961), and "Meaning," *Philosophical Review* 66, no. 3 (July 1957): 377–388.

8. John King-Farlow's comments, questions, and examples, presented to me in private correspondence, have been very helpful.

9. Some writers explicitly restrict the criteria "for an offense" and "of an offender" to standard cases of punishment under a legal system. See, for example, H. L. A. Hart, "Prolegomenon to the Principles of Punishment," *Proceedings of the Aristotelian Society* 60 (1959–60).

10. See Samek, "Punishment: A Postscript," 221.

11. This mistake has led to the erroneous view that the concept of punishment cannot apply to offenses that merit a punishment for which there is no legitimate authority. Specifically with respect to moral offenses, it has been claimed that the concept of punishment is not applicable at all because (according to J. D. Mabbott) for moral offenses, God alone has the status necessary to punish the offender. ("Punishment," *Mind* 48 [190]: 152–167)

12. This assumption finds explicit expression in Kurt Baier's claim that the necessary preliminary conditions of the practice of punishment—he calls it the "game" of punishment—are rule making, penalization, finding guilty of a breach of a rule, and pronouncing sentence. See Baier, "Is Punishment Retributive?"

13. John Kleinig has argued that punishments are only typically and not always necessarily associated with certain features. When one of these features is absent from a particular act of punishment, though we may still correctly talk of "punishment," our description should be qualified in some way (by saying, for example, "He was undeservedly punished"). John Kleinig, *Punishment and Desert* (The Hague; Martinus Nijhoff, 1973), chapter 2.

*Tziporah Kasachkoff is professor emerita at Ben Gurion University of the Negev, Israel, and at the Graduate School and University Center, City University of New York. She coedits the American Philosophical Association *Newsletter on Teaching Philosophy* and is the recipient of the American Association of Philosophy Teachers' Award for Teaching Excellence.

Written for this book and used by permission of the author.

What Punishment Is

*by David Boonin**

---

1. 1. 1 THE NEED FOR A DEFINITION

When we talk about the moral permissibility of legal punishment, what, precisely, do we mean? A general answer to this question is easy: we mean such practices as the state's imposition of monetary fines, forced incarceration, bodily suffering, and— in extreme cases—death. A more specific answer is more difficult. Simply illustrating punishment,[1] even by appealing to clear paradigmatic examples, is not the same as defining it.

But is a more specific answer necessary for our purposes? It is tempting to suppose that it is not. As long as we all know what counts as examples of punishment, it might be said, we can move directly to the task of arguing about whether or not it is morally defensible. Indeed, one book on punishment begins by declining to offer a definition of the term for precisely this reason: "one does not require a definition of 'punishment' in order to recognize clear cases of punishment being imposed and to distinguish such cases from those in which individuals are treated in ways that, although similar to punishment in certain respects, are nevertheless something else entirely" [Montague (1995: 1)]. An "understanding" of punishment is certainly needed, Montague concedes, but one can understand punishment well enough without defining it.

While the reluctance to begin a discussion of punishment by developing a clear, specific definition is understandable, however, it is ultimately misguided. For a fully satisfactory inquiry into the moral permissibility of punishment, it is not enough to point to examples and say either that they are cases of punishment or that they are cases of something else. One must also be able to identify the properties that make them something else. If one cannot do this, then one cannot fully determine what, precisely, makes the permissibility of punishment problematic. More importantly, if one cannot do this, then one cannot satisfactorily determine whether or not a purported justification of punishment succeeds in justifying punishment or only in justifying something very much like it. [...]

Finally, and perhaps most importantly for the purposes of this book, we cannot fully disentangle the importantly related practices of punishment and compulsory victim restitution without understanding what makes some cases cases of punishment and others cases of something else. Such disentanglement is crucial to the project of this book: it is necessary to see precisely why rejecting the claim that punishment is morally permissible does not entail rejecting the claim that compulsory victim restitution is morally permissible. For all of these reasons, then, we must begin our investigation by clarifying what makes some forms of treatment cases of punishment and others cases of something else. And it is difficult to see how to do this without a definition.

[. . .]

1. 1. 3 HARM

A [satisfactory] definition . . . can be obtained by testing various conditions against our intuitive reactions to clear, paradigmatic instances of legal punishment. As already noted, such cases include monetary fines, forced incarceration, bodily suffering, and, in extreme cases, death. So, we should begin by asking what these various practices have in common.

Perhaps the most obvious quality that these practices have in common is that they are all in some way bad for the person on whom they are inflicted.[...] This point is often expressed by saying that punishment necessarily involves "pain," but this way of putting things is unsatisfactory.[...] A murderer, for example, could be executed painlessly, and this would clearly be bad for him even if he does not experience pain. The same problem arises if punishment is defined, as it sometimes is, in terms of subjecting people to experiences that are "unpleasant." Other writers have attempted to capture the sense in which punishment involves something negative for the person on the receiving end by saying that punishment involves an "evil," but this runs the risk of defining punishment as something that is, at least in itself, a wrong; and this, in turn, would violate the requirement of neutrality by begging the question against those retributivists who maintain that the treatment that punishment inflicts on an offender is not merely allowable but a positive good. Finally, some writers have defined the negative effect of punishment on the person who is punished in terms of the language of rights. Punishment, on this account, involves depriving someone of what would otherwise be a right. If one holds the view that losing a right is always bad for someone, then putting things in terms of rights poses no real difficulties for an analysis of punishment as something that is bad for someone. But if, as seems plausible to me, there can be cases in which a person loses a right but is not made worse off by this loss, then such cases would seem to provide a good reason not to link punishment to rights by definition. A woman who is physically incapable of becoming pregnant, for example, might still have a legal right to an abortion, and if depriving her of that right would in no way be bad for her, it is difficult to see how it could count as punishing her. It therefore seems more sensible to say that acts of punishment all, in some way, make the person who is punished worse off than she would otherwise be. If an offender received a monetary prize for her offense, or a paid vacation, a relaxing massage or life-extending therapy, for example, we would not be inclined to say that she had been punished for her transgression. And so, a natural starting point in generating a definition of punishment is to say that punishment *harms* the person who is punished, where harming someone means making her worse off in some way, which includes inflicting something bad on her or depriving her of something good. I will refer to this as the "harm requirement."

1. 1. 3. 1 The Beneficial Consequences Objection

A critic of the harm requirement might object that this requirement neglects the beneficial long-term consequences that punishment can have for the person who is punished. Adler, for example, who rejects the claim that harmfulness is an essential property of punishment, appeals to what he calls the "conscientious punishee," the offender "who wants to submit to punishment, who believes that she can achieve reconciliation, atonement, expiation, renewed innocence, greater moral knowledge, or some other good by undergoing the punishment" (Adler, 91). Indeed, [...] a number of writers have claimed not only that punishment ultimately benefits the offender who is punished, but that the moral permissibility of punishment is grounded in this very fact. A definition of punishment that incorporates the harm requirement would therefore seem to beg the question against such a position, ruling out the possibility that punishment might be justified as ultimately good for the person punished by definitional fiat. This, in turn, would violate the neutrality requirement established earlier, rendering the definition unacceptable.

This objection to the harm requirement is understandable, but it is also mistaken. The harm requirement maintains that for a certain treatment to count as a punishment, it must harm the recipient. But it is neutral on the further question of whether or not being subject to such a harm might produce beneficial consequences in the future, including beneficial consequences that are great enough to outweigh (and perhaps even to justify) the immediate harmful ones. Consider, for example, a child who is spanked as a (nonlegal) punishment for having hit another child. The parent who punishes a child in this way may believe that spanking will make him understand more fully why what he did was wrong, and that this, in turn, will contribute to the child's moral development in various important ways. If this is so, then spanking the child now will ultimately benefit him in the future. But all of this is perfectly consistent with the harm requirement. Indeed, it presupposes it. For if spanking the child does benefit him in this way, then this will be so precisely because it involves inflicting a harmful treatment on the child as a means of demonstrating to him how it feels to be on the receiving end of such harmful treatment. If the spanking were not harmful to the child (if, for example, it felt just like being pleasingly caressed), then it would not have the desired educative effect of showing what it is like to be a victim of wrongful treatment in the first place. So, considerations of the possible long-term benefits of punishment provide no reason to reject the harm requirement. If anything, they provide further reason to accept it.[6]

1. 1. 3. 2 The Masochist Objection

A second objection to the harm requirement is that it is subject to refutation by counterexample. Most people, for example, strongly dislike being physically beaten. But some people, apparently, do not. Most people would find incarceration highly unpleasant. But some people, perhaps, would not, and others, depending on their circumstances, might find it preferable to the available alternatives. And so, it might be urged, we can say at most that punishment involves treatments that are *typically* harmful or that are considered undesirable by most people, but we cannot say that this is so of punishment in every instance. You and I might strongly prefer not to be whipped, for example, and so this punishment would be harmful to us, but a masochist might enjoy a beating; and, if he did, it would remain a form of corporal punishment nonetheless. Since such cases apparently involve acts that are acts of punishment but that do not harm their recipients, they seem to demonstrate that the harm requirement is not accurate over an important (even if somewhat limited) range of cases.[...]

The objection that appeals to cases such as the masochist rests on two claims: that in such cases the treatment in question does not harm the recipient and that it counts as punishment nonetheless. A defender of the harm requirement might reject the objection's first claim and argue that even if the masochist enjoys being beaten, a beating is still something that is objectively harmful to him. Similarly, even if a homeless or insecure person prefers the security of prison to the unpredictability of life on the outside, one could argue that the restriction on his freedom of movement is objectively a grave harm to him even if he doesn't particularly mind it.

But even if the objection's first claim can be sustained in a significant range of cases, the second should be rejected outright. For if we concede that the masochist is not harmed by being whipped or that the homeless person is not harmed by being imprisoned, then we have two good independent reasons to conclude that he is not punished either. And if he is not punished, of course, then even if he is not being harmed, he cannot serve as a counterexample to the claim that punishment requires harm.

The first reason to believe that these attempted counterexamples fail in this way arises because there is a conceptual symmetry between punishment and reward. What is true of punishment in one direction, that is, must be true of reward in the other. Yet, in the case of reward, it should be clear that a person has not been rewarded for doing a good deed if the treatment that she receives in response does not in fact end up benefiting her. Suppose, for example, that I give you a piece of candy because you did me a favor last week, but the candy causes a severe allergic reaction. We might say that I tried to reward you for your good deed or that I intended to reward you, but we would not say that you had, in fact, been rewarded. And we would not say this precisely because you had not been benefited. Since it seems reasonable to presume that reward and punishment are symmetrical in this respect, this provides support for the claim that the offender who is not actually harmed by the treatment he or she receives is not actually punished by it.

The second reason to believe that without real harm there is no real punishment arises from cases in which we believe that no harm is done because of some particular fact about the treatment itself. When a stay in a minimum-security prison for white-collar criminals seems to resemble nothing more than an all-expenses-paid vacation at a comfortable resort, for example, people do not consider the offender to have been punished and they complain about his being treated so leniently for precisely this reason.[...] Our intuitive response to punishments that seem clearly nonharmful and to attempts to reward that clearly do not benefit both vindicate the claim that the harm requirement is a core component of our concept of punishment. And so, the apparent counterexamples to the harm requirement, in which it seems that a person is punished but is not harmed, in the end do not undermine the harm requirement but once again reinforce it.

I think that these considerations suffice to defend the harm requirement from what might be called the "masochist objection," but there is one more concern that might be raised at this point. For if we agree that the masochist who is not harmed by his whipping is not punished by it either, it can seem that we must therefore conclude that whipping is not a form of punishment after all. And that result can seem sufficiently counterintuitive to force us back to the conclusion that the masochist really is being punished and that punishment therefore really does not require harm. This worry about my rejection of the masochist objection is understandable, but it is ultimately misguided. The reason is that there is a crucial difference between saying that a particular person has been subjected to a form of treatment that is a form of punishment and saying that this person has, in fact, been punished. And even if it is possible that some people are not harmed by being subjected to forms of treatments that are uncontroversially characterized as forms of punishment, this does not mean that we must say that such people are actually punished by such treatments.

Since this response to the objection may at first seem puzzling, an analogy may be of use. Consider a doctor who administers a sedative to a patient. An essential property of a sedative is that it makes people sleepy. But just as there are some people who may be delighted by some forms of punishment, there may be some people who are stimulated by some forms of sedatives. If the doctor gives such a drug to such a patient, then what she gives the patient might still be properly characterized as a sedative because of its general properties, but this does not mean that in giving the sedative to this particular patient she actually sedates the patient. Similarly, if the state inflicts a form of corporal punishment on someone who is not harmed by it then while it may be proper to continue to refer to this treatment as a form of punishment (since it is a form of treatment that does, in general, harm people), this does not mean that in administering it to this particular offender the state will in fact be punishing him. It will, at most, be attempting to punish him.[...]

1. 1. 3. 3 The Community Service Objection

A final objection to the harm requirement also turns on the aim that it is subject to refutation by counterexample. While the masochist objection focuses on anomalous people who seem not to be harmed by treatments that would harm most of us, this objection focuses on a somewhat anomalous punishment that seems not to harm most people. In particular, the objection maintains that while the harm requirement may be consistent with several of the most commonly recognized forms of punishment, it fails to account for cases of a less standard but still uncontroversially punitive treatment: cases in which an offender is sentenced to perform community service.[...] Adler, in particular, has argued that, at least for offenders who want to accept their punishment because they believe they will benefit from it in the long run, mandatory community service is a genuine form of punishment but is not harmful in any significant way to the offender (Adler, 91–2). Adler points out that community service can include many behaviors that are not undesirable or unpleasant, such as coaching a sports team or working with handicapped people, and cites a study showing that many offenders continue to volunteer for such projects after their sentences have been completed. If mandatory community service can be both punitive and nonharmful, then the harm requirement must again be rejected.

But it is the community service objection itself that must be rejected. This objection to the harm requirement fails to take in to account the difference between, say, coaching a soccer team made up of disadvantaged children and being compelled to coach such a team.[...] If I have always wanted to coach such a team and you give me the opportunity to do so, then you benefit me. If I would prefer to do something else and you coerce me into coaching the team, then you harm me even if I end up enjoying myself and want to continue coaching the team after my sentence has been served. An offender who is forced to do something she would otherwise not do is thereby harmed; for this reason, such offenders fail to serve as counterexamples to the harm requirement. If an offender who has always wanted to coach such a team is required to do so, then it may well be true that he is not harmed. But for the reasons given in the previous section, it would also seem right to conclude that he is not thereby punished.

1. 1. 4 INTENTIONAL HARM

I have argued thus far in defense of the harm requirement. If subjecting a particular offender to a particular treatment does not harm her, then even if the treatment is, in general, a form of punishment, she has not been punished. The harm requirement accurately captures part of what is distinctive about punishment. It helps, for example, to distinguish correctly cases of punishment from cases of reward. But the harm requirement alone is not enough. For there are practices that involve inflicting the same kinds of harm that are inflicted in cases of punishment but that are clearly not cases of punishment. Consider, for example, the following two pairs of cases:

1. Larry marries Laverne and is charged a fee for processing his marriage license.

2. Moe marries both Betty and Veronica and is charged a fine for violating antipolygamy laws.

3. Curly is found not guilty of murder by reason of insanity and is confined against his will for the rest of his life.

4. Shemp is found guilty of murder and is confined against his will for the rest of his life.

In all four cases, a person does an action and is then harmed by the state as a result. Furthermore, the kind of harm that is incurred in (1) is the same as the kind incurred in (2), and the kind incurred in (3) is the same as the kind incurred in (4). But while (2) and (4) are clearly cases of punishment, (1) and (3) are clearly not.

Several considerations are required to account fully for the difference between (2) and (4), on the one hand, and (1) and (3), on the other. For the purposes of this section, however, we can focus on one feature: that which arises from the distinction between intentionally causing a harmful effect and foreseeably causing a harmful effect. Consider a patient who has been diagnosed with cancer and encouraged to undergo chemotherapy. She is told that the chemotherapy will have two effects: it will kill the cancer cells and it will cause hair loss. When this patient agrees to the procedure, she does so with the intention of killing the cancer cells. She foresees that this will also cause hair loss, but this is not her intention. This can be cashed out in counterfactual terms. If the chemotherapy would kill the cancer cells but not cause hair loss, she would still undergo it. If it would cause hair loss but not kill the cancer cells, she would not. Because of these facts, we can say that she intends to kill the cancer cells but merely foresees that she will lose her hair.

This same distinction can be applied to the question of the role that inflicting harm plays in the institution of punishment. When a person is found not guilty of murder by reason of insanity, the state may determine that to protect the public, he must be locked up in a mental institution. In doing so, the state recognizes that its action will seriously harm the person,[...] but harming him is not its intention. Its intention is merely to protect the public, and it would lock him up even if this did not harm him. Similarly, when the state charges a fee for processing a marriage license, it understands that the cost imposes harm on those getting married, but this is not its intention. Its intention is merely to recover the costs involved in processing the relevant paperwork, and it would charge the same fee even if, for some reason, couples getting married benefited from paying it.[...] When the state punishes someone, on the other hand, it inflicts various harmful treatments on him *in order* to harm him. It is not merely that in sentencing a prisoner to hard labor, for example, we foresee that he will suffer. Rather, a prisoner who is sentenced to hard labor is sentenced to hard labor *so that* he will suffer, and if a given form of labor turned out to be too pleasant and enjoyable, he would be sentenced to some other form of labor for precisely that reason. As Benn puts it, the "unpleasantness" of punishment is not merely an incidental byproduct or side effect of it, but rather is "essential" to punishment (Benn, 8).[...]

This is not to insist, it is important to emphasize, that the offender's suffering must be intended for its own sake. That would reduce punishment to sadism.

Rather, it is to maintain that the punisher intends to harm the recipient of the punishment and does not merely foresee it, even if this harm is, in turn, intended for the sake of some further end. When a parent punishes her child in a nonlegal context by spanking him, for example, the pain inflicted on the child is not simply a foreseen side effect of the spanking, as it might be in the case of the pain caused by removing a splinter. If the splinter came out painlessly, the parent would not reinsert it in order to pull it out again in a more painful manner, but if the first spank was too mild to cause any pain, the parent would spank again, and harder. But while the parent who spanks her child thus clearly intends the pain that she causes and does not merely foresee it, she causes the pain not as an end in itself, but rather for the sake of some further end, such as educating the child or deterring him from committing similar infractions in the future.[15] It might at first seem odd to think that whether or not an act is an act of punishment could depend on facts about the intentional states of the punisher, but on reflection it should seem clear that this must be so. If you see an adult hitting a child, for example, you cannot know if the adult is disciplining the child or simply attacking the child without knowing the reason. If you see a uniformed official forcing a laborer to lift a heavy rock, you cannot know whether what you see is a prisoner being punished or a slave being exploited without knowing why the laborer is being forced to lift the rock.[...] And so, if you see an offender being subjected to a harmful treatment, you cannot know whether or not he is being punished without knowing why the offender is being so treated.[...]

As a result of these considerations, we must accept what I will call the "intending harm requirement": for an act to be a punishment, it must be done with the intent of harming the person being punished. Accepting this requirement is necessary to illuminate fully the difference between punishment, on the one hand, and such practices as charging user fees and requiring pretrial detention, on the other. Many examples can be used to support this basic point. Governments quarantine some of their citizens; call some of them for jury duty; conscript some of them into the military; subject some of them to curve taxation, and zoning regulations; build new highways or airports that adversely affect the quality of life of some of them; and so on. In all of these instances, and many more, the state acts in the full understanding that the act will harm some of its citizens. Clearly, though, none of these cases involves the state's punishing some its citizens. And part of what explains this is that the harm in these cases is foreseen but not intended.[...] The intending harm requirement, therefore, is needed to produce a fully illuminating definition of punishment.

[...]

1. 1. 5 INTENTIONAL RETRIBUTIVE HARM

So punishment involves, at the least, intentional harm. But it also involves more than this. If I punch you in the nose to make you suffer, then I harm you, and do so intentionally, but I do not punish you. This is because I am not harming you in response to some transgression of yours. So, an additional requirement is this: to be a punishment, an act must involve intentionally harming someone *because* he previously did a prohibited act. And since we are concerned in this book with legal punishment in particular, we can be more specific: to be a legal punishment, an act must involve intentionally harming someone *because* he previously did a legally prohibited act, which means that he is responsible for having done the act and that he had no valid legal excuse for doing so.[...] Call this the "retributive requirement."[...] The retributive requirement is needed to distinguish cases of punishment from cases of mere gratuitous injury. It therefore seems plainly well motivated. Is there any reason to reject it?[...]

1. 1. 5. 1 The Mistaken Verdict Objection

One reason to reject the retributive requirement might seem to arise from the following simple fact: sometimes innocent people are mistakenly convicted of offenses they did not commit and serve sentences for those offenses. It thus seems clear that sometimes innocent people are punished. Yet, if the retributive requirement is correct, there can be no such thing as punishment of the innocent, since by definition punishment involves punishing someone for an offense she actually committed. Since there seem plainly to be cases in which the innocent are punished, and since the retributive requirement seems unable to account for this fact, it seems plain that the retributive requirement must be rejected.[...]

This reasoning, however, is misleading. This can perhaps be most clearly seen by again appealing to the structural symmetry between punishment and reward. Suppose that I have lost my beloved dog and have offered a $500 reward for her safe return. As you walk into my front yard for a visit one afternoon, she comes bounding up the steps, and I mistakenly conclude that you have found and returned her. So, I give you the $500. Clearly, what you have received from me is a benefit, and you have received it from me for just this reason. So, it is clearly true that you have been intentionally benefited by me. But even though this is true, it is not true that you have been rewarded by me, anymore than it would be true that you have been repaid by me if I had given you the money under the mistaken impression that I had borrowed it from you last week and now owed it to you. I may believe that I am rewarding you for something, I may intend the money to be a reward, but in fact what I am giving you is not a reward. And it is not a reward (or a repayment) precisely because you have done nothing to be rewarded (or repaid) for. The same is therefore true in the case of punishment. If you are mistakenly convicted of an offense you did not commit, then the judge may believe that she is punishing you and may throw you in jail with this intention, but the harm she imposes on you cannot, strictly speaking, be a punishment. An innocent person can suffer the harms caused by a particular punishment but cannot, strictly speaking, be punished. As Quinton, among others, has recognized, "the infliction of suffering on a person is only properly described as punishment if that person is guilty" (Quinton, 59).[...]

The claim that an innocent person cannot, strictly speaking, be punished seems to be correct. Indeed, it seems to be as clearly correct, and for the same basic reason, as is the claim that a person who has not loaned money to someone cannot, strictly speaking, be repaid. And if the claim is correct, then the mistaken verdict objection to the retributive requirement must clearly be rejected. But it is important to emphasize that the retributive requirement can be construed in a slightly different way so that it retains its basic force even if the objection is sustained.[...] In Section 1.1.4, I noted that the intentional harm requirement can be construed in two different ways: as the requirement that an act cause harm and that the harm be caused intentionally, or as the requirement that an act be intended to cause harm, regardless of whether it does so. And although I maintained that the former, stronger version of the requirement should be accepted, I noted that even in the latter, weaker version, it was sufficient to generate the problem of punishment, and so stipulated that I would accept the weaker version at least for the sake of the argument. The same can be done here with the retributive requirement. On a strong reading, the requirement is that to be a punishment, an act must be retributive. This would require punishment to involve harm that is both retributive and intentional. On a weak reading, the requirement is that to be a punishment, an act must be *intended* as retributive even if it turns out not to be because the recipient of the treatment is innocent. This would require punishment to be intentional retributive harm rather than retributive intentional harm. As for the harm requirement I believe that the retributive requirement should be accepted in its strong version. But, again as for the harm requirement, I believe that the weak version is sufficient to generate the problem of punishment. It is difficult enough to justify the claim that it is morally permissible for the state to act with the intention of harming someone because he is believed to have broken the law. It doesn't matter whether or not the person believed to have broken the law did, in fact, do so.

1. 1. 5. 2 The Consequentialist Objection

A second objection to the retributive requirement, so understood, maintains that it violates the neutrality condition that any reasonable definition of punishment must satisfy. The objection runs as follows. Some attempted justifications for the practice of punishment are essentially "backward-looking" in nature. The considerations they appeal to as a justification for punishment lie in facts about what was true prior to the time that the punishment is imposed. On one retributivist account, for example, punishing an offender now is justified because the offender deserves to be punished, and the offender deserves to be punished because, in the past, the offender committed a wrongful act. So, a retributivist of this sort would have no objection to the stipulation that to count as a punishment, the act must be done because the recipient of the punishment acted in a certain way in the past. But other attempted justifications for punishment are essentially "forward-looking" in nature. On a typical consequentialist account of punishment, for example, punishing an offender now is justified because it will deter the offender and others like her from committing such infractions in the future. A defender of such a theory might therefore object to the claim that to count as a punishment, the act must be done because of the offender's past behavior. Rather, on this account, it must be done because of future benefits that will accrue from doing it. And so, according to this consequentialist objection, the retributivist requirement makes the definition of punishment beg the question against consequentialist theories. This means that any definition that incorporates the requirement will fail the neutrality test and will therefore be unacceptable.[...]

This consequentialist objection to the retributive requirement fails because it neglects the distinction between the nature of punishment and the justification of punishment.[...] Consider again the concept of "repayment." Essential to its nature is that repayment involves paying someone back or a previously bestowed benefit. If I give you ten dollars and you have never provided me with any good or service, then my giving you the ten dollars cannot count as an act of repaying you. This is a claim about the nature of repayment. This claim, however, is completely neutral on the question of what, if anything, justifies the claim that repayment is a morally commendable way to behave. In particular, it is neutral about whether the practice is justified on backward-looking grounds (e.g., "because he is owed the money") or on forward-looking grounds (e.g., "because repaying people generates trust, which creates future benefits to society"). And the same is true of punishment. Legal punishment involves driving a line on the basis of essentially backward-looking features—the line between those who have (or are believed to have) committed a legal offense in the past and those who have (or are believed to have) not—and then treating that line as morally relevant in determining how such people may permissibly be treated in the present. The claim that this is an essential feature of legal punishment, however, is neutral on the question of what, if anything, renders legal punishment morally permissible. And it is neutral on this further question precisely because it is neutral on the question of what, if anything, makes the line that it draws morally relevant. It is consistent with the retributivist view that the line is morally relevant because it separates those who deserve to suffer from those who do not, for example, but it is equally consistent with the consequentialist view that the line is morally relevant because of the good consequences that follow from drawing it there. Including the retributive requirement in our definition of punishment is therefore dictated by considerations of accuracy and illumination and is not overturned by considerations of neutrality.

1. 1. 6 Reprobative Retributive Intentional Harm

The result of the discussion to this point is that punishment involves acting with the intention of harming someone because she has (or is at least believed to have) committed an offense. These requirements are needed to distinguish accurately between cases of punishment and various cases that do not involve punishment. They do so in a manner that helps to illuminate what is distinctive about punishment. And they do so in a manner that is neutral on the question of whether or not punishment is justified and, if it is, on what grounds it is justified. There are two reasons, however, to hold that we are still short of an adequate definition. The first is that there are other differences between some of the pairs of cases previously discussed that these requirements fail to illuminate. The second is that there are other pairs of cases, not yet discussed, that these requirements fail to distinguish accurately. A definition based solely upon the requirements of harm, intention, and retribution, therefore, is still insufficiently illuminating and accurate.

To begin with the first consideration, let us return to the case of paying a fee when you voluntarily marry to one person versus paying a fine when you voluntarily marry more than one person at the same time. A fine is clearly a punishment, while a fee is clearly not. Part of the difference between a fine and a fee is illuminated by attending to the distinction between intending harm and merely foreseeably bringing it about, and part of it is illuminated by appealing to the fact that a fee is charged for doing a legal act, while a fine is charged for doing an illegal one. But focusing exclusively on these two differences threatens to obscure a further relevant difference between the cases. When the state charges you a fee to process your wedding license, it is in no way expressing disapproval of your decision to get married. But when the state imposes a fine on you from violating antipolygamy laws, part of what it is doing is expressing its disapproval of your behavior. And the same is true of the other cases that in part helped to motivate the intentional harm requirement. When we imprison someone because he committed an offense, for example, we are in part admonishing him for his behavior. When we quarantine someone because she has contracted a highly contagious disease, on the other hand, we impose a similar kind of harm on her, but in no way do we mean to express disapproval of her. These considerations demonstrate that a fully illuminating definition of punishment must include a further requirement: to count as a punishment for an offense, the act must express official disapproval of the offender. As Duff and Garland put it, punishment "involves an essential element of condemnation" (Duff and Garland, 13).[...] Call this the "reprobative requirement."

The second reason for accepting the reprobative requirement arises from consideration of a further case. If a definition of punishment limited to considerations of harm, intention, and retribution is insufficiently precise, then there will be cases in which an offender is harmed intentionally and because he committed a legally prohibited act but that are still not cases of punishment. I believe that there can be such cases and that, even though they are more contrived than those discussed to this point, they provide further valuable support for the reprobative requirement.

So, consider first the fact that there seem to be contexts in which the deliberate infliction of pain is meant to convey approval rather than disapproval. There is, for example, the practice of hazing within fraternities, as well as painful initiation rites within gangs and other clubs and organizations. As part of such a practice, the authorized leader of a group might deliberately inflict painful treatment on a new member, say by branding him with a hot iron, and the painfulness of the treatment might well be intentional and not merely foreseen. That is, if the treatment didn't cause pain to the recipient, then it could not fulfill its function as a rite or initiation (the iron, for example, would have to be made hotter if it didn't hurt the first time). But, at least in the sort of case I am concerned with here, the message conveyed by the harsh treatment would be one of approval rather than disapproval. This is how it is understood by the person who inflicts the pain, by the person on whom the pain is inflicted, and by the other members of the relevant group. Now consider the case of a gang that requires potential new members to break the law- say, by stealing a car—in order to be eligible for initiation. In this case, the leader of the gang who brands the new member with a hot iron after the new member steals a car deliberately inflicts painful treatment on the new member precisely because he broke the law. Clearly, this is not a case of the new member being punished for his offense. But, just as clearly, this assessment cannot be justified without adding the reprobative requirement to the definition of punishment.

The need for the reprobative requirement is perhaps less immediately apparent than the need for some of the other elements of our definition. But once the need becomes apparent, it is difficult to imagine a convincing objection to it. One might, at first, be tempted to object that the requirement begs the question in favor of one particular justification of punishment: that punishment is justified as a means of expressing or communicating society's disapproval of the offender's act. But, like the consequentialist objection to the retributive requirement considered in Section 1.1.5.2, this objection confuses the question of what punishment is with the question of what makes punishment permissible. The reprobative requirement maintains that part of what makes an act a punishment is that it expresses official disapproval of the offender's behavior. But this requirement is entirely neutral on the question of whether or not this feature of punishment, or any other feature of it, renders it morally permissible.[...]

1. 1. 7 AUTHORIZED REPROBATIVE RETRIBUTIVE INTENTIONAL HARM

The discussion to this point has focused on how punishment affects the person punished and on what reasons are given for it. The question of who is doing the punishing has been passed over. Does this question matter? If we were looking for a definition of punishment in general, this question would potentially become somewhat complicated. Some philosophers have argued that if acts of the sort that I have described are carried out by private citizens, then they cannot qualify as punishment for that very reason, but only as something like vigilante justice. Primoratz for example, has argued that "by definition, punishment is determined and executed by those *authorized* to do so" [(Primoratz, 84); see also Benn)]. Others, however, have argued that such acts should still be construed as punishment, though perhaps as unauthorized and impermissible punishment. Still others have puzzled over the question of whether or not a person can punish himself or whether a wrongful act can, in effect, be its own punishment.[...] For our purposes, however, we can sidestep these particular problems. This book is concerned with the permissibility of legal punishment, and where I have used the term "punishment," it has been as shorthand for "legal punishment." And whatever we might think about the coherence or existence of other forms of punishment, it is clear that a punishment cannot be a legal punishment, in particular, unless it is carried out by an authorized agent of the state acting in his or her official capacity.[...] Call this the "authorization requirement."

The case for the authorization requirement, understood as a necessary condition for legal punishment, is overwhelming. In the absence of such authorization, there is no reason to think of an act as a legal punishment, even if there is reason to think of it as a punishment of some sort. The only objection to the requirement that I am aware of maintains that it begs the question in favor of the moral permissibility of punishment and thus violates the neutrality condition established as one of the conditions for an acceptable definition. But this objection rests on the assumption that if an act is legally authorized, then it is morally permissible. And this assumption is plainly false. The authorization requirement is therefore consistent with definitional neutrality.

[...]

1. 1. 8 PUNISHMENT VERSUS RESTITUTION

I have argued that legal punishment should be defined as authorized intentional reprobative retributive harm. In arguing for this definition, I have claimed that it does the best job of accurately distinguishing between cases of punishment and other cases, and that it does so in an illuminating and neutral manner. In developing this argument, I have used examples of practices other than punishment, including curfews, quarantines, pretrial detention, gratuitous infliction of harm, and so forth. I have, however, deliberately refrained from appealing to one further case: compulsory victim restitution. I have done this precisely so that the definition of punishment arrived at will not have been influenced ahead of time by preconceptions about the relationship between punishment and restitution. Having arrived at a satisfactory definition of punishment, however, we must now ask: given this definition, what should we say about the practice of compelling an offender to make restitution?

Let us begin with an example. Larry vandalizes Moe's car by painting obscene words on it and breaking the windshield. Larry is caught and found guilty. The judge orders Larry to compensate Moe for the harm he has caused. She forces Larry to remove the spray paint from Moe's car, to pay the costs of replacing the windshield, to pay the costs involved in Moe's renting a car while his is in the shop, and to compensate him for the inconvenience and emotional distress Larry caused him. This seems clearly to be a case of compulsory victim restitution. Is it also a form of punishment?

Clearly, the act satisfies the authorization requirement. The judge is a legally authorized official acting in her official capacity. Clearly, it satisfies the retributive requirement. She orders Larry to do these things because Larry vandalized Moe's car. It seems equally clear that the judge's act satisfies the reprobative requirement. The act at the very least, expresses the view that Moe is entitled to have his car returned to its original condition, which means that Larry was not entitled to damage it, which in turn means that Larry did something that he was not entitled to do. And finally, it seems clear that the judge's act harms Larry. Larry is made worse off by having to give Moe some of his money and spending some of his time cleaning up Moe's car. In all of these respects, the judge's act of forcing Larry to make restitution to Moe satisfies the definition of punishment we have arrived at. Indeed, for some theorists, these similarities between punishment and restitution seem to be sufficient to conclude that restitution is a form of punishment.[...]

But this conclusion is premature. For one further question remains: in imposing this burden on Larry, does the judge act with the intention of harming Larry? As we saw in Section 1.1.4, distinguishing between harm and intentional harm is necessary in order to account fully for the difference between, for example, fees and fines. If the answer to this question is yes, then restitution is more like a fine than a fee and is a punishment. If the answer is no, then restitution is more like a fee than a fine and is not a punishment.[...]

The answer to the question is this: there is no one answer that covers every case in which a judge compels an offender to make restitution to his or her victim. In some cases, the judge's intent may be to impose a cost on the offender. She may say, for example, that she wants Larry to suffer the drudgery involved in cleaning the paint off Moe's car so that Larry will come to see how wrong his act was. In this case, part of the judge's motivation for imposing the cost on Larry is, indeed, punitive. Following Barnett, we can refer to cases of this sort as cases of "punitive restitution" (Barnett, 219–20). But this need not be true of all cases. In some cases, the judge's reasoning may be that Larry must pay the money because he owes it to Moe. In this case, the judge foresees that paying Moe will impose a cost on Larry in the same way that she might foresee that enforcing the terms of a contract will impose costs on one of the parties to the contract, but this fact plays no role in her decision. Following Barnett, we can refer to cases of this sort as cases of "pure restitution" (Barnett, 220). An argument against the moral permissibility of punishment, therefore, will also provide an argument against punitive restitution. But it will provide no reason to reject pure restitution. And this fact will become important toward the end of our investigation.

[...]

NOTES

1. Unless otherwise noted, when I say "punishment" in this book, I mean "legal punishment.'
[...]

6. It is possible, of course, that a proponent of the objection might insist that the benefits of submitting to punishment are immediate rather than delayed. But if the recipient of a given treatment is benefited at the moment that the treatment begins, it is not clear what reason we would have for considering it to be a punishment in the first place. If a pleasant caress on the child's back benefits him immediately and also somehow teaches him that it is wrong to hit other children, for example, then it may well serve the same purpose as a spanking for educative purposes, but it would clearly fail to count as punishment and so would again fail to provide a counterexample to the harm requirement.

[...]

15. That the parent intends the harm only as a means and not as an end, it may be worth pointing out, does not undermine the counterfactual analysis of intentions presented here. A critic might point out that there is a counterfactual situation in which the parent would not harm the child: if the parent could achieve her ultimate end of educating or deterring the child without harming him, after all, surely she would. But this fact does not pose a problem for the claim that there is an important difference between the spanking case and the splinter-removing case. What matters is that in the spanking case but not in the splinter case, the parent has, in fact, chosen to use pain as a means to achieve her end, even if, in both cases, she would prefer not to.

REFERENCES

Adler, Jacob. 1991. *The Urgings of Conscience: A Theory of Punishment*. Philadelphia: Temple University Press.

Barnett, Randy. 1985. "Restitution: A New Paradigm of Criminal Justice." In *Punishment and Rehabilitation*, second edition, ed. Jeffrie G. Murphy. Belmont, CA: Wadsworth.

Benn, Stanley I. 1985. "Punishment," In *Punishment and Rehabilitation*, second edition, ed. Jeffrie G. Murphy. Belmont, CA: Wadsworth.

Duff, R. A., and D. Garland. 1994. "Introduction: Thinking About Punishment." In *A Reader on Punishment*, ed. R. A. Duff and D. Garland. Oxford: Oxford University Press.

Montague, Phillip. 1995. *Punishment as Societal-Defense*. Lanham, MD: Rowman and Littlefield.

Primoratz, Igor. 1989. *Justifying Legal Punishment*. Atlantic Highlands, NJ, and London: Humanities Press International.

Quinton, Anthony M. 1969. "On Punishment." In *The Philosophy of Punishment*, ed. H. B. Acton. London: MacMillan.

*David Boonin is an associate professor of philosophy at the University of Colorado, Boulder. He is the author of *A Defense of Abortion* and *Thomas Hobbes and the Science of Moral Virtue* and has written numerous articles on a variety of topics in ethics and applied ethics.

Part 2:

Can Punishment Be Justified?

In the preceding section, we considered the kinds of criteria that are reasonable to use for applying the concept of punishment. While the authors of these articles did not agree on whether certain criteria were necessary or sufficient, they all assumed that punishment involved the intentional infliction of some kind of harm. Thus, before debating the specific issues of punishment for juveniles, we need to ask whether it is ever justified to inflict harm or suffering on juveniles intentionally.

And before we do this, we need to ask a more general question. We must now ask what justifies us in ever doing harm to any other person, whether that person is a juvenile or an adult. If intentionally harming another person is generally assumed to be bad, what, if anything, makes punishment morally permissible? Once we pose this question, it becomes clear that the burden of proof must be on the advocate of punishment to demonstrate that intentionally inflicting harm on another person is in some context permissible. If there are no good arguments for this position, then all punishment—whether of juveniles or adults—is morally wrong.

Traditionally, there have been three main attempts to justify punishment. Perhaps the oldest, which still has many contemporary advocates, is the retributive theory of punishment. Put simply, this theory claims to be an argument for retributive justice, which sees punishment as the appropriate and just response to a previous harm done by the offender. For the retributivist, punishment is retrospective. It looks back to the amount of harm that the offender inflicted on another person to determine the proportionate harm—an "eye for an eye" but not two eyes for an eye—that should be inflicted on the offender. For the retributivist, punishment is not something that is done for the sake of bringing about good consequences but precisely for its own sake. The retributivist insists that justice demands that the offender be punished, that she simply deserves to be punished for the wrong that she did. End of story.

In contrast to the retributivist theory, the consequentialist or utilitarian theory of punishment is prospective, in that it looks not to the past but to the future. For the consequentialist, or utilitarian, punishment is justified if and only if it brings about beneficial results, unjustified if it brings about bad results.[1]

49

For the consequentialist, punishment may be justified if it serves to deter other persons from committing the same offense (deterrence theory) or if it serves to incapacitate an offender who we have reason to believe will be dangerous if free (incapacitation theory). However, for the consequentialist, the gain in favorable consequences must be weighed against the pain and suffering inflicted on the offender and against the pain and suffering that often results from the offender's incarceration—for example, the pain and suffering that members of her family or friends might undergo. Furthermore, the form and level of punishment should be determined not by some abstract idea of proportionality but by its ability to bring about these beneficial consequences.

A third major attempt to justify punishment is the rehabilitative or moral education theory of punishment. The advocate of this theory is interested in morally changing the wrongdoer. The assumption behind it is that most if not all wrongdoers can come to see that they have done wrong and can be brought to want to do right in the future. For the moral education advocate, what kind of punishment is appropriate depends on what will be really effective in morally changing the offender.

Certain standard objections are raised to each of these theories. The retributivist may be accused of advocating revenge, and, unless the punishment exactly reproduces the act of the offender (for example, raping the rapist), it is by no means clear how to decide what level of punishment is proportionate to the offense committed. An objection often leveled against the utilitarian is that utilitarianism might justify punishing a person the judge knows to be innocent if it will serve to deter others from doing what the innocent person is accused of doing. Also, a utilitarian might justify an "unjust" level of punishment (for example, a very harsh penalty for a relatively minor offense) on the grounds that it more effectively deters crime. The advocate of rehabilitation needs to show why inflicting suffering or otherwise causing harm to offenders will make them better persons or why they should not simply receive some form of psychotherapy instead of punishment.

There are, of course, other theories of punishment in addition to the three major ones indicated above. Punishment may be justified as an expression of disapproval and condemnation or as a form of self-defense, and there are a number of hybrid solutions that combine elements of different theories of justification.

In the first article in this section, "The Retributive Theory of Punishment," Jonathan Jacobs presents a contemporary defense of the retributive theory of punishment based on the values of liberal democracy. He begins by distinguishing between vengeance/retaliation and retribution and then argues that retribution, rather than taking pleasure in the suffering of the offender, is the only theory of punishment that takes seriously the value of respect for persons and that, therefore, treats the offender as a rational agent responsible for her actions. Jacobs also compares retributivism with consequentialism and argues that the latter misses the intrinsic importance of desert (what the offender deserves as a result of her actions) and proportionality and that only retributivism properly captures the point of punishment. In sum, Jacobs argues that the retributive theory of justice is best suited to the values of the liberal democratic political order.

Michael Lessnoff, in "Two Justifications of Punishment," defends a hybrid theory of punishment; specifically, he argues for a utilitarian/deterrence theory that embraces certain features of the retributive theory. His defense of this hybrid theory rests on a distinction between the functions of two kinds of justifications for punishment. The first attempts to answer the question, why punish? The second addresses the question, what entitles us to punish these people? His answer to the first question is utilitarian—punishment reduces wrongdoing. His answer to the second is retributive—that people guilty of the wrongdoing deserve to be punished in proportion to their degree of guilt.

In "Much Respect," Paul Butler defends a very different hybrid theory of punishment, which he calls a "hip-hop" theory of punishment. Drawing on the comments and lyrics of a number of hip-hop artists and on his understanding of hip-hop culture, Butler argues for a theory of punishment that has retribution as its object but is limited by certain utilitarian concerns. Among these concerns are the recognition that drug laws are severely and overly harsh; the recognition of the role of the environment in determining the criminal conduct of the lawbreakers; the effect of mass incarceration on third parties, particularly the dependents of the incarcerated persons and more generally on the communities from which they come (especially African American communities); the way in which racial and other forms of bias enter into how crime is understood and enforced; the way in which African Americans are disproportionately represented in American prisons; and the way in which the American prison system dehumanizes people. As a result of these utilitarian social concerns, Butler identifies a number of utilitarian principles that should be incorporated within a retributive framework and that would limit it, among them that people should not be punished for using or selling drugs, that punishment should be imposed only by people within a community, and that prison should not be the main form of punishment.

In the last article in this section, "Retributive Punishment and Revenge," Karsten J. Struhl, who is one of the coeditors of this book, argues that there is no clear way to distinguish retribution from revenge and that retributive punishment is largely motivated by the emotions of revenge. On this basis, he further argues that legal retributive punishment is best understood as a form of controlled revenge. Struhl concedes that this does not necessarily count against the justifica-tion of punishment, since whether revenge is necessarily bad is itself debatable. In fact, one of the possible political implications of Struhl's analysis is that we should be willing to affirm the revenge elements in the criminal justice system. In doing so, we might have the prosecuting attorney officially represent both "the people" *and* the victim, and we would allow the victims to express their vindic-tive emotions more completely as well as having input and perhaps even some measure of veto power in every phase of the legal process—during the criminal investigation, plea bargaining, the jury trial, and especially during the sentencing phase. These are, in fact, some of the demands of the victims' rights movement. On the other hand, if we think revenge is bad, and if revenge does indeed pro-vide the motivational foundation of retributive punishment, this may provide a good reason to be suspicious of retributive theory as an adequate justification of punishment. It might also be a reason to eliminate as far as possible the retribu-tive elements in the criminal justice system.

As you read the excerpts in this section, consider some of the following questions:

- Do you agree that the burden of proof is on the person who thinks that punishment is justified? Why or why not?

- Is retribution a form of justice, or is it a disguised form of revenge? Or both? If legal retribution is to a large extent motivated by revenge, to what extent would that invalidate the retributive theory as a justification for punishment?

- With which theory of punishment are you most sympathetic—the retribu-tive, the consequentialist/utilitarian, or the rehabilitative/moral-education theory? Why? With which of these theories are you least sympathetic? Why?

- To what extent do you think that the attempt to justify punishment requires a hybrid theory? Evaluate the advantage and disadvantage of one of the hybrid theories in this section (Lessnoff or Butler).

- To what extent do you think Butler's hip-hop theory of punishment accu-rately reflects the values of hip-hop culture?

NOTE

1. Strictly speaking, utilitarianism is one form of consequentialism insofar as it is concerned with certain kinds of consequences, namely those that would reduce pain and increase pleasure for everyone involved.

The Retributive Theory of Punishment

*by Jonathan Jacobs**

Several theories compete for supplying an account of the justification and aims of legal punishment—punishment carried out with the authority of the state, in response to violations of criminal law. Moreover, in some of the theories the justification of punishment is distinguished from punishment's aim(s), while in others, aim and justification are combined. Indeed, we sometimes see reference to the "justifying aim" of punishment. Retributivism is one of the main approaches to the justification of punishment, and the present discussion will explicate the main characteristics of retributivism and make a case for it. While punishment may have some non-retributivist aims, retributivist considerations are crucial elements of the justification of punishment, especially in a liberal-democratic polity.

RETRIBUTIVISM CONCERNS JUSTICE, NOT REVENGE

It is important to distinguish retributivism from *vengeance*, and it is important to distinguish it also from severity. Vengeance involves being motivated by passion (even if one waits, and exacts vengeance in a composed, coolheaded manner), and it also typically involves anticipating, and then experiencing pleasure in harming the victim of vengeance. Vengeance is *hitting back*, causing suffering as retaliation, and often it involves little regard for proportionality or for the suitability of the vengeance in relation to that for which vengeance is sought. If, in seeking vengeance, a great deal more harm is done than was done by the original act, the seeker of vengeance may be unbothered by that or even welcome it. In fact, one may seek to exact vengeance by harming people other than the individual against whom vengeance is sought. Harming that person's family or friends may be an especially hurtful approach to seeking vengeance. Retributivism differs from vengeance in each of those regards.

First, the retributivist justification of punishment is centrally concerned with justice, not with retaliation. *Desert* is vitally important to retributivism. In that respect, retributivism is motivated differently from vengeance, and it involves a concern for justice rather than retaliation. Desert is a complex notion; there isn't some single, adequate definition that captures it completely. Desert is often closely related to claims about what justice requires, to the legitimate claims a person can assert, and to what is owed to a person. In the context of legal punishment, desert concerns the most fundamental grounds for the appropriateness of coercively imposing a deprivation of liberty or suffering of some kind, because of the wrong conduct for which one is responsible. When a person asserts a legitimate rights claim, we often say that the person is owed that to which he or she has a legitimate claim; someone (or society) has the duty to see to it that the claim is fulfilled. It might seem odd to say that an offender has a right to be punished (though that view has been defended).[1] However, retributivists argue that punishment is inflicted as deserved, as owed to a person on account of that for which that person is responsible as a voluntary agent. That claim can be asserted and defended without also including considerations about what punishment might accomplish or whether it will deter other persons from breaking the law. Retributivists typically regard what a person deserves as fundamental to the moral justification of punishment.

Also, while we might find it satisfying that justice is done, there is no place in retributivism for taking pleasure in the suffering of the person punished. A vengeful person might take considerable pleasure in causing suffering.[2] A person seeking vengeance might think that cruelty is appropriate, and that to degrade or humiliate the person against whom vengeance is sought is fitting. That is no part of retributivism. Along the same line of distinction, proportionality is very important to retributivism. Excessive, disproportionate punishment would be wrong, whereas for a person seeking vengeance, "paying back with interest" might seem perfectly appropriate.

Granted, it is very difficult to specify a satisfactory account of what constitutes proportionality in punishing; that must be conceded. Nevertheless, the retributivist strives to ascertain what is proportional in punishing because that is an important aspect of punishment being just, along with desert. The concern with proportionality is important to the explanation of why retributive punishment does not involve taking malicious pleasure in causing suffering or knowing of the suffering of the person punished. There is a crucially important difference between balancing the scales of justice and enjoying "getting back" at someone. The notion of "balancing the scales" of justice is metaphorical, but it indicates the central place of desert in retributivism. It highlights the retributivist's focus on what justice requires rather than looking to what sorts of results or consequences one or another practice of punishment might have as a basis for justifying punishment.

Justice—even more than desert—is a complex matter, and there are different sorts of justice appropriate to different issues and contexts. That is distinct from the fact that there are rival theories of justice, rival views of what justice requires. For example, one might claim that there is political justice, social justice, economic justice, and criminal justice, as well as there being rival accounts of each of those *types* of justice. The present point concerns the difference between, say, retributive justice and distributive justice. The latter concerns how benefits and burdens are allocated among the members of a society. Questions about whether an income tax should be progressive or whether entitlements (such as Social Security or Medicare) should be means-tested are questions of distributive justice. In chapter 5 of *Utilitarianism*, where John Stuart Mill is trying to show that questions of justice are ultimately decided on the basis of utility, he looks at views of distributive justice as an important test case. For instance, should workers be compensated on the basis of their productivity, or their skill, or perhaps on the basis of need or even equally? After all, don't we all have equal need for basic material necessities? Should the state plan the distribution of wealth at all, and interfere with market forces? Is that an inappropriate imposition on self-determination and liberty? Whatever the merit of Mill's argument, his discussion clearly presents the fact that there are numerous conceptions of distributive justice, each one with adherents who believe that *that* conception is *of course* the correct one, with the vital support of reason on its side. But they cannot all be correct conceptions, even if there is something to be said for each.

One might argue that we should cease thinking in terms of retributive justice and conceptualize crime and punishment in a different way, assimilating them into a broader conception of social justice. Retributivists, of course, reject that view, and they insist that to abandon retributive justice would be a serious moral error, reflecting a failure to respect the voluntary agency and accountability of individuals. (This will be discussed further below.) Perhaps no one wants to be punished; nonetheless, if we think of ourselves as deserving regard and respect as rationally self-determining agents, then (the retributivist would insist) retributivist considerations are integral to a just polity.

Defenders of retributivism often argue that it *respects* persons in a distinctive and morally significant manner. In a liberal-democratic political order it is important that as citizens, persons have the same standing before the law, and that standing should reflect the fact that persons are rational, voluntary, responsible agents. It is also important that the law should be understood to address persons as rational agents; it should not be merely an imposition on them by an agent or institution with coercive power. The values and principles shaping the law should be endorsable by those to whom the law applies. That is a crucial respect in which the polity can be said to be democratic. It is liberal in the sense that law permits and protects extensive individual rights and liberties, and there is a significant role for representation in government. In that way government reflects people's commitments and concerns, and the rule of law reflects sovereignty grounded in the people.

The nature of a liberal democratic rule of law will be discussed below in section V, but we can make a couple of basic points about it here. Liberalism is often understood in terms of the state not imposing or enforcing any comprehensive view of morality, and that is indeed a significant feature of liberalism. However, a broadly endorsed framework of values is required for there to be the scope within which individuals *have* extensive freedoms. Thus, while there is scope for a diversity of values and interests, and people have extensive individual freedoms, agreement on the values that make that sort of sociopolitical order possible is needed. The democratic element is that there is a role for citizens in electing representatives and other government officials, and representatives of the people fashion the laws under which people live. The laws are not simply imposed by an agent who is unaccountable to citizens.

Also, a liberal-democratic political order would be flawed if, for example, it assigned different groups of persons to different statuses in the polity, perhaps distinguishing between those who are free and participate in governance, and those who are ruled and have no role in governance. In a liberal-democratic polity the rule of law respects persons by protecting their freedoms and their standing, and this includes the context of criminal justice, in which procedure is governed by numerous restrictions and requirements safeguarding citizens' standing.

One of the most important, unavoidable issues a liberal polity must face is the relation between law and morality. While a liberal order does not comprehensively enforce any particular conception of a well-led life or of morality, a widely endorsed framework of values is needed to support and preserve a liberal order. Within that framework there should be extensive scope for individual liberty and for voluntary association and participation in groups and group activities of many kinds.

The relation between law and morality in a liberal polity is not the primary focus of the present discussion, though it is related to it in significant ways. The question of how the law should treat persons who violate the law involves moral issues unavoidably. For present purposes, it is important to see that there is no inconsistency between (i) the liberal order not enforcing morality comprehensively and (ii) criminal law (and criminal procedure) in a liberal polity reflecting and upholding certain moral values and principles. Moreover, these features of a liberal political order help us understand the basis for a retributivist justification of legal punishment. That justification has important moral features, but retributive punishment is not the same thing as coercively enforcing a specific morality.

RETRIBUTIVISM, DESERT, AND THE MORAL POINT OF PUNISHMENT

As indicated above, the notion of desert figures centrally in the retributivist justification of punishment.[3] Because the notion is so strongly relevant to punishment, even critics of retributivism often seek to include a retributive constraint in their theories. A theory of punishment paying no regard to whether the persons punished have actually committed crimes would be morally suspect in a basic respect. That is why desert tends to have a place in any of the plausible approaches to justifying punishment.

For instance, suppose a theorist is defending a consequentialist conception of punishment, and suppose that deterrence and reform of offenders are among the theorist's key considerations.[4] A consequentialist maintains that actions are not intrinsically right or wrong; they are right or wrong on the basis of whether they bring about certain sorts of states of affairs. They are right or wrong on the basis of their consequences. Of course, a consequentialist has to not only make the case for that approach to moral theory but also make a case for what it is about the consequences of actions that matters. For instance, a hedonistic utilitarian (Jeremy Bentham and Mill are the two most famous ones) argues that it is the pleasure and pain brought about by actions that we are to look to in moral evaluation and decision. Mill argued that people desire pleasure and pleasure alone for its own sake, and that what is desired for its own sake is what we are to regard as good. We all desire happiness, and he interpreted happiness in hedonistic terms; that is, in terms of pleasure. He was careful to avoid endorsing vulgar hedonism, and he argued that there are qualitatively superior and inferior pleasures. But he held a hedonist theory of value, and he wedded that to a consequentialist form of moral theory. (A consequentialist does not have to be a hedonist or even a utilitarian. However, hedonistic utilitarianism is the most influential and best-known form of consequentialism.)

The theorist defending a consequentialist justification of punishment will not focus on desert in the same way a retributivist does, even if the consequentialist assigns some role to desert, perhaps arguing that there are good *consequentialist* reasons in favor of punishing only persons known (or carefully judged) to be guilty of the offenses with which they have been charged. A consequentialist can maintain that only persons *who deserve* to be punished *should be* punished, because there are undesirable consequences of abandoning that condition. People might be fearful of being arrested, though known to be innocent. They might lose confidence in the integrity of the courts. And so forth. The consequentialist is likely to insist that this does not make the view a mixed view, including retributivist considerations as well as consequentialist ones. Instead, the insistence on desert is included because there would be little confidence in criminal justice if persons known to be innocent could be punished knowingly and if *having violated the law* was not a necessary condition for suffering the imposition of criminal sanction. People in such a society would probably live in a constant state of anxiety and insecurity, knowing that even if they are blameless, they still might be subject to punishment if the authorities believed that some net benefit could come of it. From a utilitarian perspective, such a state of affairs would have considerable disutility.

H. L. A. Hart includes retributivist-seeming features in a non-retributivist account of punishment. He wrote:

> the injunction "treat like cases alike" with its corollary "treat different cases differently" has indeed a place as a prima facie principle of fairness between offenders, but not as something which warrants going beyond the requirements of the forward-looking aims of deterrence, prevention and reform to find some apt expression of moral feeling. Fairness between different offenders expressed in terms of different punishments is not an end in itself, but a method of pursuing other aims which has indeed a moral claim on our attention; and we should give effect to it where it does not impede the pursuit of the main aims of punishment.[5]

Thus, in punishing more serious crimes more severely, we are aiming to do what we deem to be required to effectively check more serious evils, and we do this in a way that meets public demands for denunciation of serious crimes. This involves considerations of fairness across two dimensions: (i) across the dimension of treating what is alike in a like manner, and (ii) across the dimension of responding with more severity to graver offenses. It could be argued that neither of these essentially depends on endorsement of retributivism because there are good consequentialist reasons for inclusion of such conditions.[6]

This is an example of how a non-retributivist can domesticate what appear to be distinctively retributivist considerations to non-retributivist theory. When utilitarians argue on grounds of utility that only offenders should be punished, that *sounds* like retributivist "just deserts," but the reasons given are utilitarian reasons. Consequentialist justifications can accommodate the principle that severer offenses merit severer penalties, and at the same time require that punishments be no severer than is necessary to promote desirable social ends. This is a strategy with considerable appeal if one is concerned that retributivism—in its rejection of consequentialist considerations—is "good for nothing." While the retributivist insists that punishment based on desert reflects a requirement of justice, the objector argues that if society is going to cause people to suffer, it needs a clear idea of what is gained by doing so, even when those who suffer are known to be guilty of crimes.

We need to distinguish retributivism that maintains that punishing offenders is a requirement of justice from retributivism that maintains that deserving punishment is a ground for imposing it, though it is not necessarily a second moral failing if we fail to punish the offender. Immanuel Kant famously held the view that morality requires that all criminals should be punished, that desert (the fact of guilt) was a necessary and sufficient condition for punishment.[7] Many contemporary retributivists argue that while desert is a necessary condition of justified punishment, it is not morally necessary that all persons known to be guilty be punished. There may be reasons for withholding punishment in some cases. This does not mean that whether or not to punish is a matter of simple discretion. It means that there can be additional relevant considerations without thereby making the justification of punishment consequentialist.

A retributivist does not have to claim that retribution is an aim of punishment, if by "aim" we mean some state of affairs to be brought about, or intended to be brought about, by it. A retributivist might assert that punishment "balances the scales" of justice, that is, it does what justice requires in response to wrongdoing. This can be explained in non-consequentialist terms; it is not a matter of maximizing some sort of desired end or some specific type of state of affairs. Consequentialism is concerned with maximizing of that kind, whereas retributivist considerations concern what punishment normatively *is*, or what is done *in* punishing. That is not the same as looking at the matter in terms of what punishment *brings about*. If we "balance the scales" of justice in the retributive sense, what is crucial is the character (the motive and the form) of the response to wrongdoing rather than some desirable end *brought about* by what we do. The retributivist claims that the contextually relevant demands of justice are not to be interpreted in consequentialist terms. Perhaps educational policy or policy concerning the maintenance and improvement of infrastructure (sewers, roads, bridges, utilities, etc.) is appropriately interpreted in consequentialist terms. There are desirable ends we wish to bring about or perhaps even to maximize (given the need to balance their costs against the costs and benefits of other desirable ends). That is a sort of concern different from our concern with justifying the imposition of criminal sanction.

Thus, the retributivist does not include the desert condition on consequentialist grounds. Rather, it has independent weight; it is intrinsically important, and not included only because its inclusion is likely to lead to outcomes that are more desirable. It might be objected that, even if retributivist considerations have weight in their own right in regard to punishment, there is a criminal law in the first place, and there is criminal sanction in the first place, *so that there will be less crime*, less violence, less harm, fewer violations of people's rights, and fewer unwelcome intrusions on their spheres of autonomy. Thus, it might be argued that *the overall institution of criminal law* is justified in consequentialist terms, though particular judgments concerning who should be punished are driven by considerations of desert.[8]

That is an important suggestion, and it can be a way to show that there are necessary roles for consequentialism and retributivism in the overall conception of legal punishment. Still, the retributivist could argue that the significance of retributivism is more pronounced than that view suggests. It is true that the purpose of criminal law is to prevent people harming others, and that is, in a broad, highly general sense, a concern with what is or could be brought about by criminal justice. But the retributivist could say that retributivism captures and expresses the *point* of punishment, which is not the same thing as the overall aim or purpose of a criminal justice system.[9] Aim concerns what we hope will be brought about by an action or a practice. If one holds that punishment is justified by the fact that punishing offenders deters those persons from committing further crimes and deters other persons from committing crimes, that would be an articulation of punishment's justifying aim. It is justified (in that view) by the difference it makes, by the consequences of instituting the practice in contrast to not instituting it.

Many retributivists have asserted that it is a principle of reason or a clear moral intuition (not a hunch or guess but a non-inferential moral proposition) that if a person commits a wrongful action that person deserves to be punished. And, indeed, many people agree that this is a basic and evident proposition. However, there are many people who claim that they not only do not find it to be evident, but they do not even think it is *true*. The defense of retributivism need not rest on its principle being rationally evident or non-inferentially basic. Another approach to the issue is in terms of how retributivist considerations are connected with other principles and commitments concerning the distinctive, constitutive capacities of rational agents. For example, one might argue that no political order that failed to respect human beings as persons—as having a kind of intrinsic dignity separate from price and from what a human being can be used for—is morally permissible or legitimate. Conjoin to that the notion that a legal order should be such that the values and principles structuring it should be intelligible and endorsable by persons living under that rule of law, and that persons should have the ability to comply with the law, and we can see how a retributivist justification of punishment can emerge from that group of claims and convictions. Retributivism, it is argued, uniquely recognizes and responds to the standing and the agency of human beings.

The point is not that "anyone can see" that criminal conduct merits punishment imposed as suffering. Instead, it is that there is a network of concepts including agency, voluntariness, responsibility, desert, and respect, and the connections between them are the basis for certain normative considerations and considerations concerning how it is appropriate to treat persons. For instance, a person who knowingly, voluntarily does good for others merits gratitude. Similarly, a person who knowingly, voluntarily causes harm to others merits resentment. Gratitude and resentment are mere affect, and are not efficacious features of moral life unless persons act in ways appropriate to their expression. Moreover, it is simply a mistake to insist that resentment is always "toxic," always unhealthy, or an emotion we should seek to suppress or somehow eliminate. In fact, it can be argued that resentment, when directed at the proper objects, for the proper reasons, and to the proper extent, is crucial for the preservation of justice. Our resentment of needless, avoidable harm, and our resentment of deliberate unfair treatment, and so forth, are crucial to upholding principles of justice.[10] The absence or suppression of resentment of such harms would not be a mark of moral maturity; it would indicate a lack of commitment to justice. This sort of explication of important normative considerations can be plausibly employed in making the case for retributive punishment. Merely reporting resentment and merely noting that one merits being resented would be a kind of moral playacting rather than a willingness to do what is in fact justified, which is, in many cases, a matter of meting out punishment.

This is not offered as a fully adequate account of retributive punishment. It is a suggestion of lines along which such an account can be sketched out. It is an indication of how retributive punishment can be explained and justified in terms of the ethical significance of important features of human beings and human action. The justification of retributive punishment is not limited to a moral intuition or a putative rationally evident truth, which, as we know, many people simply do not share.

The defender of retributivism can argue that punishment is not justified by the difference made by it but by the moral rightness of responding to ill-desert with an imposition of suffering (even if the suffering is limited to the temporary loss of certain liberties). Punishment has a morally justifying point in itself, distinct from the difference it might make to future conduct. Thus, we can distinguish between what morally justifies punishment and asking the question of the overall purpose of criminal laws and the institutions and practices of criminal justice.

Retributivists often argue that if we justify punishment on the basis of what we hope to accomplish by punishing offenders we thereby fail to respect persons in the morally required manner. This is because consequentialist justifications legitimize an action or a practice on the basis of what is likely to be brought about by it. If there were good empirical reasons for believing that quite long sentences would dramatically reduce car theft, we might conclude that the benefit "purchased" by lengthy sentences is sufficient to justify them, even if, in most thefts of automobiles, no one is seriously harmed and cars are often recovered without significant damage. It appears that, in principle, consequentialist justifications are not constrained by considerations of proportionality in the way retributivism is. Moreover, it is in fact unclear how effectively specific sentences deter specific classes of criminals and crimes. It is unclear to what extent certain sentences are disastrous for some offenders while they are little more than a strategy of bringing crime within prison walls for others, and so on. Because of how complex the relevant issues are, and because of how difficult it is to measure the relevant matters with precision and confidence, claims about what punishment is aimed at, *when offered as part of a justification of punishment*, are vulnerable on epistemic grounds, independently of any moral reservations we might have about consequentialist justifications.

It must be granted that a consequentialist can insist that only offenders should be punished. This is because the practice of inflicting punishment on people known to be innocent would almost surely lead to widespread anxiety and suspicion regarding the authorities and the courts. The same reply can be made with respect to highly disproportionate sentences. The overall, long-term, undesirable consequences might easily outweigh the desirable ones. But it is thinking of justification in terms of a balance of consequences that the retributivist regards as mistaken. The retributivist maintains that a consequentialist calculation—even if it is empirically accurate—is an inappropriate approach to the issue. Indeed, the retributivist would argue that even if inflicting punishment on people known to be innocent had considerable net social benefits, it would still be wrong. It would be inconsistent with what persons *deserve* regardless of what might or might not be beneficial.

RETRIBUTIVISM, CONSEQUENCES, AND THE COMPLEXITY OF SENTENCING

Critics of retributivism often argue that, even if it can be successfully distinguished from vengeance (or from a socially sanitized, institutionally regulated version of vengeance), there remains something dubious in it, and that is the fact that it justifies a practice that knowingly causes suffering (that is, punishment) without regard to whether or not it does any good. The critic finds that feature of retributivism morally objectionable or, at the very least, quite problematic. When what is at issue is infliction of suffering, shouldn't the justification of it at the least ensure that the practice does some good? The point is that even if we could ascertain what punishments are proportional to which crimes, surely the justification of inflicting punishment requires that it do some good, if it is to be justified.

Retributivists are not deaf to this concern. It is not as though consequences are of no interest whatsoever. If certain practices of criminal sanction were retributively justified and also did some good (say, in terms of deterrence or in terms of motivating ethical self-correction or at least compliance with the law on the part of those punished) that would be welcomed by the retributivist. But again, the retributivist insists that it is a mistake to justify the infliction of suffering via punishment on the basis of what *else* might happen as a result, or on the basis of expected benefit. Punishment is one part of a complex of institutions and practices of criminal justice, and that complex exists because of the difference it makes to society overall. Nevertheless, the retributivist argues that any sentencing of an individual is to be justified on the basis of what that offender *did* and what the offender deserves for having done *that*. That is a fundamental normative claim with significance in its own right. Facts about desert are crucial in regard to the suitability of punishing any particular person *at all*, and they are crucial in regard to what punishment is *appropriate* to that person's criminal conduct.

That is not to say that commitment to a retributivist justification of punishment makes it any easier to know *what* specific punishment is appropriate. Moreover, it must be granted that offenders differ widely in sensibility, in regard to how they respond to being punished. For some persons punishment is a dreadful experience, a blow to their self-esteem, and an occasion for serious self-reflection and evaluation of one's own character. The reflection might lead to renewed resolve to comply with the law through seeing more clearly the soundness of the values informing it. Or it may lead to depression and a badly wounded personality. For others, imprisonment may be something of a rite of passage, a mark of attaining adulthood of a sort, and it could even strengthen the prisoner's self-esteem through the notion that "doing time" is evidence of one's rejection of the authority of the law. Serving in prison might elevate one's standing in certain social groups or gangs.

A great many other responses are possible, and how one's working life is affected, how one's relations with family and friends are impacted, and the difference made to one's standing in the community can figure in all sorts of ways for many kinds of reasons. It is possible to try to anticipate a prisoner's sensibility on the basis of the specific populations to which the person belongs. A twenty-two-year-old, well educated, physically unimposing, first-time offender is very likely to fare less well in a prison environment of intimidation, blackmail, gang-related social structure, and so forth than a thirty-eight-year-old who has "done time" four times and is preceded by a reputation for getting his way by devious manipulation and sheer force. It is fairly clear that the experience of incarceration is likely to be more traumatic and damaging for the former of the two. Nevertheless, statistics regarding groups will not yield precise, certain predictions, and people's reactions and behavior can be surprising in the best and in the worst ways. While there are many reliable relevant generalizations, there are still significant epistemic impediments to highly specific predictions of the consequences of specific penal practices. There are too many factors, too many influences, too many contingencies affecting what actually happens to particular individuals and how they respond.

Yet it might seem that for punishment to be fair, account should be taken of sensibility. If person P is impacted in such a way that he or she feels deeply ashamed and filled with remorse, shouldn't that response be acknowledged and perhaps be a consideration in favor of parole or release at an earlier time than would be suitable for person P*, who takes pride in doing "hard time" and in joining others who feel scorn for the law? On the one hand, it can be argued that fairness requires that persons who commit similar offenses deserve similar sentences. On the other hand, it can be argued that fairness requires that account should be taken of the offender's response to punishment (including the severity of an offender's suffering); otherwise, it is as if we are meting out quite different degrees of punishment for similar offenses.

The variability of sensibility is not necessarily the basis for a strong objection to retributivism. The latter can hold that one important aspect of fairness is that there should be consistency or near-consistency in sentencing. This is because, even if different persons would respond quite differently to being punished, it is important to have consistency in the norms that people are expected to honor. Everyone can know what the law says, and can know that it applies to everyone similarly. There is fair warning with regard to liability to punishment. It is not as though it is a mystery what counts as an offense or even what sentences are likely to follow conviction. In any case, it is impossible to fashion a criminal justice system that is responsive to the particularities of every individual's character and circumstances, and such a system is not a necessary condition of fair criminal justice.

Current law (at least in the United States) takes sensibility into account to some extent, at least insofar as there is often discretion in sentencing. The utterly unrepentant offender may be sentenced more severely than the offender who exhibits remorse and acknowledgment of the wrongfulness of the crime. It might be difficult to tell reliably when an offender's show of remorse is genuine and when it is manipulative. Good behavior while serving a sentence may be clearer evidence of whether the offender is at least willing to be steadily compliant with rules, whether or not the person has had a crisis of conscience or has undergone a process of ethical self-correction. Thus, there are various opportunities for some aspects of sensibility to be taken into account.

However, it remains important to recognize that, even with discretion in sentencing, it can happen that offenders' response to being imprisoned can vary quite dramatically. Differences in sensibility might remain significant despite the opportunities for the criminal justice system to weigh it and respond to it. Many offenders may simply have no idea of how they will respond to being punished. Sentencing judges may feel they cannot make confident predictions regarding the issue. The retributivist can point out that this sort of uncertainty does not bedevil retributivism in a uniquely damaging way. It is simply a difficulty encountered by any approach to justifying punishment. And, again, it is not a plausible requirement of criminal justice that it should punish individuals in a manner uniquely suited to the particularities of each person. No system of law and social institutions could even pretend to do that. The epistemic obstacles simply cannot be overcome. That does not imply that whatever we do is unfair. We have an obligation to be fair in the ways in which it is possible to be fair, not in every logically conceivable way.

Perhaps a more troubling objection to retributivism is that, in many cases, not just the offender suffers as a result of punishment. Those dependent on the offender can suffer as well, and they do not deserve to suffer. Depending on the circumstances, the imprisonment of a parent, spouse or partner, or a son or daughter who has been providing care could be disastrous for other family members or close associates of the prisoner. In *Why Punish?* Nigel Walker writes:

> Those who object to utilitarianism because it seems to condone the punishment of the innocent . . . might ask whether the harm done every day to prisoners' dependants in the name of retributive sentencing does not amount to the same thing.[11]

He says that "the retributive sentencer cannot escape this dilemma."[12] That may be so, and retributivism has to acknowledge the reality of what Walker calls "obiter punishment." This is distinct from another category of possible impacts of punishment, such as loss of employment opportunities and income, damaged friendships, social stigma, and so on. Earlier I noted the distinction between the aim and the justification of punishment, and that is relevant here in the sense that the retributivist's primary, direct concern is with desert rather than foreseen (or unforeseen) consequences and the balance of benefits and costs of specific penal practices. Making that distinction will not make the difficulties of unintended consequences disappear; they are still real, and they can matter powerfully in people's lives.

Still, retributivism is no worse off than other justifications with respect to "obiter punishment." It is always possible to widen the context of morally relevant ramifications and to add new descriptions of the circumstances, descriptions that extend beyond a narrowly legal focus on that specific offense as conceived by the law, and that particular offender's sentence and responses to it. That widening is a way to continue to generate additional "yes, but what about . . ." questions. It is never the case that what is going on, or what results from what is going on, is limited to what is captured and expressed by the specific legal description applied by criminal justice. There will always be additional descriptions, and many of them will describe unwanted and unintended effects. That fact is made no more bearable by a justification for punishment that is non-retributivist. There could be consequences of many kinds, extending well into the future and affecting many people who had no involvement with the crime being punished. A conseqen- tialist might argue that at least that approach takes such matters into account. But that is also the source of a weakness of consequentialism, namely, it includes no principled basis for discriminating what is directly relevant to punishing the crime committed from everything else causally impacted by punishing the crime.

How far out should we try to track the consequences of practices and policies? Why should all manner of consequences be taken into account when the question to be answered is a question of *criminal justice in a liberal polity*? I emphasize that because it highlights the appropriateness of concern with respect for persons as voluntary, accountable agents. The more our attention sprawls over the multitude of radiating consequences, the more we put at risk the focus on values of great significance in a liberal polity. The more the consequentialist seeks to take into account those effects, the more problematic becomes the resulting determination of what criminal justice requires insofar as the factors shaping that determina- tion may have little to do with criminal justice.[13] We will have a bit more to say regarding this issue in the final section of the discussion.

As a final comment here on the issue of whether retributivism is objectionably inattentive to consequences, it can be said that obiter punishment and incidental harms to the sanctioned offender (such as stigma, loss of job opportunities, and so forth) are not eliminable. The justice of this or that action or practice cannot ensure that it is *totally* just in the sense that there is no injustice in what eventu- ates. But retributivist justification is minimally vulnerable to being interpreted as a bet that our luck will be good if we punish, that is, that punishing brings about net gains. Consequentialist justifications depend on luck in the respect that there is always looseness and uncertainty concerning the relation between any consequentialist justification and the actual states of affairs brought about by the practice. Retributivist justification is not subject to luck and contingency in the same way because it is not dependent on bringing about some particular result or state of affairs. It can welcome desirable consequences, but it is not dependent on them.

RETRIBUTIVISM AND SOCIAL CONDEMNATION

In recent years, attention has been drawn to the significance of expressivist considerations in the justification of punishment.[14] According to an expressivist view, a chief difference between imposing a penalty (or a tax or a licensing requirement) and punishing is that the latter involves an expression of denunciation, censure for having violated an important value or norm. The conduct in question merits indignation and is not just undesirable or inconvenient; it is antithetical to important socially shared values such that regular conventions for asserting society's commitment to them are appropriate. Joel Feinberg has argued that with regard to certain types of conduct a guilty verdict is not enough, and an expression of condemnation is not enough; punishment is needed as an authoritative disavowal of the conduct.

He argues that punishment serves the socially useful function of vindicating the law when it has been violated. Anything short of the imposition of punishment would be merely symbolic and would fail to preserve the distinction between what is unwelcome and what is wrong in a manner that is unacceptable as a violation of important values. He argues that punishment has symbolic significance, and that is how it is distinguished from a penalty. The difference is not just a matter of severity; after all, penalties can be quite substantial. Nor is it simply a matter of a penalty being a "price" that one pays. Being fired from employment because of unsatisfactory performance is quite different from paying a parking ticket, and in neither case (unless the situation is quite extraordinary) are condemnation and censure appropriate. We could say that loss of employment is a "price" of poor performance, but we can still see the difference between those cases. What distinguishes both of them from punishment is the role of the expression of resentment and condemnation in the latter.

The emphasis on the role of denunciation is well placed. In general, a liberal polity criminalizes and punishes conduct it finds unacceptable because of how it threatens participants in that order and is not merely objectionable as a nuisance or out of step with popular fashion or etiquette. There are often costs to engaging in the latter kinds of conduct, but society does not respond with denunciation as a way of asserting and sustaining an important norm or value.

Feinberg argues that expressivism avoids some of the stubbornly persistent problems facing retributivism. Chief among them is the issue of how to fit punishments to crimes. Feinberg claims that trying to fit punishments to the moral blameworthiness of the offender just cannot be done in a conclusively satisfactory way. We simply cannot tell whether we are getting it right or not, and reasonable disagreement is always possible. Contrariwise, we can do much better at telling whether a sentence expresses society's condemnation and resentment. The expressivist account is a way to give clarity to the meaning of punishment without undertaking the impossible task of apportioning the severity of punishment to the blameworthiness of the offender. Penalties and punishments are authoritative deprivations for failures, but the latter involves a condemnatory aspect that the former does not. It is not a question of how burdensome is the deprivation, and in any event, that will differ significantly across different individuals. Instead, the main point is that punishment involves condemnation.

Feinberg concedes that numerous difficulties remain. However, he holds that conventions of disapproval can be articulated with more clarity and consistency than attempts to proportion pain to blameworthiness. Punishment is a "conventional device for the expression of attitudes of resentment and indignation, and of judgments of disapproval and reprobation. . . ."[15] That is why hard treatment is required in response to certain kinds of conduct. Mere censure or disapproval would fail to express society's condemnation. Feinberg argues that if an alternative to hard treatment, an alternative to the infliction of pain, could effectively perform the function of expressing condemnation, then that alternative should be considered. There is no retributive requirement that punishment should involve hard treatment; it's just that we have no other suitable convention.

There are several conceptions of the justification of punishment that include retributivist elements *and* elements concerning communicative features. R. A. Duff has developed such an account.[16] In his view punishment is to address the offender as someone able to acknowledge the correctness of the values reflected in the law, the wrongness of his or her own conduct, and the justice of punishment. That complex acknowledgment can—and hopefully will—motivate the offender to undertake a process of ethical self-correction and reconnection with correct values. The entire complex communicative character of this conception of punishment depends on punishment being deserved, but clearly Duff believes that there is more to punishment than "just deserts." Duff's view includes a retributivist core, but he connects it with additional elements concerning the relations between offenders and the community, and with certain views about the moral psychology of criminal sanction and how it is intended to motivate a corrected conception of values and a corrected disposition to act on the part of persons punished.

Duff interprets punishment as having an important role in reconnecting offenders with the values of the society, and he accepts "hard treatment" (incarceration) as uniquely suited to motivate a kind of secular penance by which the offender's alienation from the community is overcome.[17] It is not just that hard treatment is the most suitable convention we have, but that, given human nature, we know that deserved suffering is normatively appropriate. It can motivate acknowledgment of one's offense and motivate a process of secular penance, of ethical self-correction. Duff's view is a good example of a position in which retributivism is integral but, at the same time, punishment is a complex communicative act, which, when it succeeds, realizes certain goods for the offender and the community. This is neither pure consequentialism nor pure retributivism.

Duff's communicative account illustrates how retributivism can include an expressive aspect recognizing the significance of condemnation as a feature of punishment. For Duff, that aspect is part of a complex mode of address, which appeals to the offender's reason. There is at least some communicative dimension to retributivism generally in the respect that the law and criminal sanction are thought to address persons as rational agents and are held to reflect values and principles persons could rationally endorse. It is in the complexity of that mode that Duff's view includes elements that go beyond what is essential to retributivism. For Duff it is important that punishment should be understood as part of a conception of community in which persons respect each other and have a measure of concern for the well-being of the community in general. Punishment is not simply rejection from the community but a way of declaring that the offender's relation to the community has been damaged by his or her conduct. Through the sting of punishment the offender can be motivated to restore relations with the community through ethical self-correction. That is more than a prudential decision to comply with the law; it is a restored commitment to what are now recognized as the correct values governing life in that community.

Retributivist theories differ from expressivist theories in that the former place the emphasis on punishment as deserved and as fitting. Retributivists acknowledge the difficulty of ascertaining proper proportionality but accept that difficulty as setting a task requiring constant critical consideration rather than seeing it as rendering fitness of punishment to crime hopelessly mysterious or confined to metaphor (such as "balancing the scales of justice" or "righting a wrong," etc.). Moreover, retributivists do not regard hard treatment merely as the penal convention we rely on. They regard the suffering that punishment causes as a crucial part of what makes deserved punishment genuine. The point is not to worsen or damage the offender but to address the offender in a way that respects rational agency and demonstrates the reality of accountability. Voluntary, intentional agents are accountable for conduct that violates certain values and principles, and as accountable, they are liable to sanction.

Retributivist theories differ from communicative theories in that the latter often involve what we might call "thicker" commitments regarding the nature of political community and the individual's relations to other members of it. It is plausible to suggest that one's approach to the justification of punishment is likely to be shaped and oriented by one's conception of the polity. Retributivism is well suited to conceptions of the liberal polity in which there is considerable scope for individual autonomy, and while people may have many sorts of significant relations to each other, criminal justice is not directly concerned with restoring any specific conception of community life other than that required by the liberal rule of law.

Duff's conception of punishment is part of a larger conception of a liberal polity of a certain type, in which persons' mutual concern for each other's moral character and concern for the common good are pronounced features of civil society. That is not to say that he advocates people extensively policing each other's souls. Instead, he is making the case for a polity in which the notion of a morally informed community has a central place. There is more to this conception of liberalism than protected spheres of individual liberty.

RETRIBUTIVISM, THE LIBERAL POLITY, AND THE DIGNITY OF PERSONS

There are several reasonable conceptions of the liberal polity, and some of those conceptions may not involve the commitments we find in Duff's view. In addition, not only are there multiple reasonable conceptions of the liberal order, there are numerous different reasons people might have for *supporting* a liberal order, and it is not clear that just one type of consideration or one unique method of argument justifies the liberal polity.[18] In fact, one of the merits of a liberal order is that it can accommodate a measure of disagreement about those important matters. This does not mean that people have an unqualified right to reject the law or to decide which laws to obey and which to flout; however, civil disobedience may be justified in some circumstances. (The questions of *which* circumstances, and what *forms* of disobedience, are important issues of political and moral thought.) After all, even a liberal-democratic polity can make bad or unjust law.

While there are likely to be persistent disputes regarding some matters of law—the possession and use of various drugs is one such issue in the United

States—criminal law in a liberal polity should reflect widely endorsed values and principles. Even when that is the case, it will not resolve all questions of the relation between law and morality. But a liberal polity can accommodate a measure of disagreement on some such matters, and such disagreement can fuel important political and moral debates, and in that respect can be healthy.

Also, it is important to recognize that a great many matters having to do with the character of relations between people and the sorts of concern they have for each other have to do with the character of civil society rather than the liberal rule of law as such. The way that one understands the relations between civil society and the basic form of the polity can have significant implications for how extensive one takes the relations between criminal justice and justice more comprehensively construed to be. If one believes that many aspects of civil society should also be regarded as politically significant, it is likely that one will also think that criminal justice needs to be understood as one aspect of a more general, multi-aspect conception of justice overall. (Sometimes this is referred to as "social justice," though at present the expression tends to be used to connote a specific policy agenda, typically including extensive claims about redistribution of wealth.)

Regardless of the diversity of conceptions of a liberal order, criminal law and criminal justice in a liberal democracy involve important commitments to respecting persons as capable of understanding the reasons for what is required, broadly endorsing the values informing what is required, and understanding the justice of criminal sanction when persons violate the law. Kant famously marked the distinction between *persons* and *things* as the distinction between what has dignity (and is owed respect as rationally autonomous) and what has a price (and is such that something else can be substituted for it).[19] Even if one does not accept Kant's metaphysical basis for the distinction, or his specific conception of rational autonomy, the normative point of Kant's distinction is recognizably important and has considerable moral and political significance.

Kant is not the sole origin of a distinction between the dignity of persons and the type of value that things that are non-persons can have. There are biblical roots for the notion of human beings as being like God, inasmuch as the former are created in the image of the latter, possessing intellect and will. Moreover, religiously grounded ethics often holds that each person has equal standing before God; no one is intrinsically superior to anyone else, and all are owed respect. There are also ancient philosophical conceptions in which the possession of reason is a basis for human beings' capacity for voluntary action guided by conceptions of the good. Such views involve the claim that there are, in fact, objective goods (and evils) for human beings. (There is no guarantee that people will acquire and seek to actualize *correct* conceptions of the good. However, the capacity to act on the basis of understanding—whether correct or not—is a crucial feature of a human being.) Thus, multiple currents of thought supply elements for a conception of human beings as having morally and politically significant standing, standing that law should respect.

The point is not that one may simply pick whichever view one prefers but that there are substantial conceptual resources for explicating why criminal law should *address* or relate to persons in certain ways rather than simply *apply* to or be imposed on them. It is worth observing that some of the most important sources of the conception of persons' standing in a liberal democracy were not themselves committed to that form of political order. But that does not disqualify them as valuable resources for understanding liberal democracy.

A conception of a liberal-democratic polity in which the fundamental principles of liberalism are protected against erosion by democratic process will be one in which the rule of law is restrained in regard to enforcing or imposing any specific conception of a well-led life or of moral excellence. It will take the liberal dimension as seriously as it takes the democratic dimension. In John Stuart Mill's defense of liberty he was concerned with the way in which the tyranny of majorities could effectively repress minorities, eccentricity, and ways of life and interests not consonant with popular taste and convention. He was right to be concerned, and that concern can be extended to the ways in which the political process itself can be employed so as to encroach on individual liberties, though doing so with the political "mandate" of democratic process. Democratic processes can yield illiberal results, and it is not as though any result achieved by the ballot is therefore politically just or suitable to the liberal polity. Preservation of the liberalism of liberal democracy is a challenging task and not something that can be taken for granted.

Given the retributivist's central concern with desert, it might seem that retributivism's approach to justifying punishment is limited in its suitability to only certain more libertarian conceptions of the polity (that is, theories in which the powers of the state are more rather than less limited). A consequentialist approach might be more accommodating in regard to the sorts of policy aims punishment is intended to serve. A frequent criticism of retributivism is that it is an implausibly narrow view and it fails to come to grips with the multiple social and economic issues relating to the causes of crime and the life circumstances of many offenders. Critics (whether consequentialists or not) sometimes urge that punishment should be seen in a larger, more complex context of social issues. There is an important sense in which the way one sees criminal sanction is something rather like a barometer for how one sees the relations between political order and the social world. The answer to the questions, "What justifies criminal sanction, and what should we expect from it?" can indicate much about one's view of the scope of legitimate state power and the role of the state in shaping society.

The retributivist is not willfully blind to the larger social context of crime and punishment. However, the retributivist is likely to argue that there are basic issues of principle concerning crime and criminal sanction, and that we obscure them or improperly complicate them by integrating them with other types of concerns to which other considerations of justice are relevant. Many retributivists would argue that we should not assimilate criminal justice to a larger, more comprehensive conception of justice. The principles and features distinctive of criminal justice warrant their own focus, which is what retributivism provides, and it does so in a manner intended to be responsive to, and to preserve, liberal principles and ideals. It does this through its focus on the accountable agency of individuals and regard for their moral standing. The retributivist might argue that attempting to resolve social problems through criminal justice confuses matters and blurs the normative focus of *both* contexts.

Adding more types of considerations to the justification of punishment and connecting it with other aspects of justice are likely to enlarge the authority of political institutions over criminal sanction because more policy aims will be involved. Granted, that is precisely what is desired by many defenders of the view that criminal justice should be seen as one aspect of a more comprehensive conception of justice. Critics of the view argue that it invites a substantial risk to liberal principles, as it makes desert and its core notion of individual accountability just one factor among many others in determining what should constitute criminal justice. If one wished to endorse a view in which the state has extensive commitments and powers in regard to the social world—thus, more policy and less civil society—and to also be committed to an austere retributivist conception of punishment, considerable additional explanation would be required. Given one's other commitments, retributivism might seem out of place. It would not be straightforwardly inconsistent with the rest of the view, but the overall account would need to be carefully explicated.

As a final point, even if one is committed to an austere conception of retributivism and to quite limited state powers, there remain the following difficulties. The first is that determining what are to count as the fundamental rights of persons in a liberal polity may not be feasible apart from substantive moral commitments and commitments concerning the chief goods of a well-lived life. The second is that the notion of desert may be inseparable from the notion of character-based moral blameworthiness (and praiseworthiness, too).[20] That is problematic because it suggests that even the most restrained liberal polity will, in its criminal justice institutions and practices, be making judgments about people's "insides"—their characters, and not just their conduct.

In response to the former point we should note that we have, in a way, already addressed it by observing that even a liberal polity depends on a widely endorsed framework of values and principles. That does not make the difficulty disappear, but it is at least acknowledged and accepted as a feature of a liberal polity. Such a polity faces the persistent challenge of restraining the tendency to expand the rule of law over more and more departments of life in illiberal ways. One way to describe that extension would be to say that the liberal polity must guard against state policy encroaching more and more on civil society, shrinking the sphere of voluntary activity. However benign the state's intentions, it does what it does through coercive power, and that is a fundamental reason why the spontaneity and voluntariness characteristic of civil society can be threatened by the expansion of policy.

The second point may appear to put liberalism at risk in a more threatening way because of what it suggests about the danger to individuals' moral independence. In order to make determinations of desert, the law has to judge offenders on the basis of features of inner moral character, and it is not difficult to see illiberal potential in that. Those features make the difference between negligence and careful premeditation, and they can be very important to questions concerning motives. However, here again, it is possible to be accommodative without undermining liberalism.

The law does indeed need to make various distinctions concerning motive, intention, knowledge, reasonableness, negligence, and so forth in order to be adequately discriminating in attributing culpability, given the complex texture of agency. In principle, reference to what Kant called "inner wickedness" may be necessary, even though a liberal polity's rule of law is not an instrument for encouraging virtue. The distinctions can help guide judgment in ways that respect individuals' "insides," though they can also be abused in ways that lead to punishing people for *what they are like* and not just *what they have done*. Thus, the distinctions are not inherently inimical to liberalism, though it is crucial to guard against the potential for abuse of persons via their use.

At the outset we explained how retributivism differs from vengeance. Moreover, retributivism does not necessarily advocate harsh punishment. It insists on proportionality, *not* severity. It is possible to defend a retributivist conception of punishment and *also* support fixed ceilings on punishment. For example, one might argue that no crime should be punished with a sentence greater than ten years of imprisonment. That ceiling should not be set arbitrarily; even if there is no "natural" fit of punishments to crimes, there is a vitally important difference between a carefully reasoned matching of punishments to crimes and a schedule of such things without a reasoned basis.

What sentences are appropriate to which crimes is a complex, very difficult question, and critics of retributivism are right to point out there just is no evident, *a priori* or rationally compelling way to answer it. The retributivist need not claim that retributivism renders answering the question easy or uncontroversial. Rather, the retributivist claims to offer the justification of legal punishment most suited to a political order in which individuals are to be regarded and treated as rational, voluntary agents, responsible for their actions and able to conform with the requirements of the law. Retributivism supplies what it takes to be the most normatively sound justification for punishment.

NOTES

1. Herbert Morris defended such a view in "Persons and Punishment," in *Monist* 52 (1968).

2. Nietzsche famously argued that punishment originated as a practice of exacting a form of debt from a person whose conduct was regarded as undesirable and damaging to the group. He also argued that, despite all the moralistic overtones of philosophical and religious conceptions of punishment, it is a way of expressing vengeance and power over those punished. See his *The Genealogy of Morals*, especially its "First Treatise." Numerous sources in the history of philosophy and political thought have important resonances in contemporary theorizing about the liberal polity. Those sources range from Aristotle to Locke to Mill to Rawls and Nozick, with many others in between. There are several rival theories of liberalism involved in current debates about political forms and institutions and state powers. Plus, there are rivals to *liberalism* as a basic political form. As a matter of historical fact, the vast majority of states in the world have not been liberal or liberal-democratic states.

3. Among contemporary theorists, Andrew Von Hirsch and Jeffrie Murphy are among the most influential defenders of a desert-based approach to punishment.

4. Jeremy Bentham developed perhaps the "purest" consequentialist justification of punishment, one faithful to his rigorous hedonic utilitarian principles. See chapters 11–15 of *The Principles of Morals and Legislation* (Amherst, NY: Prometheus Books, 1988).

5. H. L. A. Hart, *Punishment and Responsibility* (Oxford: Oxford University Press, 1995), 172.

6. A consequentialist approach does not exclude considerations of fairness or proportionality. However, to the extent that it includes them, they are explained in consequentialist terms, and they are not regarded as justified by rational principle or on the basis of normative considerations, other than the fact (if it is a fact) that there are benefits to including them. For a discussion of the main approaches to ethical theory and the chief differences between them see my *Dimensions of Moral Theory: An Introduction to Metaethics and Moral Psychology* (Malden, MA: Blackwell, 2002).

7. See Kant's "On the Right of Punishing" in his *The Philosophy of Law: An Exposition of the Fundamental Principles of Jurisprudence as the Science of Right*.

8. Hart writes:

   Much confusing shadow-fighting between utilitarians and their opponents may be avoided if it is recognized that it is perfectly consistent to assert *both* that the General Justifying aim of the practice of punishment is its beneficial consequences *and* that the pursuit of this General Aim should be qualified or restricted out of deference to principles of

Distribution which require that punishment should be only of an offender for an offence. (*Punishment and Responsibility*, p. 9)

9. I develop at greater length this, and some of the following objections to consequentialist justifications of punishment in "Luck and Retribution," *Philosophy* 74 (October 1999): 535–555.

10. Adam Smith presents an especially important account of the role of resentment in the appropriate concern with justice. See *The Theory of Moral Sentiments*, pt. 3, chap. 4.

11. Nigel Walker, *Why Punish?* (Oxford: Oxford University Press, 1991), 107.

12. Ibid.

13. There is an important contemporary debate over the issue of whether criminal justice should or should not be integrated into a more comprehensive conception of justice. For treatment of the issues in dispute see *From Social Justice to Criminal Justice: Poverty and the Administration of Criminal Law*, ed. William Heffernan and John Kleinig (New York: Oxford University Press), 2000.

14. See Joel Feinberg, "The Expressive Function of Punishment," in *A Reader on Punishment*, ed. R. A. Duff and David Garland (New York: Oxford University Press, 1994), 71–91.

15. Ibid., 74.

16. Duff's work has been quite influential in recent debates concerning both the justification and the aim of punishment. Also, Duff has connected those issues with important topics in moral psychology and political theory. His communicative theory is presented in *Punishment, Communication, and Community* (New York: Oxford University Press), 2001.

17. Duff developed his account of punishment motivating a kind of secular penance in *Trials and Punishments* (Cambridge: Cambridge University Press, 1986).

18. In recent decades a number of important conceptions of liberalism and the liberal political order have been developed. John Rawls's *A Theory of Justice* has been especially influential in regard to reinvigorating the debate about liberalism and the just liberal order. Amartya Sen's *The Idea of Justice* is a much-discussed contemporary work. See also *Perfection and Neutrality: Essays in Liberal Theory*, ed. S. Wall and G. Klosko, and Joseph Raz's *The Morality of Freedom* for discussion of some of the most significant contemporary approaches to liberal theory.

19. See Immanuel Kant, *Grounding for the Metaphysics of Morals*, trans. James Ellington (Indianapolis: Hackett, 1993). There he makes the distinction between persons and things, and between dignity and price. Also, one of his formulations of the fundamental criterion of right action, the moral law, is in terms of the distinctive form of respect owed to persons (as rationally autonomous beings).

20. On both of these points see Jeffrie G. Murphy, "Legal Moralism and Liberalism," in *Character, Liberty, and Law: Kantian Essays in Theory and Practice* (Dordrecht: Kluwer, 1998), 89–118, and "Legal Moralism and Retribution Revisited," in *Punishment and the Moral Emotions: Essays in Law, Morality, and Religion* (New York: Oxford University Press, 2012), 66–93.

*Jonathan Jacobs is chair of philosophy at John Jay College of Criminal Justice, director of the Institute for Criminal Justice Ethics, and a member of the doctoral faculty of philosophy at the CUNY Graduate Center. Much of his work addresses moral and political questions concerning criminal sanction in a liberal polity. He also works on medieval moral psychology and metaethics, exploring how theistic commitments inform those issues. He has been awarded grants and fellowships from the National Endowment for the Humanities and the Littauer Foundation and is a Life Member of Clare Hall, Cambridge. He is the author of nine books and over seventy articles.

Written for this book and used by permission of the author.

Two Justifications of Punishment

by Michael Lessnoff*

Every developed society has a system of law; that is, of rules prescribing the infliction of various deprivations, minor and severe, on persons who behave in specified ways. Law, in other words, entails punishment.

That organized society thus deliberately imposes suffering on certain of its members inevitably calls for justification. Historically, two major, and conflicting, justifications of punishment have been suggested—the retributive theory, and the utilitarian theory. I wish to argue that the latter is essentially correct, and that this has been obscured by an ambiguity of the word 'justification.'

By 'the retributive theory,' I mean the view that what justifies the suffering inflicted by punishment is the moral culpability of the behaviour that is punished; that persons who have committed morally wrong acts (or at least seriously culpable ones), and only such persons, ought to be punished; and that the severity of punishment ought to be, so far as possible, in proportion to the moral culpability of the act punished.[1] On this view, the *consequences* of punishment, other than the immediate deprivation suffered by the criminal, are irrelevant to its justification.

On the utilitarian view, by contrast, it is entirely by its beneficial consequences that punishment is justified, and not by any obligation to visit suffering on the perpetrators of immoral acts; specifically, punishment is justified in so far as it tends to reduce the occurrence of crimes, that is, of seriously undesirable or bad acts.[2] Punishment may reduce the occurrence of bad acts in two ways: namely, through fear—the discouraging effect on those contemplating criminal acts of the possibility of suffering legal sanctions as a result (commonly called deterrence); or through moral education—the salutary effect of punishment on the moral personality of the individual punished, or of members of society generally, so that they become disinclined, for reasons of moral principle, to perform acts of the kind punished.[3]

I am here concerned with utilitarian and retributive theories *of punishment*, and not with utilitarianism or retributivism as broader ethical theories. Nothing is implied by either of the theories I am considering as to what, in general, is the criterion of morally good or bad action. The kinds of action that the utilitarian thinks bad, and wishes to reduce through punishment, he may hold to be bad on any ground at all, including intuition or divine revelation; the kind of action that the retributivist thinks immoral, and on whose perpetrator he wishes to visit suffering, he may, equally, hold to be immoral on any ground whatever, including the unhappiness or other bad consequence that they cause. Indeed, the kinds of action whose occurrence the utilitarian seeks to reduce through punishment could quite possibly be precisely the same kinds of action as call, in retributivist eyes, for the infliction of suffering on their perpetrators, and for the same reasons. Nor is either the utilitarian or the retributivist necessarily committed to upholding punishment at all: the utilitarian will abandon it if convinced it does not reduce crime; and the retributivist will do the same if he believes morally culpable acts to be non-existent (as might be the case if he were also a determinist).

What, now, of the merits of the two opposed theories, retributive and utilitarian? Two separate issues have to be disentangled here—one moral, one logical. If a man believes that perpetrators of morally culpable acts ought to suffer, regardless of the consequences, we may think him a barbarian, but we cannot prove him wrong. On the other hand, there may be no moral disagreement between adherents of the contending theories, but only confusion as to what the implications of the theories are. We arrive, here, at the familiar challenge thrown by the retributionists in the face of their adversaries; if it is the desirable consequences of punishment that justify it, and not the fact that the victim has committed a wrong act, why not, on appropriate occasions, punish an innocent man, pretending that he is guilty, if the desirable consequences can be brought about thereby? It is useless for the utilitarian to reply that punishment of the innocent is unlikely to reduce crime, and that therefore utilitarianism could not endorse it: for, apart from the dubious accuracy of the premise, the charge that the utilitarian has to counter is that his theory *would* countenance punishment of the innocent *if* this produced desirable consequences. If a theory *could*, in possible circumstances, justify punishing the innocent, it may well be an immoral theory.

Nor is it of much use to argue, as some utilitarians do, that their theory cannot justify punishment of the innocent, because there is no such thing—because 'punishment' *means* inflicting suffering on a person guilty of an offence, for that offence.[4] For, the relevant sense of 'guilt' is here *moral* (not merely legal) guilt; and to deny that there can be legally correct punishment of morally guiltless acts is to deny that a law can be unjust, which is absurd. Utilitarians would do better to defend themselves by saying that their theory is an answer, not to the question, 'What justifies punishment?,' but to the different question 'What justifies punishment of the (morally) guilty?' This simple modification would more satisfactorily achieve the desired result of preventing the utilitarian theory from justifying punishment of the innocent. It also has the advantage of exposing rather clearly the real moral issue between the opposed theories of punishment.

For the thoroughgoing retributionist answer to the question, 'What justifies punishment of the guilty?' is 'Their guilt, simply,' while the utilitarian answer is 'The tendency of the punishment to reduce the occurrence of wrong acts.' Choice between these two answers depends, of course, on a value judgment; perhaps to most people the utilitarian answer seems more humane and therefore preferable.

But utilitarianism is charged, not only with possibly justifying punishment of the innocent, but also with possibly justifying savage punishment of the guilty, if this were an effective way of reducing crime. At this point a retributive theory may still seem preferable, for it at least limits the severity of punishment, admittedly in a rather vague way, by the degree of moral culpability of the offence. But this difficulty has been solved by Professor Hart,[5] through his distinction between the General Justifying Aim of punishment and its Principles of Distribution (determining who may be punished, and how much). The General Justifying Aim of punishment as a social institution, as of any social institution, is the purpose it serves, the benefit it secures, the good it does. For a thoroughgoing retributionist, the General Justifying Aim of punishment is to ensure that wrongdoers suffer as they deserve; for a utilitarian, it is to diminish the amount of wrongdoing. All social institutions that are deliberately established or maintained have a General Justifying Aim (a manifest function, in the language of the sociologist Robert Merton[6]); only some of them involve questions of distribution also. In the case of punishment, by its very nature, this second question arises as well. As Hart shows, a contention that the point of institutionalizing *some* system of punishment is to reduce wrongdoing, by no means determines who is to be punished, or how much (in other words, does not determine precisely *what* system of punishment should be institutionalized): for the pursuit of a goal does not imply that one neglects all other values. Since punishment involves the infliction of suffering on individuals, the rights of individuals are obviously relevant to its distribution. The Principles of Distribution that most people, perhaps, would accept, lay down that punishment should be imposed only on persons guilty of an offence, and should not be more severe than the moral culpability of the offence justifies. It is here that the idea of retribution properly comes into the picture; but, as Hart stresses, holding to retribution in the distribution of punishment does not entail the conclusion that retribution is the General Justifying Aim of punishment, nor is it inconsistent with the view that its General Justifying Aim is utilitarian.

What, then, is the justification of punishment? Punishment has in common with a good deal of human behaviour the fact that it causes harm, suffering, inconvenience, etc., to individual victims. Such behaviour may be institutionalized or purely private. A commonplace example of the latter kind is causing noise late at night, thus preventing one's neighbours from sleeping. Imagine such a case actually to happen—X plays his record-player until 3 a.m., so that Y cannot sleep. Suppose now that a third party asks X to justify his behaviour. X, let us say, replies as follows: "My friends and I get a lot of pleasure from the music; and anyway Y has always been a rude and unfriendly neighbour." Here X has given two justifications for his behaviour; yet they are totally different in type. The word 'justification' is ambiguous. The pleasure derived from the music is X's Justifying Aim for his behaviour; the past rudeness and hostility of Y is no such thing, but rather the consideration that, in X's eyes, permits him to ignore (or at least override) Y's interests. The first half of X's reply can be taken to be an answer to a question such as 'What good does your behaviour do?' (though probably no such question was intended in the imaginary example); the second half, to such a question as 'What entitles you to treat a person in that way? (i.e., to hurt him)?' The former may be called the question of *teleological* justification, the latter that of *entitling* justification.

A similar dichotomy of justifications is applicable to many social institutions. Take, for example, the institution, in our own society, of compulsory purchase of private property by public authorities. Like punishment, and like causing noise late at night, this causes some suffering (or at least inconvenience) to individuals, and hence demands justification. Again, two kinds of justification can be given for the practice as it exists in our society: first, that compulsory purchase is necessary for the sake of economic development, amenity, etc.; second, that those whose property is taken from them receive fair compensation. Here, economic development and amenity are teleological justifications, while fair compensation is the entitling justification that (allegedly) reconciles the pursuit of these goals with justice to the individual. Clearly the case of punishment is precisely parallel: the teleological justification (Hart's General Justifying Aim) is the reduced occurrence of wrongful acts; the entitling justification is the guilt of the offender. Thus Hart's distinction between a utilitarian General Justifying Aim of punishment and partly retributive Principles of Distribution, takes its place as one example of a larger family of distinctions, between teleological justification and entitling justification of behaviour that causes suffering or inconvenience to individuals.

The problem of entitling justification is more or less the problem of avoiding injustice in the pursuit of goals, however admirable. It is a crass error to make a natural entitling justification serve as a teleological justification; and this, surely, is what could happen if anyone deduced from the fact that unjust punishment can be avoided only by punishing only the guilty, the conclusion that the aim of punishment is to make the guilty suffer. Such a view is no more plausible than the corresponding view that the aim of compulsory purchase is to compensate the expropriated for inconvenience suffered. Although the question, 'What justifies punishment?' is ambiguous, the correct answer to the question 'Why punish?' is utilitarian. It is in this sense that the utilitarian theory of punishment is essentially correct.

If these considerations are correct, it follows that there is less difference between punishment and other institutions involving the exercise of state authority than has sometimes been thought—such institutions as quarantine, taxation, or military conscription. These are all institutions which involve inconvenience and even hardship to individuals; all of them, therefore, require both a teleological and an entitling justification. In the case of conscription, for example, the typical teleological justification would be that it is necessary for the defence of the nation, or (less respectably) to extend its boundaries; the entitling justification, that defence (and expansion) benefit the conscripted individual also. This, however, is not sufficient for an adequate entitling justification; also required is that the burdens of conscription are fairly distributed among the population. As for taxation, the teleological justification is complex: partly, that taxation is necessary to finance all the useful services that the state provides; partly, that it is used to redistribute wealth more equally. The entitling justification is, partly, that those who pay tax benefit from the services provided; and, in so far as this is not so (redistributive taxation by definition means that some taxes are paid by certain individuals for the benefit of others), that it is just that the relatively rich should be made to pay for benefits for the relatively poor. In the case of quarantine regulations, the teleological justification is obvious enough, but an entitling justification might appear to be lacking. However, I believe this is not the case—the entitling justification is that the harm done to the individual is slight, both absolutely and in relation to the harm that might be done to others by the absence of such regulations.

The case of redistributive taxation shows that the teleological justification of a social institution need not be utilitarian—in this case, it is rather the achievement of greater social justice. It would, therefore, be more plausible to say that the justification of taxation is retributive, than that the justification of punishment is; for, if retribution means giving each individual his just deserts, then it is at least partly the purpose of redistributive taxation to proportion each individual's share of the wealth of the community more nearly to his just deserts than the market, according to one (admittedly controversial) view of justice, can do. Redistributive taxation also shows that where the teleological justification of an institution is that it does justice (or rather, corrects injustice), no *separate* entitling justification is needed—rather, the two kinds of justification coincide. But this is what one would expect, since, as was pointed out above, the problem of entitling justification is the problem of avoiding injustice to individuals in the pursuit of goals. If retribution were the teleological justification of punishment, it would be its entitling justification also—but I have argued that here the teleological justification is utilitarian.

Another way to illuminate what seems to be the true relationship between retributive and utilitarian considerations in regard to punishment is to invoke the distinction, commonplace in sociology, between goals and norms.[7] Norms are socially sanctioned rules of behaviour, which impose obligations on individuals and restrictions on actions. Some norms prescribe what must be done, others forbid what must be avoided (these are prohibitions). Typical prohibitions forbid lying and stealing, and taboo incest. Such norms do not specify what goals individuals or groups may aim to achieve, but they do forbid, first certain goals, secondly certain means to permitted goals. They license the pursuit of legitimate goals, subject to certain restrictions as to means. For example, in our own society business firms may pursue maximum profit so long as they do not use force, fraud, etc., to that end. The point of the norms prohibiting force and fraud is mainly to avoid injustice to other individuals. This precisely parallels the situation in regard to the institution of punishment. Punishment is a means to the goal of reducing wrongdoing; but it is only a legitimate means if it avoids injustice to individuals, and the rights of individuals are protected by restrictive norms which prohibit the punishment of the innocent, and unduly severe punishment even of the guilty. In regard to punishment, utilitarian theory states the goal (aim, purpose) of the institution, while retributivism states merely one of the norms that govern the pursuit of this goal, as of all goals.

The view of the justification of punishment taken in this paper might be called a two-stage one: first, one asks what general goal is (supposedly) forwarded by punishing; secondly, one asks why, and in what circumstances, one is entitled to forward that goal by means of punishment. It may, therefore, be worthwhile to distinguish this approach from another two-stage analysis, which also concludes that utilitarianism gives the correct answer to one stage, while the correct answer to the other requires retributionism. This is the theory (associated above all with John Rawls)[8] which depends on a distinction between justifying a rule, and justifying an act. Rawls distinguishes the question, 'Why put J in jail?' from the question 'Why put people in jail?' The answer to the first question is something like 'Because J robbed the bank'; the answer to the second, 'In order to protect society against wrongdoing.' Hence, Rawls concludes, utilitarian considerations are sufficient to answer the questions "whether or not to use law rather than some other mechanism of social control, . . . and what laws to have and what penalties to assign"; but the working of a system of law in particular cases must be retributive in form, since by definition applying a law means punishing persons who have broken it, and only them. In other words, the justification of a particular act of punishment is retributive; the justification of a rule of law that prescribes punishment is utilitarian.

Unfortunately, Rawls' formulation seems both confused and mistaken. Whether to use law rather than some other means of social control is a different issue from what laws to have and what penalties to assign: the first is not a question of what rules to have, but of whether to have a particular *kind* of rules; the second is a question of what particular rules of that kind to have. Only the second sort of issue is properly described as the justification of rules; and neither issue can properly be settled solely by reference to the consequences of the application of such rules (i.e., to utilitarian considerations); although, *if* such rules are justified, it is quite correct to describe the justification as utilitarian (in the teleological sense of 'justification'). The effectiveness of law and punishment as a means of social control does not suffice to justify the use of these techniques; for it may be that they impose suffering on people unjustly. Such would be the view of a retributivist who is also a determinist and so believes there is no such thing as moral culpability—hence, for him, there should be no punishment. Again, if one believes that there is both a teleological (utilitarian) and an entitling (retributive) justification for the use of punishment, one cannot decide what laws to have and what penalties to assign on utilitarian considerations alone; that would be to invite penalties of unlimited severity, if this were an efficacious means of social control. In the total design of a particular system of punishment—in deciding on the rules that constitute it—the pursuit of the goal of social control must be governed by the restraints required to ensure justice to individuals, that is, by *retributive rules* (i.e., *rules* dictated by retributive principles) that limit the permissible severity of penalties (Hart's remarks on mitigation and excuse are relevant here, for the application of these concepts in law is governed by *rules*).[9] Laws of strict liability seem immoral to many people because they flout such retributive rules for the sake of beneficial consequences. As for the justification of particular acts of punishment, Rawls' formulation fails to do justice to either the retributive or the utilitarian aspect of the matter. For Rawls, such acts of punishment are justified if prescribed by a law which itself has a utilitarian justification. Since laws cannot be justified in the way that Rawls supposes, this must be amended to the formula that an act of punishment is justified if prescribed by justified rules of law. This shows that the retributive element in the justification of an act of punishment cannot be reduced to the condition that the act is prescribed by a rule. On the contrary, it is necessary that the act of punishment be inflicted only on one who is *morally* guilty, and that the severity of the punishment reflect the degree of guilt. It is in this sense that the justification of an act of punishment is retributive—but so it is equally of a rule of law that prescribes punishment, and of the practice of punishment as such. Conversely, the justification of an act of punishment is also necessarily utilitarian, since without such acts (in appropriate cases) a system of punishments could not exist, and the beneficial consequences of punishment would not exist either—each individual punishment makes its contribution to the total effect. In other words, in regard to the justification of punishment, the correct distinction is not between different aspects of punishment, but between different senses of 'justification.' Every aspect of punishment—act, rule, and practice—requires a dual justification; that is, a teleological justification and an entitling justification.

NOTES

1. This is roughly the view of Kant, *Philosophy of Law* (Edinburgh, 1887), pp. 195–8.
2. I exclude from consideration an alternative utilitarian formula, namely, that punishment is justified because (or if) it improves the total balance of pleasure over pain, or anything of the kind, since such a balance is in principle incalculable, and any attempt to optimize it therefore chimerical.
3. Individual moral education through punishment is sometimes called *reform*; general moral education seems usually to be intended by those who see the function of punishment as the *denunciation* of crime.
4. For example, see Benn and Peters, *Social Principles and the Democratic State* (London, 1959), p. 182; A. Quinton, "On Punishment," in P. Laslett (ed.), *Philosophy, Politics and Society*, first series (Oxford, 1956), p. 86.
5. See his "Prolegomenon to the Principles of Punishment," in P. Laslett and W. G. Runciman, *Philosophy, Politics and Society*, second series (Oxford, 1962).
6. See his *Social Theory and Social Structure*, revised ed. (Glencoe, Illinois, 1957), pp. 19–85.
7. See Merton, *op. cit.*, pp. 131–61.
8. See his "Two Concepts of Rules" in P. Foot (ed.), *Theories of Ethics* (London, 1967).
9. *Op. cit.*

*Michael Lessnoff is an associate research fellow at the School of Social and Political Sciences at the University of Glasgow, Scotland. He is the author of a number of books in political philosophy, including *Political Philosophers of the Twentieth Century*, *The Spirit of Capitalism and the Protestant Ethic: An Enquiry into the Weber Thesis*, and *Ernest Gellner and Modernity*.

Lessnoff, Michael. "Two Justifications of Punishment." *Philosophical Quarterly* 21, no. 83 (April 1971): 141–148.
Reproduced with permission of Blackwell Publishing Ltd.

Much Respect: Toward a Hip-Hop Theory of Punishment

by Paul Butler*

If I ruled the world, imagine that . . .
I'd open every cell in Attica, send 'em to Africa. . . .
If I ruled the world, imagine that
I'd free all my sons, I'd love 'em love 'em baby

—Nas[1]

INTRODUCTION: THE HIP-HOP NATION[2]

This Article imagines the institution of punishment in the hip-hop nation. My thesis is that hip-hop can be used to inform a theory of punishment that is coherent, that enhances public safety, and that treats lawbreakers with respect. Hip-hop can improve the ideology and administration of justice in the United States.

For some time the debate about why people should be punished has been old school: Each one of four theories of punishment—retribution, deterrence, incapacitation, and rehabilitation—has acceded to prominence, and then lost its luster. Hip-hop offers a fresh approach. It first seems to embrace retribution. The "unwritten law in rap," according to Jay-Z, is that "if you shoot my dog, I'ma kill yo' cat . . . know dat/For every action there's a reaction."[3]

Next, however, comes the remix. Hip-hop takes punishment personally. Many people in the hip-hop nation have been locked up or have loved ones who have been. Punishment is an exercise of the state's police power, but it also implicates intimate family relationships. "Shout outs" to inmates—expressions of love and respect to them—are commonplace in the music and visual art. You understand criminal justice differently when the people that you love experience being "locked down all day, underground, neva seein' the sun/Vision stripped from you, neva seein' your son."[4]

The hip-hop theory of punishment acknowledges that when too many people are absent from their communities because they are being condemned by the government, prison may have unintended consequences. Retribution must be the object of punishment, but it should be limited by important social interests. In a remarkable moment in American history, popular music is weighing the costs and benefits of punishment. As we listen to the radio, watch music videos, dance at clubs, or wear the latest fashion, we receive a message from the "black CNN."[5] Hip-hop exposes the current punishment regime as profoundly unfair. It demonstrates this view by, if not glorifying law breakers, at least not viewing all criminals with the disgust which the law seeks to attach to them. Hip-hop points out the incoherence of the law's construct of crime, and it attacks the legitimacy of the system. Its message has the potential to transform justice in the United States.

[. . .]

IV. Punishment: The Remix

[. . .]

This project is not intended to suggest that hip-hop culture has explicitly constructed a theory of punishment. The claim is more limited, but still, I hope, profound. Thousands of hip-hop songs consider crime and punishment. These voices are worth listening to—they evaluate criminal justice from the bottom up.[102] Our current punishment regime has been designed from the top down, and that, in part, explains why many perceive it to be ineffective or unfair. We might punish better if the ghetto philosophers and the classic philosophers met. They address many of the same issues in punishment, including causation, harm, responsibility, excuse, and justification.

We would see that Erykah Badu, Snoop Dogg, and Jeremy Bentham have a lot in common. Immanuel Kant and Jay-Z would get along well, but their differences would be instructive. Not all of the artists are brilliant theorists, although some of them are. They represent, however, a community that has borne the brunt of the world's 200-year experiment with prison. That community knows much, has laid it down on tracks, and now attention must be paid.

We should not look to hip-hop culture for an entirely new justification of punishment. Hip-hop culture does not create out of whole cloth, and neither do the philosophers, scholars, and lawmakers who have articulated the current punishment regime. The art of hip-hop is in the remix. Thus some hip-hop overtly responds to trendy theories of punishment. The "broken window" theory of law enforcement, for example, has had a profound impact on the ghetto and thus on hip-hop culture.[103] Other elements of hip-hop can be interpreted as unconscious shout-outs to scholars of whom the artists probably are not aware. Foucault's influential history of the prison reverberates throughout hip-hop theory, as does the new criminal law scholarship on third party interests in criminal law and the effects of mass incarceration. Hip-hop culture, though, is post-postmodern. In fact, some of its characteristics, especially its embrace of retribution, seem startlingly old-fashioned.

I want to begin a discussion about a hip-hop theory of punishment by focusing on three classic problems in punishment theory. Why do we punish? What should we punish? How should we punish? I will identify six principles from hip-hop culture that address these issues.[104] First, the purpose of punishment should be retribution. Second, punishment should be limited (but not determined) by utilitarian concerns, especially the effect of punishment on people other than the lawbreaker. Third, punishment should be designed to "catch" the harm caused by rich people more than poor people. Fourth, people probably should not be punished for using or selling intoxicants. Fifth, punishment should be imposed only by people within a community, not outsiders. Sixth, prison should be used sparingly as an instrument of punishment.

A. Why Punish?

I ain't God but I'll pretend.

—Eve[105]

1. Retribution and Respect in Hip-Hop.

Hip-hop lyrics exhibit a strong conviction that wrongdoers should suffer consequences for their acts. In the words of Jay-Z: "Now if you shoot my dog, I'ma kill yo' cat/Just the unwritten laws in rap—know dat/For every action there's a reaction."[106] The culture abounds with narratives about revenge, retaliation, and avenging wrongs. The narrator in Eve's *"Love is Blind"* kills the man who abuses her close friend.[107] Likewise, Nelly warns "if you take a life, you gon' lose yours too."[108]

At the same time, hip-hop culture seems to embrace criminals. In Angie Stone's *"Brotha,"* for example, she sings, "To everyone of y'all behind bars/You know that Angie loves ya."[109] To an incarcerated person Jay-Z seeks to "send . . . some energy" because "if he's locked in the penitentiary . . . . They all winners to me."[110] This kind of warm acknowledgement of the incarcerated is commonplace in hip-hop, and virtually unheard of in other popular culture, which largely ignores the two million Americans in prison.

The most important civic virtue in the hip-hop nation is respect. One of the culture's contributions to the English language is the verb "dis," which means "to disrespect."[111] To dis someone is worse than to insult them—it is to deny his or her humanity. Hip-hop vocabulary also includes the term "props"—to give props is to afford proper respect.[112] The misogyny and homophobia in some hip-hop makes it difficult to claim a universal value of respect for all persons.[113] Virtually all hip-hop, however, connotes a respect for the dignity of lawbreakers.

In attempting to reconcile hip-hop's impulse for righting wrongs with its respect for dignity—even the dignity of criminals—a criminal law scholar immediately thinks of retribution. This justification of punishment is premised on the idea of "just deserts."[114] When one harms another, justice requires that she be harmed in return. Retributivists believe than punishment communicates respect for the criminal by recognizing him as a moral agent and respect for the victim by avenging his harm.

The Bill of Rights codifies the retributive concern for the criminal's humanity. The Eighth Amendment prohibits the state from punishing criminals in a manner that is inconsistent with their dignity. The Supreme Court has also interpreted the Eighth Amendment as requiring that criminals not be punished disproportionately to their crime, although it has given lawmakers wide latitude in determining what proportionate punishment is.[115]

How would a profound respect for the humanity of criminals change the way we punish them? It might require a more meaningful concept of proportionate punishment than the Supreme Court has currently endorsed.[116] Harsh sentences for drug crimes, for example, are premised on utilitarian, not retributive, justifications.[117] Such penalties have been the subject of much criticism in the hip-hop community. They have been defended by police and lawmakers on the ground that they keep drugs out of low-income and minority communities. If this assertion is true, it would not persuade retributivists, who require proportionality even when disproportionate punishment is socially useful.[118] While I will later suggest that the hip-hop nation probably would not punish drug users, if it did, its embrace of retribution means they would be punished significantly less than they are now.[119]

Hip-hop theory would reject or modify some elements of retribution. Assaultive retribution, for example, is premised on hate of the criminal, which is the opposite of the hip-hop perspective.[120] More significantly, however, some theories of retribution are premised on a world in which benefits and burdens are distributed equally; it is just to punish the criminal, the argument goes, when he upsets the balance.[121]

The hip-hop nation does not share this world view; it sees benefits and burdens as allocated in an uneven and racialist manner. Through this lens, the "choice" of a poor person to sell drugs has a different and less blameworthy social meaning than the choice of a middle class person to engage in, say, insider trading.[122] In "Dope Man," Jay-Z raps, "I grew where you hold your blacks up/Trap us, expect us not to pick gats up/Where you drop your cracks off by the Mack Trucks/Destroy our dreams of lawyers and actors/Keep us spiralin', goin' backwards."[123]

Hip-hop culture, like retributive philosophy, emphasizes the importance of moral autonomy and free agency.[124] Both posit that people who freely choose to do wrong should be punished. Where hip-hop theorists and traditional retributivists diverge, however, is on how to determine responsibility for individual acts. Hip-hop culture emphasizes the role of environment in determining conduct, whereas classic retributivist theory focuses on individual choice. In essence, hip-hop culture discounts responsibility when criminal conduct has been shaped by a substandard environment. OutKast, for example, asserts "knowing each and every nigger sellin', but can you blame/The fact the only way a brother can survive the game."[125]

The hip-hop analysis does not deny that the poor are moral agents; it is instead a quasiscientific or empirical claim about the nature of free choice. In the words of NWA:

[A] nigga wit' nothin' to lose
One of the few who's been accused and abused
Of the crime of poisonin' young minds
But you don't know shit 'til you've been in my shoes[126]

2. Hip-Hop Utility: Third Party Interests and the Effects of Mass Incarceration.

> What you gonna do when they come for you
> Work ain't honest but it pays the bills
> What we gonna do when they come for you
> God I can't stand life withoutcha
>
> —Erykah Badu[127]

Punishment has had a profound effect on some American communities.[128] There are neighborhoods where so many men are locked up that a male presence seems palpably absent.[129] It approaches gross understatement to note that a community feels it when, as for African Americans, more young men are in prison than in college.

Hip-hop is concerned with the collateral effects of punishment. It acknowledges that even when punishment is deserved, there may be severe and unintended consequences. Dorothy Roberts has described three ways that mass incarceration harms the African American. It damages social networks, infects social norms, and destroys social citizenship[130]

Hip-hop has catalogued a number of these harms. Damage to social networks, especially, is a consistent theme. Makaveli, for example, notes that families suffer when incarcerated parents cannot provide for their children. He states: "My homeboy's doin life, his baby mamma be stressin'/Sheddin' tears when her son, finally ask that questions/Where my daddy at? Mama why we live so poor?"[131]

Should such consequences be considered when an individual offender is punished?[132] Classic retributivists believe that social considerations are immoral. The message from hip-hop, on the other hand, is that such considerations are essential.[133] Hip-hop culture advocates retribution—but not at all costs. If the consequence of making people pay for their crimes is the decimation of a community, then retribution is less important.

Professor Darryl Brown observes that "mitigating third-party interests...is necessary to maintain the legitimacy of criminal law, even as conflicting commitments to distributive fairness, retributive justice, and crime prevention necessitate some punishment."[134] Brown notes that when federal prosecutors believe that a corporation has committed a crime, they may decline prosecution upon consideration of "collateral consequences, including disproportionate consequences to shareholders and employees not proven personally culpable."[135] A recent decision by the Supreme Court of Canada applied similar analysis to punishment of native people in Canada.[136]

Hip-hop culture suggests broad support for such an approach in the United States, especially as applied to minority communities. In practice, consideration of collateral consequences might lead to sanctions other than incarceration. When prison is appropriate, sentences might be shorter, or family leave could be allowed. Prisoners might be allowed to work to support their families. The goal would be sentencing targeted not just to the individual offender, but to his entire community.

In practice, a hip-hop construct of punishment would combine retributive and utilitarian justifications but differently than the prevailing mixed-theory model, which assumes that the aim of punishment is utilitarian, but with retributive limits.[137] In the hip-hop construct, the objective of punishment would be retribution—but with utilitarian limits.

B. What to Punish?

Ain't no Uzi's made in Harlem.

—Immortal Technique[138]

1. Who's Bad?

Consider the following facts: In the United States, approximately half of the people in prison are African American.[139] A black male born in 1991 has a 29% chance of being imprisoned, compared to a 16% chance for a Hispanic male, and a 4% chance for a white male.[140]

If punishment is being allocated properly, these statistics suggest that half of the most dangerous or immoral Americans are black, even though African Americans make up only about 12% of the population. It means that black men pose such a threat that they must be locked up at a rate more than seven times that of white men, and that Hispanic men must be locked up at four times the rate. The person who has confidence in the American criminal justice system probably has an unfavorable view of blacks and Latinos and a more positive view of whites.

The hip-hop nation rejects this view. It does not see morality or dangerousness as allocated along the race and class lines that the prison population suggests. A frequent theme in hip-hop is that the law does not correctly select the most deserving candidates for punishment. Specifically the law does not properly weigh the immorality posed and danger caused by white elites. On the other hand, it exaggerates the threat posed by the poor and by minorities. From this perspective, blameworthy conduct by privileged white people or the government often goes unpunished.

Thus Ice-T jokes that "America was stole from the Indians/Show and prove, what was that?/A straight up nigga move."[141] Immortal Technique complains that "families bleed because of corporate greed."[142]

Hip-hop artists sometimes accuse the state of complicity in crime. In "*Gun Music*," Talib Kweli raps, "You know who killing it, niggas saying they militant/ The only blood in the street is when the government spilling it."[143] In another song, Kweli provides an example: "[The police] be gettin' tips from snitches and rival crews/Doin them favors so they workin for the drug dealers too/Just business enforcers with hate in they holsters/Shoot you in the back, won't face you like a soldier."[144]

Of course, complaints that criminal law is selectively enforced against blacks and other minorities are familiar, and not only in hip-hop culture. Hiphop's indictment of criminal justice goes further; it identifies bias in the way that crime is constructed as well as the way that it is enforced.

Some hip-hop artists have suggested that lawmakers define crime in a way that does not challenge powerful corporate interests—even when corporations cause harm. KRS, in "*Illegal Business*," explains: "In society you have illegal and legal/We need both, to make things equal/So legal is tobacco, illegal is speed/ Legal is aspirin, illegal is weed."[145] It is legal for a corporation to make a gun. Business people responsible for the sale of defective products are not typically prosecuted—even if the products cause death or severe injuries. Nicotine and alcohol distributors are licensed by the government; in the case of tobacco there are even government subsidies for growers. Sellers of other drugs, including argu-ably less harmful ones, are punished. Hip-hop suggests that some of the existing distinctions between legal and illegal conduct, and between crimes and torts, are unprincipled.

Hip-hop sometimes presents poor minorities as relatively powerless in the grand scheme. "Right or wrong... I don't make the law," Erykah Badu explains to her criminal-minded lover in "*Danger.*"[146] In this view, actual bad actors—including people who profit from widespread alcoholism, tobacco sales, and the demand for guns—are politically powerful. The fact that their injurious conduct is not punished helps explain hip-hop's lack of confidence in American criminal justice.

2. Hip-Hop and Drugs: Keeping It Real.

In hip-hop culture, the idea that minorities are selectively prosecuted sometimes seems to border on paranoia. In the case of drug offenses, however, this perception is accurate. According to statistics compiled by the U.S. government, blacks are about 15% of monthly drug users.[147] Yet, they accounted for 33% of drug possession arrests[148] and more than 70% of people incarcerated for drug use.[149] Just because you are paranoid, the old joke goes, doesn't mean they're not out to get you.

The fact that drug offenses are selectively prosecuted in the African American community informs the hip-hop perspective on drug criminalization, but it is only one factor among many. A persistent critique of hip-hop culture is that it glorifies the use of illegal drugs. Upon closer examination, we see that this is partly true.

Hip-hop culture suggests that recreational drugs like marijuana and ecstacy enhance the quality of life and that they are fun.[150] The Notorious B.I.G. raps: "Some say the x, make the sex/Spec-tacular."[151] Hip-hop stars Ja Rule, Missy

Elliott, and Tweet collaborated on a song called "X" which extols the virtues of having sex under the influence of ecstacy.[152]

Marijuana, though, is the hip-hop nation's intoxicant of choice. In a classic song, Snoop Dogg raps about the pleasure of driving through his neighborhood sipping alcohol and smoking weed.[153] The scholar Michael Eric Dyson describes marijuana as "the necessary adjunct to ghetto fabulousness .... Getting high is at once pleasurable and political: It heightens the joys to be found in thug life while blowing smoke rings around the constraints of the state."[154]

Indeed there are probably more hip-hop songs critical of the harm posed by alcohol than by other soft drugs. Public Enemy, for example, compared the large cans of malt liquor sold in low-income communities to a "gun to the brain."[155]

Hip-hop offers a more nuanced, and less consistent, perspective on "hard" drugs. Some critics have observed that more respect is accorded sellers than users. 2Pac (a.k.a. Tupac Shakur), for example, criticizes his addict parent for being a "part time mutha."[156] In another song, however, he praises street corner dealers for raising him when his father was not present.[157]

Other hip-hop artists are angrier at drug sellers. Ice Cube raps, "And all y'all dope-dealers ... You're as bad as the po-lice—cause ya kill us."[158] He goes on to castigate dealers for "[e]xploitin' us like the Caucasians did/For 400 years—I got 400 tears—for 400 peers/Died last year from gang-related crimes."[159]

Still, there is sympathy for why some people sell drugs. Biggie Small facetiously dedicated his autobiographical song "Juicy" to the people who called the police when he was "just tryin' to make some money to feed [his] daughters."[160] Kanye West raps about being "forced to sell crack" because there "ain't no tuition for having no ambition/and ain't no loans for sittin' your ass at home."[161]

Ultimately hip-hop acknowledges the poor consequences that drugs can have on individuals and communities. The culture is not as quick as some scholars to label drug crimes "victimless." Acknowledging these costs, however, does not inevitably lead to a belief that drug offenders should be punished. Because of the environmental factors that contribute to drug use and sales, the government's perceived complicity in the availability of drugs in the ghetto, the fact that the state allows the sale of potentially harmful drugs like tobacco and alcohol, and the selective enforcement of the drug laws in minority communities, the hip-hop consensus seems to be against punishment of drug offenders.[162] In this view, the state may have a legitimate interest in controlling the use and sale of some drugs. First, however, the government bears the burden of proving that it can regulate drugs in a manner free of racial bias and that the benefits of regulation will not be outweighed by the costs.[163]

C. How to Punish?

1. Punishment from Inside.

> *Freedom and power to determine our destiny* . . .
> Black juries when our brothers are tried in court
>
> —Paris[164]

Hip-hop artists frequently express suspicion of discretion exercised by people outside their community, especially white elites. This concern is conveyed most often in critiques of the police. In "*99 Problems*," Jay-Z wonders if he is stopped by the police because he is young, black, and wearing his hat low on his head.[165] Grand Puba recalls driving on the New Jersey turnpike:

> [When a police officer] looked over, caught the shine from the rim of the Rover/You know his next move (sound of police siren) pull it over . . . I pulls over to the right hand shoulder/Look through the rearview he got his hand on his holster/He had this look "how this black nigga this car?"/ You know these cracker state troopers don't know rap stars.[166]

Many artists also worry about discretion by sentencing authorities. Big L raps that "There are too many young black brothers doin life bids/Cause justice means 'just us white kids.'"[167] This concern is supported by empirical evidence that blacks and Hispanics receive more severe sentences than whites for the same crime.[168]

Efforts by lawmakers to constrain discretion, however, seem to have exacerbated inequities. The Federal Sentencing Guidelines are one example. Professor Charles Ogletree writes,

> [The United States Sentencing Commission's failure] to consider the offender's personal characteristics places too great an emphasis on the harm caused by the offender's act and too little emphasis on circumstances that would serve to mitigate the punishment. The Commission should have realized that it is a *person* who stands before the bar to accept the punishment imposed by the court.[169]

Mos Def echoes Professor Ogletree's concern about wholesale justice: "Yo, it's one universal law but two sides to every story/Three strikes and you be in for life, mandatory/And even if you get out of prison still livin/Join the other five million under state supervision/This is business, no faces just lines and statistics."[170]

One response, from a hip-hop ethos, might be a requirement that punishment be imposed by people within the community. In the context of trials, Professor Sheri Lynn Johnson has observed "the most obvious counterbalance to the bias of white jurors is the mandatory inclusion of black jurors in the decision-making process."[171] Professor Johnson's recommendation could be extended to sentencing. Thus, a defendant would have the right to jurors from his community, and these jurors would have sentencing authority.[172]

Advocacy of this kind of reform has been a consistent theme in hip-hop. In "Escape from Babylon," Paris outlined a ten-point plan that included black juries for African American defendants.[173] Similarly, Nas has recommended that "the streets be the court—and corners hold the trial."[174]

"Representation" is an important theme in hip-hop culture. One "represents" by conducting himself or herself in a way that makes the community proud. Representation implies responsibility. In sentencing lawbreakers, representation of the hip-hop community would enhance the expressive value of punishment and give it a legitimacy it now lacks.

2. Prison.

I hold this slow and daily tampering with the mysteries of the brain, to be immeasurably worse than any torture of the body.

—Charles Dickens[175]

Prison is an instrument of punishment that is approximately 200 years old. It was designed in an attempt to punish criminals in a more humane way than killing them or harming their bodies.[176] How successful has the experiment been?

The hip-hop nation is better situated to answer the question than virtually any other community in the world. The United States incarcerates more people than any country other than Russia.[177] The majority of its inmates are African American and Hispanic.

Hip-hop became popular during the same period that the prison population experienced its greatest expansion. From 1972 to 1997, the prison population increased by 500%—from 196,000 to 1,159,000 inmates.[178] The rate of violent crime actually decreased during this time, but the number of people locked up for nonviolent offenses rose sharply.[179]

The experiences of the two million people now incarcerated in the United States have been documented more in hip-hop than in any other medium. The portrait is ugly. To Nas, prison is "the belly of the beast" and "the beast love to eat black meat/And got us niggaz from the hood, hangin' off his teeth."[180]

The virtually universal view in the hip-hop nation is that punishing people by locking them in cages for years is a miserable public policy. Incarceration is cruel because it is dehumanizing. It is counterproductive because, as discussed in Part III, it has been used so promiscuously in minority communities that it has lost its value as deterrence. The scholar Robin Kelley summarizes the hiphop perspective as follows: "Prisons are not designed to discipline but to corral bodies labeled menaces to society; policing is not designed to stop or reduce crime in inner-city communities but to manage it."[181]

The artists put it more eloquently: In the words of Beanie Sigel "I know what it's like in hell/I did a stretch in a triflin' cell.... [L]ocked down all day, underground, neva seein' the sun/Vision stripped from you, neva seein' your son."[182] Immortal Technique says "sleeping on the floor in cages starts to fuck with your brain/The system ain't reformatory , it's only purgatory."[183] DMX describes "the frustration, rage, trapped inside a cage."[184]

Hip-hop often depicts incarceration as being driven by profit rather than public safety. Its analysis is that it is socially expedient to warehouse people whose problems are difficult or expensive to treat, especially when there are economic benefits to the (largely white and rural) communities where prisons frequently are situated. This concern is supported in part by the rise in the prison population during an era in which violent crime decreased. The hip-hop perspective is reminiscent of Kant's critique of utilitarianism—that it is immoral to punish people as a means of benefiting society. According to some artists, that is the real meaning of the punishment regime. GangStarr complains: "The educational system presumes you fail/The next place is the corner then after that jail."[185] Mos Def suggests a "prison-industry complex" that supports a "global jail economy."[186] Ras Kass explains: "It's almost methodical, education is false assimiliation/Building prisons is more economical."[187]

CONCLUSION: WORD IS BORN

Hip-hop culture ascended to national prominence in the post-civil rights era. For the hip-hop nation, one of the enduring lessons of the civil rights movement is that the criminal law was used as an instrument of racial subordination. Images of civil rights activists getting locked up (or brutalized by the police) are common in hip-hop culture, especially music videos.

Hip-hop artists express some of the same concerns as traditional civil rights activists about criminal justice. Both vigorously protest racial profiling by police. Unlike civil rights culture, hip-hop does not practice a politics of respectability. It is less bourgeois. It champions the human rights of criminals as enthusiastically as the rights of the falsely accused. It is as concerned with fairness for drug sellers as for law-abiding middle-class people who are stopped by the police for "driving while black" or "driving while brown." Ultimately, hip-hop culture's reforms focus more on substantive than procedural issues (criminal law more than criminal procedure). Accordingly hip-hop activists may be better equipped to protest the crack cocaine sentencing regime, felony disenfranchisement, or recidivist statutes than organizations like the NAACP. They are also more willing to use nontraditional tactics to change the laws.

At the same time, hip-hop culture is post-postmodern. Some hip-hop artists seem more optimistic about the potential of the United States to achieve justice than some critical theorists. There is more faith in the potential of the rule of law, even if that potential is not now realized. Some hip-hop artists are less suspicious of capitalism than are many postmodernists. Hip-hop ultimately, however, seems more rooted in critical theory than traditional jurisprudence. It embraces instrumentalist tactics and is deeply suspicious of authority.

One serious deficiency in hip-hop is its endemic sexism and homophobia. Can any credible theory of justice be based on a culture that routinely denigrates more than half the population? The answer must be "no." In order for hip-hop to command the moral authority that, at its best, it deserves, it must address subordination within the hip-hop nation. The problem besmirches hip hop's extraordinary aesthetic achievement and detracts from its important evaluation of criminal justice. Hip-hop music and videos, especially, contain the kind of depictions of gender and sexuality that we might expect of adolescent boys.

The increasing prominence of women rappers provides limited cause for hope.[188] Hip-hop has a long way to go, however, before its constructive political analysis is not compromised by lyrics, visual images, and attitudes that put down a considerable portion of its own community.

This Article is a beginning. It is an early attempt to fashion a hip-hop jurisprudence. In hip-hop culture there is a tradition of answer raps—of provocative responses to provocative words. I look forward to those responses.

Notes

1. Nas, *If I Ruled the World*, on It Was Written (Sony Records 1996) (lyrics available at Original Hip-Hop (Rap) Lyrics Archive, *at* http://www.ohhla.com/anonymous/nas/written/ruled.nas.txt (last visited Mar. 28, 2004)).

2. The hip-hop nation consists of artists, students, workers, activists, and scholars. For a discussion of the distinction between the hip-hop generation and Generation X, see Gary Mendez, *Confessions of a Gen Xpatriate: Pledging Allegiance to the Hip-Hop Generation, at* http://www.horizonmag.com/3/gen-xpatriate.asp (last visited Mar. 28, 2004).

3. Jay-Z, *Justify My Thug, on* The Black Album (Roc-A-Fella Records 2003) (lyrics available at Original Hip-Hop (Rap) Lyrics Archive, *at* http://ohhla.com/anonymous/jigga/theblack/justify.jyz.txt (last visited Mar. 4, 2004)).

4. Beanie Sigel, *What Your Life Like*, on THE TRUTH (Def Jam Records 2000) (lyrics available at Original Hip-Hop (Rap) Lyrics Archive, *at* http://ohhla.com/anonymous/beanie/thetruth/whatlife.sig.txt (last visited Mar. 7, 2004)).

5. The phrase comes from Chuck D, of the rap group Public Enemy. *See* The History of Hip-Hop, *at* http://www.headbob.com/hiphop/hiphophistory.shtml (last visited Mar. 28, 2004).

[...]

102. *See* Alan David Freeman, *Legitimizing Racial Discrimination Through Antidiscrimination Law: A Critical Review of Supreme Court Doctrine*, 62 MINN. L. REV. 1049 (1978) (contrasting the "victim" and "perpetrator" perspectives in antidiscrimination law); Mari J. Matsuda, *Looking to the Bottom: Critical Legal Studies and Reparations*, 22 HARV. C.R.-C.L. L. REV. 323 (1987) (arguing for the inclusion of the voices of those at the "bottom" in legal scholarship).

103. For a discussion of the "broken window" theory of law enforcement, see James Q. Wilson & George L. Kelling, *Broken Windows*, ATLANTIC MONTHLY, Mar. 1982, at 29. For a reaction from hip-hop to former New York City mayor Rudolph Giuliani's endorsement of "zero tolerance" policing, see Brand Nubian, *Probable Cause*, on FOUNDATION (Arista Records 1998) (lyrics available at Original Hip-Hop (Rap) Lyrics Archive, *at* http://ohhla.com/anonymous/brnubian/found/probable.brn.txt (last visited Mar. 7, 2004)) ("I ain't do shit! Jakes lock a nigga with a weed clip...Now Giuliani wanna talk about the 'Quality of Life'/Think he got the right to follow me at night/with no probable cause, other than my skin is black like yours.").

104. This theory is constructed from my reading of the values and concerns expressed in hip-hop culture. It is not intended to be definitive or exhaustive. It is intended to provoke debate.

105. Eve, *Love Is Blind*, on RUFF RYDERS' FIRST LADY (Interscope Records 1999) (lyrics available at Original Hip-Hop (Rap) Lyrics Archive, *at* http://ohhla.com/anonymous/eve/firstldy/is_blind.eve.txt (last visited Mar. 5, 2004)).

106. Jay-Z, *supra* note 3.

107. Eve, *supra* note 105.

108. Nelly, *Nellyville*, on NELLYVILLE (Universal Records 2002) (lyrics available at Original Hip-Hop (Rap) Lyrics Archive, *at* http://ohhla.com/anonymous/nelly/ville/nv.nel.txt (last visited Mar. 5, 2004)). For other examples of retributivism, see Notorious B.I.G., *Somebody's Gottta Die*, on LIFE AFTER DEATH (Bad Boy Records 1997); Mystikal, *Murder 2*, on UNPREDICTABLE (Jive Records 1997).

109. Angie Stone, *Brotha*, on MAHOGANY SOUL (J-Records 2001) (lyrics available at Lyrics Time, Angie Stone Lyrics—Brotha (Remix), *at* http://www.lyricstime.com/lyrics/2682.html (last visited Feb. 4, 2004)).

110. Jay-Z, *supra* note 77.

111. A definition can be found at urbandictionary.com, http://www.urbandictionary.com/define.php?term=dis&f=l (last visited Mar. 5, 2004) (displaying the results of searching the term "dis").

112. A definition can be found at urbandictionary.com, http://www.urbandictionary.com/define.php?term=props&f=l (last visited Mar. 5, 2004) (displaying the results of searching the term "props").

113. *See* Michelle Goodwin, *The Economy of Citizenship*, 76 TEMP. L. REV. 129, 192 (2003) (discussing misogyny in rap music and noting how "Ice T, Ice Cube, Dr. Dre, Snoop Dogg, N.W.A., Slick Rick, Jason Lewis, UGK and many more contribute to the denigration of women").

114. For a famous exposition of retribution, see IMMANUEL KANT, THE PHILOSOPHY OF LAW 194–98 (W. Hastrie trans., 1887) (1797) ("Even if a Civil Society resolved to dissolve itself...the last Murderer lying in the prison ought to be executed before the resolution was carried out .... This ought to be done in order that every one may realize the desert of his deeds ....").

115. *See generally* Lockyer v. Andrade, 538 U.S. 63 (2003) (upholding the constitutionality of a defendant's sentence to two consecutive terms of 25 years to life for stealing $68.84 worth of videotapes from a K-Mart store); Harmelin v. Michigan, 501 U.S. 957 (1991) (upholding a defendant's sentence of life without parole for possession of cocaine).

116. See *Andrade*, 538 U.S. at 63.

117. See, *e.g.*, Sara Sun Beale, *What's Law Got To Do with It?: The Political, Social. Psychological and Other Non-Legal Factors Influencing the Development of (Federal) Criminal Law*, 1 BUFF. CRIM. L. REV. 23, 56 (1997) ("It seems doubtful whether drug offenses evoke the strongest retributive impulses. It seems more likely that three strikes and mandatory minimum legislation [for drug offenses] is based upon a deterrent view of the purpose of criminal sanctions."); Ilene H. Nagel, *Structuring Sentencing Discretion: The New Federal Sentencing Guidelines*, 80 J. CRIM. L. & CRIMINOLOGY 883, 914 n.190 (1990) ("[I]n the area of crimes related to drugs, crime control goals rather than just deserts seemed to prevail ....").

118. Michael S. Moore, *The Moral Worth of Retribution, in* RESPONSIBILITY, CHARACTER AND EMOTIONS 179 (Ferdinand Schoeman ed., 1987) ("[R]etributivists [are]... committed to the principle that punishment should be graded in proportion to desert ....").

119. For an expanded argument that retributive punishment would lower sentences for drug crimes, see Paul Butler, *Retribution, for Liberals*, 46 UCLA L. REV. 1873, 1884–88 (1999).

120. See Joshua Dressler, *Hating Criminals: How Can Something That Feels So Good Be Wrong?*, 88 MICH. L. REV. 1448, 1451–53 (1990) ("The most famous exponent of assaultive variety [of retributivism] is James Stephen, who claimed that 'it is morally right to hate criminals.' Under Stephen's view, punishment is justified without any consideration of the criminal's rights or best interests ....").

121. See HERBERT MORRIS, ON GUILT AND INNOCENCE 34 (1976) ("It is just to punish those who have violated the rules and caused the unfair distribution of benefits and burdens. A person who violates the rules has something others have—the benefits of the system—but by renouncing what others have assumed, the burdens of self-restraint, he has acquired an unfair advantage. ... Justice—that is punishing such individuals—restores the equilibrium of benefits and burdens by taking from the individual what he owes, that is, exacting the debt.").

122. See Kelley, *supra* note 92 ("Moreover, economic restructuring resulting in massive unemployment has created criminals out of black youth, which is what gangsta rappers acknowledge. But rather than apologize or preach, they attempt to rationalize and explain.").

123. Jay-Z, *Dope Man, on* VOLUME 3: THE LIFE AND TIMES OF S. CARTER (Roc-A-Fella Records 1999) (lyrics available at Original Hip-Hop (Rap) Lyrics Archive, *at* http://ohhla.com/anonymous/jigga/volume_3/dope_man.jyz.txt (last visited Mar. 5, 2004)). For a similar perspective, see ICE CUBE, KILL AT WILL (Priority Records 1990)).

124. "[R]etributivism is based on the view that humans generally possess free will (or, perhaps more usefully, the capacity for free choice), and, therefore, may justly be blamed when they choose to violate society's mores." JOSHUA DRESSLER, UNDERSTANDING CRIMINAL LAW 16 (3d ed. 2001) (footnotes omitted).

125. OutKast, *Mainstream*, On ATLIENS (LaFace Records 1996) (lyrics available at Original Hip-Hop (Rap) Lyrics Archive, *at* http://www.ohhla.com/anonymous/outkast/atliens/main.otk.txt (last visited Mar. 5, 2004)).

126. NWA, *100 Miles and Runnin'*, on 100 MILES AND RUNNIN' (Priority Records 1990) (lyrics available at Original Hip-Hop (Rap) Lyrics Archive, *at* http://www.ohhla.com/anonymous/nwa/100_mile/100_mile.nwa.txt (last visited Mar. 5, 2004)).

127. Erykah Badu, *The Other Side of the Game, on* BADUIZM (Universal Records 1997) (lyrics available at Original Hip-Hop (Rap) Lyrics Archive, *at* http://ohhla.com/anonymous/badu/baduizm/other.bdu.txt (last visited Mar. 5, 2004)).

128. See Dorothy E. Roberts, *The Social and Moral Cost of Mass Incarceration in African American Communities*, 56 STAN. L. REV. 1271 (2004) (appearing in this Symposium).

129. See Todd R. Clear, *The Problem with "Addition by Subtraction": The Prison Crime Relationship in Low-Income Communities, in* INVISIBLE PUNISHMENT: THE COLLATERAL CONSEQUENCES OF MASS IMPRISONMENT 181, 184 (Marc Mauer & Meda Chesney-Lind eds., 2002) (describing urban areas in which one in four men is incarcerated).

130. Roberts, *supra* note 128.

131. Makaveli, *White Man'z World, on* THE DON KILLUMINATI: THE 7 DAY THEORY (Interscope Records 1996) (lyrics available at Original Hip-Hop (Rap) Lyrics Archive, *at* http://ohhla. com/anonymous/2_pac/don_kill/whiteman.2pc.txt (last visited Mar. 5, 2004)). For a discussion of the impact of mass incarceration on social norms, *see supra* Part III.

132. *See* Darryl K. Brown, *Third-Party Interests in Criminal Law*, 80 TEX. L. REV. 1383 (2002) (discussing ways in which "the practice of criminal law . . . accommodates concerns for collateral consequences to third parties").

133. Kant wrote:

> Juridical Punishment can never be administered merely as a means of promoting another Good either with regard to the Criminal himself or to Civil Society, but must in all cases be imposed only because the individual on whom it is inflicted *has committed a Crime.* For one man ought never to be dealt with merely as a means subservient to the purpose of another . . . .

KANT, *supra* note 114, at 195 (emphasis in original).

134. Brown, *supra* note 132, at 1384.

135. *Id.* at 1387 (quoting Memorandum from Eric H. Holder, Jr., Assistant Attorney General, to all U.S. Attorneys and Heads of Department Components pt. II (June 16, 1999)).

136. *See* R. v. Gladue, [1999] S.C.R. 688 (Can.).

137. Many scholars justify a mixed theory of criminal punishment. They distinguish between, on the one hand, the general justifying aim of the criminal law and, on the other hand, the rules of criminal responsibility that determine who should be punished and how severe the punishment should be. Many have argued that general aim of the criminal law . . . is to deter unwanted behavior. Nonetheless, some of these same utilitarians apply retributive concepts of just deserts in determining *whether* and *how much* to punish a particular person . . . .

DRESSLER, *supra* note 124, at 22–23 (emphasis in original).

138. Immortal Technique, *Peruvian Cocaine, on* REVOLUTIONARY VOLUME 2 (Nature Sounds Records 2003) (lyrics available at Original Hip-Hop (Rap) Lyrics Archive, *at* http://www. ohhla.com/anonymous/immortal/rev_vol2/peruvian.tch.txt (last visited Mar. 5, 2004)). Immortal Technique quotes this line from the movie NEW JACK CITY (Warner Bros. 1991).

139. *See* MAUER, *supra* note 12, at 124.

140. *See id.* (citing BONCZAR & BECK, *supra* note 12).

141. Ice-T, *Straight Up Nigga, on* O.G. ORIGINAL GANGSTER (Warner Brothers Records 1991) (lyrics available at Original Hip-Hop (Rap) Lyrics Archive, *at* http://www.ohhla.com/anonymous/ ice_t/og/straight.ict.txt (last visited Mar. 5, 2004)).

142. Immortal Technique, *Speak Your Mind, on* REVOLUTIONARY VOLUME 1 (Viper Records 2001) (lyrics available at Original Hip-Hop (Rap) Lyrics Archive, *at* http://ohhla.com/anonymous/ immortal/rev_vol1/speak_yr.tch.txt (last visited Mar. 5, 2004)).

143. Talib Kweli featuring Cocoa Brovaz, *Gun Music, on* QUALITY (MCA Records 2002) (lyrics available at Original Hip-Hop (Rap) Lyrics Archive, *at* http://ohhla.com/anonymous/t_kweli/ quality/gunmusic.tab.txt (last visited Mar. 5, 2004)).

144. Talib Kweli, *The Proud, on* QUALITY, *supra* note 143 (lyrics available at Original Hip-Hop (Rap) Lyrics Archive, *at* http://ohhla.com/anonymous/t_kweli/quality/theproud.tab.txt (last visited Mar. 5, 2004)).

145. Boogie Down Productions, *Illegal Business, on* BY ALL MEANS NECESSARY (Jive Records 1988) (lyrics available at Original Hip-Hop (Rap) Lyrics Archive, *at* http://ohhla.com/anonymous/ boogiedp/by_all/business.bdp.txt (last visited Mar. 4, 2004)).

146. Erykah Badu, *Danger, on* WORLDWIDE UNDERGROUND (Motown Records 2003) (lyrics available at Erykah Badu Lyrics—Danger, *at* http://www.azlyrics.com/lyrics/erykahbadu/danger. html (last visited Mar. 5, 2004)).

147. *See* MAUER, *supra* note 12, at 147.

148. *See id.* at 146.

149. *See* Thomas, *supra* note 83.

150. For an insightful analysis of hip-hop's treatment of marijuana and crack cocaine, see Ted Sampsell-Jones, *Culture and Contempt: The Limitations of Expressive Criminal Law*, 27 SEATTLE U. L. REV. 133, 163–67 (2003).

151. Notorious B.I.G. featuring R. Kelly, *Fuck You Tonight*, *on* LIFE AFTER DEATH, *supra* note 108 (lyrics available at Original Hip-Hop (Rap) Lyrics Archive, *at* http://ohhla.com/anonymous/ntr_big/l_aftr_d/fuck_you.big.txt (last visited Mar. 7, 2004)).

152. Ja Rule featuring Missy Elliot & Tweet, *X*, *on* PAIN IS LOVE (Sony Records 2001) (lyrics available at Original Hip-Hop (Rap) Lyrics Archive, *at* http://ohhla.com/anonymous/ja_rule/painlove/x.jah.txt (last visited Mar. 7, 2004)).

153. Snoop Dogg, *Gin and Juice*, *on* DOGGYSTYLE (Death Row Records 1993) (lyrics available at Original Hip-Hop (Rap) Lyrics Archive, *at* http://ohhla.com/anonymous/snoopdog/dogstyle/ginjuice.snp.txt (last visited Mar. 5, 2004)).

154. MICHAEL ERIC DYSON, HOLLER IF YOU HEAR ME: SEARCHING FOR TUPAC SHAKUR 239 (2001).

155. Public Enemy, *1 Million Bottlebags*, *on* APOCALYPSE 91 ... THE ENEMY STRIKES BACK (Def Jam Records 1991) (lyrics available at Original Hip-Hop (Rap) Lyrics Archive, *at* http://ohhla.com/anonymous/pb_enemy/apoc_91/1mil_bag.pbe.txt (last visited Mar. 5, 2004)).

156. 2Pac, *Part Time Mutha*, *on* 2PACALYSPE Now (Jive Records 1992) (lyrics available at Original Hip-Hop (Rap) Lyrics Archive, *at* http://www.ohhla.com/anonymous/2_pac/2pclypse/parttime.2pc.txt (last visited Mar. 5, 2004)).

157. 2Pac, *Dear Mama*, *on* ME AGAINST THE WORD (Jive Records 1995), (lyrics available at Original Hip-Hop (Rap) Lyrics Archive, *at* http://www.ohhla.com/anonymous/2_pac/matworld/dearmama.2pc.txt (last visited Mar. 5, 2004)).

158. Ice Cube, *Us*, *on* DEATH CERTIFICATE (Priority Records 1991) (lyrics available at Original Hip-Hop (Rap) Lyrics Archive, *at* http://ohhla.com/anonymous/ice_cube/death/us.cub.txt (last visited Mar. 5, 2004)).

159. *Id.*

160. Notorious B.I.G., *Juicy*, *on* LIFE AFTER DEATH, *supra* note 108 (lyrics available at Original Hip-Hop (Rap) Lyrics Archive, *at* http://www.ohhla.com/anonymous/ntr_big/ready_to/juicy.big.txt (last visited Mar. 5, 2004)).

161. Kanye West, *We Don't Care*, *on* COLLEGE DROPOUT (Roc-A-Fella Records 2004) (lyrics available at Kanye West Lyrics—We Don't Care, *at* http://www.azlyrics.com/lyrics/kanyewest/wedontcare.html (last visited Mar. 5, 2003)).

162. *See* Sampsell-Jones, *supra* note 150.

163. This is an example of hip-hop's mixed theory of punishment at work. The culture's retributive instinct argues for punishment of drug offenders who harm others, for instance, cocaine sellers. The utilitarian limitations on punishment, however, including the number of minority men who would be incarcerated under an exclusively harm-based regime, militates against punishment.

164. Paris, *Escape from Babylon*, *on* THE DEVIL MADE ME DO IT (Tommy Boy Records 1990) (lyrics available at Original Hip-Hop (Rap) Lyrics Archive, *at* http://ohhla.com/anonymous/paris/thedevil/escape.prs.txt (last visited Mar. 5, 2004)).

165. Jay-Z, *99 Problems*, *on* THE BLACK ALBUM (Def Jam Records 2003) (lyrics available at Original Hip-Hop (Rap) Lyrics Archive, *at* http://ohhla.com/anonymous/jigga/theblack/99_probs.jyz.txt (last visited Mar. 5, 2004)).

166. Brand Nubian, *Probable Cause*, *on* FOUNDATION (Arista Records 1998) (lyrics available at Original Hip-Hop (Rap) Lyrics Archive, *at* http://ohhla.com/anonymous/brnubian/found/probable.brn.txt (last visited Mar. 7, 2004)).

167. Big L, *Fed Up wit the Bullshit*, on LIFESTYLEZ OV DA POOR AND DANGEROUS (Sony Records 1995) (lyrics available at Original Hip-Hop (Rap) Lyrics Archive, *at* http://www.ohhla.com/anonymous/big_l/lifestyl/fedupwit.bgl.txt (last visited Mar. 5, 2004)).

168. *See* MAUER, *supra* note 12, at 138–40.

169. Charles J. Ogletree, Jr., *The Death of Discretion? Reflections on the Federal Sentencing Guidelines*, 101 HARV. L. REV. 1938, 1953 (1988); *see also* Albert W. Alschuler, *The Failure of Sentencing Guidelines: A Plea for Less Aggregation*, 58 U. CHI. L. REV. 901, 937 (1991) ("Aggregated sentences, whether chosen by a legislature or by a sentencing commission, seem likely to be more severe than individualized sentences.").

170. Mos Def, *Mathematics*, on BLACK ON BOTH SIDES (Rawkus Records 1999) (lyrics available at Original Hip-Hop (Rap) Lyrics Archive, *at* http://ohhla.com/anonymous/mos_def/black_on/math.mos.txt (last visited Mar. 7, 2004)).

171. Sheri Lynn Johnson, *Black Innocence and the White Jury*, 83 MICH. L. REV. 1611, 1649 (1985).

172. *See* Morris B. Hoffman, *The Case for Jury Sentencing*, 52 DUKE L.J. 951 (2003) (advocating juror sentencing).

173. Paris, *supra* note 164.

174. Nas, *Nas Is Coming*, on IT WAS WRITTEN (Sony Records 1996) (lyrics available at Original Hip-Hop (Rap) Lyrics Archive, *at* http://ohhla.com/anonymous/nas/written/coming.nas.txt (last visited Feb. 28, 2004)).

175. LAWRENCE M. FRIEDMAN, CRIME AND PUNISHMENT IN AMERICAN HISTORY 80 (1993) (quoting CHARLES DICKENS, AMERICAN NOTES 146 (Penguin 1972) (1842)).

176. For a concise history of prison, see MAUER, *supra* note 12, at 1–14. For a deeper analysis, sec FOCCAULT, *supra* note 88.

177. *See* MAUER, *supra* note 12, at 23 figs. 2–3.

178. *See id.* at 19.

179. *See id.* at 19–37.

180. DMX, Method Man, Nas & Ja Rule, *Grand Finale*, on BELLY SOUNDTRACK (Def Jam Records 1998) (lyrics available at Original Hip-Hop (Rap) Lyrics Archive, *at* http://ohhla.com/anonymous/misc/hip-hop/grfinale.bly.txt (last visited Mar. 4, 2004)).

181. Kelley, *supra* note 92, at 118.

182. Beanie Sigel, *supra* note 4.

183. Immortal Technique, *Revolutionary*, on REVOLUTIONARY VOLUME I, *supra* note 142 (lyrics available at Original Hip-Hop (Rap) Lyrics Archive, at http://ohhla.com/anonymous/immortal/rev_vol1/revolut.tch.txt (last viewed Feb. 28, 2004)).

184. DMX, *Who We Be*, on THE GREAT DEPRESSION (Universal Records 2001) http://www.ohhla.com/anonymous/dmx/thegreat/whowebe.dmx.txt (last visited Mar. 5, 2004)).

185. GangStarr, *Conspiracy*, On DAILY OPERATION (Chrysalis/ERI 1992) (lyrics available at Original Hip-Hop (Rap) Lyrics Archive, *at* http://www.ohhla.com/anonymous/gngstarr/daily_op/conspire.gsr.txt (last visited Mar. 28, 2004)).

186. Mos Def, *supra* note 170.

187. Ras Kass, *Ordo Abchao (Order Out of Chaos)*, on SOUL ON ICE (Priority Records 1996) (lyrics available at Original Hip-Hop (Rap) Lyrics Archive, *at* http://ohhla.com/anonymous/ras_kass/sl_onice/abchao.rsk.txt (last visited Mar. 5, 2004)).

188. For an analysis of black women rappers and sexual politics in rap music, see ROSE, *supra* note 49, at 146–82.

* **Paul Butler** is a professor of law at The George Washington University Law School. He is frequently consulted on issues of race and criminal justice. He has published in many scholarly journals, and his work has been featured on *60 Minutes, Nightline,* and other evening news programs. He has been awarded the Soros Justice Fellowship.

Retributive Punishment and Revenge

by Karsten J. Struhl*

The move from cultures of revenge to societies with criminal justice systems and retributive punishment is undoubtedly a progressive historical development. However, it is by no means the case that revenge has disappeared. In this essay, I shall argue that revenge conceals itself precisely in legal retributive punishment. I also argue that legal retributive punishment is a substitution of public for private revenge and, therefore, a form of controlled revenge. I shall also explore the implications of these claims, implications that move in two very different political directions—as a reason to allow the victim more opportunity to express and exercise her emotions of revenge in the legal system; and as a reason to be suspicious of the retributive theory of punishment and the way in which it manifests itself in the criminal justice system.

From the Informal Code of Revenge to Legal Punishment

Most ancient societies as well as some contemporary ones have an informal code of revenge. If someone causes some kind of harm to another, the individual who has been harmed has a right to retaliate and, in fact, is expected to retaliate. If someone causes some kind of harm to another's family members, friends, or members of another's tribe, the aggrieved individual has not only a right but an *obligation* to avenge this harm by harming the offender or perhaps those close to him—in effect, to pay him or her back. This is what has sometimes been called "the revenge ethic," which, "simply put, makes justice the personal responsibility of the person insulted or hurt or, if that person is dead, of someone closely related to him, almost invariably a close blood relative."[1] However, there was often an implicit if not explicit understanding that the revenge ethic follows, at least in a rough way, the *law of talion*, which prescribes that the retaliation be proportional to the offense. The *law of talion* gives revenge an internal limit—yes, an "eye for an eye," but not more than that, not "two eyes for an eye."

There were several problems, however, with this informal revenge system. The first, of course, was that the guilt or innocence of the party to be harmed was left to the avenger to decide. The second was that the appropriate degree of harm to be inflicted on the offender was also left to the avenger. What this meant in practice is that the *law of talion* was often exceeded. In fact, some cultures deliberately exceeded it, assuming that a blood debt had to be paid with interest.[2]

A third problem was that the target of vengeance was not necessarily only the individual wrongdoer but might include close kin and even the entire clan or tribe to which the wrongdoer belonged. In fact, a member of the offender's family (or even of some larger social grouping) *rather than the offender himself* might be chosen as the target. In Montenegro, a seventy-year-old man explains, "You have killed my son, so I killed yours. I have taken revenge for that, so I now sit peacefully in my chair."[3] For the Yanomamo of Brazil the target can be anyone within the offender's community.[4] The explanation for this point of view in indigenous communities and ancient societies is bound up with their way of understanding the relation of the individual to the family and the community. In contrast to how we view it, given our modern sensibility, the individual's identity and responsibility is not seen as independent of his or her family or community identity and responsibility. As Charles K. B. Barton, a lecturer on police ethics and justice at Charles Sturt University in Australia, explains, "Any member of the offending group constitutes a legitimate target for revenge, because they are all guilty on account of their shared group identity."[5] However, for our modern sensibilities, only the individual wrongdoer is taken to be responsible, and therefore it seems unjust to harm anyone else.

A fourth and perhaps the most important problem with the informal culture of revenge was the possible negative consequences of taking revenge, the most common being the possibility of an escalating cycle of violence. This is related to the previous problems. If the avenger took what seemed like revenge with interest, it would then be incumbent on the recipient of the avenger's wrath to take revenge against the avenger, perhaps also with interest. In fact, the taking of revenge and thus exceeding the *law of talion* might be built into the logic of the informal revenge system. Arindam Chakrabarti, who is a professor of philosophy at the University of Hawai'i at Manoa, argues that, for the avenger, the original harm was more than harm simple, since the original harm was unprovoked, undeserved, and unexpected. Thus, in order to get even, the avenger tries to increase the quantity and severity of the harm; but this will motivate the original perpetrator to retaliate for the increase. Thus, "one never gets even by retaliation. The revenge spiral keeps continuing, turning into blood feuds, keeping old wounds fresh rather than helping them heal."[6] And as these blood feuds can target members of the family and community as well as the specific perpetrators and avengers, the revenge cycle tends to draw in more and more people and may continue indefinitely.

The historical solution to these problems was to create a system of laws that separates legal punishment from revenge and insists that the would-be avenger must allow the law to punish the offender. The idea is that retributive punishment within the legal system substitutes justice for revenge. The criminal justice system, it is argued, subjects the offender to justice, not revenge. The offender is judged guilty or innocent of the crime by an impartial jury or judge, and the judge then decides, within legally stipulated limits, what punishment is proportionate to the crime. In so doing, the element of revenge is removed, and the crime now is seen as a crime against the society, which demands justice, not revenge. In short, legal retributive punishment is not revenge. I shall suggest shortly why I think that this view is mistaken.

Two Tales of the Transformation of
Revenge into Legal Punishment

A number of ancient stories and myths testify to the ambivalence that ancient societies had toward revenge. One of the most famous is the story of the House of Thebes, which found its way into the three plays that constitute Aristophanes's *Oresteia*. The background story that informs the three plays is a brother's revenge. Thyestes had an affair with the wife of his brother Atreus, who was the king of Argos. Atreus initially banishes Thyestes but later invites his brother to a feast where he serves him, as a main course, a dish composed of the ground-up flesh of Thyestes's children. When Thyestes finally realizes what he has eaten (the hands and the heads of his children were at the bottom of the dish), he puts a curse on all the descendants of Atreus. The first to experience the effects of this curse is Atreus's son, Agamemnon, whose wife, Helen, is taken to Troy by Paris. Agamemnon then assembles a fleet of ships to sail to Troy and attack the Trojans. However, before arriving at Troy, the fleet is stalled for lack of a strong wind, and an event occurs that is taken as an omen and is interpreted as saying that Agamemnon must sacrifice his daughter Iphigenia in order that the strong winds return. Iphigenia is subsequently sacrificed, the ships reach Troy, and Troy is defeated. However, when Agamemnon returns triumphant from Troy, his wife Clytemnestra murders him in retaliation for his killing their daughter. She is assisted in this murder by Aegisthus, whom she has taken as a lover during Agamemnon's absence. Aegisthus, who is also the only surviving son of Thyestes, has now also avenged the murder of his two brothers by Agamemnon's father.

As the tale of revenge continues, Orestes, Clytemnestra's son, who had fled the kingdom when his mother subsequently married Aegisthus, now returns and, with the encouragement of his sister Electra, kills his mother, in part for the murder of his father. But the story does not end here, as the Furies, who are the demonic avengers of matricide, torment Orestes and drive him nearly mad. At this point, Apollo enters the scene and brings Orestes and the Furies to Athens, where Athena sets up a court system and a jury to try Orestes. In this jury trial, the Furies act as the prosecutor, both testifying against Orestes and cross-examining him, and Apollo speaks in his defense. After testimony, the jury of twelve Athenians is equally divided, and Athena herself casts the deciding vote in Orestes's favor, thereby acquitting him. The Furies are furious and cry: "The earth is overthrown. Our laws are obsolete.... You violate creation! You dishonor the voice of the blood and the earth."[7] But Athena implores them, "Let your rage pass into understanding... promising a fair tomorrow,"[8] and promises them an honored place in this new system where they can always sit and watch the proceedings, at which point they become magically transformed into the Eumenides, or "the kindly ones." The moral point seems to be that the cycles of revenge can be quieted by the introduction of an impartial legal system. But it is important to note that in this tale, the spirit of revenge, while it has been tamed, can still sit within the courthouse. It is also important to note that, at the trial of Orestes, the Furies were allowed the role of prosecutor. We might also wonder whether, without the magic of Athena, the spirit of revenge can so easily be transformed into "the kindly ones."

Let us now move to a more modern tale, one that is told by John Locke in the late seventeenth century. In his *Second Treatise on Civil Government*, Locke posits a state of nature in which there are natural laws that give all human beings natural rights. In the state of nature, Locke writes, everyone has the right of life, liberty, health, and property, and those who violate the rights of a fellow human can be punished by any other human being. Thus, in addition to the aforementioned rights, everyone in the state of nature has an additional right—the right to punish whoever violates another person's rights.

The state of nature poses a number of problems that require human beings to enter into a voluntary agreement with one another—a social contract that by consent of all creates a society where the people are collectively sovereign. The social contract also establishes a government to legislate and administer the laws and to protect the rights that exist in the state of nature, except for one right—the right to punish. One of the reasons that it is reasonable to move from the state of nature to the social contract is that individuals in the state of nature—most of whom Locke believes would have an innate understanding of natural law and would wish to respect each other's natural rights[9]—tend to be partial to their own interests. As a result, while everyone in the state of nature has a right to punish those who violate the natural rights of others, it is likely that the punisher will exact a punishment that exceeds the harm caused by the offense, that "ill-nature, passion, and revenge will carry them too far in punishing others; and hence nothing but confusion and disorder will follow."[10] In other words, the punisher will become an avenger who exceeds the *talion*, which will then generate the kinds of problems discussed in the previous section. Thus, while according to Locke we keep most of our rights even as we enter the social contract—the contract having as part of its purpose to enforce those rights—the individual must give up entirely the right to punish either in her own behalf or on the behalf of others. The social contract provides the basis for a system of laws, among which are criminal statutes that mandate specific penalties for specific crimes, the penalty being proportionate to the offense.

However, that the individual no longer has the right to punish raises two questions. The first is whether, as in the *Oresteia*, there are at least some trace elements of revenge existing in the criminal justice system. The second is whether the criminal justice system should, in some way, seek to act as an avenger on behalf of the victim. Locke's social contract tale does not explicitly answer these questions. On the one hand, it suggests that the system of laws will now become a substitute for revenge and that the point of punishment is not to avenge the victim but to punish the lawbreaker in the name of the society as a whole. In so doing, what is established is *retributive justice* in place of revenge. On the other hand, insofar as the social contract expresses the will of the people, the system of laws may be interpreted as a substitute for *private* revenge but not a substitute for revenge as such. In this second interpretation, the function of the criminal justice system will be to create a form of *public* revenge that institutionalizes the *law of talion* so that punishment will not exceed the bounds of the crime. While the victim gives up the personal right of revenge, the state seeks revenge in her behalf. There is also a third possible interpretation, which is that revenge was never at issue. In this interpretation, the right to punish in the state of nature is not about the right to avenge the wrongdoing but the right to act in behalf of retributive justice against those who have violated the laws of nature by violating the rights inscribed in those laws. Of course, this interpretation, like the first, assumes a clear distinction between retribution and revenge. Whether such a clear distinction can be made is what we now need to examine.

CAN RETRIBUTION BE DISTINGUISHED FROM REVENGE?

That retribution can be distinguished from revenge is a standard assumption in the United States and other liberal Western democracies. For example, soon after al-Qaeda's 2001 attack on the World Trade Center, President George W. Bush explained to FBI employees in the following words why the United States would attack the Taliban: "Ours is a nation that does not seek revenge, but we do seek justice."[11] As I am writing this article, President Barack Obama has released the following statement in reaction to the beheading of two Americans and a British citizen by the "Islamic State in Iraq and Syria" (ISIS): "We will work with the United Kingdom and a broad coalition of nations to bring the perpetrators of this outrageous act to *justice* [emphasis mine]."[12] When, in *Furman v. Georgia* (1972), capital punishment in the United States was determined to be unconstitutional,[13] Supreme Court Justice William Brenan wrote, "We have no desire to kill criminals simply to get even with them."[14]

The American philosopher Robert Nozick has famously claimed that there are at least five ways to distinguish revenge from retributive punishment. First, revenge is a response to "an injury or harm or slight" that need not be a wrong, while "retribution is done for a wrong." Second, revenge has no necessary limits, whereas retribution "sets an internal limit" that administers punishment proportionate to the harm caused by the offender. Third, revenge is always personal; it is a response to something done to oneself or someone to whom one has a close personal tie, such as a family member, "whereas the agent of retribution need have no special or personal tie to the victim of the wrong." Fourth, revenge produces a feeling of pleasure in the avenger at the suffering of the wrongdoer, whereas retribution need not involve any feeling other than "pleasure at justice being done." Finally, revenge need not assume any principle of generality, whereas retributive punishment assumes "general principles" whereby the same kinds of injuries in "other similar circumstances" will merit the same kind of punishment.[15]

A number of philosophers have added several more possible distinctions to this list. For example, Robert J. Stainton suggests that "whereas seeking revenge need not be communicative . . . exacting retribution *must* be an act of communicative behavior."[16] Jonathan Jacobs writes, "Retributivism is motivated differently from vengeance, and it involves a concern for justice rather than retaliation."[17] In fact, perhaps the majority of philosophers and legal theorists today insist that there is a fundamental distinction between retributive punishment and revenge.[18] This, however, does not mean that the distinction is correct. In fact, there are good reasons to think it is not correct.

At least four of Nozick's distinctions can be rather easily challenged. Consider his contrast that retribution is always a response to a wrong, while revenge is a response to an injury, harm, or slight that may not be a wrong. First, it is not clear what exactly the distinction is. To count as revenge, the avenger must think that in some way he or she is avenging something that is wrong. It would be odd to say of someone that there is nothing he did that was wrong, but I took my revenge anyway. Leo Zaibert, who is a professor of philosophy at Union College, gives an example of a teacher who is very cold to a student, because the student does not laugh at her jokes; the teacher says that her conduct is her attempt to "pay him back." If, however, the teacher does not consider the student's not laughing at her jokes wrong, then we would not call this either revenge or punishment. Perhaps it is simply a desire to inflict pain, or an expression of her insecurities. "But if she truly believes that there is absolutely *nothing* wrong with the student not laughing at her jokes, and she still . . . makes the student suffer, then her victimizing the student is in a sense gratuitous. . . . Revenge and punishment are never *gratuitous* inflictions of suffering."[19] And certainly when what is being avenged is something much more serious—perhaps a rape or a murder—the avenger will certainly claim that she is avenging a wrongdoing.

Consider Nozick's second distinction, that only retribution has an internal limit. However, as we have seen from our earlier discussion of cultures of revenge, revenge is also generally understood to have some kind of internal limit. Even if the limit allows for the revenge to be taken against some person other than the offender—perhaps a member of the offender's family—there is still an assumption of some rough kind of proportionality. Even revenge with interest implicitly recognizes the *talion* as the principle on which to add the interest. If the "act of revenge" is way out of proportion to the harm to which the agent is responding, we would be hard-pressed to call it revenge.[20] We would be more likely to call it an act of sadistic cruelty or the act of a deranged mind. Of course, the internal limit of revenge depends in large part on the norms of the social group of which the avenger is a member. But what legal retributive punishment is considered fitting for the crime is also a question of the norms of the society that stipulates that punishment.

Closely related to the question of proportionality and having an internal limit is the fifth distinction that Nozick makes, concerning the principle of generality—that retribution is committed to a general principle that similar cases of harm are to be treated similarly, whereas revenge need not be committed to such a principle. However, to the extent that revenge is committed to the *law of talion* in at least a rough form (even allowing for some payback interest), it will treat like cases at least relatively alike; and any reasonable review of legal punishment will show that a great many similar cases are punished quite differently. As Zaibert correctly observes, "baldly to assert that the avenger cannot possibly be committed to treating like cases alike and that the punisher is always committed to treating like cases alike smacks of mere stipulation."[21]

What can we say about Nozick's third claim, that the avenger always has a personal tie to the victim, whereas the agent of retribution need not have a personal tie? At first glance this seems to be a strong point of contrast. In fact, we might go further and say that the agent of *legal* retribution should not have any personal tie to the victim, for if she does, that would undermine the idea of the impartiality of the law. However, this contrast suffers from an ambiguity. Does personal mean "private," as opposed to "public"? If so, it raises a further question concerning exactly how to distinguish the private sphere from the public sphere. Or does personal mean "intimate"?[22] But then there are obviously degrees of intimacy, and what is intimate in one context may not be intimate in another. If I meet a member of my country in a foreign country, I may feel a certain sense of intimacy, although I might otherwise have very little in common with her. Perhaps the distinction is simply that revenge is taken on behalf of a family member or close friend. However, while this is often the case, it would not be odd to say that someone took revenge simply out of a sense that an injustice was done to someone she knew who was not a friend or family member, or even someone she only knew about. Perhaps, then, the distinction is simply between what the state officials do and what private individuals do. This distinction is clear enough, but it begs the question, for we still want to know whether officials acting in the name of the state are involved in an act of revenge. It is precisely my contention that legal punishment contains at least elements of revenge.

We come now to Nozick's fourth distinction—that the avenger takes pleasure in the suffering of the individual that she harms, whereas retribution need not involve any feeling other than the pleasurable satisfaction that justice is being served. Jonathan Jacobs reiterates this claim in even stronger terms. "There is no place in retributivism for taking pleasure in the suffering of the person punished. A vengeful person might take considerable pleasure in causing suffering. A person seeking vengeance might think that cruelty is appropriate, and that to degrade or humiliate ... is fitting."[23] Notice that, for Jacobs, retribution not only does not need to take pleasure in the suffering of the person punished, but that taking such pleasure is *incompatible* with retributivism. In either case, whether in Nozick's softer form or Jacobs's stronger claim, the implication is that revenge is all about the desire for and subsequent pleasure in the suffering of the target of revenge, whereas the main point of retribution is not pleasure but a rational response to an evil.

I think this distinction is at the core of the other distinctions, as well as the concerns of many philosophers and legal theorists who distinguish retribution from revenge. It is also the underlying rationale for the concerns of politicians and judges who insist that what motivates them is not revenge (bad) but retribution (good). In this way of thinking, revenge is taken to be essentially emotionally based and hence irrational, while retribution is rational, emotionally neutral, and on the side of the angels. That is why revenge is seen as primarily a response to an injury rather than to something that is morally wrong; why it is seen as setting no internal limits; why it is assumed that it has no general principles that guide it; why it is regarded as something personal rather than impartial. That is why, to consider Stainton's suggested distinction mentioned above, it can be assumed that revenge does not necessarily communicate anything (irrational emotional acts need not be attempts to communicate), while retribution as a rational act seeks to communicate a relation between the wrongful act of the offender and her punishment. That is also why retribution is aligned with justice, and revenge is seen as an impulsive act of retaliation that is not motivated by justice. Thus, the deeper question is whether it is possible to separate emotion and rationality in such a way that revenge is tied to the kind of emotional pleasure experienced when contemplating, seeing, or knowing about the suffering of the offender, while retribution does not seek or experience such pleasure. In order to answer this question, we need to explore more thoroughly the motivation for revenge and for retribution and determine whether it is really possible to distinguish the two.

THE MOTIVATION FOR RETRIBUTION AND THE MOTIVATION FOR REVENGE

There is something odd about suggesting that motivation for any kind of meaningful action is based on pure rationality. Even when we make decisions based on clear rational thinking, the thinking must begin with certain goals that have an emotional underpinning. Reason may guide us in refining those goals and in considering the ways in which certain actions are likely or unlikely to further these, but it does not provide the basis for the goals themselves. Furthermore, emotions themselves are rarely simply irrational, as they often assume certain ideas about people and the world; and surely our moral thinking is guided by at least one of our emotional reactions to certain kind of situations.[24] This is especially true when it comes to thinking about issues of revenge and retributive punishment, as both are guided by one of the same emotions that arise as a response to some real or presumed wrongdoing. "Both the avenger and the (retributive) punisher feel some sort of indignation, outrage, or a feeling of that tenor, as a result of what they perceive to be an instance of wrongdoing. This is why the emotion of indignation has been so central in moral philosophy."[25]

The nineteenth-century British philosopher John Stuart Mill claimed that, in the case of the desire to punish, "the sentiment of justice appears...to be the animal desire to repel or retaliate a hurt or a damage to oneself or to those with whom one sympathizes, widened so as to include all persons, by the human capacity of enlarged sympathy and of intelligent self-interest."[26] What Mill is claiming is that the sense of retributive justice is built on three emotions. The first is the natural desire to retaliate against those who cause us to suffer. The second, not specifically mentioned but implied, is to retaliate against those who harm someone we know and with whom we sympathize. The third is a form of sympathy that is so enlarged that it includes all humanity, which I think might be better to call "compassion." It is this enlarged sympathy or compassion that gives to retributive justice its universal standing. The process from the desire to retaliate for the harm that one has personally received to retributive justice assumes an extension of one's identity to create a wider circle of concern. Thus, retributive justice is built on extending the desire to retaliate against anyone who has caused harm to oneself to a desire to retaliate against anyone who has caused suffering to those smaller circles of concern (family, friends, neighbors, etc.) with whom one identifies; and, finally, to a much greater extended desire based on one's identification with and compassion for all humanity, a desire to retaliate against anyone who has harmed another human being.[27] There is, of course, a rational element involved in this extension, since we must assume that the harm is undeserved and that therefore it is the individual who caused the undeserved harm who deserves to suffer. If Mill's account is plausible, then it is reasonable to believe that retributive justice is a response to certain emotions of which a basic component is the desire to make the offender suffer for the harm caused to oneself and then to those one cares about in this universally enlarged sense. It would follow that our sense of retributive justice entails that we take pleasure in anticipating, experiencing, or knowing about the suffering of those who caused others to suffer. That is why, in jury trials, the prosecutor attempts to invoke empathy with the victim and to get the jury to feel a sense of personal horror at the nature of the crime. In short, the "intuition" of retributive justice is grounded in the same emotions of moral outrage and the desire to retaliate that motivate revenge.

This same point can be made by looking at the motivation for revenge. Revenge is not a mindless activity. It cannot simply be lashing out at someone. The avenger cannot seek or get revenge without a concept of revenge, without at least understanding what it means to seek revenge. A corollary of this point is that "lower animals can't genuinely seek (or get) revenge," although they "can intend harm to another.... But unless they have the concept REVENGE— which, arguably, no lower animal does—, they can't seek revenge."[28]

Furthermore, as I have already indicated in my discussion of revenge cultures, there is a moral underpinning built into the idea of revenge. The avenger assumes that she has been wronged and, within some general limits, takes revenge in proportion to the wrong that has been done her. Michael Davis, who is a professor of philosophy at the Illinois Institute of Technology, offers the following definition of revenge: "Revenge is openly inflicting on the wrongdoer the same kind of harm he wrongly inflicted (because he wronged his victim in that way)."[29] Davis proposes this definition in part to distinguish revenge from retribution, suggesting that retribution generally does not insist that the payback be the "same kind of harm," for example, raping the rapist. However, it seems to me that this also is not essential to revenge, so that we can modify his definition by substituting the phrase "inflicting on the wrongdoer some comparable harm." In either case, however, the concept of revenge entails the moral idea that, in some rough way, punishing should be according to what one deserves.

It might be immediately objected that this is a stipulative definition and that the concept of revenge should be defined in a morally neutral way. Indeed, there are several thinkers who have done just that. Here is one example of such a definition offered by the British political philosopher Brian Rosebury: "An act of revenge is any deliberately injurious act against another person which is motivated by resentment of an injurious act or acts performed by that other person against the revenger, or against some other person or persons whose injury the revenger resents."[30] On the basis of this morally neutral definition, Rosebury distinguishes "between revenge motivated by an act which the avenger both resents and judges to be morally unjustified, and an act which she merely resents as harming or afflicting her, irrespective of any moral judgment."[31]

I would make two observations about Rosebury's definition and its implications. First, even if we accept Rosebury's definition, it is still the case that, on his account, there is one kind of revenge where the avenger believes she is responding to a moral wrong done to her or some other person. Thus, one kind of revenge—the revenge motivated by an act that the avenger not only resents but *judges to be morally unjustified*—cannot be distinguished from retribution on the grounds that only retribution is in response to what the punisher believes is a moral wrong. Second, while we may indeed sometimes use the term "revenge" to refer to acts that are morally unjustified and to which the avenger does not even offer a pretense of moral justification, this concept of revenge does not fit very well with the meaning of revenge within the cultures of revenge. As we have seen, revenge cultures assume that revenge must be for a reason that is recognized by the community and that it must be in some proportion to the offense. Of course, specific acts of revenge may be unjust, at least by the standards of justice of modern liberal democracies—but so, for that matter, may be decisions of a court of law. In fact, the same codes of "harsh justice" and honor that motivate revenge in cultures of revenge may be inscribed into law.[32] However, we recognize that "operating under the guise of law doesn't automatically render the decrees of the court just. The same is true of revenge. Revenge that is unjust or excessive is not revenge, any more than stoning or beheading as a penalty for adultery can be recognized as justice in a moral universe.... [T]he injustice of the court suffers from the same failing as unjustified revenge."[33] In other words, it is possible to judge revenge according to the same standard by which we judge legal retributive punishment. Was there an offense that deserved to be punished? Was the punishment out of proportion to the offense (either too much or too little)? Of course, what is an offense and what is the deserved punishment may differ with different cultures. But this is as true of the idea of legal retribution as it is of revenge.

I have said a number of things about the concept of revenge and offered some reasons that it has a moral element embodied within it, however imperfectly it is executed. What about the concept of retribution? To what extent does it contain the emotion of retaliatory payback? The British philosopher John Cottingham discusses nine theories that are labeled "retributive" but suggests that the most basic of these is "repayment theory." In fact, the idea of repayment is the original meaning of "retribution," as the etymology of the term is from the Latin *re* + *tribuo*, which literally means "to pay back." However, it is not clear how to justify this repayment theory, as it "is not so much a theory as a *metaphor*, a metaphor which ... cuts remarkably little ice as a justificatory device."[34]

The theory that is closest to and perhaps entailed by the repayment theory is "the desert theory," which claims that the reason for punishment is simply that it is deserved. Again, it is not entirely clear how to justify this theory, since it tends to be reduced to a tautology—that punishment is justified because it is deserved. But why it is deserved is rarely explained beyond the idea that someone who does something wrong "deserves" to be punished. In fact, it is often the case that the retributivist will declare that the offender deserves to be punished simply because, having done something wrong, she deserves to be punished. For example, the Canadian philosopher and law professor Dennis Klimchuk argues that retributive punishment has no goal beyond retribution itself, that it is *not* inflicted on the criminal wrongdoer to promote some other social good. "The *core idea* of retributivism is the idea that those who commit criminal wrongdoings deserve punishment (simply) in virtue of their having done so."[35] Michael Moore, who is professor of philosophy and law at the University of Illinois, also insists that "we are justified in punishing because and only because offenders deserve it."[36]

The idea of desert is closely connected to the idea of responsibility, which in turn is connected to the idea that the agent has freely chosen to act as she did. Jonathan Jacobs argues that punishment is deserved whenever the offender is responsible for her actions, which means that she must be a voluntary agent.

"Retributivists argue that punishment is inflicted as deserved, as owed to a person on account of that for which that person is responsible as a voluntary agent."[37] If the offender is not responsible for her actions because they were not under her voluntary control, then she does not deserve to be punished.[38] However, it is not clear why being responsible for an intentional harmful action entails that one *deserves to suffer*. Perhaps it is the debt theory that provides the reason.

The idea that the offender deserves to be punished for an intentional voluntary action and must, therefore, be paid back for her wrongdoing also assumes that she has a debt to pay for her wrongdoing. The punishment is the payback. To pay back is to repay a debt. Wrongdoers need to be punished because their wrongdoing has put them in debt. But to whom does the offender pay this debt, and what is the currency of this debt? For legal retribution, the answer is that the offender needs to pay a debt to society, and the currency of this debt is her suffering. This can be easily recognized once we assume a proportion between the wrongdoing and the debt that is to be paid, for there can be no assessment of proportion unless there is some common currency; and since the debt was accrued by causing wrongful suffering, the debt must be repaid by the suffering of the offender in proportion to the suffering that she caused. However, if this is the case, the retributive punisher must desire that the wrongdoer be punished, which entails that she desire that the wrongdoer should suffer. On what is that desire based? The answer given by the pure retributivist is our *intuition* that the wrongdoer must be paid back in kind, that she *deserves* to be paid back in kind, that the wrongdoer by doing wrong has acquired a debt that she must pay and that *this debt can only be repaid by her suffering*. However, the retributivist will often claim that she gets no joy in this suffering as such—at most the only pleasure is that of seeing that justice is done. We might perhaps be suspicious of such an intuition. On what is that intuition based? The retributivist might answer that it is based on moral insight, an intuition that reveals the nature of justice.

However, intuitions are notoriously suspect, especially in matters of morality. We recognize that different cultures often have very different moral values concerning a great many things. The moral intuitionist reply is that however different these values are, there are certain intuitions that are universal, and their being universal provides support for claiming that they point to objectively valid moral truths. Perhaps this is so, but is this the case with respect to intuitions about legal retribution? I think there is good reason to think that our intuitions about retribution, desert, and responsibility are not universal.

We have already seen that revenge cultures have different intuitions about who is the legitimate object of revenge and what kind of revenge can be done in response to an offense. How radically different are these intuitions? Based on an analysis of ethnographic studies of revenge cultures, which he calls "honor cultures," Tamler Sommers, who is a professor of philosophy at the University of Houston, argues that these cultures have "radically different intuitions regarding responsibility and punishment."[39] In honor cultures, the focus is on the person who has been wronged, not the person who has done the wrong. After an offense has occurred, pressure is put on the victim or a member of the victim's family to avenge himself (generally the onus of responsibility is put on the male) and his family. What is at stake is his honor and the honor of his family, and if he does not seek revenge soon, he is dishonored and scorned, and he may soon become the target of abuse by others.[40] As we have seen, the target of revenge need not be the same person who committed the offense, and, in some cases, preserving the honor of oneself and one's family takes the form of revenge against the members of the offender's family. Sommers offers the following reason for this: "The important thing is that the injured party retaliates against *someone*, someone who bears a connection to the offender. Otherwise, honor is lost. . . . [T]here is no prohibition against punishing relatives or associates of the offender, since the primary function of retaliation is to restore the reputation of the offended party."[41]

This, of course, is quite different from our attitude about punishment and responsibility in what he calls our "institutionalized cultures." The responsibility to punish, for us, is not put on the victim or the victim's family. On the contrary, neither the victim nor the members of the victim's family are allowed to administer punishment, and we do not believe that anyone but the wrongdoer deserves to be punished. The temptation is to say that honor cultures are not yet "mature," or that they are simply "irrational." However, as Sommers observes, the norms of honor cultures are very functionally rational. "In honor cultures, the retributive dispositions serve primarily as deterrent directed at individual or family. If you are known as someone who is outraged at the slightest insult . . . then potential offenders are far less likely to take advantage of you."[42] Thus, if Sommers is correct in his assessment of honor cultures, our intuitions about responsibility, punishment, and desert are not universal, and therefore there is no reason to assume that they give us a special access to moral truth.

Since most retributivists can provide no justification for their understanding of punishment beyond the intuitions that the wrongdoer deserves to suffer in relation to the suffering for which she was responsible, and since there is no reason to believe that these intuitions are universally shared, this suggests that there must be something else going on. If we do not have such intuitions for rational reasons, and the retributivist nonetheless insists that they must point to some moral truth, it is likely that they are rooted in certain emotions that the retributivist may not want to recognize. The most likely candidate for the emotions that might be behind these intuitions are the emotions that motivate revenge. These include the desires to retaliate against the wrongdoer *and* to get pleasure in his or her suffering. In what we think of as our more "civilized" society, these emotions and desires are transformed into an institutionalized form so that a third party takes the role of the avenger but with the institutional pretense of being impartial and emotionally neutral. These emotions and desires are then hidden from us behind the sanctity of law and legal retribution. If we were to allow ourselves to recognize them for what they really were, we might be less comfortable with the idea of legal retribution, for what they suggest is that the meaning of punishment in our so-called civilized society is essentially a *controlled form of revenge*. I will say more about this shortly.

LEGAL RETRIBUTION AS CONTROLLED REVENGE: WHAT RIGHTS SHOULD THE VICTIM HAVE?

Let us recall Locke's analysis of the right to punish. For Locke, the social contract retains all our natural rights except the right to punish the offender. This right is now taken by government, and the victim of the offense must accept the verdict of the criminal justice system established by the government. One possible interpretation of this analysis, which we have suggested earlier, is that legal retribution is not a substitute for revenge as such but only a substitute for *private* revenge. Or perhaps, more to the point, it transforms *private* revenge into *public* revenge. What this means is that while the victim is no longer permitted to avenge the wrong directly, the criminal justice system will take revenge on her behalf. The government assumes the role of the surrogate avenger. And it is the avenger not only for the victim but also for the public whose sense of moral outrage is often grounded in a blood lust for retaliation. Only it is not called "revenge" but "justice." What this does, in effect, is sanitize the revenge and establish the pretense that such public revenge is no longer revenge but something else, something that is not subject to the messy and volatile emotions of revenge.

However, the emotions of revenge always threaten to break through the veneer of legal punishment. When shocking crimes are discussed in the public media, the public's cry for "retribution" and "punishment" can reach a fever pitch. We sometimes learn, in retrospect, that this created a "rush to judgment" and that the alleged offender, after being convicted, is later found to be innocent. When criminals are given the death penalty and subsequently executed, there are often celebrations by members of the public who are unrelated to the victim or the victim's family. The Furies that are given an honored place in Athena's court do not always remain the Eumenides, "the kindly ones." They are easily roused, and they refuse to sit quietly on the sidelines. This creates a problem for the criminal justice system—whether to maintain the illusion that legal retribution is not revenge, or to allow the revenge motive a freer play. There are several ways to respond to this problem. One way is to insist that since revenge is already built into the idea of legal retribution, we should affirm it and, in fact, strengthen its force. This is one of the goals of what is called "the victims' rights movement."

The victims' rights movement has emerged in response to what its members consider the marginalization of the victim in the criminal justice system. Victims have no legal standing to question the decisions of the criminal investigators, the prosecutor, or the judge. Steven Eisenstat, who is a professor of law at Suffolk University, discusses a number of problems that result from this.[43] First, decisions made by the district attorney's office, which may result in dropping the charges or acquittal, are not subject to victims' consent. Second, the criminal investigators and law enforcement officers may make errors that can result in acquittal or dismissal of charges and that leave the victim without any legal recourse other than tort remedies. Third, the victims have no say in how the case against the offender is developed or pursued in the court. Fourth, the prosecutor has the power to make a plea-bargaining agreement that usually gives the criminal wrongdoer a far lesser penalty than what would be commensurate with the victim's suffering, and the victim simply has to accept this. Finally, the victim has no legal standing in the determination-of-sentencing process.

The underlying problem is that the government and the prosecution represent "the people" and not the victim. The assumption is that the crime is fundamentally a crime against the society as a whole, and, as Eisenstat himself acknowledges, there is some element of truth to this. We all, in a way, suffer when there is a wrongful criminal act, for we know that any one of us could have been the victim of that act, and so we feel the insecurity of the criminal's being able to act with impunity. "Yet, who could reasonably argue that the person who has actually been mugged, robbed, raped, or beaten, has not suffered at least as great, if not a greater harm. He is suffering now."[44] The problem is not that private vengeance needs to be curbed for the sake of society as a whole. The problem, as Eisenstat and others in the victims' rights movement see it, is that the law has gone too far in the other direction, refusing to give the victim any reasonable kind of standing in the legal process. The "law has (d)evolved from the laudable purpose of seeking to eliminate the ravages of revenge, to where today, the law denies victims standing to even petition courts to enforce punishments which have been lawfully imposed upon their convicted wrongdoers."[45] Thane Rosenbaum, who is a law professor at Fordham Law School, puts this problem succinctly in social contract terms.

People would never have surrendered their right to seek self-help [their own right of revenge] had they believed that the honor they had lost, the suffering they had endured, would become irrelevant to the legal process. ... They wouldn't have imagined that the social contract meant that the harms done to them could no longer be taken personally. It's one thing for the law to serve as the exclusive punisher. It's quite another to presuppose that individuals no longer claimed an emotional stake in those punishments.[46]

One of the ways that the emotions of revenge are sometimes allowed to enter in the legal procedure is in the sentencing phase of the criminal trial. "And when emotion is introduced into the sentencing decisions, the dry concept of legal retribution begins to beat with the quickening pulse of moral revenge."[47] The most obvious way in which this is done is through victim impact statements.[48] Victim impact statements are statements presented to the judge with the intent to influence the sentencing decision. They attempt to articulate the horror of the crime and the impact that it has had on their lives. If the primary victim has been murdered, then the family and friends are considered also victims, who articulate the way in which that murder has impacted their lives. Victim impact statements also give the victims a space to discharge their emotions and to feel that in some small way they have been heard. Their use in this phase of the trial is an implicit admission that the passions of revenge—the vindictive passions—are at least a component of legal retribution. "Victim impact statements... are yet another side door into the law that invites the emotions of revenge inside the courtroom without the violence and imprecision that society fears in situations of privatized violence."[49] However, at present, this is only a very tiny side door. While most states in the United States permit victim impact statements, the victim often is only allowed to submit a written statement, which as far as she knows may never be read by the judge. Also, if the victim is allowed oral testimony, she is often cautioned against being "too emotional," and, in any case, the victim has no say in what sentence the offender receives.

What the victims' rights movement and thinkers like Eisenstat and Rosenbaum advocate is that the victim be given at least a significant seat in the sentencing process, and that widening the scope of victim impact statements is a good place to start. While Eisenstat agrees that there should be no victim involvement in the guilt phase of the criminal justice process, he suggests three procedural mechanisms that might be introduced into the sentencing phase, each of which increases the victim's role. First, at the very least, the victim should have an opportunity to make recommendations about the defendant's sentence. Currently, only a few states allow this. Second, the victim could be given the status of a legally recognized party to the sentencing hearing, although the actual decisions would still be made by the judge or the jury. Third, and the most radical of his proposals, the victim would decide the actual sentence within the federal or state guidelines of what could be the maximum sentence. Rosenbaum's proposals are even more radical. He suggests that victims be allowed to speak and ask questions during plea bargaining; that they would have a right to directly question witnesses and speak during the jury trial (or hire a special counsel to do so who would represent only them); that they could appeal lower court decisions and have veto power over the sentence; and that prosecutors would announce that they represent both the people *and* the victim.

While I would ultimately reject at least the more radical of these proposals, it is not because I do not have sympathy with the victims. I do think there should be a place within the criminal justice system where the victim can express her emotions and feel that they are heard. And I agree that the victim does need to feel that, in some way, the legal system represents her and not simply the people. However, to give the victim actual power to make decisions or to veto them would allow not just revenge but *private* revenge to return. The Furies may need their moment of expression, and they should not feel that they must always sit on the sidelines; but it would be a mistake to give them a key role in the process by which guilt or punishment is determined. We can acknowledge that legal retribution is animated by revenge without giving up the aspect of the criminal justice system that addresses the volatile nature of private revenge—to transform it into a more controlled public revenge.

Still, there is a problem that has yet to be discussed. If my analysis is correct and legal retribution is a form of controlled revenge, then one direction we can take is to give the voice of victim's revenge motives a larger hearing. However, there is another implication of my analysis, which is that rather than affirm and increase the revenge element within legal retributive punishment, we might question the idea of retribution, precisely because it is rooted in the emotions of revenge. In other words, rather than accept revenge as a necessary part of the criminal justice system insofar as it is the basis for the idea of retribution, we might question the retributive aspects of the criminal justice system that necessarily carry revenge into that system. It is this direction I want to explore in the last section of this essay.

REVENGE, RETRIBUTION, AND THE HERMENEUTICS OF SUSPICION

For the retributivist, punishment is not something that is done for the sake of something else but precisely because the offender deserves it. However, retribution is not the only justification for legal punishment. Other theories of punishment see punishment as justified in terms of some other social good—for example, deterrence, incapacitation, rehabilitation. Retribution, however, stands alone as a theory of punishment that insists that the consequences of punishment are not relevant to whether or not we should punish. The eighteenth-century preeminent German philosopher Immanuel Kant famously insisted that "even if a civil society were to dissolve itself by common agreement of all its members . . . the last murderer remaining in prison must first be executed."[50] These lines are often quoted, but Kant's reasoning is sometimes forgotten. It is not merely that those who deserve to be punished must be punished even if there are no good social consequences. It is also that a particular consequence, which Kant calls "bloodguilt," would arise if the punishment *were not to be carried out*. Thus, those who in this thought experiment are about to dissolve their social bonds must execute the last murderer so that "the bloodguilt thereof will not be fixed upon the people; for if they fail to do so, they may be regarded as accomplices in this public violation of justice."[51] What interests me about Kant's reason is the idea that not only those who are charged with execution, but all the people in the society, will be mutually involved in a "bloodguilt." What is suggested here is a fundamental connection between retribution and guilt, and, given the connection between retribution and revenge that I have discussed above, it would follow that there is also a connection between revenge and guilt.

Up to this point in the discussion, I have emphasized reasons to be suspicious of the claim that the motives of retribution are fundamentally different from the motives of revenge and also to be suspicious of the claim that the retributive punisher does not get pleasure from the suffering of those who are punished. I now want to suggest that there are reasons to be suspicious of revenge, not because it is "irrational," but because it follows a rationality of cruelty and what the nineteenth-century German philosopher Friedrich Nietzsche called *ressentiment*, which one commentator describes as "a self poisoning of the mind which . . . leads to a constant tendency to indulge in certain kinds of value delusions. . . . The emotions concerned are revenge, hatred, malice, envy, the impulse to detract, and spite."[52] For Nietzsche, punishment can be traced back etymologically to the connection between guilt and debt—*Shuld* (guilt) and *Schulden* (to be indebted). What came first historically was not moral guilt but the contractual relation between creditor and debtor in which the debtor promised that if she could not repay the debt, the creditor had a right to inflict pain on her. "In 'punishing' the debtor, the creditor shares a seigniorial right. . . . [H]e is given a chance to bask in the glorious feeling of treating another human being as lower than himself. . . . Thus compensation consists in a legal warrant entitling one man to exercise his cruelty on another."[53] And again, "[I]n what sense could pain constitute repayment of a debt? In the sense that to make someone suffer was a supreme pleasure."[54] Thus, for Nietzsche, there is a fundamental relation between punishing the guilty party and the cruel enjoyment of watching or knowing that another human being is suffering. This hermeneutic analysis would cast a very different light on Kant's understanding of the "bloodguilt" that would be visited on those who would not carry out the punishment of the "last murderer."

I cannot in the space of this essay continue to explain Nietzsche's insightful and provocative analysis. My point here is to suggest that insofar as retributive punishment is rooted in the emotions of revenge, and insofar as revenge is rooted in these other unhealthy emotions—for example, envy and cruelty—there is good reason to be suspicious of legal punishment to the extent that it is based on retributive ideas. In other words, in contrast to the victims' rights movement, which affirms and wishes to extend the revenge element in the criminal justice system, there are reasons to go in the other direction—to expunge as far as possible the retributive elements from the criminal justice system.

To develop this position further, I want to begin with some observations of Michael Moore, who although he is a firm retributivist, recognizes that there are reasons to be suspicious of retributivism. Moore, in contrast to many other retributivists, is well aware that retribution has strong emotional components, but he does not consider emotions necessarily an impediment to the truth of a moral theory. In fact, he claims that emotions "are our main heuristic guide to finding out what is morally right."[55] Emotions might be an impediment, however, if they distort our understanding of moral truth, and he concedes that "non-virtuous" emotions would often do this. He further concedes that if our retributive inclinations are contaminated by the emotions of *ressentiment*, this would count significantly against retributivism. "If Nietzsche is right in asserting that our retributive beliefs are always motivated by the emotions of *ressentiment* and right that the possession of these emotions makes us less virtuous, then we have grounds to reject retributivism as a philosophy of punishment."[56] Moore even concedes that our retributive inclinations are often based on such emotions as envy, jealousy, and even projection of guilt. Nonetheless, Moore argues that retributivism can also be motivated by the "virtuous emotions" of guilt and concern for others. Here is how it works: You learn of some horrible wrongdoing, and you ask yourself what you would feel if you did that horrible act. Moore's answer is that most of us would feel overwhelming guilt, and that to feel guilty would be to recognize that we are guilty and—here is the first punch line—"to feel guilty is to judge that we must suffer."[57] The second punch line is that from our own guilt we recognize that it is appropriate for whoever did that horrible action to suffer. In effect, we extrapolate from the guilt in our own case, which Moore takes to be a virtuous emotion, to what the offender deserves.

Moore's analysis is challenged by Jeffrie G. Murphy, who is a professor of philosophy and law at Arizona State University and who, although also a retributivist, calls himself a "reluctant retributivist." He is reluctant because, like Moore, he is aware of the way in which *ressentiment*, which he identifies with "spiteful and malicious envy," motivates our retributive inclinations and also because he thinks that Moore's attempt to defuse the Nietzschean challenge by appeal to "virtuous" guilt feelings fails. Specifically, Murphy argues that "guilt fares just as badly as *ressentiment* as an honorable emotional basis for retribution."[58] Guilt may be neurotic and destructive if projected onto others. "A person might use his own imagined guilt feelings to demand very serious punishment for conduct that is . . . objectively trivial or even unobjectionable—e.g., masturbation or homosexuality or romance outside a particular religious or ethnic or racial group."[59] And it is not clear how we can separate this irrational guilt from some assumed "rational guilt" except by insisting that the latter is based on the idea of what one deserves for wrongdoing. But then, the whole argument is circular.

Murphy also offers another challenge to the vindictive emotions that motivate retribution. There is, he says, a slippery slope from deciding that someone has an evil character and therefore deserves punishment, to cruelty. The slippery slope works this way: It is not just your action but your character and intentions that make you deserve punishment. Therefore, you have a vicious character. Therefore, "you are rotten and evil to the core," and, finally, "you deserve whatever cruel indignity I choose to inflict on you."[60]

CONCLUDING REFLECTIONS

It seems to me that the Nietzschean challenge to retributivism is a strong challenge to the revenge impulses that provide the ground for retributive punishment. Revenge may, in some sense, be a natural inclination, but it is not a healthy or "virtuous" one. It also is an inclination that can easily slide toward excessive cruelty and dehumanization of the other. Insofar as the retributive punishment contains these revenge motives, it is not surprising that our criminal justice system tends to reproduce and reinforce the brutality and dehumanization that is largely responsible for the kinds of criminal actions the criminal justice system seeks to eradicate. While certain problems of private revenge have been solved by institutional public revenge, they tend to reemerge in the punitive cruelty of the police, of the courts, of the lawmakers, and especially of the prison system. Thus, even though I have great sympathy for the victims of horrendous crimes who feel cast to the side by the criminal justice system, even though I think their pain needs to be acknowledged, I do not think that the best solution to this is to reinforce and extend the revenge motives within legal retributive punishment. We need to find a way that can compassionately acknowledge the pain of the victim, that allows the victim to express her emotions and be heard, and that simultaneously recognizes the humanity of and feels compassion for the criminal offender. If we want to have a more caring society with less crime and less inhumanity, we would do well to find ways of holding the criminal responsible without inflicting suffering on the theory that we must do so, whatever the consequences, simply because the offender deserves it. Of course, we can anticipate that we will continue to hear the words of the Furies: "The earth is overthrown. Our laws are obsolete.... You violate creation! You dishonor the voice of the blood and the earth." And while we can acknowledge this voice, we should respond with the words of Athena: "Let your rage pass into understanding... promising a fair tomorrow."

NOTES

1. Ian Johnston, "Lecture on the Oresteia," https://records.viu.ca/~Johnstoi/introser/aeschylus. htm.
2. Thane Rosenbaum notes that in Cambodian culture, the *talion* is considered insufficient. "If there is a revenge debt to be repaid, the honor culture of Cambodia requires that interest be paid along with principal—tacked on as a bonus, for the trouble of having to undertake the laboriously and emotionally wrenching work that is demanded of the avenger. Call it an eye for an eye, plus interest." Thane Rosenbaum, *Payback: The Case for Revenge* (Chicago: University of Chicago Press, 2013), 177.
3. Christopher Boehm, *Blood Revenge: The Anthropology of Feuding in Montenegro* (Lawrence: University Press of Kansas, 1984), 54.
4. Rosenbaum, *Payback*, 182. Rosenbaum discusses a number of other contemporary groups who assume that the legitimate target for revenge includes members of the wrongdoer's family—the Berbers, the Jibara Indians of Ecuador and Peru, and the Maori of New Zealand.
5. Charles K. B. Barton, *Getting Even: Revenge As a form of Justice* (Chicago: Open Court, 1999), 67.
6. Arindam Chakrabarti, "The Moral Psychology of Revenge," *Journal of Human Values* 11, no. 1 (April 2005): 34.
7. Aeschylus, *The Oresteia*, trans. Ted Hughes (New York: Farrar, Straus and Giroux, 1999), 187.
8. Ibid., 188.
9. This entails that most human beings are morally decent. However, Locke acknowledges that some are not and at one point even suggests that "were it not for the corruption and viciousness of degenerate men there would be no need... that men should separate from this great and natural community, and associate into lesser combinations." John Locke, *Second Treatise on Civil Government* in *Social and Political Philosophy*, ed. John Somerville and Ronald E. Santoni (New York: Doubleday, 1963), 186.
10. Ibid., 173.
11. Quoted in Rosenbaum, *Payback*, 7.

12. Quoted in "Video from ISIS Shows Killing of British Hostage," *New York Times*, September 14, 2014, 17.

13. This decision was subsequently reversed in *Gregg v. Georgia* (1976).

14. Quoted in Rosenbaum, *Payback*, 197.

15. Robert Nozick, *Philosophical Explanations* (Cambridge, MA: Harvard University Press, 1981), 366–368.

16. Robert J. Stainton, "Revenge," CRÍTICA, *Revista Hispanoamericana de Filosofía* 38, no. 112 (April 2006): 19.

17. See Jonathan Jacobs, "The Retributive Theory of Punishment," in this book, 53.

18. For other philosophers who distinguish between retributive punishment and revenge see Anthony Flew, "The Justification of Punishment," *Philosophy* 29, no. 111 (October 1954): 291–307; Jon Elster, "Norms of Revenge," *Ethics* 100, no. 4 (July 1990): 862–885; and Ted Honderich, *Punishment: The Supposed Justifications* (New York: Harcourt, Brace & World, 1967).

19. Leo Zaibert, "Punishment and Revenge," *Law and Philosophy* 25, no. 1 (January 2006): 95.

20. Zaibert makes a similar point by imagining a scenario in which a rancher whose barn is burned seeks "revenge" by dropping an atomic bomb on the state of Wyoming in order to kill the arsonist. Ibid., 97–98.

21. Ibid., 99. Zaibert may, however, be overstating the case with respect to Nozick's claim, since Nozick is claiming that the avenger *need not* assume any principle of generality, which means that he acknowledges that revenge may sometimes assume such a principle. However, insofar as Nozick's claim suggests a clear distinction between revenge and retributive punishment, the fact that revenge generally or at least often assumes some rough proportion between the harm caused by the offender and the harm caused by the avenger undermines his point. Zaibert goes on to argue that the prototypical vigilante is guided by certain principles by which, while taking *justice* into her own hands, she will avenge similar cases of injustice in a roughly similar way.

22. I am once again indebted to Zaibert for this line of reasoning, although my specific argument is somewhat different.

23. See Jacobs, "The Retributive Theory of Punishment," in this book, 54.

24. I know that I am going against Kant's assumption that it is possible to act from a pure sense of duty motivated *entirely* by our rational understanding of universal moral law. I cannot take the space here to defend my claim that moral thinking is always guided at least in part by our emotional reactions. I can simply say that Kant's assumption makes no senses from a naturalist perspective, which sees our moral ideas rooted in the evolutionary development of our moral responses. Reason clearly has a role to play in refining these moral responses, assessing consequences, etc., but it is not pure reason.

25. Zaibert, "Punishment and Revenge," 113.

26. John Stuart Mill, *Utilitarianism* (New York: Library of Liberal Arts Press, 1957), 65.

27. It is possible to enlarge the circle of concern even more, extending our concern to nonhuman animals. Mill himself recognizes this, as he summarizes his discussion of the utilitarian standard by noting that it would have as its goal the greatest amount of pleasure and the least amount of pain "secured to all mankind; and not to them only, but, so far as the nature of things admits, *to the whole sentient creation* [italics mine]." Ibid., 16. From this it would follow that retributive punishment would also include the desire to retaliate against anyone who has harmed those nonhuman animals with whom we sympathize. Animal welfare and animal rights law would provide a mechanism for doing this.

28. Stainton, "Revenge," 8. Stainton, however, makes clear in a footnote that he is not claiming that higher animals such as apes lack the concept of revenge.

29. Michael Davis, "Revenge, Victim's Rights, and Criminal Justice," *International Journal of Applied Philosophy* 14, no. 1 (Spring 2000): 123.

30. Brian Rosebury, "Private Revenge and Its Relation to Punishment, *Utilitas* 21, no. 1 (March 2009): 4.

31. Ibid., 3.

32. In Saudi Arabia in 2010, a man was sentenced to have his spinal court severed. In Afghanistan, men and women can be sentenced to public execution by stoning for committing adultery. In Pakistan, a woman who reports that she was raped and cannot provide four witnesses to testify that she was raped can be charged with adultery. For these and other similar examples see Rosenbaum, *Payback*, chap. 6.

33. Rosenbaum, *Payback*, 159.

34. John Cottingham, "Varieties of Retribution," *Philosophical Quarterly* 29, no. 116 (July 1979): 245. Cottingham's nine theories of retribution are: repayment theory, desert theory (she deserves to be punished), penalty theory (she broke the law and knew it), minimalism (no one should be punished unless guilty), satisfaction theory (retribution satisfies the victim's passion for revenge), fair play (not to punish would be unfair to those who have restrained themselves from doing such an action), placation theory (punishment appeases the wrath of God),annulment theory (annul the crime and right the wrong), and denunciation theory (the community denounces the crime).

35. Dennis Klimchuk, "Retribution, Restitution, and Revenge," *Law and Philosophy* 20, no. 1 (January 2001): 83.

36. Michael Moore, "The Moral Worth of Retribution," in *Philosophy of Law*, 6th edition, ed. Joel Feinberg and Jules Coleman (Belmont, CA: Wadsworth, 2000), 747.

37. Jacobs, "The Retributive Theory of Punishment," in this book, 54.

38. There is no assumption here of metaphysical free will. A soft determinist, or compatibilist, can coherently distinguish between voluntary and involuntary actions.

39. Tamler Sommers, "The Two Faces of Revenge: Moral Responsibility and the Culture of Honor," *Biology and Philosophy* 24, no. 1 (January 2009): 37.

40. Ibid., 42. Among the Albanian highlanders, a man who does not quickly kill the offender will find that other men will attempt to sleep with his wife and that his daughter does not have good prospects for marriage.

41. Ibid., 42. Among the Inuit, revenge for murder takes the form of killing not just the murderer but all his kin.

42. Ibid., 39.

43. Steven Eisenstat, "Revenge, Justice, and Law: Recognizing the Victim's Desire for Vengeance As a Justification for Punishment," *Wayne Law Review* 50, no. 4 (Winter 2005): 1115–1170.

44. Ibid., 1143.

45. Ibid., 1147.

46. Rosenbaum, *Payback*, 193–194.

47. Ibid., 216.

48. In 1991, the Supreme Court in *Payne v. Tennessee* ruled that victim impact statements were admissible in cases where the death penalty was at stake and that the character of the victim and the significance of the harm caused to the victim could be part of the statement. This decision overturned a previous 1987 Supreme Court decision, *Booth v. Maryland*, that argued that victim impact statements were in violation of the Fourteenth Amendment, which requires due process and equal protection under the law.

49. Rosenbaum, *Payback*, 223.

50. Immanuel Kant, *The Metaphysical Elements of Justice*, trans. John Ladd (Indianapolis: Bobbs-Merrill, 1965), 102.

51. Ibid.

52. Max Scheler, *Ressentiment*, trans. William Holdheim (New York: Free Press, 1961), 45–46. The idea of *ressentiment* occurs in many of Nietzsche's writings, but especially important is his *The Genealogy of Morals*. In that work Nietzsche analyzes *ressentiment* as an unhealthy state of mind rooted in a feeling of impotence and a desire to retaliate against those who are powerful, to denigrate them as evil, and to take pleasure in the imagined or real suffering that their punishment would bring about. Thus, the key emotions of *ressentiment* are feelings of impotence, envy, and cruelty.

53. Friedrich Nietzsche, *The Genealogy of Morals*, in *"The Birth of Tragedy" and "The Genealogy of Morals,"* trans. Francis Golffing (New York: Doubleday, 1956), 196–197.

54. Ibid., 197.

55. Moore, "Moral Worth of Retribution," 752.

56. Ibid., 761.

57. Ibid., 765.

58. Jeffrie G. Murphy, *Punishment and the Moral Emotions: Essays in Law, Morality, and Religion* (New York: Oxford University Press, 2012), 23.

59. Ibid., 27.

60. Ibid., 88–89. Given these arguments, it is not clear why Murphy remains a retributivist, even a reluctant one.

*Karsten J. Struhl** teaches political and cross-cultural philosophy at John Jay College of Criminal Justice (CUNY) and the New School for Public Engagement. He has coedited *Philosophy Now, Ethics in Perspective,* and *The Philosophical Quest: A Cross-Cultural Reader.* He writes about human nature, just war theory, problems of revenge and punishment, global ethics, visions of communism, ecology, Marxism, and Buddhist philosophy.

Written for this book and used by permission of the author.

Part 3:

Should Juveniles Receive a Different Kind of Punishment Than Adults?

When the juvenile justice system was originally established in the nineteenth century, its goal was to treat juveniles differently than adults. The rationale was that juvenile offenders, because they were impulsive and lacked the maturity to appreciate fully the risks and consequences of their actions, were less culpable than adult offenders and were in need of special care and attention. On the basis of this rationale, the juvenile justice system set up special courts, which, if it was deemed necessary to incarcerate juveniles, put them into special juvenile detention centers. The emphasis was less on deterrence than rehabilitation.

This, however, began to change by the late 1970s, as the general public became increasingly worried about juvenile crime, whose rates seemed to be increasing. By the 1980s, this perception had created a "moral panic." The media was full of examples of horrifying crimes committed by young people, and there was considerable discussion about "super-predator" juveniles who would rob, rape, and kill with almost no reason. The result was that the public began to demand severe punishment for juvenile offenders, and so states began passing laws that made it easy to transfer young people from juvenile to adult courts and then to try them as adults. As Bree Langemo, whose article we will discuss shortly, observes, "currently, all states allow the transfer of juvenile defendants to adult court for certain crimes. In forty-one states, juvenile defendants, fourteen years old or younger, may be transferred to adult courts under certain conditions. In twelve states, there is no minimum age for the transfer of juveniles to adult court, which, theoretically, permits a child of any age to be waived into adult court." It is important to add that if a juvenile offender is convicted in adult court, he or she will, in most cases, be sent to an adult prison. The result of this trend is that more and more juveniles are being tried and punished as adults.

The question then arises, should this trend be continued or reversed? Should juveniles who commit certain crimes be given the same kind of punishment as adults? The attempt to answer this question creates a fierce debate between those who think that there should be "adult time for adult crime," no matter how old or young the offender, and those who insist that juveniles are fundamentally·

different from adults and should therefore be treated differently and receive a different kind of punishment.

Ernest van den Haag's article, "Thinking About Crime Again," argues that juvenile offenders should be tried as adults and given the same kind of sentences adults would receive for their crimes. His article is a reflection on two books by one of the leading criminologists, James Q. Wilson. In those books, Wilson argued that rehabilitation does not work and that the point of punishment was to deter crime. However, he also argued that beyond a certain point, punishment does not have a deterrent effect, and therefore he proposed what might be called "selective incapacitation"—that "low rate" offenders should be given shorter sentences in order to make more space for "high rate" offenders.

In his reflections on Wilson's arguments and proposal, Van den Haag first notes his agreement with Wilson that rehabilitation does not work and that criminals can be deterred. However, he also indicates his disagreement with Wilson concerning the severity of punishment. In contrast to Wilson, Van den Haag believes that the more severe the punishment, the more it has a deterrent effect.

Van den Haag also challenges Wilson's "selective incapacitation" proposal and offers his own proposal for deterring crime, which focuses on juvenile offenders. He argues that since most criminals begin their career as juveniles, the best way to reduce crime overall is to abolish all juvenile courts and to try young offenders as adults. Juveniles, he argues, should no longer have the immunity of their youth to protect them from the consequences of their action, as "the immunity we have sentimentally given juveniles does not deter them from crime and even lures them in into self-destructive and antisocial criminal careers." Van den Haag does, however, stipulate that those under thirteen who commit criminal acts should be placed under the supervision of parents or social agencies. However, anyone over thirteen who committed criminal acts would be treated as an adult in the criminal justice system.

Bree Langemo's article, "Serious Consequences for Serious Juvenile Offenders: Do Juveniles Belong in Adult Court?," is a good example of the other side of the debate, since she argues that juveniles should not be tried in adult courts and that they should receive a different kind of punishment than adults. In this article, Langemo first discusses the history of the juvenile justice system and notes how the recent trend "has been to restore the pre-reformation view that juvenile defendants should be treated as adults in order to punish and deter juvenile crime." She then describes each of the methods used to place juveniles in adult court—judicial waiver (the prosecutor can petition the judge); automatic transfer, which through statutes can bypass the juvenile courts entirely; and prosecutorial discretion, in which the prosecutor can unilaterally decide that the juvenile should be prosecuted as an adult. Her overall point with respect to these methods is to demonstrate how easy it now is to mandate juveniles to adult courts. The result is that more and more juveniles end up being incarcerated in adult prisons, where they "face serious physical and emotional harm at the hands of their adult counterparts." This, in turn, means that "embittered juvenile offenders are often returned to society in a worse condition than when they entered the adult institution." They also are better prepared to commit crimes, as they often learn advanced criminal skills in prison.

Langemo offers four reasons why juveniles should not be subject to the serious consequences of being tried and convicted in adult court. First, she argues that the recent trends are based on misconceptions, as, in fact, juvenile crime is not rising, and juveniles placed in juvenile detention facilities are less likely to commit crimes after being released than juveniles placed in adult prisons. Second, she argues that the methods used to place juveniles in adult courts have a number of serious flaws, among which are the potential for abuse and discrimination based on the biases of the prosecutor and the judge. Third, adult courts are not sensitive to the special needs of juveniles, who often find the proceedings of an adult court situation unintelligible. "In addition, judges, prosecutors, and defense attorneys in adult court often do not have the specialized training to meet the special needs of juveniles as they often do in juvenile court." Finally, simply put, the fact is that juveniles are not adults. They do not yet have the emotional maturity of adults and therefore should not be treated as adults.

The articles by Van den Haag and Langemo represent the two opposing poles of the debate. Their differences are not just differences about factual matters but also fundamental philosophical differences. Van den Haag speaks from the conservative punitive position that sees severe punishment as an answer to crime on the assumption that striking fear into potential or actual offenders will be more likely to deter crime than any other method. As for juvenile offenders, the point is to make it clear that they will suffer the full penalty of the law for their criminal actions, that they will not be given a penalty discount because of their age. In contrast, for Langemo, the assumption is that our primary goal should be to rehabilitate the young offender, to be sensitive to his or her needs and lack of maturity, and that therefore we should return to the original goals of the juvenile justice system.

As you read the excerpts in this section, consider some of the following questions:

- What are the negative and positive consequences of trying juveniles in adult courts?

- What would you propose to reduce the crime rate in the United States? Do you think that treating juvenile offenders as adults helps to reduce the crime rate?

- What should the courts do with children under thirteen who commit offenses? Do you think these children understand the consequences of what they are doing or the difference between right and wrong?

- At what age should people be held accountable for their actions?

- Should juveniles receive a different kind of punishment than adults? If so, what should that punishment be? Is there an alternative to punishment for juveniles who commit crimes?

Thinking About Crime Again

*by Ernest van den Haag**

James Q. Wilson has been regarded as a leader of American criminology—we have more criminologists (and more crime) than most countries—at least since he collected his work in *Thinking About Crime* eight years ago. Deservedly so: his essays continue to throw a bright beam of light on the current tangle of obscure and sometimes obscurantist theories and statistics. The publication of a revised and greatly enriched edition of *Thinking About Crime*,[1] coinciding, as it does, with the appearance of *Crime and Public Policy*,[2] a compendious volume he edited, confirms Wilson's status, and is cause for both celebration and critical evaluation of some of his policy proposals. For Wilson is policy-oriented above all.

Thus, he strenuously argues that it is possible to influence events without knowing their causes. This is a point that should be obvious: one can extinguish a fire without knowing what caused it. Indeed, we often learn about causes from cures: if ingesting a chemical cures a disease, we may learn that the disease was caused by a lack of that chemical.

Even if likely to be correct, theories of crime causation do not help much at present. We know that a disproportionate number of crimes is committed by young males. But even if we wanted to, we could do little to reduce the proportion of young males in the population. Our knowledge helps us understand some fluctuations of the crime rate and to explain (in part) why the black crime rate is higher than the white crime rate: there is a higher proportion of young males in the black than in the white population. There is not much to be done about that either.

In one of the essays included by Wilson in *Crime and Public Policy*, Travis Hirschi brilliantly links crime to the control, or rather lack of control, of families and other groups over their members, particularly the young. Perhaps we will find ways of changing harmful family behavior or of replacing family emotional bonds in the future. For the time being nobody knows how to do it: the policy consequences even of correct causal theories are quite limited. Therefore, knowing about crime control is more important, at present, than knowing about crime causation.

Unfortunately, many hitherto influential criminologists have been less interested in controlling crime than in justifying social reforms by way of theories, usually unsubstantiated, about crime causation. They insist that social injustice is to blame for crime, not criminals. Crime is merely the punishment for our sins: poverty, inequality, "labeling" deviants, racism. Criminologists who think this way often have opposed building prisons; indeed they have opposed all crime-reducing measures other than the social reforms—in extreme cases the revolution—which their ideology (usually some variant of egalitarianism) demands. Everything else they regard as, well, irrelevant. It is, of course, to them, though not necessarily to crime reduction.

Wilson gives short shrift to theories blaming crime on the injustices of society. As a fine essay by Richard B. Freeman in *Crime and Public Policy* shows, the relationship between crime and unemployment is quite weak. Lack of money (as distinguished, I would say, from the presence of the wish for it) has little to do with crime: released convicts who are subsidized do not commit fewer crimes than released convicts who are not subsidized.

Nor do rehabilitation programs work. Summarizing research done by many hands, Wilson persuasively concludes that such programs—we have an infinite variety of them—rarely make any difference to the behavior of convicts upon release. Whatever the cost of the program, the rate of recidivism is unaffected. Wilson also finds that the behavior of convicts after being released from prison is no worse than the behavior of offenders who had been diverted to supervision (work release, probation) without imprisonment. So much for the "prisons are schools of crime" theory, which has helped many reformers—not to speak of the convicts themselves—to blame prisons for the crimes they punish.

Fortunately, however (another point Wilson strenuously argues that should be obvious), most criminals are quite deterrable. They respond to incentives and disincentives as people usually do, the cost of crime (mainly punishment multiplied by the likelihood of suffering it) being the disincentive, the advantage expected from crime being the incentive.[3]

To be sure, some offenders—not the most successful ones—may be so far gone that they are not discouraged by anything. But I would be content to deter the offenders who commit crimes because they expect a net advantage. The net advantage differs from person to person, according to character and opportunity. Punishments cannot ever be made harsh enough to discourage all prospective criminals. Yet even actual offenders seem to be quite responsive to punishment (and therefore to credible threats), as shown by their sedulous attempts to avoid it.

What weakens deterrence is that criminals succeed in avoiding punishment most of the time. Crime pays: for most offenders committing crimes is a rational response to the expected net advantage. According to Wilson, only three out of a hundred felonies ever lead to imprisonment. In New York such offenses as car theft, minor muggings, and minor burglaries have been *de facto* decriminalized. That is, they are hardly ever punished, as is evident when the number of these offenses is compared with the number of persons imprisoned for them (fewer than ten per year for car theft in the last few years).

What then is to be done? In view of the cost, Wilson is properly skeptical about increasing rates of arrest. And arrest rates certainly matter. So, however, do our scandalously low conviction and punishment rates, which Wilson does not mention. Even when caught, criminals are rarely punished. And the threat of punishment, however severe, becomes ineffective when it becomes incredible, whether because of low apprehension or because of low punishment rates.

But what about increasing the severity of punishment? Wilson seems illogical when he contends that added severity of punishment would not increase deterrence, whereas a higher probability of suffering it would. If one commits a high number of crimes every year, it cannot make much difference whether in a three-year period one is caught and punished twice, serving one year each time, or once, serving two years. Only for the amateur who commits a few crimes a year is there a difference: he might escape punishment altogether, if the probability of apprehension were low. But Wilson throughout focuses on career criminals.

I stress the importance of the severity of punishment for a more general reason as well. People who buy tickets to a lottery, as many of us do, are persuaded by the size of the prize; they discount the low probability of winning it. Might not disincentives work as incentives do?

If so, for persons tempted to commit crimes, the size of the threatened punishment could be dissuasive, despite the low probability of suffering it. They would discount the low probability of punishment, just as lottery-ticket buyers discount the low probability of winning the prize. I could be wrong: but only if fear and hope lead to different discounts—if the improbability of winning in a lottery is discounted more and the improbability of losing, of being punished for a crime, is discounted less.

Be that as it may, there must be an optimal (most deterrent) combination of punishment size and the probability of suffering it.[4] Neither, therefore, can be neglected. Surely, trivial punishment, even if inflicted with high probability, will not deter. Thus the popular clamor for severity does not seem unreasonable to me.

In another instance as well Wilson clings too closely to statistics. While favoring foot patrols by policemen because they reduce petty nuisances by prostitutes, vagrants, drug dealers, drunks, groups of rowdy youths, etc., and thereby enhance a sense of order and civility, Wilson points out that increasing such patrols does not reduce crime. He bases this conclusion on experimental comparisons between similar areas, some with frequent foot patrols and others without, which show no difference in crime rates. But the increased foot patrols in question lasted only for one or two years. If they were continued for ten or twenty years, might not the orderly environment produced by them reduce the crime rate? No environmental change is likely to modify criminal habits once they have been formed, but when it comes to the *formation* of habits, an orderly environment—if it lasts long enough to influence the outlook of the young—may well reduce crime by favoring noncriminal habits.

Although he believes in deterrence as a way to control crime, Wilson believes in incapacitation more. "Almost no one doubts that incapacitation works: a man in prison cannot harm persons outside." On the (questionable) assumption that imprisoned criminals are unlikely to be replaced, he also seems to identify a reduction of the number of crimes committed by each prisoner, or by all prisoners, with a reduction of the crime rate.

The same assumption explains why, for some time now, prosecutors have tried to focus on career criminals in securing convictions and long-time imprisonment. By keeping career criminals behind bars, prosecutors hope to decrease the crime rate. But as Wilson points out, career criminals tend to be identified only after they have been convicted often and are reaching the end of their criminal careers. Most criminals become less active as they reach middle age, and before middle age few are convicted often enough to be identified as career criminals. Therefore Wilson proposes to imprison for a long time not (or not only) those who have the most convictions, but the offenders who are most likely to commit additional crimes in the future.

Peter Greenwood (another contributor to *Crime and Public Policy*) has made careful investigations in California (and others have indirectly confirmed his results elsewhere) concluding that, on the basis of such indications as juvenile convictions, drug use, etc., one can predict, with an 81-percent success rate, who will be a "low-rate" offender (committing slightly more than one burglary and slightly less than one robbery annually) and who will be a "high-rate" offender (no fewer than 93 burglaries and thirteen robberies per year). Greenwood calculates that if all convicted high-rate robbers and burglars served seven years in prison (most now serve less), "the number of robberies in the state would drop by about 20 percent." If the time served by low-rate robbers and burglars were reduced simultaneously to two years (most now serve longer), there would be no increase in the prison population.

Accordingly, Wilson proposes a system of "selective incapacitation" which would involve "keeping sentences for [low-rate offenders] short so as not to consume scarce prison space needed [for the high-rate offenders]." In effect, "Most offenders would probably have their sentences shortened and the space thereby freed would be allocated to the small number of high-rate offenders whom [sic] even the most determined opponents of prison would probably concede should be behind bars."

Wilson is aware of many potential objections to his proposal for selective incapacitation, ranging from doubts about the identification of high- and low-rate offenders to objections against punishing convicts for what they are likely to do, in addition to punishing them for what they have already done. He deals as well with these objections as one can. But he does not deal seriously with objections that seem more serious to me.

One concerns prison space, the scarcity of which he takes for granted. It requires between $50,000 and $75,000 to build a prison cell and about $15,000 a year or more to keep a prisoner in it. Wilson does not mention that these outrageous costs—which help explain the scarcity—are the effect not of uncontrollable factors, but of mismanagement. Expensive locations for construction are selected on entirely unwarranted grounds. Available buildings, unless built as prisons, are not utilized. Security features, included in all prisons, are needed only in some. Further, prisons, properly managed, could be self-supporting. But prisoners are given no incentives, and often no opportunity, to do productive work.

Under these circumstances I think it is misleading to base policy proposals on the scarcity of prison space, as though it were an altogether exogenous and unavoidable fact—although, even at the present cost, imprisonment is cheaper than the increase in crime to be expected if we did with less imprisonment. The trouble is that the cost of imprisonment is borne by taxpayers, whereas most of the cost of crime is borne by the victims.

Another objection concerns Wilson's belief that imprisoned criminals will not be replaced. This seems quite unrealistic. Suppose the most active dentists, shirtmakers, prostitutes, burglars, or car thieves in New York were incapacitated. I am sure that after a short drop the rates of dentistry, shirtmaking, prostitution, burglary, or car stealing would remain unaffected. These rates do not depend on whether particular persons engage in these activities, or are incapacitated. Rather, the rates depend on the net advantage actual practitioners obtain, and prospective practitioners expect, from these activities, compared to other activities available to them.

Expected comparative net advantage determines both the number of jewelers and of jewel thieves, of cars and car thieves. Incapacitation determines neither. If the expected comparative net advantage remains unchanged, so will the rate of activity, regardless of who is, or will be, active or incapacitated. If the advantage rises, so do the crimes. More of the gold chains people wear around their necks were snatched from them when the gold price was higher. In this respect, unlawful occupations do not differ from lawful ones except that some of the latter, such as dentistry, require training and a license, whereas burglary does not. It is easier to become a burglar.

But are there enough people ready to be enticed to replace the criminals currently practicing when they are incapacitated? Not everybody is willing and able to become a burglar or a dentist. And the net advantage of dentistry or burglary certainly is different for each person, depending on his moral preferences, his dexterity, and his situation in life, which determine the range of his other opportunities.

Yet experience indicates that there are enough potential dentists, or burglars, to replace any incapacitated ones if the average net advantage rises enough. These potential dentists or burglars were not lured into dentistry or crime before, because the average net advantage sufficed to attract neither more nor fewer than the current number of practitioners. But if more than the usual number of actual or potential practitioners were incapacitated, the rate of dentistry or burglary would drop temporarily. This would increase the net advantage to the remaining practitioners (the price of dental care, or of stolen goods, would rise), encouraging more new ones to enter, until enough did to decrease the net advantage once more to a level which would diminish the inflow of new entrants. Since the expected comparative net advantage is the benefit over cost, it can be influenced by increasing the cost—in the case of crime, the expected punishment. But incapacitation *per se*—i.e., apart from its punitive sideeffects—plays no role.

I am not claiming that prospective dentists or burglars will engage in elaborate rational calculations to determine which profession to enter. Nonetheless, such calculations are useful in explaining their behavior, just as they help to explain the behavior of people migrating, or doing any number of other things.

The actual or future high-rate offenders Wilson wants to incapacitate are indeed responsible for a high proportion of crimes: 6 percent of the criminal population commits about a third of all crimes. I have suggested why I think that their incapacitation will not affect the crime rate. But what about the low-rate offenders who commit the remaining two-thirds of all crimes? By reducing their punishment, Wilson's selective incapacitation would, I fear, encourage these low-rate offenders and actually increase the aggregate crime rate.

Wilson appears to believe that the high-rate offenders he wants to incapacitate start their criminal careers as identifiable future highrate offenders. This seems unrealistic. They are likely to start as lowrate offenders and work their way up.

They become high-rate offenders only because they find their offenses rewarding. And their offenses will be the more rewarding the milder the punishments they suffer initially, while they are still low-rate offenders. Wilson proposes to make their sentences shorter than they are now. This would encourage more nonoffenders to become offenders and more lowrate offenders to become high-rate offenders.

In discussing his proposal for selective incapacitation, Wilson scarcely mentions deterrence. He may well be right to neglect any deterrent effect on those he wants to incapacitate. Once offenders are identifiable as prospective high-rate offenders, they are likely to be too committed to be deterred by threats of punishment.

But Wilson is not right to neglect the decrease in deterrence to be expected from his proposal to shorten the imprisonment of lowrate offenders. They are deterrable precisely because they do not have—at least not yet—the characteristics of high-rate offenders. Low-rate offenders now average one burglary and one robbery a year. They will average more, once the threat of punishment is reduced; and there will be more of them. This could more than offset any likely decrease of the crimes committed by highrate offenders.

Wilson is on much better ground with non-market-dependent crimes such as rape, or the taking of money by violence or fraud (as opposed to market-dependent crimes like burglary and car theft in which the proceeds can only be realized when they are sold). The rate of non-market-dependent crimes is determined, as is the rate of all crimes, by the comparative net advantage expected, which can be influenced by changing the cost—the punishment threatened. (There will be more rapes if the threatened punishment is a $5 fine than if it is five years in prison.) But since the rapist is himself the consumer of his proceeds, there is no market for rape. Incapacitated rapists, unlike incapacitated dentists or burglars, would not automatically be replaced, since their incapacitation would not raise the advantage of the crime to the remaining rapists and attract new offenders. Hence, incapacitating prospective high-rate rapists could reduce the rate of rape. However, unlike Wilson, I would not want to reduce the time served by lowrate rapists. To do so would encourage some to become high-rate rapists and it would also increase the total number of rapists.

Do I have anything reasonably feasible to propose that would reduce the crime rate, as Wilson's selective incapacitation would not, without overly increasing the prison population? I do.

As Wilson notes, most criminals start their careers as juveniles. They are given effective immunity from serious punishment by our juvenile-court system, which is supposed to rehabilitate rather than punish them but does neither. The immunity we have sentimentally given juveniles does not deter them from crime and even lures them in into self-destructive and antisocial criminal careers. My first and most radical proposal is to do away with the juvenile-court system.

When children under thirteen commit offenses, they should be dealt with by parents and—where parental control is demonstrably lacking—by social agencies acting *in loco parentis*. Persons over thirteen should be dealt with by the laws and courts provided for adults (though for obvious reasons juveniles should be imprisoned separately from adults). Counsel would remain free to try to persuade the court that his young client is incompetent. But incompetence should no longer be assumed automatically on the basis of age.

At present most first offenders get probation. The first crime is on the house—a prospect that does not discourage first offenses. Still, I would not object to the practice, were it individualized, so that probation were given only when the first offense was really a first offense, and not just the first (non-juvenile) conviction.

A second conviction, at any rate, demonstrates that the first did not discourage the offender. It should lead to serious punishment regardless of whether or not the convict himself is likely to become a highrate offender. Since most crimes are committed by young males (under thirty-five and often under twentyfive), punishment for young second offenders should be harsh enough to deter them and their peers from pursuing criminal careers. For second offenses, youth should be a reason for severity rather than a ground for leniency.

But where would I get the prison space, Wilson—indeed most criminologists—will ask at this point? There are two answers. In the short run my proposal would indeed exacerbate the crowding. Shortages of space would have to be dealt with by shortening the sentences of offenders over thirty-five to whatever degree necessary to make room for the younger convicts. Perhaps the simplest way to carry out this change would be to order parole boards not to consider anyone under thirtyfive for parole (with few exceptions) and to grant parole more generously to older convicts.

In the long run I expect that the proposed policy would deter more from crime than the present policy. As a result, we might have a greater proportion of criminals in prison (since they would serve longer sentences) but fewer criminals altogether and therefore not necessarily more convicts in prison than we now have.

Let me summarize. I do not expect much from selective incapacitation and think shortening the sentences of low-rate offenders would be counterproductive. But if we abolished juvenile courts and gave lengthy sentences to young offenders, particularly second offenders, I believe we could deter them from crime and thus reduce the crime rate, even if, for reasons of space, we would have to shorten the sentences of older offenders.

Until the current century the ancient profession of medicine probably killed as many patients as it cured. In its first hundred years the young science of criminology has done no better. But it is developing faster than medicine did. Wilson's work—and fortunately he is not alone—bids fair to lead to debate, reexamination, and policy changes which may actually increase the cost of crime to criminals and reduce it for society.

Notes

1. Basic Books, 293 pp., $19.95.
2. Institute for Contemporary Studies, 334 pp., $21.95.
3. Perhaps an experiment might help. Let us significantly reduce the salary of any criminologist whenever he publishes an article against deterrence. If, thereupon, fewer such articles appear, deterrence works: criminologists can be deterred. And, since the unwritten articles would have been wrong, we would lose nothing by their nonappearance. If the number of articles against deterrence does not diminish, they would be correct. But, once more, we would lose nothing, since we would have the articles. However, in this case, I would concede that some criminologists are undeterrable. (The criminologists whose salaries were reduced were compensated by their psychic enjoyment of their writing or of their financial suffering—else they would not have opted for it.)
4. The statistics Wilson relies on are not relevant to the question he addresses. They compare combinations of severity and probability, allowing only the uncontested conclusion that some combinations are less than optimal and may become optimal by increasing probability rather than severity. Given the current low probability of apprehension, this is likely to be the case for infrequent offenders (the majority) but not for the frequent offenders Wilson is concerned with. However, the two groups are not separated in the statistics he uses.

*__Ernest van den Haag__ (1914–2002) was a professor of jurisprudence and public policy at Fordham University. He was a strong proponent of capital punishment. His works include *Punishing Criminals: Concerning a Very Old and Painful Question* and (with John P. Conrad) *The Death Penalty: A Debate.*

Van den Haag, Ernest. "Thinking About Crime Again." *Commentary* 76 (December 1983): 73–76.

Reprinted from COMMENTARY, December 1983, by permission; copyright © 1983 by Commentary, Inc.

Serious Consequences for Serious Juvenile Offenders: Do Juveniles Belong in Adult Court?

by Bree Langemo*

I. INTRODUCTION

"The child savers who invented the juvenile justice system a century ago are probably spinning in their graves knowing that children are once again being incarcerated in adult jails and prisons."[1] Adult punishment and incarceration of juvenile offenders is the result of the current view that juvenile offenders should be treated as adults. While the original goal of the juvenile justice system was to rehabilitate juvenile offenders,[2] the recent trend has been to restore the pre-reformation view of treating juvenile offenders as adults in order to punish and deter juvenile crime.[3] To accomplish this goal, states have made it easier to waive juvenile defendants into adult court by utilizing one of three methods: judicial waiver, automatic transfer, or prosecutorial discretion.[4] States have implemented a variety of methods to increase the amount of juvenile defendants tried in adult court rather than juvenile court such as the following:

1. expanding the types of cases and offenders judges can transfer for adult trials after a hearing;

2. lowering the age of criminal jurisdiction;

3. shifting the transfer decision from judges to prosecutors; and

4. increasing the number of offenses and types of offenders that are automatically tried in criminal courts as mandated by legislatures.[5]

The effect of placing juvenile defendants in adult court includes, among many things, the juvenile being subject to adult punishment, including the death penalty and life without parole.[6] While juveniles convicted of serious criminal offenses committed at the age of fifteen or under are safeguarded from being executed,[7] sixteen and seventeen-year-old juveniles convicted of serious crimes are not.[8] In addition, juveniles convicted of serious criminal offenses committed at any age under eighteen may be sentenced to life without parole, the second most severe punishment next to the death penalty.[9] Once convicted, a serious juvenile offender sentenced as an adult is incarcerated in an adult institution in nearly all states.[10] As will be shown, juveniles in adult institutions face serious physical and emotional harm from older inmates[11] and are more likely to commit suicide.[12]

This article suggests that juvenile defendants should not be placed in adult court for four main reasons: (1) recent trends are based on misconceptions; (2) methods used to place juveniles in adult court have significant flaws; (3) adult courts are not sensitive to the needs of juveniles; and (4) juveniles are not adults. This article then makes three proposals. Juvenile courts should be made to be better equipped to handle serious juvenile offenders by increasing available resources. Also, serious juvenile offenders should be given blended (or split) sentences to restore the focus on rehabilitation. Finally, juvenile inmates should be placed in facilities separate from adult inmates. Accomplishing these three proposals would result in a restoration of the original goal of the juvenile justice system to rehabilitate juveniles, but would do so in a better equipped juvenile justice system.

II. Background

A. History of the Juvenile Justice System

Prior to 1899, juvenile courts were nonexistent, and juvenile defendants were tried in the same court and received the same punishment for their crimes as their adult counterparts.[13] The only protection offered to juvenile defendants was the common law doctrine of infancy, which provided the following:

> The common law infancy gradations conclusively presumed that children less than seven years of age lacked criminal capacity, regarded those fourteen years of age and older as fully responsible adults, and created a rebuttable presumption of incapacity for those between seven and fourteen years of age. The presumption of incapacity was strongest at the age of seven and diminished gradually until it disappear[ed] entirely at the age of fourteen. The common law based the presumption of incapacity on chronological age and not some subjective "mental age." The presumption of incapacity for those under fourteen placed the burden on the prosecution to prove criminal responsibility.[14]

At the end of the nineteenth century, a progressive reformation aimed for significant policy changes in the treatment of juvenile defendants and sought a juvenile court system that acted as the *parens patriae*, or the juvenile's ultimate parent.[15] The view of the treatment of juvenile defendants shifted from punishing juveniles as adults to rehabilitating delinquent children into better persons.[16] In 1899, Illinois established the first juvenile court by enacting the Juvenile Court Act, which sought "not to adjudicate guilt or fix blame, but to investigate, diagnose, and prescribe treatment."[17] By 1925, juvenile courts were established in all but two states.[18] In 1938, the Federal Juvenile Delinquency Act was enacted, providing for judicial discretion in transferring juvenile defendants to juvenile court.[19] Under the Federal Juvenile Delinquency Act, federal prosecutors were also given the discretion to try juvenile defendants in juvenile court unless the offense was punishable by death or life imprisonment.[20] By the middle of the 1940s, all states had created juvenile court systems.[21]

The goal of the juvenile court statutes was to treat, supervise, and rehabilitate juvenile defendants "under the belief that juveniles were less blameworthy and less morally culpable for their actions than adults" based on scientific, sociological, moral, and educational factors.[22] However, the "save the children" approach may not have been intended to include all juveniles who commit crimes, such as serious violent offenders, but rather to seek the rehabilitation of juveniles who commit minor criminal offenses.[23] The juvenile court's rehabilitative goal began to close its focus by the late 1970s, and the focus on punishment and deterrence of juvenile crime was again instituted.[24] As juvenile courts were criticized for being too lenient with juveniles committing serious crimes, the transfer of juvenile defendants from juvenile court to adult court became easier in over half the states starting in 1976.[25] An increase in serious juvenile crimes, including homicide and gun offenses, in the mid-1980s resulted in "[w]idespread misgivings about the ability of juvenile courts either to rehabilitate serious young offenders or simultaneously to protect public safety . . . ."[26] Such misgivings led to more juvenile defendants being transferred to adult court and being subject to adult punishment.[27] These "get tough" measures "de-emphasized rehabilitation and individualized consideration of the offender, stressed personal and justice system accountability and punishment, and based transfer and sentencing decisions on the seriousness of the offense and prior record."[28]

B. Recent Trends in the Juvenile Justice System

"[S]erious juvenile offenders 'should be thrown in jail, the key should be thrown away and there should be very little or no effort to rehabilitate them.'"[29] These were the sentiments of Florida Congressman Bill McCollum, a main sponsor of the Violent Crime Control and Law Enforcement Act of 1994, which allows juveniles, thirteen or older, to be prosecuted in adult court.[30] The recent trend in the juvenile justice system has been to restore the pre-reformation view that juvenile defendants should be treated as adults in order to punish and deter juvenile crime.[31] The number of juvenile defendants transferred to adult court increased by forty-two percent (42%) from 1985 to 1994.[32] In addition, "get tough" policies on juvenile crime have multiplied since the middle 1990s and have included "lowering the age at which minors can be waived out of juvenile court into adult court, making that waiver less restrictive, and punishing more minors alongside adults for a growing variety of crimes."[33]

Reasons offered for the recent trends are "that juvenile crime rates are rising, the juvenile justice system has failed, and the public is better protected by treating minors as adults."[34] Recent trends are also the result of politicians feeling pressured to punish juvenile crime more severely due to "[t]he publicity of the heinous acts some minors...committed[,]...creat[ing] an anxious climate in which there [was] a looming sense of danger that a 'superpredator' youthful offender [was] at large."[35] Expert predictions that the worst is yet to come and that the clock is ticking towards an increase in "superpredator" violent crimes has created a climate of "time is running out."[36] Each media display of a "superpredator" crime results in increased political pressure to punish juvenile crime rather than to rehabilitate juvenile offenders.[37]

Currently, all states allow the transfer of juvenile defendants to adult court for certain crimes.[38] In forty-one states, juvenile defendants, fourteen-years-old or younger, may be transferred to adult courts under certain conditions.[39] In twelve states, there is no minimum age for the transfer of juveniles to adult court, which, theoretically, permits a child of any age to be waived into adult court.[40] Recent trends clearly show a shift from the rehabilitation of juvenile offenders to the punishment of juvenile offenders as adults: the result is juveniles being transferred to adult court.

III. Methods Used to Place Juveniles in Adult Court

Juvenile defendants do not have a constitutional right to a juvenile court.[41] Juvenile courts are created by state legislatures, which results in a diverse range of defining jurisdiction, powers, and purposes for juvenile courts.[42] "Because juvenile courts exist only as creatures of the legislature, what lawmakers create, they also may take away."[43] While specific procedures vary considerably from state to state, a juvenile defendant can be brought into adult court in three basic ways: judicial waiver, automatic transfer, or prosecutorial discretion.[44]

A. Judicial Waiver

Judicial determination is the most common method of waiving a juvenile defendant into adult court.[45] In the judicial waiver process, a juvenile court judge will make a case-by-case assessment by conducting a transfer hearing to determine whether a juvenile should be transferred into adult court.[46] In *Kent v. United States*,[47] the United States Supreme Court formalized the judicial waiver process and held that a juvenile court must provide a juvenile with procedural due process protections when making such a "critically important" decision.[48] The Court held that

> there is no place in our system of law for reaching a result of such tremendous consequences without ceremony—without hearing, without effective assistance of counsel, without a statement of reasons. It is inconceivable that a court of justice dealing with adults, with respect to a similar issue, would proceed in this manner. It would be extraordinary if society's special concern for children, as reflected in the . . . Juvenile Court Act, permitted this procedure. We hold that it does not.[49]

Thus, the Court held that a juvenile must be given an opportunity for a hearing in which a juvenile is entitled to the assistance of counsel, and that a juvenile court must provide a statement of reasons and considerations when transferring a juvenile to adult court.[50] In an appendix to the decision, the Court provided a list of determinative factors to be considered by a juvenile court judge when deciding whether to transfer a juvenile to adult court.[51] The Court stated that "[a]lthough not all such factors will be involved in an individual case, the Judge will consider the relevant factors in a specific case before reaching a conclusion to waive juvenile jurisdiction and transfer the case to [adult court] for trial under adult procedures . . . ."[52] This list of determinative factors consisted of the following:

1. The seriousness of the alleged offense to the community and whether the protection of the community requires waiver[;]

2. Whether the alleged offense was committed in an aggressive, violent, premeditated or willful manner[;]

3. Whether the alleged offense was against persons or against property, greater weight being given to offenses against persons especially if personal injury resulted[;]

4. Prosecutive merit of the complaint, i.e., whether there is evidence upon which a Grand Jury may be expected to return an indictment . . . [;]

5. The desirability of trial and disposition of the entire offense in one court when the juvenile's associates in the alleged offense are adults . . . [;]

6. The sophistication and maturity of the juvenile as determined by consideration of his home, environmental situation, emotional attitude and pattern of living[;]

7. The record and previous history of the juvenile, including previous contacts with . . . law enforcement agencies, juvenile courts and other

jurisdictions, prior periods of probation to this Court, or prior commitments to juvenile institutions[;]

8. The prospects for adequate protection of the public and the likelihood of reasonable rehabilitation of the juvenile (if he is found to have committed the alleged offense) by the use of procedures, services and facilities currently available to the Juvenile Court.[53]

Some states have incorporated the *Kent* factors either by statute or adjudication in their criteria for judicial waiver.[54] Other states focus on a juvenile's "'amenability to treatment' and instruct the judge to examine the youth's criminal sophistication, potential to be rehabilitated, delinquency history, prior interventions, and the seriousness of the offense."[55] Still others concentrate on

"the best interests of the juvenile and the public" and mandate an
inquiry into the seriousness of the offense, the culpability of the juvenile
in committing the offense, the prior record, the juvenile's programming
history, the adequacy of punishment or programs in the juvenile justice
system, and the dispositional options available.[56]

In any case, a juvenile court judge has discretion and need not give equal weight to each factor.[57] Judicial waiver into adult court may be limited to serious offenses or restricted by a minimum age, but some states impose neither limitation, leaving it to the discretion of the juvenile court judge.[58]

The waiver process typically consists of the prosecutor filing a transfer motion, which initiates a hearing to waive jurisdiction from juvenile court to adult court.[59] In some states, juvenile defendants may initiate a hearing by requesting a transfer.[60] Unless a statute provides otherwise, juvenile defendants are not allowed to waive themselves into adult court.[61] The waiver hearing, while informal, is adversarial, allowing the submission of evidence and cross-examination.[62] However, the rules of evidence are not followed strictly, and the juvenile court judge's decision may be based on "'informal but reliable evidence' including hearsay testimony."[63] The juvenile court judge then determines "whether probable cause exists to believe that the child committed an offense," and if so, "whether to retain juvenile court jurisdiction or to transfer the child for criminal prosecution."[64] Most states do not allow the juvenile to appeal this decision until there has been a final judgment on the merits, i.e., a criminal conviction.[65] However, the prosecution is allowed an immediate appeal when the juvenile court judge declines to transfer the juvenile because criminal prosecution is precluded, under the Double Jeopardy Clause of the Fifth Amendment of the United States Constitution, once the juvenile has been tried and convicted as a delinquent in juvenile court.[66]

B. Automatic Transfer

"Because juvenile courts exist only as creatures of the legislature, what lawmakers create, they also may take away."[67] Statutes may automatically waive juvenile defendants into adult court, bypassing juvenile court altogether.[68] Statutory exclusion "simply removes from juvenile court jurisdiction youths of a certain age and charged with certain offenses or in conjunction with a prior record."[69] "If a legislature defines juvenile court jurisdiction to include only those youths below a jurisdictional age and whom prosecutors charge with a non-excluded offense, then, by statutory definition, all other chronological juveniles are 'adult' criminal defendants."[70]

Automatic transfer is utilized in more than half of the states through legislation, and typically excludes older juveniles, who are charged with the most serious crimes, from juvenile court jurisdiction.[71] For example, some states exclude juveniles, sixteen and older, from juvenile court jurisdiction when they are charged with a capital offense or murder.[72] In other states, juveniles, fourteen or older, are excluded from juvenile court jurisdiction when they are charged with a capital offense.[73] Other serious offenses excluded from juvenile court jurisdiction by statute include arson, kidnapping, aggravated robbery, or criminal sexual conduct.[74]

Jurisdictions differ on the issue of whether to sentence a minor as a juvenile or as an adult when the minor, who is automatically waived into adult court after being statutorily excluded from juvenile court, is convicted of a non-excluded, lesser-included offense in adult court.[75] Some jurisdictions provide that "the excluded offenses also subsume all lesser included offenses and that once the state tries a youth as an adult, he cannot invoke the post-verdict sentencing benefits of the juvenile court."[76] Other states conclude that "a youth convicted of a lesser-included, non-excluded offense should be sentenced as a juvenile unless the state conducts a post-conviction waiver hearing to decide whether to sentence him as an adult."[77]

Juvenile defendants have unsuccessfully challenged "'automatic adulthood' as a denial of due process [in that] they do not receive the procedural safeguards required by *Kent,* and as a violation of equal protection because exclusion on the basis of the alleged offense constitutes an arbitrary legislative classification."[78] The due process claim is based on "the lack of judicial review of prosecutors' charging decisions that result in their removal to criminal court."[79] However, courts will not review prosecutorial decisions on whether to charge juvenile conduct as a misdemeanor or felony "because the constitutional doctrine of separation of powers denies the judicial branch the power to compel or control the executive branch in . . . discretionary matters."[80] In addition, "[c]ourts uniformly reject [equal protection] claims, noting that classification on the basis of offenses involves neither an inherently suspect class nor an invidious discrimination, and the loss of juvenile court treatment does not infringe upon a fundamental right or 'preferred liberty' that requires strict judicial scrutiny."[81]

Criminal court judges in more than half of the statutory exclusion jurisdictions are allowed to "transfer back" or "reverse waive" juvenile defendants to juvenile court "for trial or sentencing, or to impose a juvenile or 'youthful offender' sentence in lieu of an adult criminal sentence."[82] A criminal court judge makes such a decision "under provisions that recreate the *Kent*-style proceedings that originally impelled states to adopt offense exclusion...laws."[83]

C. Prosecutorial Discretion

With prosecutorial waiver, a prosecutor unilaterally determines whether a juvenile should be prosecuted as an adult or a juvenile based on whether probable cause exists that the juvenile committed the crime.[84] Concurrent jurisdiction in juvenile and criminal courts for certain offenses provides prosecutors with the discretion to "'direct file' or charge youths of certain ages with the same offense in either forum."[85] Prosecutorial waiver statutes are adopted in approximately ten states, and eight of these ten states provide no standards or criteria to guide a prosecutor's discretion.[86] Only two states instruct prosecutors to consider *Kent*-like factors in exercising their discretion.[87] Prosecutorial discretion is not subject to judicial review because it "is itself an incident of the constitutional separation of powers, and that as a result the courts are not to interfere with the free exercise of the discretionary powers of the prosecutor in his control over criminal prosecutions."[88]

Juvenile defendants have unsuccessfully challenged prosecutorial waiver statutes on due process and equal protection grounds.[89] Courts have held that:

> [T]he juveniles' due process challenge [is rejected] by noting that unlike the situation in Kent, where the juvenile court had original and exclusive jurisdiction, they do not possess any protected interest in being subject to the jurisdiction of the juvenile court and therefore enjoyed no right to procedural protections .... [T]he juveniles' equal protection analysis [is rejected] by emphasizing that many statutes impose different penalties for the same course of conduct and prosecutors enjoy discretion to choose among such alternatives as long as they do not do so on a discriminatory basis.[90]

With one exception, prosecutorial waiver statutes have consistently been upheld.[91] In that one exception, a "direct file" statute was rejected by the Utah Supreme Court "because it denied waived juveniles the uniform operation of state laws... [by] allow[ing] prosecutors to charge some youths with serious offenses in juvenile court while prosecuting other youths charged with identical offenses in criminal court."[92] The Utah Supreme Court demanded that "the lawmakers specify relevant criteria and not create a system which allowed prosecutors' random and unsupervised decisions to create the classification."[93]

Criminal court judges in many states are allowed to "transfer back" or "reverse waive" juvenile defendants back to juvenile court "for trial or sentencing, or to impose a juvenile or 'youthful offender' sentence in lieu of an adult criminal sentence."[94] Such a decision is made "under provisions that recreate the Kent-style proceedings that originally impelled states to adopt ... direct file laws."[95]

IV. Effect of Juveniles Being in Adult Court

When a juvenile is in adult court, the court proceedings will often be longer and slower, which may result in the juvenile waiting in jail longer if bail is not or cannot be posted.[96] While a juvenile has the right to a jury trial in adult court,[97] a juvenile in adult court loses rights extended to juveniles in juvenile court.[98] Juvenile anonymity and confidentiality is reduced or eliminated in adult court, whereas juvenile proceedings typically are confidential for the remainder of the juvenile's life.[99] However, some states have now eliminated juvenile confidentiality even when in juvenile court.[100] Under federal law, juveniles are fingerprinted and photographed when they commit "adult felonies."[101] In addition, juveniles are deprived of certain civil rights when they are convicted as adults, including disqualification from public employment and limitations on other opportunities, such as the right to vote.[102] Perhaps the most significant effect of a juvenile being in adult court is the consequence of adult punishment and incarceration.

A. Adult Punishment

"A waiver decision is essentially a sentencing choice between the adult offender's punitive criminal forum and the ... rehabilitative juvenile choice."[103] A juvenile defendant convicted in adult court for a serious criminal offense may be exposed to life without parole as a mandatory sentence, or execution for offenses committed as a juvenile.[104] While juveniles convicted of serious criminal offenses committed at the age of fifteen or under are safeguarded from being executed,[105] juveniles convicted of serious crimes committed at the age of sixteen or seventeen are not.[106] Juveniles convicted of serious criminal offenses committed at any age under eighteen may be sentenced to life without parole, the second most severe punishment next to the death penalty.[107]

Thirty-eight states and the federal government (both civilian and military) ... have statutes authorizing the death penalty for [juvenile] capital crimes . . . . Of those forty death penalty jurisdictions, eighteen jurisdictions (45%) have expressly included age eighteen at the time of the crime as the minimum age for eligibility for that ultimate punishment. Another five jurisdictions (13%) have included age seventeen as the minimum. The other seventeen death penalty jurisdictions (42%) use age sixteen as the minimum age, either through an express age in the statute (five states) or by court ruling (twelve states).[108]

Since 1973, two hundred and twenty-four juveniles convicted of serious criminal offenses have been sentenced to death.[109] Twenty-one of these juvenile offenders sentenced to death have been executed.[110] Currently, the United States is the only country in the world to execute juvenile offenders.[111]

While juveniles who commit serious criminal offenses when they are fifteen years or under cannot be sentenced to death,[112] they may be sentenced to life without parole.[113] Only a few states currently prohibit the sentencing of juveniles who commit crimes while under the age of sixteen to life without parole.[114] The majority of states permit the imposition of life without parole or even mandate it upon conviction of juveniles in adult court.[115] For example, in Washington, eight-year-olds can be subject to life without parole,[116] and ten-year-olds in Vermont can also be sentenced to life without parole if convicted in adult court.[117] In Florida, Lionel Tate, at twelve years old, killed a playmate and was tried in adult court and convicted of first degree murder.[118] The conviction carries a mandatory life without parole sentence.[119]

Life without parole sentences "are effectively immune from constitutional attack" in the majority of states and the federal courts.[120] Most courts do not subject life without parole sentences to the proportionality analysis under the Eighth Amendment with the rationale being that "punishment is a legislative prerogative—and that society is well within its rights to impose harsh punishment on juvenile offenders in response to their atrocious crimes[,]"[121] and that "the offenders before [these courts] are 'adults,' and have been properly certified as such."[122]

While some states consider youthfulness as a mitigating factor, it is only one factor of many considered when imposing a sentence and is within the judge's discretion.[123] Under federal sentencing guidelines, youthfulness, as a mitigating factor, is explicitly rejected.[124]

B. Incarceration

A juvenile offender convicted in adult court may be subject to straight adult incarceration, graduated incarceration, or segregated incarceration.[125]

In straight adult incarceration, juveniles are placed in adult prisons and subject to the same treatment and programs as adult convicts. Graduated incarceration places the juvenile in a separate institution from adults until they reach a specified age, as dictated by statute. Upon reaching that age, the juveniles are removed from the separate facility and placed into an adult facility. The segregated system of incarceration isolates the youthful offenders from older offenders by housing them in separate facilities for the term of their stay. Juveniles under the segregated system will never co-habitate with adult offenders, even after they have reached the age of majority.[126]

In almost every state, a juvenile offender sentenced as an adult is incarcerated in an adult institution with other adults if the juvenile offender is of a certain age or other youthful offenders are sentenced as adults.[127] Juvenile offenders in adult institutions face serious physical and emotional harm at the hands of their adult counterparts.[128] Juvenile offenders in adult facilities are "five times more likely to be sexually assaulted, twice as likely to be beaten by staff, and fifty percent more likely to be attacked with a weapon than minors in juvenile facilities."[129] In addition, suicide attempts are 7.7 times more likely by juveniles in adult institutions than juveniles in juvenile facilities.[130]

As a result of such abuse, embittered juvenile offenders are often returned to society in a worse condition than when they entered the adult institution.[131] While juveniles in adult institutions are often not provided with educational or recreational facilities, they are schooled in crime by older inmates who instruct the juvenile offenders in advanced criminal skills and share criminal contacts.[132] As a result, juveniles in adult institutions are more likely to reoffend than juveniles placed in juvenile facilities.[133]

V. Juvenile Defendants Should Not Be in Adult Court

Americans were shocked when the media reported that nine-year-old Cameron Kocher killed his seven-year-old neighbor, Jessica Carr, by shooting her with a gun he had taken from his parents' locked cabinet.[134] But many were just as shocked to learn that Kocher would be tried as an adult after his transfer request to juvenile court was denied.[135] Did Kocher understand at nine years old what he had done? Should such juvenile defendants be in adult court and treated as adults? For the reasons that follow, I maintain that juvenile defendants should not be in adult court.

A. Justifications for Recent Trends Are Based on Misconceptions

Justifications offered for the recent trends in treating juvenile defendants as adults are based on misconceptions. Justifications for the recent trends include "that juvenile crime rates are rising, the juvenile justice system has failed, and the public is better protected by treating minors as adults."[136] In fact, the juvenile crime rate is not rising, the juvenile justice system has not failed, and the public is not necessarily better protected by treating minors as adults.[137]

Due to the vast media attention of certain violent crimes committed by juveniles, politicians felt pressured to create more punitive measures in "an anxious climate in which there [was] a looming sense of danger that a 'superpredator' youthful offender [was] at large."[138] It was predicted by criminologists that between 1992 and 2010, the violent crime rate of these superpredators would double.[139] Current data do not support this prediction.[140] Rather, the following has occurred:

- For offenders age 13 and under, the number of homicide arrests in 2000 was only 38% of the number in 1994 just 6 years earlier[;]

- The numbers fell similarly for offenders ages 14 to 17, with the 1,492 homicide arrests in year 2000 constituting only 36% of the 4,115 homicide arrests in 1994[;]

- Homicide arrests [of] all persons under age 18 as a percentage of all homicide arrests has fallen from the peak of 16.2% in 1994 to only 6.8% in 2000.[141]

Despite the statistics showing a drop in serious juvenile crime, jurors and some judges continue to believe that serious juvenile crime is a widespread epidemic.[142] In fact, legislative action to make juvenile crime more punitive by treating juvenile defendants as adults occurred after the juvenile violent crime rate started to show a dramatic decline.[143] Thus, the "get tough" policies have not effectuated the decrease in juvenile crime.[144]

The misconceived idea that juvenile crime rates are rising has led to the further misconception that the juvenile justice system has failed. The central goal of the juvenile justice system is to rehabilitate. To this extent, the juvenile justice system has not failed in that juvenile offenders in juvenile justice facilities are less likely to recidivate than juvenile offenders in adult institutions.[145] "Thus, the research suggests that the get tough trend is counterproductive in the effort to reduce crime; sending juveniles to adult prisons results in more crime, not less."[146]

In addition, sentencing juveniles to tough adult prison terms ignores the cause of the problem and only acknowledges the symptom. Serious juvenile offenders are typically emotionally disturbed and require serious psychological intervention.[147]

With legislative focus on holding juveniles criminally responsible, the chances of psychological intervention have not improved.[148] In fact, "the demand for out-patient mental health care for minors far exceeds the supply, and the need for services is ever increasing."[149] Each year, the demand for juvenile mental health services doubles while the availability of interventions remains limited.[150] Thus, the focus on making juvenile crime more punitive has detracted from the prevention of juvenile crime through providing psychological intervention.

Finally, the public is not necessarily better protected by treating minors as adults because incarcerating juveniles in adult prisons has led to increased recidivism rates.[151] Where the juvenile is not sentenced to life without parole or the death penalty, substantial research has shown that criminal behavior is accentuated after a juvenile offender is released from an adult institution.[152] Research has also shown that juveniles transferred to adult court and punished as adults after conviction were "three times more likely to reoffend and reoffended sooner than those kept in the juvenile court system."[153] While some politicians may be pleased that the juvenile incarceration rate has increased, so has the arrest rate for crimes committed by juvenile offenders after release.[154]

Thus, the reasons offered for the recent trends in treating juvenile defendants as adults are based on misconceptions in that the juvenile crime rate is not rising, the juvenile justice system has not failed, and the public is not necessarily better protected by treating minors as adults.[155]

B. Methods Used to Place Juveniles in Adult Court Have Significant Flaws

The three methods used to place juveniles in adult court each have significant flaws. Judicial waiver provides the most due process protection for juveniles[156] and allows for a case-by-case assessment of each juvenile, thus, taking into account individual characteristics of juveniles.[157] Juvenile court judges work closely with juvenile issues and are knowledgeable of the best treatment for juveniles by examining each juvenile case on an individual level.[158] The juvenile offender is given individual consideration based on the juvenile's particular conduct and needs as opposed to a waiver process based on the juvenile's offense only.[159] However, judicial waiver rests on the discretion of a judge, creating the potential for abuse and invidious discrimination.[160] Judicial waiver may be inconsistently applied and can have serious detrimental effects on juveniles.[161] In addition, prosecutors may "use the potential for transfer and the ability to appeal transfer decisions as a bargaining chip[, and a] minor could be tempted to plead guilty to a lesser offense rather than risk being transferred to the adult court or wait in juvenile court through an appeal if he could not afford bail."[162]

Statutory exclusion is a "rational, non-discretionary, and easily administered" method of placing a juvenile defendant in adult court.[163] However, statutory exclusion is offense-oriented and fails to take into consideration individual circumstances, including individual capacity, of the juvenile.[164] Once a juvenile is automatically transferred into adult court, a juvenile is often before a trial judge who tends to lack the experience with juvenile defendants that juvenile court judges generally possess.[165] Statutory exclusion has the potential for abuse where a prosecutor charges the juvenile with an offense subject to automatic transfer to adult court in order to place the juvenile in adult court rather than charging the juvenile with a lesser offense that would leave the juvenile in juvenile court.[166] While a juvenile in some states has the opportunity to request a "transfer back" to juvenile court, the burden is on the juvenile to prove that he or she should be transferred back.[167] In addition, while Kent-style proceedings are held, the decision is made by a trial court judge who usually lacks the experience of a juvenile court judge.[168]

Prosecutorial waiver may make for a more convenient system and may circumvent the more inconvenient judicial waiver process, which includes a hearing and appellate review.[169] However, the potential for abuse is significant when the discretion to place a juvenile in adult court lies solely in the hands of the prosecutor.[170] A main criticism of prosecutorial waiver is that it "strip[s] the judiciary of its independent jurisdictional role in the adjudication of children by granting the charging authority the unbridled discretion to unilaterally determine which forum has jurisdiction . . . [and thus,] depriv[ing] children . . . [of] the judicial counterweight which they are constitutionally entitled to receive."[171] Prosecutorial waiver fails to examine the individual circumstances, including the individual capacity, of each juvenile as the prosecutor makes his decision on no set of established criteria.[172] Moreover, a prosecutor's discretion is not appealable and is only subject to review by the public through the political process.[173] Consequently, the prosecutor's decision may not be based on the best interests of the juvenile, but instead will often be politically motivated.[174] Again, while in some states a juvenile has the opportunity to request a "transfer back" to juvenile court, the burden is on the juvenile to prove that he or she should be transferred back.[175] Although Kent-style proceedings are held, the decision is made by a trial court judge who usually lacks the experience of a juvenile court judge.[176]

Thus, each of the three methods used to place juveniles in adult court has significant flaws, and none of the methods should be utilized since juvenile defendants will suffer severe consequences as a result of being placed in adult court inappropriately.

C. Adult Court Is Not Sensitive to the Needs of Juveniles

The environment of an adult court is not sensitive to the needs of juvenile defendants. Juvenile defendants face a more incomprehensible legal environment in adult court than in juvenile court.[177]

> The degree of the child's inability to comprehend the adult system will inevitably result in challenges to [the] youngsters' fitness to stand trial based upon developmental considerations, an issue which juvenile courts can sometimes avoid .... [C]hildren do not grasp "abstract legal concepts" such as "rights" generally understood by adults[,]... [and] children's understanding of the trial process is poorer than that of adults. Children often have difficulty "separating defense attorney functions from court authority." Finally, "pre-adolescents are significantly less capable of imagining risky consequences of decisions."[178]

When deciding whether to go to trial in adult court or take a negotiated plea bargain, juveniles often do not understand the consequences of such decisions due to their inability to measure the likelihood of conviction or the impact of the length of a sentence upon their lives.[179] In addition, judges, prosecutors, and defense attorneys in adult court often do not have the specialized training to meet the special needs of juveniles as they often do in juvenile court.[180]

D. Juveniles Are NOT Adults

"[Y]outh are not yet adults developmentally, emotionally, or physically."[181] A juvenile defendant in adult court must suffer the life-altering consequences of being treated as an adult rather than as a juvenile. Juveniles should not be treated as adults in that they are not adults. Society has deemed individuals under the age of eighteen to be incapable of making many wellreasoned decisions involving the consumption of alcohol, the use of tobacco, and the act of gambling as well as the decision to marry or to vote.[182] Juveniles are protected by society from making and from suffering the consequences of such decisions.[183] In contradiction, "society has also demanded that some of these same minors be forced to confront the most serious adult consequences for crimes that they commit or for decisions that they have made in their admittedly lesser capacity."[184] As a result, juveniles "are tried and punished by society as adults when society has clearly indicated that they are not considered adults."[185]

VI. Proposed Solutions

I propose that juvenile courts be revitalized to be better equipped to handle serious juvenile offenders by increasing their available resources. "The juvenile justice system embodies the beliefs that juveniles are less culpable than adults, are more able to grow, and should be given assistance and the opportunity for reha-bilitation."[186] Adult courts do not embody such beliefs and are oriented towards retribution and punishment rather than rehabilitation.[187] Ironically, the juvenile justice system was first established to counter the severe consequences of punish-ing juveniles as adults.[188] The original "save the children" approach may not have envisioned juveniles who commit serious, violent crimes, envisioning instead the rehabilitation of juveniles who commit minor criminal offenses.[189] Consequently, juvenile courts may not have been originally structured to deal with juveniles who commit serious criminal offenses, such as murder, but the fact that society is now faced with new challenges amongst their youth just means that juvenile courts must adapt.[190]

> The new (real and perceived) challenges faced by juvenile courts—increased caseloads, a population with more access to lethal weap-ons, more public attention focused on the work of juvenile courts as a consequence of the notoriety of some delinquent behavior, the need to strengthen families and schools, the involvement of young children in a drug trade dominated by adults, and peer pressure displacing family systems—all raise questions about the efficacy of a juvenile court model which was created in a different era. However, the fact that we face new challenges—e.g., changes in family systems—simply means that juvenile courts must adapt to a changing reality for children and families. This is exactly what the founders of the juvenile court attempted with the cre-ation of the court and its associated social service providers.[191]

Juvenile courts should be expanded to include the adjudication and incarcera-tion of serious juvenile offenders by better equipping juvenile courts. Juvenile courts need to be equipped with more staff who are highly skilled and highly motivated. Juvenile court staff should have significant education, training, and experience in both the physical and mental attributes of juveniles. Staff education and training should continue on a regular basis in order for the staff to maintain up-to-date knowledge. Staff should also assist in collecting and developing social and psychological information on juveniles. Improving juvenile courts can be accomplished through better funding. Political pressure on our legislators can obtain the funding necessary to rejuvenate our juvenile courts as "[l]egislators are free to construct systems for providing justice for children...."[192] The future of juvenile courts should be based on the following goal:

[J]uvenile courts must preserve individualized decision-making with respect to the culpability and developmental needs of children, while insisting on appropriate imposition of responsibility. Post-disposition, we must develop ways of moving away from institutionalized "treatment" of children to community-based programs designed to support children and families and to build self-esteem and competencies. The juvenile court must be transformed in a way that permits and indeed requires children to be treated as *our* autonomous and individual children, and which provides for the public safety. This requires changes in the ways that juvenile courts adjudicate and dispose of cases. It requires a reorganization of services for children so that the interest of children—not those of institutions or agencies—prevail.[193]

Once our juvenile courts are rejuvenated, they will be well-equipped to adjudicate and incarcerate serious juvenile offenders. In addition, I propose that juvenile defendants be given split sentences to restore the focus on rehabilitation, and propose that juvenile defendants be placed in facilities separate from adult inmates.

Split sentencing is the imposition of a juvenile sentence and an adult sentence on a juvenile convicted of serious crime.[194] The split sentence consists of a juvenile sentence and an adult sentence that is stayed until the juvenile completes the juvenile sentence, at which point, the judge will vacate the adult sentence if it is determined that the juvenile has been rehabilitated.[195] When it is not clear that the juvenile defendant can be rehabilitated, split sentencing allows the court to retain jurisdiction and determine whether the juvenile has been rehabilitated by age twenty-one, and at the same time, gives juveniles the opportunity to utilize rehabilitation programs available only in the juvenile justice system.[196] Split sentencing promotes the original goal of the juvenile court system in rehabilitating juveniles and also protects the public in that the adult sentence will be activated if it is determined that the public will not otherwise be safe.[197] In addition, the juvenile is not automatically treated as an adult.[198] Split sentencing has been utilized in Alaska, Arkansas, Florida, Illinois, Kansas, Massachusetts, Michigan, Minnesota, Missouri, Montana, New Mexico, and Oklahoma.[199]

Juveniles should not be placed in facilities with adults because to do so is unsafe and prevents rehabilitation. Juveniles in adult institutions face serious physical and emotional harm from older inmates[200] and are more likely to commit suicide.[201] Under split sentencing, juvenile defendants should be able to serve their juvenile sentence in facilities separate from adults for safety reasons and rehabilitation purposes. If the court finds that the juvenile has not been rehabilitated and thus, activates the adult sentence, juveniles could be placed in adult facilities as provided under graduated incarceration.[202]

In addition, the American Bar Association (ABA) requires that safety be a central concern for incarcerated juveniles and requires that special steps be taken to protect these juveniles.[203] The ABA requires that incarcerated juveniles be classified by specially trained staff taking into consideration "age, social history, institutional history, previous record, physical and mental development, and the charged offense."[204] The ABA also demands compliance with the following regarding staff and training:

> Administrative staff and people in policy making positions dealing with youth in the adult system should have education, training, and experience regarding the distinctive characteristics of children and adolescents. Staff hired to supervise youth should be trained to understand both the physical and psychological components of adolescence. Pre-service and in-service training should be provided to all staff, and those hired should have an understanding of treatment and rehabilitation. Additional areas of training include the special needs of female offenders, minority offenders, offenders with gender identity issues, and youth who are sex offenders or the victims of sexual assault or other abuse. Staff should be sensitive to issues of sexual harassment of inmates.[205]

The ABA demands compliance whether juveniles are incarcerated with adult inmates or not.[206] In addition, the ABA provides that incarcerated juveniles should be provided educational and religious services, physical activities, physical and behavioral health care, adequate nutrition, and family visitation.[207] Compliance with these ABA standards is essential for the safety and rehabilitation of incarcerated juveniles.

VII. CONCLUSION

Nearly two hundred thousand juveniles are transferred to adult court every year, and over seven thousand juveniles are incarcerated in adult prisons.[208] Juveniles should not be subject to the serious consequences of being tried and convicted in adult court for four main reasons: (1) recent trends are based on misconceptions; (2) methods used to place juveniles in adult court have significant flaws; (3) adult courts are not sensitive to the needs of juveniles; and (4) juveniles are not adults. Rather than place juveniles in adult court, juvenile courts should be rejuvenated to be better equipped to handle serious juvenile offenders by increasing their available resources. In addition, juvenile defendants should be given blended or split sentences to restore the focus on rehabilitation and should be placed in facilities separate from adult inmates. If successful, the original goal of the juvenile justice system to rehabilitate juveniles would be restored, but in a better equipped juvenile justice system.

Of course, the best way to protect juveniles from adult punishment and incarceration is to prevent juvenile crime in the first place. "Many people have lost faith in prevention programs because of the perceived rise in juvenile crime, but some legislators still believe it makes more sense to invest in programs to reach juveniles before they commit crime than to spend more money building new prisons."[209] Effective preventive programs involve the family and the community and identify "at-risk" juveniles.[210] Predictors of "at-risk" juveniles include:

1. early, troublesome, dishonest, aggressive, or antisocial behavior;

2. poor parental guidance and stability;

3. criminal parents and siblings;

4. broken homes and early separations;

5. social deprivation stemming from a low economic level; and

6. school failure resulting from low intelligence or achievement, and absenteeism.[211]

Identifying "at-risk" juveniles can aid in preventing violent crime through early intervention. One successful juvenile intervention program is California's Project Heartbeat.[212] This program provides mental health services and includes parents and school officials in developing treatment plans for each juvenile.[213] The program's goal is that "[t]hrough early identification of children in need of intervention and by involving all interested parties in treatment, the county hopes to prevent disturbed youth from proceeding down a path towards violent crime."[214] Federal funding allows Project Heartbeat to meet this goal.[215]

While preventative programs won't solve the problem, they may prevent adult punishment and incarceration for some "at-risk" juveniles. Most importantly, preventative programs may save some victims. "We as a society are forgetting our role in the product that is our youth [and]... are blind to the lessons learned as recently as one hundred years ago about the dangers (to society at large as well as to juveniles) of punishing juveniles alongside adults."[216] If we cannot prevent juvenile crime, let us at least try to rehabilitate our youth. Let us not forsake these juveniles as they are not a lost cause.[217]

NOTES

1. Wanda Mohr et al., *Will the Juvenile Court System Survive?: Shackled in the Land of Liberty: No Rights for Children*, 564 ANNALS AM. ACAD. POL. & SOC. SCI. 37, 42 (1999).

2. Jennifer A. Chin, *Baby-Face Killers: A Cry for Uniform Treatment for Youths Who Murder, From Trial to Sentencing*, 8 J.L. & POL'Y 287, 294–95 (1999).

3. *See id.* at 298–99.

4. See BARRY C. FELD, JUVENILE JUSTICE ADMINISTRATION 179 (Thomson West 2003).

5. Task Force on Youth in the Criminal Justice System, American Bar Association Criminal Justice Section, *Youth in the Criminal Justice System; Guidelines for Policymakers and Practitioners* 1 (2001), *available at* http://www.abanet.org/crimjust/pubs1reports/index.html [hereinafter *Youth in the Criminal Justice System*].

6. *See* FELD, *supra* note 4, at 218–19.

7. *See* Thompson v. Oklahoma, 487 U.S. 815, 838 (1988) (holding that it was unconstitutional as cruel and unusual punishment under the Eighth Amendment to execute a juvenile who was under the age of sixteen at the time the serious offense was committed).

8. *See* Stanford v. Kentucky, 492 U.S. 361, 380 (1989) (holding that it was not unconstitutional as cruel and unusual punishment under the Eighth Amendment to execute a juvenile who was sixteen or seventeen years old at the time the serious offense was committed).

9. *See* Wayne A. Logan, *Proportionality and Punishment: Imposing Life Without Parole on Juveniles*, 33 WAKE FOREST L. REV. 681, 708–09 (1998). "Despite the fact that [life without parole] is second only to the death penalty in terms of its severity, Eighth Amendment proportionality challenges brought by juveniles against such sentences have met with limited success in state courts, and no success in the federal system." *Id.* at 684 (footnote omitted).

10. FELD, *supra* note 4, at 222.

11. Lisa S. Beresford, *Is Lowering the Age at Which Juveniles Can Be Transferred to Adult Criminal Court the Answer to Juvenile Crime? A State-by-State Assessment*, 37 SAN DIEGO L. REV. 783, 821 (2000).

12. Jarod K. Hofacket, *Justice or Vengeance: How Young Is Too Young for a Child to Be Tried and Punished as an Adult?*, 34 TEX. TECH. L. REV. 159, 173 (2002).

13. *See* Beresford, *supra* note 11, at 788; Chin, *supra* note 2, at 291.

14. FELD, *supra* note 4, at 32–33.

15. *See* Beresford, *supra* note 11, at 789.

16. Chin, *supra* note 2, at 292.

17. *See* Beresford, *supra* note 11, at 789.

18. *Id.* at 790.

19. Chin, *supra* note 2, at 293–94.

20. *Id.* at 294 n.28.

21. *Id.* at 294.

22. *Id.* at 294–95.

23. *See* Thomas F. Geraghty, *Justice for Children: How do We Get There?*, 88 J. CRIM. L. & CRIMINOLOGY 190, 215 (1997).

24. Beresford, *supra* note 11, at 790.

25. *Id.*

26. FELD, *supra* note 4, at 176.

27. *Id.*

28. *Id.*

29. Beresford, *supra* note 11, at 784 n.5 (quoting Florida Congressman Bill McCollum).

30. *Id.*

31. *See* Chin, *supra* note 2, at 298–99.

32. Beresford, *supra* note 11, at 790. "In 1985, the total number of juvenile cases transferred was 7200. In 1994, that number increased to 12,300 ...." *Id.*

33. Hofacket, *supra* note 12, at 163 (footnote omitted).

34. *Id.* at 164.

35. *Id.*

36. Logan, *supra* note 9, at 681–82.

37. *See id.* at 681–83.

38. Chin, *supra* note 2, at 299.

39. Mohr, *supra* note 1, at 41.

40. Logan, *supra* note 9, at 689.

41. FELD, *supra* note 4, at 199.

42. *Id.*

43. *Id.*

44. *Id.* at 179.

45. *Id.*

46. FELD, *supra* note 4, at 179.

47. 383 U.S. 541 (1966).

48. *Id.* at 561–62.

49. *Id.* at 554.

50. *Id.* at 561–62.

51. *Id.* at 566–67.

52. *Kent*, 383 U.S. at 567–68.

53. *Id.* at 566–67.

54. FELD, *supra* note 4, at 185.

55. *Id.* at 188.

56. *Id.* at 189 (citing MICH. COMP. LAWS ANN. § 712A.4 (West 2003); MINN. STAT. ANN. § 260B.125 (West 2000)).

57. *Id.* at 185.

58. *Id.* at 185–86.

59. FELD, *supra* note 4, at 186.

60. *Id.* This typically occurs when the juvenile wants a jury trial. *Id.*

61. *Id.*

62. *Id.* at 189.

63. *Id.* at 191.

64. FELD, *supra* note 4, at 187–88.

65. *Id.* at 197.

66. *Id.*

67. *Id.* at 199.

68. *See id.* at 199.

69. FELD, *supra* note 4, at 199.

70. *Id.* at 199–200.

71. *Id.* at 200.

72. *Id.* at 179 (citing MINN. STAT. ANN.§ 260B.015 Subd. 5 (West 2000)).

73. *Id.* at 200 (citing MD. CODE ANN., COURTS & JUDICIAL PROCEEDINGS § 3-804 (West 2000)).

74. FELD, *supra* note 4, at 180(citing ALASKA STAT. § 47.12.030 (Michie 2000); D.C. CODE ANN. § 16-2301 (2000)).

75. *Id.* at 205.

76. *Id.* at 205–06.

77. *Id.* at 206.

78. *Id.* at 200.

79. FELD, *supra* note 4, at 200–201.

80. *Id.* at 202.

81. *Id.* at 204–05.

82. *Id.* at 212–13.

83. *Id.* at 213.

84. *See* FELD, *supra* note 4, at 208.

85. *Id.* at 207.

86. *See id.* at 208.

87. *Id.* at 208 (citing NEB. REV. STAT. ANN. § 43–276 (Michie 1997); WYO. STAT. ANN. § 14-6-273(b)(i)-(vii) (Michie 1997)).

88. *Id.* at 209.

89. FELD, *supra* note 4, at 210.

90. *Id.*

91. *Id.* (citation omitted).

92. *Id.* at 210–11.

93. *Id.* at 211.

94. FELD, *supra* note 4, at 212.

95. *Id.* at 213.

96. Beresford, *supra* note 11, at 820. Adult proceedings can be longer and slower due to the increase in caseload of juvenile defendants without additional resources. *Id.*

97. *See* FELD, *supra* note 4, at 186.

98. Beresford, *supra* note 11, at 821.

99. *Id.*

100. *Id.* In California, a juvenile's name can be disclosed if he is over fourteen years old and has committed certain offenses. *Id.* In Arizona, juvenile proceedings are open to the public. *Id.* at 821 n.272.

101. *Id.* at 821.

102. *Id.*

103. Hofacket, *supra* note 12, at 171 (internal quotations omitted).

104. *See* FELD, *supra* note 4, at 218–19.

105. *See Thompson,* 487 U.S. at 838 (1988) (holding that it was unconstitutional as cruel and unusual punishment under the Eighth Amendment to execute a juvenile who was under the age of sixteen at the time the serious offense was committed).

106. *See Stanford,* 492 U.S. at 380 (1989) (holding that it was not unconstitutional as cruel and unusual punishment under the Eighth Amendment to execute a juvenile who was sixteen or seventeen years old at the time the serious offense was committed).

107. *See* Logan, *supra* note 9, at 708. "Despite the fact that [life without parole] is second only to the death penalty in terms of its severity, Eighth Amendment proportionality challenges brought

by juveniles against such sentences have met with limited success in state courts, and no success in the federal system." *Id.* at 684.

108. Victor L. Streib, *Executing Juvenile Offenders: The Ultimate Denial of Juvenile Justice,* 14.1 STAN. L. & POL'Y REV. 121, 136–37 (2003) (citations omitted).

109. *See id.* at 123. Offenders began to be sentenced to death in 1973 under the current death penalty system. *Id.* at 122.

110. *Id.* at 126. However, three hundred and sixty-five (365) juvenile offenders have been executed since 1642. *Id.*

111. *Id.* at 139.

112. *Thompson,* 487 U.S. at 838.

113. *See* Logan, *supra* note 9, at 690.

114. *Id.*

115. *Id.* at 690–91 (footnote omitted).

116. *Id.* at 691 (footnote omitted).

117. *Id.*

118. Dana Canedy, *As Florida Boy Serves Life Term, Even Prosecutor Wonders Why,* N.Y. TIMES, Jan. 5, 2003, at 1.

119. *Id.*

120. Logan, *supra* note 9, at 714.

121. *Id.* at 722.

122. *Id.* at 721.

123. *See* FELD, *supra* note 4, at 220–21.

124. *Id.* at 220 (citing U.S. SENTENCING GUIDELINES MANUAL § 5H.1 (1995)).

125. Chin, *supra* note 2, at 332.

126. *Id.* (footnotes omitted).

127. FELD, *supra* note 4, at 222.

128. Beresford, *supra* note 11, at 821.

129. *Id.* at 821–22.

130. Hofacket, *supra* note 12, at 173.

131. Beresford, *supra* note 11, at 819.

132. Hofacket, *supra* note 12, at 173.

133. Beresford, *supra* note 11, at 819.

134. *See* Anthony DePalma, *Grieving for Dead Girl, Town Asks: Should Boy, 10, Face Murder Charge?,* N.Y. TIMES, Aug. 26, 1989, at 6.

135. *See id.*

136. Hofacket, *supra* note 12, at 164.

137. *Id.* at 164–67.

138. *Id.* at 164.

139. Beresford, *supra* note 11, at 790–91.

140. *Id.* at 791; *see also* Robert E. Shepherd, Jr., *Recapturing the Child in Adult Court,* 16 A.B.A. CRIM. JUST. 58, 58 (Winter 2002) ("[J]uvenile crime has dropped significantly over the past several years, despite the media references to 'young thugs,' 'youthful predators,' or 'super-predators.'").

141. Victor L. Streib, Execution and Life in Prison Without Parole for Kids Who Kill, A Global Approach to Ending Juvenile Injustice 2–3 (Dec. 6–7, 2002) (unpublished manuscript on file with author, Ohio Northern University College of Law); *see also* Robert E. Shepherd, Jr.,

Recapturing the Child in Adult Court, 16 A.B.A. CRIM. JUST. 58, 58 (Winter 2002) ("[J]uvenile crime has dropped significantly over the past several years, despite the media references to 'young thugs,' 'youthful predators,' or 'super-predators.'").

142. Shepherd, *supra* note 140, at 58.

143. *See* Hofacket, *supra* note 12, at 164–65 (footnotes omitted).

144. *Id.* at 165.

145. *Id.* at 166 (footnotes omitted).

146. *Id.*

147. John Kip Cornwell, *Preventing Kids from Killing,* 37 HOUS. L. REV. 21, 74 (2000).

148. *Id.*

149. *Id.* at 70 (footnote omitted).

150. *Id.*

151. *See* Hofacket, *supra* note 12, at 166–67.

152. Beresford, *supra* note 11, at 822.

153. *Id.* at 819.

154. *Id.*

155. Hofacket, *supra* note 12, at 164–67.

156. *Id.* at 168–69.

157. *See* FELD, *supra* note 4, at 179.

158. Beresford, *supra* note 11, at 805.

159. *See id.*

160. *Id.* at 806.

161. *Id.* at 805; *see also supra* Section IV discussion.

162. *Id.* at 806.

163. Hofacket, *supra* note 12, at 169.

164. *Id.* at 169.

165. Beresford, *supra* note 11, at 813.

166. *Id.* at 812.

167. *Id.*

168. *Id.* at 813.

169. *Id.* at 816.

170. *See* Beresford, *supra* note 11, at 816.

171. Hofacket, *supra* note 12, at 170–71.

172. *Id.* at 169.

173. Beresford, *supra* note 11, at 817.

174. *See* Hofacket, *supra* note 12, at 171.

175. Beresford, *supra* note 11, at 812.

176. *Id.* at 813.

177. *See* Geraghty, *supra* note 23. at 222.

178. *Id.*

179. *Id.* at 226.

180. *See id.* at 228.

181. *Youth in the Criminal Justice System, supra* note 5, at 33.

182. Hofacket, *supra* note 12, at 161.

183. *Id.*

184. *Id.*

185. *Id.*

186. *Id.*

187. Hofacket, *supra* note 12, at 164.

188. *Id.* at 165.

189. *See* Geraghty, *supra* note 23, at 215.

190. *Id.* at 216;

191. *Id.* at 215–16 (footnotes omitted).

192. *Id.* at 229.

193. *Id.* at 229–30 (footnote omitted).

194. Beresford, *supra* note 11, at 826.

195. *Id.*

196. *Id.* at 826–27.

197. *Id.*

198. *Id.* at 827.

199. Beresford, *supra* note 11, at 827.

200. *Id.* at 821.

201. Hofacket, *supra* note 12, at 173.

202. *See generally* Chin, *supra* note 2, at 332.

203. *Youth in the Criminal Justice System, supra* note 5, at 22.

204. *Id.*

205. *Id.* at 21 (footnotes omitted).

206. *Id.* at 21.

207. *See id.* at 27–31.

208. *Youth in the Criminal Justice System, supra* note 5, at 1.

209. Beresford, *supra* note 11, at 822.

210. *Id.* at 822–23.

211. *Id.* at 823.

212. Cornwell, *supra* note 147, at 71.

213. *Id.* at 71–72.

214. *Id.* at 72.

215. *Id.*

216. Hofacket, *supra* note 12, at 187 (footnote omitted).

217. *See id.*

*Bree Langemo is dean of business, public service, and social sciences at Pikes Peak Community College.

Langemo, Bree. "Serious Consequences for Serious Juvenile Offenders: Do Juveniles Belong in Adult Court?" *Ohio Northern University Law Review* 30, no. 1 (2004): 141–165.

Used by permission.

Part 4:

Should Juveniles Ever Receive a Life Sentence Without Parole?

As Frank Butler, a professor of criminal justice and one of the authors in this section, suggests, during the late 1980s and 1990s "a moral panic prevailed in the United States with regard to youth criminality." This was a time when the news media publicized horrible crimes committed by teenagers. For example, in April 1989 there was continual media coverage of a twenty-eight-year-old investment banker who, while jogging in New York City's Central Park, was brutally raped and severely beaten almost to the point of death. The jogger herself was initially in a coma, and when she awakened she had no memory of the attack. Since several other robberies had occurred that evening in Central Park involving teenage perpetrators, the assumption was that this too was the result of teenage gang activity. Eventually, five African American teenagers were brought to trial and convicted of the crime. Most people were sure that these young people were guilty, and it wasn't until 2002 that their convictions were vacated when another man confessed to the crime, and DNA evidence confirmed that he was indeed the perpetrator.

During this same period, a number of academics developed theories about a new generation of "severely impoverished juvenile super-predators...capable of committing the most heinous acts of physical violence for the most trivial reasons."[1] Given this climate of opinion, legislators in a number of states passed laws that mandated life without parole (LWOP) for juveniles who were found guilty of certain crimes. In practice this law was used in the following way. A prosecutor petitioned a judge to certify a juvenile as an adult. If the judge agreed, the defendant no longer had the protection afforded to juveniles, and if he or she was found guilty of certain kinds of crimes, the judge was required to pronounce the sentence of life without parole. In other words, the judge had no discretion in sentencing. In many states, these juveniles may not have themselves committed the crime for which they were being tried. For example, some states have felony murder rules that hold a defendant guilty of murder if a death occurs during the course of a felony, even if the defendant is only an accomplice. Thus, a fourteen-year-old who may simply have been present during a robbery in which someone was killed could be convicted of murder and sentenced to LWOP.

What is the situation today? To understand this, we need to consider three Supreme Court decisions. The first was *Roper v. Simmons*, which in 2005 abolished the death penalty for juveniles on the grounds that they were not sufficiently mature to be held to the same standards of responsibility as adults. That decision drew on scientific research demonstrating that the personalities of juveniles are not fully developed. The second was *Graham v. Florida* (2010), which concluded that it was unconstitutional to sentence juveniles to LWOP if they were not convicted of homicide. *Graham v. Florida* used some of the reasoning of *Roper v. Simons* as a precedent. Justice Anthony M. Kennedy, writing for the majority, specifically argued that "juveniles are more capable of change than adults, and their actions are less likely to be evidence of 'irretrievably depraved character' than are the actions of adults." In other words, the court reasoned that, at least with respect to non-homicidal crimes, juveniles were more capable of being rehabilitated. The ruling, however, still left twenty-eight states with laws mandating LWOP for juveniles who were convicted of capital crimes.

This brings us to the third relevant Supreme Court decision, which in June 2012 combined two cases—*Miller v. Alabama* and *Jackson v. Hobbs*, the legal citation being *Miller v. Alabama* (2012). Both Evan Miller and Kuntrell Jackson were sentenced to LWOP when they were fourteen. Miller and an older friend had robbed a fifty-two-year-old neighbor, who was intoxicated, beaten him, and then set fire to the neighbor's home, a trailer, with the neighbor inside. Miller was convicted of murder and was sentenced to LWOP, because, according to Alabama law, LWOP is mandatory if the death results from arson. Jackson was waiting outside while his friends were robbing a video store. One of his friends shot and killed the clerk. Because Jackson was an accessory to the murder and had a prior record of shoplifting, he was convicted of murder and given a mandatory sentence of LWOP.

Miller v. Alabama went beyond *Graham v. Florida* and ruled that mandatory LWOP was unconstitutional under the Eighth Amendment, which forbids "cruel and unusual punishment." It did not, however, argue that LWOP was itself unconstitutional but only that mandating it was unconstitutional. What the 5–4 majority decision did was to give judges discretion in whether or not to apply a sentence of LWOP on an individual basis. The majority decision, which was written by Justice Elena Kagan, did, however, insist that the judges "take into account how children are different, and how those differences counsel against irrevocably sentencing them to a lifetime in prison" and, specifically, that they take into account such characteristic of juveniles as "immaturity, impetuosity, and failure to appreciate risks and consequences," as well as such circumstances as "the family and home environment that surrounds him—and from which he cannot usually extricate himself—no matter how brutal or dysfunctional." In other words, judges are urged to apply LWOP sparingly, but they nonetheless can decide to give a LWOP sentence on a case by case basis.

It is not yet clear to what extent the *Miller* decision will change the situation. There are about twenty-five hundred juveniles in the United States with sentences of LWOP, two thousand of whom were given this sentence as the result of mandatory LWOP laws.[2] In principle, these two thousand cases could be reviewed. However, as of June 2014, two years after the ruling, most of the twenty-eight states that had such laws have not attempted to change them, and, of the states that made statutory changes, very few have allowed the juveniles serving these sentences to apply for a new sentence. In fact, the Supreme Court decision was never clear about whether the decision should apply retroactively. Cara H. Drinan, as associate professor of law at the Catholic University of America, summarized the situation in the following way: "States are going through the motions of compliance, but in an anemic and hyper-technical way that flouts the spirit of the decisions."[3] The reason for this is not difficult to ascertain. American citizens are divided on this issue, which is not simply a legal issue or a scientific issue, although legal precedence and scientific research do inform our thinking about these issues. It also raises deep emotional and moral issues. All these issues are addressed by the readings in this section.

The three articles in this section view LWOP from different viewpoints: the first from the vantage point of the families of victims who support LWOP, and the last two from the vantage point of legal and criminal justice thinkers who oppose LWOP. The first selection, by Thomas R. McCarthy, is just what its title states: his brief of amicus curiae that was presented to the *Miller* court in behalf of the National Organization of Victims of Juvenile Lifers. This organization is a national victims' rights organization that represents and is composed of the families of victims murdered by juveniles who were sentenced to LWOP.

In this brief, McCarthy argues that LWOP is an appropriate sentence for juvenile murderers. His first argument is that when juvenile murderers receive such sentences, the families of the victims are able to achieve some "measure of finality." However, if LWOP were not an available sentence, "these families would be forced to relive the fact of the murder over and over as they prepare for and participate in parole hearing," which would cause great harm to their mental and physical health and put them in a state of fear that the killer of a loved one would be released. McCarthy's second argument is that it would be especially unfair to the victim's families if those previously sentenced to LWOP were now to become eligible for parole. "The criminal justice system promised these victims [the family of a victim is, in effect, also a victim] that the killer would never be released. Having obtained legal finality, these victims were able to move on." Furthermore, since the family members assumed that the juvenile murderer would be put away for life, they would have had no reason to retain records of information that might enable them to oppose parole effectively. In all, McCarthy's brief insists that taking away the option of LWOP for juveniles convicted of murder or, worse, allowing those sentenced to LWOP to be eligible for parole would be manifestly unfair to the families of the victims.

The second selection, by Frank Butler, implies an argument in its title: "Extinguishing All Hope." For a young person to know that he has no chance of ever being released from prison is to create a psychological state of hopelessness, which is a kind of moral death. Butler also presents the result of a set of interviews conducted at a large men's prison with eleven prisoners sentenced to LWOP. One of his conclusions is that these prisoners come from traumatic environments, dysfunctional families, and, because they were alienated from mainstream values, often found associations with people on the street who brought them to criminality. Although this article was written before the *Miller* decision, the overall point is that putting a young person in a situation of hopelessness for the rest of his or her life is especially unjust when it ignores the abusive childhood situation and the specific circumstances of the crime.

The last article in this section, "Life Without Parole for Children," by Victor Streib and Bernadette Schrempp, looks carefully at some of the social scientific and brain research that suggests that youthful offenders are less responsible for their actions than adults and that they have a greater potential for growth and change. For example, the authors summarize research that demonstrates "that the parts of the brain in the frontal lobe associated with regulating aggression, long-range planning, abstract thinking, and, perhaps, even moral judgment are not sufficiently developed in adolescents to support these functions." Given these studies, they conclude that we cannot predict what an individual may become on the basis of what he or she did as a juvenile, and therefore we have no way of knowing whether or not a juvenile offender should be kept in prison in later years.

As you read the excerpts in this section, consider some of the following questions:

- Imagine that you have done something terrible as a teenager. Do you think that you should be held responsible for the rest of your life for what you did?

- To what extent do you believe that the family of the victim should have a say in whether a juvenile offender should be sentenced to LWOP? Is applying the *Miller* decision retroactively to those serving LWOP sentences unfair to the family of the victim?

- To what extent should the social scientific and neurobiological research be relevant to deciding whether juveniles should receive sentences of LWOP?

- As Streib and Schrempp observe, "the United Nations Convention on the Rights of the Child (CRC) includes an absolute prohibition of life without parole sentences for crimes committed by juveniles under the age of 18." To what extent should international law be relevant to determining whether or not LWOP is a legitimate sentence?

NOTES

1. Randy Hertz, "Why Life Without Parole Is Wrong for Juveniles," *Nation*, posted March 13, 2012, http://www.thenation.com/article/166773/why-life-without-parole-wrong-juveniles.

2. "US Supreme Court Bans Mandatory Life Without Parole for Youth," National Center for Youth Law, http://www.youthlaw.org/juvenile_justice/6/us_supreme_court_bans_mandatory_life_without_parole_for_youth/.

3. Quoted in Erik Eckholm, *New York Times*, January 20, 2014.

Brief of Amicus Curiae: The National Organization of Victims of Juvenile Lifers in Support of Respondents

*by Thomas R. McCarthy**

INTEREST OF AMICUS CURIAE[1]

The National Organization of Victims of Juvenile Lifers ("NOVJL") is a national victims' rights organization comprised of the families of victims murdered by juvenile offenders who were tried and sentenced as adults because of the horrific nature of their extremely violent crimes. NOVJL works to find other victims of violent juvenile offenders tried and sentenced to life imprisonment in order to ensure that their voices are part of the national discussion concerning the imposition of life sentences on juveniles and to support each other as victims of the devastating acts of criminally violent teens. NOVJL works to protect and preserve victims' rights through public policy advocacy at both the federal and state levels and by filing amicus briefs in cases that bear on victims' rights. *See Graham v. Florida*, 130 S. Ct. 2011 (2009).

At the time of our nation's founding, crime victims were actively involved in the administration of justice. Indeed, early American criminal prosecutions generally were brought by the victim. *See* D. Beloof & P. Cassell, *The Crime Victim's Right to Attend the Trial: the Reascendant National Consensus*, 9 LEWIS & CLARK L. REV. 481, 484–85 (2005). But as the criminal justice system transformed to a public-prosecution model, victims' rights often were overlooked. A task force commissioned by President Reagan to assess the treatment of crime victims in the criminal justice system found that these victims "have been overlooked, their pleas for justice have gone unheeded, and their wounds—personal, emotional and financial—have gone unattended." President's Task Force on Victims of Crime, Final Report, Washington, D.C.: U.S. Government Printing Office, Dec. 1982.

Victims' rights groups, buoyed by the work of the Task Force, succeeded in restoring many of the rights of victims in the criminal justice system. Now, every State in the Union either has enacted legislation or amended its constitution (or in some cases both) to expressly guarantee victims' rights.[2]

Congress also has enacted multiple statutes to protect the rights of crime victims, including the Victim and Witness Protection Act of 1982, the Victim's Rights and Restitution Act of 1990, and the Crime Victims' Rights Act of 2004, which among other things ensures "[t]he right to be reasonably heard at any public proceeding in the district court involving release, plea, sentencing, or any parole proceeding." 18 U.S.C. § 3771(a)(4).

Thus, both the States and Congress have recognized the importance of preserving the role of victims and victims' families[3] throughout the criminal process, from trial to sentencing and to parole proceedings for those violent offenders that become eligible for release. After all, it is the families of the victims of juvenile murderers, and organizations such as NOVJL, that must always remind those charged with the administration of justice of the heinous acts that led these teenagers to be charged and sentenced as adults. *See* Pub. L. 97–291, § 2(a) (1) ("Without the cooperation of victims . . . , the criminal justice system would cease to function.").

INTRODUCTION

Petitioners rely on psychological and scientific research to argue that "numerous features of adolescence" make teens who commit crimes "less culpable than adults." Jackson Br. at 5. Even assuming this is true as a general matter, it has little bearing on any individual comparison. *See* The Royal Society, *Brain Waves Module 4: Neuroscience and the law*, at 13 (Dec. 2011) (Given that "[t]here is huge individual variability in the timing and patterning of brain development . . . decisions about responsibility should be made on an individual basis at this stage of development."). As one court recently remarked, "[e]ven assuming that such psychological and scientific research is constitutionally relevant, the generalizations concluded therein are insufficient to support a determination that 14-year-olds who commit homicide are never culpable enough to deserve life imprisonment without parole." *State of Wisconsin v. Ninham*, 797 N.W.2d 451, 457 (Wis. 2011) (affirming life-without-parole sentence imposed upon fourteen-year-old murderer).

Looking at the facts and circumstances of "[s]pecific cases," *Graham v. Florida*, 130 S. Ct. 2011, 2031 (2010),[4] it is quite clear that, despite their age, certain teenaged murderers are more than capable of distinguishing right from wrong and fully appreciating the consequences of their actions. Indeed, this observation is reflected in the common-law maxim *malitia supplet ætatem*: malice supplies the want of years. As illustrated below, some teen-aged murderers exhibit sufficient malice to hold them accountable as adults for their murderous acts. Thus, a prophylactic constitutional rule prohibiting the imposition of a life-without-parole sentence on *any person* under 18 years of age would be unwarranted and improper. Whether such a sentence is justified should be assessed on a case-by-case basis. *See generally Graham*, 130 S. Ct. at 2036–42 (Roberts, C.J., concurring in the judgment).

Moreover, engrafting such a rule onto the Eighth Amendment would substantially harm victims' families. When juvenile murderers are sentenced to life, victims' families are able to achieve some measure of finality, at least with respect to the legal process. But if that sentence were made categorically unavailable, even for the worst offenders, these families would be forced to relive the facts of the murder over and over as they prepare for and participate in parole hearings. For them, that process would never end, harming their mental and physical health as a result. Replacing the finality of the life-without-parole sentence with the recurring anguish of the parole process effectively imposes a sentence on victims' families—a sentence under which they must forever relive the crime that took their loved one's life and live in constant fear of a killer being turned loose.

A categorical ban on the imposition of the life-without-parole sentence on teen-aged killers would cause particular harm to the victims' families in cases in which the juvenile lifer's conviction and sentence are final. Because these families rightfully thought they had reached the end of the legal process, they would have had no reason to preserve court records or other relevant information that might bear on a parole decision. Without such information, they would be unable to mount an effective opposition to parole. Such a circumstance would render illusory the participatory rights conferred upon them and protected by the laws of all fifty states and the federal government. *See supra* note 2 & p. 3.

In sum, because the life-without-parole sentence may be constitutionally imposed on teen-aged killers under certain circumstances, categorically banning it under the Eighth Amendment would be improper. This is especially so because such a categorical approach would cause great harm to victims' families and undermine their right to participate in the criminal justice process.

ARGUMENT

I. Life Imprisonment Without Parole Is an Appropriate Sentence for Juveniles Who Commit the Most Heinous Murders.

"[T]he capacity of doing ill, or contracting guilt, is not so much measured by years and days, as by the strength of the delinquent's understanding and judgment." William Blackstone, 4 *Commentaries* 23. At common law, a fourteen-year-old was considered to have the same criminal capacity as an adult. Notwithstanding his age, the fourteen-year old was *"doli capax"* or "fully accountable for his criminal conduct." *Whitehead v. State*, 262 A.2d 316, 318 n.1 (Md. App. 1970) (citing Clark & Marshall, *Law of Crimes*, 6th Ed., § 6.12, pp. 391–394); *see also* Black's Law Dictionary 521 (8th ed. 2004) (defining *"doli capax"* as "[c]apable of committing a crime or tort; esp., old enough to determine right from wrong"). On the other hand, a child of seven years or less was considered *doli incapax*. See, e.g., *Dubiver v. City & S. Ry. Co.*, 75 P.693, 694 (Or. 1904).

Those between ages seven and fourteen were presumed to be *doli incapax*, but that presumption could be overcome if the crime committed exhibited sufficient malice:

> Between the ages of seven and fourteen years an infant is deemed prima facie to be *doli incapax*; but in this case the maxim applies, *malitia supplet ætatem*—malice (which is here used in its legal sense, and means the doing of a wrongful act intentionally, without just cause or excuse,) supplies the want of mature years.

Angelo v. People, 96 Ill. 209, 1880 WL 10095, at *2 (1880) (quoting *Broom's Legal Maxims* 232–33). "The period between seven and fourteen is subject to much uncertainty: for the infant shall, generally speaking, be judged prima facie innocent; yet if he was *doli capax*, and could discern between good and evil at the time of the offence committed, he may be convicted and undergo judgment and execution of death, though he hath not attained to years of puberty or discretion." 1 W. Blackstone, *Commentaries* 452–53 (1765) (quoted in *Com. v. Ogden O.*, 864 N.E.2d 13, 17 n.3 (Mass. 2007)).

Although the precise age at which the criminal justice system deems people *doli capax* may vary somewhat from jurisdiction to jurisdiction, *see, e.g.*, Alabama Br. at 5,[5] the maxim still holds—*malitia supplet ætatem*. And teen-aged murderers who commit crimes with sufficient malice may properly be deemed "fully accountable" for their conduct.[6]

The following examples illustrate the point. As they show, the life-without-parole sentence may be properly imposed on teen-aged murderers where malice supplies the want of years,[7] especially given that the Court not so long ago upheld a life-without-parole sentence imposed on a first-time offender who committed a nonviolent drug-possession crime, *see Harmelin v. Michigan*, 501 U.S. 957, 1002–04 (1991).[8]

1. Donald Torres (age 14)

Victims:

Harry Godt (adult)
Jennifer Godt (adult)
Jon Godt (age 4)
Jennifer Godt (age 1½)

At approximately midnight on February 24, 1989, Donald Torres broke into the home of his neighbor Harry Godt, knowing that Mr. Godt, his wife, and two young children were asleep on the second floor. Torres spread kerosene over the kitchen floor and the stairway to the second floor of the home. Using his lighter and some newspaper, Torres ignited the kerosene. From outside his apartment, Torres watched the flames spread through and engulf the Godts' home. He watched Mr. Godt run out of the house and then go back inside to attempt to save his family. Harry Godt, his wife, and their two young children all perished in the fire.

According to the State Medical Examiner, the Godts all died of asphyxia due to carbon monoxide saturation of the hemoglobin and third-degree burns that covered 90 to 95 percent of their bodies.[9] After initially denying any involvement, Torres later admitted to police that "he had intentionally started the fire to get back at Harry Godt because Godt had accused Torres of teaching [Godt's] son, Jon, to play with matches." Torres also admitted that he had known that "the Godt family was in the home when he started the fire."[10]

A Delaware jury convicted Torres of four counts of intentional first degree murder and four counts of reckless first degree felony murder. He was sentenced to eight consecutive terms of life without parole.[11]

2. Paul Dean Jensen Jr. (age 14)

Victim:

Michael Hare (adult)

Paul Jensen already had a record of shoplifting, vandalism, burglary, arson, stalking, and more when he committed premeditated murder.

On January 14, 1996, Jensen engaged in a "dry run" of his plan to rob a taxicab. At about midnight, a Pierre, South Dakota taxicab dispatcher received a call requesting a ride from Buhl's Laundry. When the taxi driver arrived, she was met by Jensen and his sixteen-year-old friend, Shawn Springer. At their request, the taxi driver took Jensen and Springer on a two-stop journey that ended only one block from where they met the cab in the first place. During the drive, Springer asked the taxi driver if anyone had ever stolen or tried to steal the cab money bag. The driver responded that if anyone did try to steal it, they could have it, as it only contained thirty dollars.

Seven days later, Jensen, his sister, and Springer entered a friend's unlocked apartment and stole some cash, a necklace, a shotgun, and a handgun that turned out to be the weapon used to kill a taxi driver five days later. On the evening of

January 26, 1996, Jensen showed the stolen handgun to a friend. He also showed the friend two or three ammunition clips. At around 11:00 pm, the Pierre taxi dispatcher received a call from Springer requesting to be picked up at the Days Inn and insisting to be picked up at "north back door." The dispatcher refused, stating that the cab would arrive at the office door. Springer indicated that there would be two passengers. When the dispatcher asked where they were going, Springer said, "Paul, where are we going?" Jensen replied, "I don't know. Fort Pierre, I guess. I don't know."

The taxi driver, Michael Hare, arrived at the Days Inn and shortly thereafter noticed Jensen and Springer coming from the back of the Days Inn. They entered the cab and directed Hare to take them to Fort Pierre. Jensen and Springer directed Hare to take them down a gravel road near Fort Pierre where the cab stopped. At this very same time, the dispatcher was trying to call Hare's cellular phone. Although Hare did not directly respond to her call, the dispatcher could hear Hare say over the cell phone: "That's all I have is thirty bucks. Take it. Take it all." The dispatcher then heard Jensen and Springer say, "That ain't all you got" and demand "everything." Hare replied, "That's all I have. They only give us thirty bucks. You can have it. Take it, take it all."

Jensen got out of the taxi with the stolen handgun drawn. He ordered Hare to exit the vehicle. After Hare got out of the vehicle, Jensen shot him in the chest. Hare fell down and pleaded for his life, yelling, "Please God, don't kill me." Jensen approached Hare and shot him once more on each side of the head, killing him. Jensen then grabbed Hare's billfold and other items, which had been placed on the hood of the taxi, and jumped into the passenger seat. Springer and Jensen drove off, leaving Hare's lifeless body at the end of the gravel road. They were apprehended shortly thereafter by police, who had been alerted to the crime by the dispatcher.

Later, while Jensen was being held in the Juvenile Corrections Center in Rapid City, he bragged to the other juveniles in his holding area about having planned and executed the murder of a taxi driver. According to the testimony of one of the juveniles, "Jensen related the story of his cold-blooded execution-style murder in a calm and unfeeling manner."[12] A South Dakota jury convicted Jensen of first-degree murder. He was sentenced to life imprisonment without parole.[13]

3. Ashley Jones (age 14)

Victims:

Deroy Nalls (adult)

Mary Nalls (adult)

Millie Nalls (adult)
Mary Jones (age 10)

In 1999, Ashley Jones and her sixteen-year-old boyfriend, Geramie Hart, plotted and executed a horrific crime that involved the murder of her grandfather and her Aunt Millie and would have involved the murder of her grandmother and her 10-year-old sister had they not miraculously survived the attack.

Hart and her ten-year-old sister Mary lived with their grandparents, Deroy and Mary Nalls. Jones's aunt, Millie Nalls, also lived in the house. Jones's family did not approve of her relationship with Hart, so she plotted with Hart to kill them, set the house ablaze, and abscond with their money.

On the night of August 29, 1999, Deroy Nalls was in the den watching television. His wife, daughter, and younger granddaughter were asleep in their rooms. Jones let Hart into the house. He was armed with Deroy's .38 caliber pistol, which Jones previously had smuggled to him. Jones and Hart entered the den, where Hart promptly shot Deroy twice in the face. Jones and Hart then moved quickly to Millie's bedroom where she had been sleeping and shot her three times. Seeing that she survived the gunshots, Jones and Hart hit her repeatedly with portable heaters, stabbed her in the chest, and set her room on fire. The pair next entered Mary Nalls's bedroom and shot her once in the shoulder, stopping only because it was their last bullet.

Jones and Hart returned to the kitchen area and discovered that Deroy was still alive. Hart hit him with various objects and stabbed him repeatedly, leaving the knife in his back. Jones then poured charcoal lighter fluid on her grandfather and set him on fire. Jones's young sister, Mary, woke up, and Jones led her into the kitchen area where she saw her grandfather on fire but still alive. Hart forced Deroy to disclose where he kept his money, and then stabbed Deroy in the throat. Jones then poured lighter fluid on her grandmother and set her on fire. Jones and Hart watched her burn, and Hart urged Jones to pour more lighter fluid on her. Young Mary attempted to flee the kitchen, but Jones grabbed her and began hitting her. Hart pointed the gun at the young girl and said, "This is how you are going to die." Jones said, "No, let me do it," and stabbed her little sister 14 times. Jones and Hart then set the house ablaze.

Jones and Hart took $300 that had been hidden beneath her grandparents' mattress and drove away in their Cadillac. Miraculously, Mary Jones survived, despite suffering a collapsed lung and multiple stab wounds. The ten-year-old had pretended to be dead until Jones and Hart fled the burning house and then heroically helped her grandmother out of the house and contacted others for help.

Jones and Hart were arrested the next morning in a hotel room, where her grandparents' car had been found in the parking lot. Jones and Hart voluntarily confessed to the murders of Jones's grandfather and aunt and the attempted murders of her grandmother and little sister.[14] Upon learning that her younger sister had survived the attack, Jones remarked "I thought I killed that bitch."[15]

Jones was convicted of two counts of capital murder and two counts of attempted murder. She was sentenced to life imprisonment without parole. The sentencing judge noted that Jones "did not express genuine remorse for her actions." The judge also noted that "while awaiting her sentencing, the defendant had threatened older female inmates in the Jefferson County Jail by telling them she would do the same thing to them that she had done to her family."[16]

4. Omer Ninham (age 14)

Victim:

Zong Vang (age 13)

Omer Ninham committed a murder that the Supreme Court of Wisconsin described as "a horrific and senseless crime [that] cannot adequately be reduced into words. The terror experienced by the victim and the hurt suffered by his family and friends is, in a word, unimaginable."[17]

On the evening of September 24, 1998, Zong Vang was riding his bike home with a bag of tomatoes his older brother had asked him to pick up from the grocery store. While riding along Webster Avenue in Green Bay, Wisconsin, Vang was approached by five teens: Ninham, 13-year-old Richard Crapeau, 13-year-old Jeffrey P., 14-year-old Amanda G., and 14-year-old Christin J.

Vang did not know any of them and had done nothing to provoke them. He just happened to encounter a group looking for a fight. Crapeau said to Ninham, "Let's mess with this kid," and Ninham responded, "'I got your back,' meaning he would back [Crapeau] up in a fight."[18]

Ninham and Crapeau began taunting Vang and quickly attacked him. Crapeau then yanked Vang's bicycle away from him, grabbed Vang's grocery bag, and threw it in the street. After Vang asked them for his bicycle back, Ninham punched Vang, knocking him to the ground.

Vang got up and attempted to flee, running towards a parking ramp at St. Vincent's Hospital, which was on the same street. The attackers chased Vang, catching up to him at the top of the five-story parking ramp. When they reached Vang, Crapeau punched him in the face. Vang repeatedly begged for mercy and asked why they were trying to hurt him. But Ninham and Crapeau continued to attack Vang.

Ninham then pinned Vang against a concrete wall, and Crapeau punched Vang in the face. As Vang cried and screamed, "Let me go," Ninham and Crapeau lifted Vang up off the ground, with Ninham holding Vang's wrists and Crapeau holding Vang's ankles. Ninham and Crapeau "then began swinging Vang back and forth out over the parking ramp's concrete wall—a drop that measured nearly 45 feet to the ground." Vang, still crying and screaming, pleaded with Ninham and Crapeau not to drop him. Crapeau then let go of Vang's feet and urged Ninham to "[d]rop him." Showing no mercy to the still-pleading Vang, Ninham let go of Vang, leaving him to plunge five stories to his death. At just that time, a bystander exiting the parking facility down at ground level heard what sounded like a "bag of wet cement hitting the pavement." Vang landed on his back on the parking ramp's paved exit lane, 12 feet from the base of the ramp.

Ninham, Crapeau, and their companions fled the scene, leaving Vang in a heap on the concrete. One of the other companions later testified that Ninham stood for several seconds looking over the edge of the wall at Vang on the ground below. Ninham then looked at Jeffrey P. and said, "Don't say nothing. Better not say shit." Rescue personnel were unable to revive Vang. The official cause of Vang's death was craniocerebral trauma resulting from his fall.

A jury convicted Ninham of first-degree intentional homicide and of physical abuse of a child for the death of the thirteen-year-old Vang. Ninham was sentenced to life imprisonment without parole.[19]

5. Scott Darnell (age 15)

Victim:

Vicki Larson (age 10)

Scott Darnell already had a record that included molesting young girls, attempted rape, and assault with a deadly weapon when he raped and murdered Vicki Larson.[20] Indeed, it was only a month earlier that Darnell had been released from incarceration and placed in the custody of a parole officer.[21] He was on an authorized absence from a correctional facility at the time he raped and murdered Vicki.[22]

On July 12, 1979, Darnell lured Vicki away from her brother's baseball game to a location in a nearby cornfield where he had already dug a shallow grave three days earlier. There, Darnell raped and strangled Vicki to death with a bandana. He then dumped her lifeless body into the pre-dug grave and buried her. In an attempt to conceal his crimes, he buried the bandana he had used to strangle Vicki. In addition, he threw his wristwatch into a nearby field in order to set up an alibi that he had been jumped and had his watch stolen.

Darnell and Vicki were the objects of an overnight search after they had been reported missing that evening. Local police came across Darnell the next morning, finding him "extremely dirty, wet and muddy." He told them that he had been jumped by two men on motorcycles who stole his watch.

Later on, Darnell confessed to the rape and murder-by-strangulation of Vicki Larson. He showed officers where he had buried his bandana and where he had thrown his watch. He also showed them the shovel that he had used to dig what would be Vicki's grave.[23]

Darnell was convicted of murder and rape at a bench trial. Darnell showed little emotion during the trial and verdict, but "joked freely with jailers and relatives during the recesses."[24] Darnell was sentenced to life imprisonment without parole. The sentencing judge remarked that Darnell's rape and murder of Vicki Larson were "exceptionally brutal."[25]

A few years later, while Darnell was in prison for the rape and murder of Vicki Larson, prison officials uncovered and thwarted an elaborate escape plan that Darnell was in the process of carrying out. In uncovering the escape, the prison officials found a letter from Darnell addressed to Judge Jeffrey O'Connor, who had been the state's attorney who prosecuted Darnell. The letter read:

> You used me, you took my life as surely as if you would of sent me to the chair.
>
> Do you wonder why I write in red? It is the color of your blood. Do you have daughters, Jeffrey? If they are young, I'll be merciful with them. As merciful as I was with Viki. But regardless, they shall die.
>
> Whether wife sons daughter or any other, they shall die in front of your eyes.
>
> And when every cry is called, every tear shed, every drop of blood spilled before your feet, it will be your turn. . . . I will keep you alive for days. But you will die finally. And I'll feed you to the dogs.[26]

II. A Categorical Ban on the Life-Without-Parole Sentence for Juvenile Killers Will Needlessly Trample on the Rights of Victims.

The Court has remarked that the life-without-parole sentence is somewhat unique. *See Graham*, 130 S. Ct. at 2027. The way in which it is perhaps most unique is that it is the *only* sentence that allows victims to obtain legal finality. The life-without-parole sentence brings them certainty by terminating the legal process. *See Menzias v. Galetka*, 150 P.3d 480, 521 (Utah 2006) (Wilkins, J., concurring) ("[A] sentence of life without parole" is "more certain for the victims."). It avoids the interminable nature of the death penalty appeal process. *See id.* (describing the "seemingly endless requirements to review, re-review, analyze, and re-analyze any possible defect in the proceedings by which those found guilty of crimes so hideous that the death penalty is imposed"). And it enables victims to avoid the recurring pain of the parole process, which forces them to relive the horrors of these heinous crimes and paralyzes them with fear that the murderers who so callously took the lives of their family members might be released.

Imposing the parole process on victims' families thus comes at a substantial cost. Each parole proceeding inflicts on them the mental and physical anguish of replaying the murder in their mind's eye as they prepare for and attend parole hearings. Worse still, they must repeat this process over and over each time the killer become eligible for parole. And throughout this process, they live in constant fear that the killer will be set loose on society. For these reasons, a life-*with*-parole sentence has been likened to "sentencing the victim and the victim's family, as well.... It's a sort of a virtual prison, because ... as long as [the killers] are in jail ... and as long as they come up for parole, we're sharing that sentence with them."[27] To create a rule prohibiting life-without-parole sentences for all teen-aged killers would thus impose real and immeasurable harm on their victims.

This rule would be particularly unfair where the life-without-parole sentence is already final.[28] The criminal justice system promised these victims that the killers would never be released. Having obtained legal finality, these victims were able to move on. While they may never fully overcome the physical, emotional, and psychological trauma of the crime itself, at least they could rest assured that the killer would no longer be a threat to them or any other innocent person. Reopening final sentences and forcing the victims to again encounter these killers through the parole process would effectively transfer the life sentence from the perpetrator of the heinous crime to his innocent victim.

Moreover, invalidating final sentences of teen-aged murderers would thwart victims' participatory rights. There is a national consensus that crime victims have a right to participate in the criminal process. "As might be expected, statutes and constitutional provisions regarding specific crime victims' rights differ across jurisdictions, but there is general agreement about which victims' rights are most important." *See* Dean G. Kilpatrick, *Interpersonal Violence and Public*

Policy: What About the Victims?, 32 J.L. MED. & ETHICS 73, 78 (2004). These are victims' participatory rights, which "are designed to parallel defendants' rights to participate in criminal proceedings" and thus include the rights "to be notified about key criminal justice system proceedings and hearings, to be present at such hearings and proceedings, and to be heard at appropriate points in such hearings and proceedings." *Id.; see, e.g.,* ALA. CODE § 15-23-79(b) ("The victim shall have the right to be notified by the Board of Pardons and Paroles and allowed to be present and heard at a hearing when parole or pardon is considered."); ARK. CODE § 16-90-1113(a)(1)(A) ("Before determining whether to release the defendant on parole, the Parole Board shall permit the victim to present a written victim impact statement concerning the effects of the crime on the victim, the circumstances surrounding the crime, the manner in which the crime was perpetrated, and the victim's opinion regarding whether the defendant should be released on parole."); *id.* § 16-90-1113(a)(1)(B) ("At the victim's option, the victim may present the statement orally at the parole hearing.").

Because the life-without-parole sentence brings closure to the legal process, victims tend not to retain court records or take steps to preserve witness testimony or other important evidence. As time passes, victims may no longer have access to key evidence and information that has particular relevance to parole proceedings. Some NOVJL members, for example, have indicated that key witnesses to the murder of a family member have passed on. Others have noted that they do not have transcripts of key proceedings, such as when the sentencing judge explained the court's reasons for imposing a sentence of life without parole. And because electronic dockets are of relatively recent vintage (and do not even exist in some places), victims may be left with no means of obtaining information that might be crucial to determining whether a murderer stays in prison or is set free.

Without access to important evidence bearing on a parole determination, the promise of victims' participatory rights is an empty one. And because "parole boards cannot make sound decisions about the release of convicts from prison without information from victims," Kilpatrick, *Interpersonal Violence and Public Policy: What About the Victims?*, 32 J.L. MED. & ETHICS 73, 74 (2004), murderers who remain dangerous to the public may be set free among an unsuspecting public.

CONCLUSION

For the reasons set forth herein, the judgments of the Alabama Court of Criminal Appeals and the Supreme Court of Arkansas should be affirmed.

NOTES

1. Pursuant to this Court's Rule 37.6, counsel for *amicus curiae* NOVJL certifies that this brief was not authored in whole or in part by counsel for any party and that no person or entity other than *amicus curiae* or its counsel has made a monetary contribution to the preparation or submission of this brief. Both parties have consented to the filing of this brief. Pursuant to Rule 37.3(a), the parties' letters so consenting have been filed with the Clerk.

2. ALA. CODE § 15-23-79; ALASKA CONST. art. I, § 24; ALASKA STAT. § 33.16.120; ARIZ. CONST. art. II, § 2.1; ARIZ. REV. STAT. ANN. § 13-4414; ARK. CODE ANN. §§ 16-90-1109, -1113; CAL. CONST. art. I, § 28; COLO. CONST. art. II, § 16A; COLO. REV. STAT. ANN. §§ 24-4.1-302(2), -302.5; CONN. GEN. STAT. ANN. § 54-203; DEL. CODE ANN. TIT. 'II, § 9416; FLA. CONST. art. I, § 16; FLA. STAT. ANN. § 960.001; GA. CODE ANN. §§ 17-17-13; HAW. REV. STAT. §§ 706-670, -670.5; IDAHO CODE ANN. § 19-5306; 725 ILL. COMP. STAT. ANN. 120/4.5; 730 ILL. COMP. STAT. ANN. 5/3-3-4; IND. CODE ANN. § 35-40-5-5; IOWA CODE ANN. § 915.18; KAN. STAT. ANN. § 22-3717; KY. REV. STAT. ANN. §§ 421.500, 421.520; LA. REV. STAT. ANN. § 46:1844; ME. REV. STAT. ANN. TIT. 17-A, § 1175; MD. CODE ANN., CORR. SERV. § 7-801; MASS. GEN. LAWS ANN. CH. 258B, § 3; MICH. COMP. LAWS ANN. § 780.769; MINN. STAT. ANN. § 243.05; MISS. CODE ANN. § 99-43-43; MO. ANN. STAT. § 595.209; MONT. CODE ANN. § 46-24-212; NEB. REV. STAT. § 81-1848; 2011 NEV. LAWS CH. 23 (A.B. 18); N.H. REV. STAT. ANN. § 21-M:8-K; N.J. STAT. ANN. § 52:4B-44; N.M. STAT. ANN. § 31-21-25; N.Y. CRIM. PROC. LAW § 440.50; N.C. CONST. art. I, §37; N.C. GEN. STAT. ANN. § 15A-1371; N.D. CENT. CODE § 12.1-34-02; OHIO REV. CODE ANN. § 5149.101; OKLA. STAT. TIT. 57 § 332.2; OR. REV. STAT. ANN. § 144.098; 61 PA. CONS. STAT. ANN. § 6140; R.I. GEN. LAWS § 12-28-6; S.C. CONST. art. I, § 24; S.C. CODE ANN. § 16-3-1560; S.D. CODIFIED LAWS § 24-15A-43; TENN. CODE ANN. § 40-38-103; TEX. CODE CRIM. PROC. ANN. art. 56.02; UTAH CODE ANN. § 77-27-9.5; VT. STAT. ANN. TIT. 13, § 5305; VA. CODE ANN. § 53.1-155; WASH. REV. CODE ANN. § 7.69.032; W. VA. CODE ANN. § 62-12-23; WIS. STAT. ANN. §§ 304.06, 950.04; WYO. STAT. ANN. §§ 1-40-204, 7-13-402; D.C. CODE §§ 23-1901, 23-1904.

3. There is a national consensus that the rights afforded to crime victims extend to the family members of murder victims. *See, e.g.*, 18 U.S.C. § 3771(e) ("For the purposes of this chapter, the term 'crime victim' means a person directly and proximately harmed as a result of the commission of a Federal offense or an offense in the District of Columbia. In the case of a crime victim who is under 18 years of age, incompetent, incapacitated, or deceased, the legal guardians of the crime victim or the representatives of the crime victim's estate, family members, or any other persons appointed as suitable by the court, may assume the crime victim's rights under this chapter."); Ala. Code § 15-23-60(19) (defining "victim" as a "person against whom the criminal offense has been committed, or if the person is killed or incapacitated, the spouse, sibling, parent, child, or guardian of the person"). For this reason, the term "victim" is sometimes used in the literature on victims' rights as including the family members of a murder victim.

4. *See also* Craig Lerner, *Juvenile Criminal Responsibility: Can Malice Supply The Want Of Years?*, 86 TULANE L. REV. 309, 339–40 (2012) ("Recounting the facts of a crime where a claim of juvenile immaturity is raised is essential in clarifying the kind of juvenile being discussed.... [It] can dispel the idea that [the teen-aged murderers] are typical adolescents; it should alert one to the possibility that [teen-aged] murderers... are atypical. So alerted, one might be inoculated from facile claims that defendants in such cases are just adolescents behaving badly.").

5. *See also* The Royal Society, *Brain Waves Module 4: Neuroscience and the law*, at 13 (Dec. 2011) ("In England the age of criminal responsibility is ten. This means that up to the age of ten a child will not be held responsible for criminal acts. From the age of ten however, in the eyes of the law, a child is accountable in the same way as an adult for their behaviour, and is deemed sufficiently mature to stand trial and to engage in legal processes.").

6. It thus is constitutionally irrelevant whether psychological and scientific research suggests that teens as a class are less responsible for their criminal conduct than adults. Jackson Br. at 5. In any event, the research on this point is inconclusive at best. *See* Stephen J. Morse, *Brain Overclaim Syndrome and Criminal Responsibility: A Diagnostic Note*, 3 OHIO ST. J. CRIM. L. 397, 409 (2006) ("The neuroscience evidence in no way independently confirms that adolescents are less responsible."); *see also* Alabama Br. at 43–48. Moreover, some of the scholarly literature on the issue actually suggests that it is not that the underdeveloped brain causes risky behavior

but that risky behavior may cause changes to the brain. *See, e.g.*, Robert Epstein, *The Myth of the Teen Brain*, Scientific Am. Mind, April/May 2007, at 58 ("There is clear evidence that any unique features that may exist in the brains of teens—to the limited extent that such features exist—are the result of social influences rather than the cause of teen turmoil.").

7. The relative rarity with which the life-without-parole sentence is imposed on teen-aged murderers demonstrates only that legislatures and prosecutors properly reserve this sentence for particularly depraved murderers. Especially given that most States provide for the possibility of life without parole for at least some teen-aged murderers, *see* Alabama Br. at 9 ("Thirty-nine jurisdictions have statutes allowing 14-year-olds to be sentenced to life without parole for aggravated murder."), the infrequency with which this sentence is opposed cannot possibly support a finding that there is any sort of national consensus against it.

8. A murderer is surely much more criminally culpable than a non-violent, first-time drug offender, principally because murder, like the death penalty, is "'unique in its severity and irrevocability.'" *Graham*, 130 S. Ct. at 2027 (quoting *Gregg v. Georgia*, 428 U.S. 153, 187 (1976) (joint opinion of Stewart, Powell, and Stevens, JJ.)); *see id.* ("The Court has recognized that defendants who do not kill, intend to kill, or foresee that life will be taken are categorically less deserving of the most serious forms of punishment than are murderers.").

9. *See Torres v. State of Delaware*, 608 A.2d 731 (Del. 1992); *Torres v. State of Delaware*, 642 A.2d 837 (Del. 1994); *Torres v. Kearney*, No. 04-109, 2005 WL 3263098 (D. Del. Dec. 1, 2005).

10. *See* Charles D. Stimson & Andrew M. Grossman, Adult Time for Adult Crimes: Life Without Parole for Juvenile Killers and Violent Teens 46 (Heritage Found. Aug. 2009).

11. *Torres*, 608 A.2d 731; *Torres*, 642 A.2d 837; *Torres*, 2005 WL 3263098.

12. *State of South Dakota v. Jensen*, 579 N.W.2d 613 (S.D. 1998).

13. *Id.*

14. *See Hart v. State of Alabama*, 852 So.2d 839 (Ala. Crim. App. 2002).

15. *See* C. Stimson & A. Grossman, *supra*, at 27.

16. *State of Alabama v. Jones*, No. CC–2000–0151, 0152 (Ala. Cir. Ct. May 25, 2001) (finding of fact from guilt phase of trial).

17. *See State of Wisconsin v. Ninham*, 797 N.W.2d 451, 457 (Wis. 2011).

18. *See id.*

19. *State of Wisconsin v. Ninham*, 797 N.W.2d 451, 457 (Wis. 2011).

20. Kris Jensen & Daniel J. Foley, *Who Failed with Scott Darnell?*, Quad-City Times (Davenport, Iowa) (Aug. 12, 1979).

21. *Larson v. Darnell*, 448 N.E.2d 249, 250 (Ill. App. 1983).

22. Kris Jensen & Daniel J. Foley, *Who Failed with Scott Darnell?*, Quad-City Times (Davenport, Iowa) (Aug. 12, 1979).

23. Craig Brown, *Witnesses Describe Darnell, Scene of Murder*, Quad-City Times (Davenport, Iowa) (Jan. 29, 1980).

24. Craig Brown, *Judge Finds Darnell Guilty of Rape, Murder*, Quad-City Times (Davenport, Iowa) (Feb. 8, 1980).

25. Craig Brown, *Murderer's Chilling Letter Never Sent*, Quad-City Times (Davenport, Iowa) (Aug. 2, 1984).

26. Craig Brown, *Murderer's Chilling Letter Never Sent*, Quad-City Times (Davenport, Iowa) (Aug. 2, 1984).

27. *Sentencing the Victim* (IVS Video Inc. 2002), PBS , Independent Lens (March 2, 2004), *available at* http://www.hulu.com/watch/55120/pbs-indies-sentencing-the-victim. In addition to the emotional and physical toll on victims, the recurring parole process forces victims to incur substantial financial costs. Victims must regularly take time off from work to attend parole hearings and pay for transportation to and from the location of the parole proceedings.

28. Although such a holding should not apply retroactively, it is possible that lower courts might wrongly conclude otherwise. *See In re Sparks*, 657 F.3d 258 (5th Cir. 2011) (holding that *Graham* applies retroactively to cases on collateral review). The retroactivity problem could be avoided entirely if the issue were properly left to the state legislatures. *See e.g.*, Texas Penal Code § 12.31(a); *Meadoux v. State*, 325 S.W.3d 189, 194 (Tex. Crim. App. 2010) (noting that "the Legislature specified that the amendment of § 12.31(a) was not to be applied retroactively").

*Thomas R. McCarthy is codirector of the Supreme Court Clinic at George Mason University School of Law. He filed an amicus brief with the Supreme Court in the *Miller v. Alabama* and *Jackson v. Hobbs* cases (2012) on behalf of the National Organization of Victims of Juvenile Lifers.

McCarthy, Thomas R. "Brief of Amicus Curiae of the National Organization of Victims of Juvenile Lifers in Support of Respondent in the Supreme Court of the United States," February 21, 2012, pp. 1–25.

Reprinted with permission from the grieving murder victims familiar with NOVJL, the National Organization of Juvenile Lifers (www.teenkillers.org).

Extinguishing All Hope:
Life-Without-Parole for Juveniles

by Frank Butler*

A criminal sentence of life with no possibility for parole is a drastic punishment, permanently banishing the recipient from social interaction in the free world for the remainder of his or her natural life. It is a sociolegal judgment that the person is essentially irredeemable. Short of the death penalty, it is unique in its finality and despair.

Such a draconian punishment naturally raises profound ethical issues with regard to how and when it is used. Those issues are particularly critical when the sentence is imposed on minors, whose psycho-social development is incomplete and who presumably will endure the punishment for the longest time. This research involves an exploration of so-called "juvenile life-without-parole" (JLWOP), especially as seen through the eyes of those who live it daily.

REVIEW OF THE LITERATURE

In the United States there are approximately 6,800 persons serving "life" sentences for crimes committed when they were juveniles. Most of them at some point will be eligible for parole consideration. Approximately one-quarter of them, however, have been deemed permanently ineligible for parole consideration (Nellis & King, 2009). These are the persons who have been sentenced to life "without parole" for crimes committed as juveniles.[1]

There is major variation among the states in their use of JLWOP. Half of all JLWOP prisoners are incarcerated by four states: Pennsylvania, California, Michigan, and Louisiana (Nellis & King, 2009). Though a few states (Alaska, Colorado, Kansas, New Mexico, and Oregon) prohibit JLWOP, 29 states mandate JLWOP for at least one crime, which most often is homicide (Nellis & King, 2009).

States also vary in the minimum age (at the time of the crime) for which JLWOP can be imposed as a punishment: thirteen states sanction any age, one state sets the minimum at 8 years, eighteen set the minimum at 10, twenty set the minimum at 12, and thirteen set it at 14 (Leighton & de la Vega, 2007). Among those serving JLWOP sentences currently, the youngest age at the time of the crime is 13. Approximately 73 persons serving JLWOP were given the sentence for crimes committed when they were 13 or 14 (Equal Justice Initiative, 2007).

Only a few nations other than the United States have persons serving sentences of JLWOP. Human Rights Watch (2005) identified only South Africa (four persons), Tanzania (one person), and Israel (between four and seven persons). The sentence technically is a potential in a variety of other countries, but there is no evidence that it is used.

The sentence conflicts with major provisions of international law. For example, life sentences for minors are prohibited under Article 37 of the United Nations Convention on the Rights of the Child (1989), which has been ratified by all countries except the United States and Somalia (UNICEF, 2010). Likewise, Article 6 of the International Covenant on Civil and Political Rights prohibits JLWOP sentences (1966). The United States ratified this covenant in 1992, with a reservation that it would try juveniles in adult court in "exceptional circumstances" (United Nations Treaty Collection, 1992). Finally, the international oversight body for the Convention Against Torture has suggested that JLWOP may constitute cruel, unusual, or degrading treatment prohibited by the convention (Equal Justice Initiative, 2007).

Academic research has explored adults' experience of life-without-parole, and there are also rich first-person accounts (e.g., Hassine, 2009; Paluch, 2004). Life-without-parole has been characterized as "unquestionably a semantically disguised sentence of death" (Villaume, 2005, p. 267) and as "death by incarceration" (Johnson & McGunigall-Smith, 2008, p. 328). The latter also describe life-without-parole as a "civil death" involving "a lifetime of boredom, doubt, and anxiety punctuated by piercing moments of insight into one's failings as a human being" (Johnson & McGunigall-Smith, 2008, pp. 329, 334). Especially because of the length and finality of the sentence, family ties commonly fade, and "[e]ach day brings mortifications that remind prisoners of their helplessness and the sheer loss of dignity they suffer in a world in which no one recognizes their inherent worth as human beings" (Johnson & McGunigall-Smith, 2008, p. 338).

JLWOP evolved from the tortured history of juvenile justice in the United States, where solicitous concern for the malleability and potential of youth tended to become ensnared in structures that served largely to advance the interests of dominant social classes (Platt, 1977; Schneider, 1992). Sentences of JLWOP were rare prior to the 1980s. From 1962 to 1981, an average of two JLWOP sentences were imposed per year. Fifty were imposed in 1989, and 152 in 1996, with a decline to 54 in 2003 (Human Rights Watch, 2005). In most of the years between 1985 and 2001, it was more likely that a juvenile, compared with an adult, convicted of murder would be sentenced to life-without-parole (Human Rights Watch, 2005).

Particularly in the late 1980s and 1990s, a moral panic prevailed in the United States with regard to youth criminality. Moral panics involve extensive publicity surrounding particular acts of social deviance, contributing to an exaggerated view of the severity and threat of the deviance, as well as general societal demonization of those who engage in similar acts of deviance (deYoung, 1998; Logan, 1999; Reinarman, 1988; Zatz, 1987).

In a moral panic, public indignation about the deviant group (sometimes termed "folk devils") appreciably exceeds the concern warranted by the immediate threat presented by the group (Cohen, 1980; Goode & Ben-Yehuda, 1994). Societal hostility toward the deviant group yields perceived imperatives to escalate punitive responses toward the group, whose values and behaviors (commonly painted in exaggerated and stereo-typical images) are deemed anathema to the morality of the larger society.

Emphasis by the mass media on violent crime by juveniles, aided by criminologist predictions of unprecedented violence by an emerging class of juvenile "super-predators," fueled public disenchantment with the rehabilitative basis of juvenile justice. Though the purported juvenile crime wave in the 1980s and 1990s was later debunked as primarily myth, the panic had lasting impact as many states facilitated transfer of youth to the more punitive adult-court and as youth generally faced more serious criminal punishments, including JLWOP (Beckett & Sasson, 2004; Kappeler & Potter, 2005).

Historically minors could be prosecuted in adult criminal court rather than juvenile court. In the 1960s, the U.S. Supreme Court established due process protections (e.g., formal consideration of the youth's maturity and rehabilitative potential) that juvenile courts needed to adhere to before transferring—or "waiving"—a juvenile to adult court (*Morris Kent v. U.S.*, 1966). However, when homicides by youth increased significantly for a short time from the late 1980s to early 1990s, due largely to easy access to firearms, most states established mechanisms to ease the transfer of youth to adult court (Mauer, King, & Young, 2004). Allowing prosecutors to file certain juvenile cases directly in adult court, and categorically excluding certain crimes from juvenile court jurisdiction by statute, were politically popular reforms (e.g., Densmore & Wahlberg, 2004). Consequently many youth who historically would have been processed through juvenile court found themselves in adult court where sentences of life-without-parole were possible. Thus, the prevalence of JLWOP sentences has existed only since the late 20th century.

Life-without-parole sentences are favored largely because they achieve permanent incapacitation of persons who have shown through at least one event that they are dangerous to society. Simultaneously they obviate a major shortcoming of the death penalty: wrongful executions.[2]

Some difficulties arise, however, in that it is notoriously difficult to predict future dangerousness, especially based on a homicide committed by a teen (Appleton & Grover, 2007). Pragmatically, incapacitating someone from the teen years until natural death—including providing minimally adequate medical care in old age—is an expensive undertaking for society (Appleton & Grover, 2007). Also, the absence of any potential for parole can mitigate some incentives for good behavior in prison (Appleton & Grover, 2007).

JLWOP ostensibly furthers the goal of general deterrence among juveniles. This effect is potentially confounded, however, by major differences in rates of use of JLWOP among the states. One particular conundrum with deterrence is the fact that 26% of JLWOP sentences are based on felony-murder convictions (Leighton & de la Vega, 2007). Felony-murder is a form of strict criminal liability that holds a defendant guilty of murder if a death occurs during the course of a felony. Even completely unintentional and accidental killings can be elevated to "murder" under the doctrine. Ignoring issues of excessive risk and culpability, felony-murder focuses simply on whether the defendant committed the under-lying felony (Fletcher, 1980/1981). Its use in the context of teens is particularly controversial, because of their general inability to consider long-term—let alone unforeseen—consequences of their actions and because peer pressure is especially powerful at this developmental stage (Flynn, 2008).

Retribution is a major goal of criminal punishment purportedly served by JLWOP: to atone for the stupendous harm resulting from their actions, the juve-nile justly deserves a drastic form of punishment. As a philosophy of criminal punishment, retribution has strong roots in Anglo-American religious traditions but also strains the tenets of those traditions. For example, its call for a form of "just vengeance" conflicts with theological ideals like mercy, redemption, and forgiveness (Forrester, 1997; Gorringe, 1996; Marshall, 2001).

[...]

One essential element of retribution is fair application: those who cause the same type of harm and are equally culpable should receive the same dose of punishment. As with other aspects of juvenile and criminal justice, however, Justitia's blindfold seems permeable to race in cases of JLWOP: 56% of JLWOP prisoners are Black, and in many states the proportion exceeds 60% (Nellis & King, 2009). Black youth serve JLWOP sentences at a rate that is tenfold that of White youth (Human Rights Watch, 2005).

Proportionality is a key requirement for retribution that is debatable in the case of JLWOP. A central tenet of proportionality is that a sentence "must correspond to the crime—not just to the harm caused by the offense, but also to the culpability of the offender" (Logan, 1998, p. 707). Since the U.S. Supreme Court abolished the death penalty for crimes committed by juveniles (*Roper v. Christopher Simmons*, 2005), JLWOP is the most severe form of criminal punishment that can be imposed for juvenile crime. Ordinal proportionality is achieved only if the most severe punishment is imposed on the most horrendous criminals. Though approximately 93% of JLWOP sentences are imposed for crimes of homicide, 59% of JLWOP sentences are for the person's very first conviction (Human Rights Watch, 2005). Also, 16% are for crimes committed by youth between the ages of 13 and 15 (Leighton & de la Vega, 2007).

Cardinal proportionality is one of the most serious issues with regard to JLWOP: is this severe degree of punishment morally appropriate for crimes committed during minority, in terms of minors' culpability? Psychological and biological research increasingly demonstrates the incomplete psycho-social development of adolescents. Teens exhibit "immature judgment—the tendency...to make choices that may be harmful to themselves or others" (Scott & Steinberg, 2003, p. 811). Their inclination toward risk and sensation-seeking rises through ages 16 and 17, then decreases significantly (Feld, 2007). Adolescent judgment is strongly affected by peer orientation, attitudes toward risk perception, temporal perspective (lack of future orientation), and capacity for self-management (impulsivity, sensation-seeking, and moodiness) (Scott & Steinberg, 2003).

The frontal lobe of the brain regulates emotions and impulses and assists with long-term planning and evaluations of risk and reward. Its development progresses throughout adolescence. Concomitantly, development of the limbic system may precipitate exceptional emotionality and susceptibility to stress (Scott & Steinberg, 2003).

Adolescents also explore and experiment with a variety of behaviors as part of the process of identity development. The teen years commonly involve "risky, illegal, or dangerous activities" (Scott & Steinberg, 2003, p. 819). Because the adolescent's character is incomplete, it would seem inappropriate to conclude that a given adolescent is hopelessly depraved, a judgment that is inherent in a sentence of JLWOP:

> Youths are more impulsive and seek novel and exciting experiences. They are short-sighted and prefer immediate rewards to delayed gratification. They misperceive and miscalculate risks and discount the likelihood of adverse consequences. They are more vulnerable and susceptible to negative peer and environmental influences. Although adolescents'

cognitive abilities compare favorably with adults', they do not develop mature judgment and self-control until early adulthood. (Feld, 2007, pp. 57–58)

Though the literature demonstrates from a macro perspective that JLWOP is a significant sociolegal and ethico-legal issue, there is scant micro-level empirical research, i.e., studies among those who are the subjects of this type of punishment: so-called "juvenile lifers."[3] The present research is an attempt to begin to address that lacuna.

Few studies examine the lives and experiences of juvenile lifers in a scholarly way; most current works are prepared for advocacy purposes. The present study was undertaken largely out of a sense of genuine ethical puzzlement: why is so extreme a punishment (categorical banishment from the free world until death, which in these cases is apt to cover a very long time period, regardless of any positive changes in the individual) visited upon persons whose neurological, psychological, and social development is commonly agreed to be incomplete?

All unjustified, unexcused killings of human beings are supremely reprehensible, but what is it about juvenile lifers' crimes that merits an absolute societal cessation of all hope for them, since that same penalty obviously is not applied to all—including adults—who are involved in similar killings? Were these adolescents' lives so extremely dysfunctional and malignant that they truly approached the atavistic super-predators of lore? Alternatively, or perhaps in combination, were there lapses or irregularities in criminal justice processes that were fateful to this particular group of juveniles, leading to or appreciably impacting their ultimate, permanent exile from the moral community? The most authentic way to begin to address these questions is in face-to-face, systematic conversation with those who live the realities every day.

METHOD

The field research for this study was conducted at the largest men's prison in a northeastern state. The prison, located outside a major city, holds prisoners with a variety of security classifications, including maximum security. This particular research was embedded in a larger study of prisoners who had experienced juvenile justice as youth.

The prison had no record of which prisoners were "juvenile lifers." Prison psychologists were able to identify a couple prisoners they knew to be juvenile lifers, and those prisoners provided the names of others. Thus, of necessity, the nonprobability sample was purposive and involved snowball sampling (Singleton & Straits, 2005). For each participant, the author was permitted to access the automated case summary in the prison's information system, but the summaries were usually sketchy and often incomplete, and they provided little useful information beyond basic demographics.

Each potential participant was issued a "call out" sheet by the prison's psychology department to report to the psychology treatment area at a particular time. (The prison specified that the research was to be conducted through its psychology department.) The author met with each man individually, explained the study and its purpose of understanding the experiences of prisoners who had experienced juvenile justice, and inquired whether the prisoner wished to participate. It was made clear that the study concerned only the prisoner's juvenile experiences, not his adult life. Participants then signed a consent form approved by the prison and the university institutional review board.

The sample of 11 prisoners ranged in age from 23 to 50. The mean age was 35; the median age was 34. Seven participants were Black; three were biracial (Black/White); and one was Latino.

Two individual interviews were scheduled with each participant. All interviews were with the author, alone with the participant, in an office with a closed door. The interviews were conducted in the prison's psychology department, usually in one of the prison psychiatrists' or psychiatric nurses' offices when they were not in. The interviews were conducted from November 2007 through January 2008. Each participant was interviewed at least twice, and each interview lasted approximately one hour.

The interviews were in-depth, semistructured, and highly open-ended (Ashkar & Kenny, 2008; Hesse-Biber & Leavy, 2007). Each participant was asked to describe his youth: his home and school experiences, his friends, his dreams for the future, his experiences of getting in trouble with the law as a minor (discussed chronologically), who or what was important to him as a youth, and whether he felt he was treated fairly in juvenile justice processes. Additionally he was asked about his present views of juvenile justice, including whether anything might be done to improve it.

The second interview with each participant was primarily a validity check: the author summarized his understanding of what the participant had said during the first interview, asked for clarification and elaboration on issues that were unclear, and allowed the participant to add any new information that was relevant. Throughout the interview processes, the author strove to remain sensitive to the moral and methodological challenges of working with members of vulnerable populations such as these men (Liamputtong, 2007).

[...]

FINDINGS

A variety of generalizations can be drawn from the experiences of the 11 juvenile lifers. Nine were raised by a single parent, usually a mother but sometimes a grandmother. Traumatic home environments were common, usually including the effects of major poverty, and 5 left home, usually by running away and usually in their early teens. Illustrative comments are:

> My mom was using cocaine. She had mood swings... My brother always sold drugs. We'd fight. He'd accuse me of taking the drugs, but later I realized my mom was taking them. (Thomas[4])

> My mom died when I was 15. That took a toll on me; the whole mindframe was "F- the world." I lost myself in drugs, money, and alcohol. (Matthew)

Most commonly the most important person in the youth's life was a female, usually his mother. Male role models were almost entirely absent. When the youths did look up to males, it was usually their friends on the street.

Seven participants explained that they had stopped going to school, usually while in 7th to 10th grade. Most commonly they had been increasingly truant and then simply ceased attending school. Usually they dropped out for the fast life of the streets. Their comments suggest a prevalence of (possibly untreated) learning and/or emotional disabilities that made school generally unappealing for them. Four participants specifically discussed serious mental illness, multiple suicide attempts, and/or inpatient hospitalizations for mental illness.[5]

Though many had attended church services and were ostensibly part of a Christian faith tradition during childhood, nearly all became alienated from religion during adolescence. Even during childhood, religion often seemed more external (e.g., forced attendance at church) than internalized.

The dream of excelling in athletics (e.g., rollerblading, boxing, baseball, football) inspired many of the youth in their early- through midteens. Often much of the youths' free time was devoted to sports practice in the hope of achieving their ambitions.

With regard to friendships, four participants emphasized that as youth they tended to associate with persons much older than themselves. The older youth/

young adults often served as role models, usually for the worse. Nearly all participants explained that their friends had a major influence on their own criminality. Representative comments are:

> I had much older friends. The older guys always said no matter what you do, they can't lock you up because you're so young. For example, they let me carry the guns. (Thomas)

> At 9 to 10 years old, I was the littlest member of the neighborhood gang; the oldest guy was 16. The crack dealers wanted kids to sell it. A friend of my older brother—a neighborhood hustler—knew pushers, and he put my name in the mix. (Philip)

> At 13 years old, I caught my first auto theft. I learned from another kid in the neighborhood... My friends absolutely influenced me getting into trouble. I felt like the odd man out. They were making $3,000 to $4,000 a week. (James)

The majority acknowledged that they were using illegal drugs, particularly marijuana, in their early years. Most commonly they started using marijuana at age 13–14 or at age 9–10.

With regard to whether the participants as juveniles were treated fairly by the police, only two participants reported that they had been "roughed up" by the police. However, six participants discussed what they perceived as psychological mistreatment during interrogation. Often they reported that they wish they had realized not to speak without having a lawyer present, and/or that they felt strongly intimidated at the time. Representative comments are:

> I went to the police station with my mom when I heard they were looking for me. I knew of my rights from TV, but at the time, I thought I didn't do anything, so I'll talk to them. I didn't think I needed a lawyer. (Andrew)

> I wasn't given the *Miranda* warnings at the police station because they said I wasn't under arrest. As a kid, I didn't think I could leave. I was there from 9 a.m. to 11 p.m. (James)

> The police did "good cop/bad cop." One threatened me about life in prison and sexual abuse in prison. Then the "good cop" said he'd just put me down as a witness to the crime. I trusted the "good cop"; he was like a godsend. I confessed. (John)

Among participants who had experiences in juvenile court, all expressed that they were baffled by the court proceedings. Representative comments are:

All I know is just talk, talk, talk. All I was saying was "all right, okay."
(Matthew)

You don't have the slightest idea what's being said; they talking back
and forth. (Bartholomew)

All participants experienced adult court when they were juveniles, at least for
the case that led to each youth's life sentence. In addition to their continuing lack
of comprehension of the proceedings, nearly all participants were highly critical
of the legal representation they had received, particularly their lawyers' degree
of involvement in their cases. Representative comments are:

My court-appointed lawyer told me he and the D.A. [District Attorney]
were best friends. (Matthew)

I only saw my lawyer twice before trial: at the preliminary hearing
and arraignment. There was no investigation or expert by my lawyer.
My lawyer didn't even put on a case: as soon as the prosecutor rested, he
rested. (Andrew)

At least four participants did not adequately comprehend the implications of
a sentence of life without parole. Commonly they faulted defense counsel for the
misunderstanding. For example:

My lawyer had me believe I'd serve 10–15 years [if I plead guilty and got
"life"]. The lawyer later said she made some mistakes early in her career.
(Peter)

My lawyer didn't explain "life sentence." Court-appointed lawyers,
they be with the D.A. The D.A. offered 10–20 years, but that seemed
too long. I couldn't see that far, thinking "I be a grown man when I get
out." (Jude)

[...]

DISCUSSION

Tragedy and turmoil are pervasive in the lives of most of the participants as
juveniles. Poverty with all of its attendant disadvantages is a major influence in
nearly all their young lives. Common also are family disruption and dysfunction,
as well as learning and behavioral challenges at school. Alienated from mainstream values represented by school and faith-traditions, the youth often found
meaning in associations with friends on the street, including older "homies" who
facilitated their initiation into illegality. Commonly this included substance abuse

very early in adolescence. Another form of escapism for them was embodied in dreams of athletic excellence.

The individual and social maladies the youth experience are not "causes" of their criminality in any deterministic sense, nor do their life experiences "excuse" their criminality. Obviously, most persons in similar situations do not become involved in criminal homicides. Nevertheless, it is valuable to recognize life circumstances like poverty, family disruption, learning challenges, social alienation, and substance abuse as *sources* for criminality, in that persons who face them are more apt to find themselves arrested, convicted, and incarcerated than those who do not (Reiman & Leighton, 2010). Though social disadvantage cannot "explain" criminality, it can certainly lend it context.

The human lives which the youth were involved in extinguishing—some very directly, some very remotely—represent annihilations that, in moral, legal, and social senses, are wrong. A core normative question posed by this research is whether those victims and society itself are best served by sentences of JLWOP.

Aside from the markedly challenged social and personal backgrounds of most participants, the research raises troubling issues about legal procedural justice: interrogation procedures that play on a youth's immaturity (see also, e.g., Feld, 2006; Rogers, Hazelwood, Sewell, Shuman, & Blackwood, 2008; Scott-Hayward, 2007); defense counsel whose efforts are incommensurate with the drastic sentence their clients potentially face; and lack of clarity in ensuring that youths comprehend the "without parole" element of JLWOP. With serious deficiencies in procedural due process such as these, the imposition of a uniquely drastic sentence as JLWOP should give pause.

The two cases grouped in star-crossed first-offenders seem to raise most starkly the ethico-legal issue of whether the sentence of JLWOP is proportional to the culpability of the offender: there is a total absence of prior criminal record, and there are a variety of factors that diminish the youth's blameworthiness, at least in comparison with how an adult would be seen as culpable in the same circumstances. Likewise, the five cases categorized as drug-addicted robbers reflect indubitably horrendous takings of human life, but the youths' compromised mental states and lack of prior serious violence would seem to militate against imposition of the most severe sentence.

The four cases described as retaliatory assaulters would seem to merit the highest levels of punishment in a retributive sense. Here there are the fewest extenuating circumstances, and the youth have a history of violence. Arguably, JLWOP would be appropriate, but still there remain indicia of juvenile immaturity and procedural shortcomings that counsel prudence before imposing so extreme a punishment.

Retaliatory assaulters may represent what proponents of JLWOP describe as a group of juveniles who "has been aggressive and antisocial from childhood and is likely to continue offending throughout the life course" (*Terrance Graham v. Florida, and Joe Sullivan v. Florida*, 2009, p. 17). Such a trajectory is purportedly "fixed" prior to adulthood, though it is difficult to identify clinically during the teen years. Proponents dispute ideas of brain immaturity in teens, preferring instead the notion that dangerous teens result from "society treating physically mature young people as if they were children, denying them adult responsibility and status" (*Terrance Graham v. Florida, and Joe Sullivan v. Florida*, 2009, p. 19).

Feld (2007, p. 64) notes that appellate courts generally do not apply full proportionality analyses in assessing JLWOP sentences:

> Although penal proportionality requires a principled relationship between the seriousness of a crime—harm and culpability—and the sentence imposed, courts focus exclusively on the gravity of the crime—harm—rather than the culpability of the actor when they conduct proportionality analyses.

Likewise, he explains that while youthfulness is a mitigating factor in death-penalty cases, it is commonly treated as an aggravating factor in sentencing minors for noncapital homicide.

Perhaps the major moral difficulty lies in the fact that youth in all three categories received the same sentence. In the state in which this study was conducted, JLWOP seems to sweep broadly, gathering significantly divergent cases into its ambit.

An invidious factor in understanding JLWOP sentences is race. All of the participants here are men of color, and nationally judges impose JLWOP on Blacks at a rate 10 times higher than on Whites (Human Rights Watch, 2005). Racial disparity is endemic to juvenile justice and becomes more concentrated as one progresses through the system (Feld, 2003). Scott and Steinberg (2003, p. 809) state that "[a] troubling explanation for the puzzling hostility toward young law violators is that attitudes are driven by racial and ethnic bias." If Black youth are seen as a social threat, it is easier to discount their immaturity and view them as more deserving of serious punishment. Ironically, this inverts the substantial research indicating that neighborhood disadvantage, neighborhood violence, and experience with racial discrimination foster later violent behavior in youth who adopt a "code of the street" (National Institute of Justice, 2009).

In its imposition on minors who commonly have histories that include severe family dysfunction, economic disadvantage, multiple trauma, and learning challenges, the morality of JLWOP is suspect. When adolescent psycho-social immaturity and propensity to risk are considered, the moral issues are compounded, especially when minors are sentenced more severely than their adult counterparts. If there are significant disparities in its use involving factors like geography and race, and if juveniles are not routinely afforded the legal protections due them in criminal cases, the ethical impediments to imposing JLWOP are substantial.

The physical, psychological, and social deprivations of imprisonment are profound. Simply on the basis of chronology, they are apt to be experienced longer by juveniles given life without parole than by similarly sentenced adults. Philosopher John Stuart Mill contended that life imprisonment is a punishment worse than even the death penalty:

> What comparison can there really be, in point of severity, between consigning a man to the short pang of a rapid death, and immuring him in a living tomb, there to linger out what may be a long life in the hardest and most monotonous toil, without any of its alleviations or rewards… (quoted in Steffen, 1998, p. 61)

JLWOP involves none of the therapeutic or transformative elements valued by moral philosophies such as virtue ethics (Sellers & Arrigo, 2009). It simply banishes a minor from free society for the duration of their natural life, without any regard for significant beneficial changes that can occur in a person's life over a span of many years. As far as society is concerned, the sentence extinguishes all hope. Proponents of JLWOP note that the possibility of clemency exists (Brief *amicus curiae* of the Criminal Justice Legal Foundation in *Terrance Graham v. Florida*, and *Joe Sullivan v. Florida*, 2009), though the actual use of clemency by elected executives would likely be exceedingly rare for any life-sentenced prisoner, short of clear evidence of actual innocence.

The present research draws upon the lived experience—in all its complexity—of a small set of juvenile lifers, recording their stories related to juvenile justice. Analyzing their narratives provides a rich understanding of sources of criminality as well as deviance within criminal processes. Obviously there is no warranty that the 11 participants are representative of all juvenile lifers, but the authenticity and detail that are possible in this type of research are easily lost in larger studies. The population is difficult to access, and institutional protocols such as prohibitions on electronic recordation are impediments.

Some will question the truth of the participants' stories. The research relies heavily on memories, which can be selective and faulty. The social constructivist nature of the research prioritizes credibility as a primary component of internal validity; the major goal is to ensure that the results are an accurate interpretation of the participants' own meaning of their experiences (Creswell, 2007). The member checking that was an integral part of the research method was intended to foster authenticity and believability in gauging whether the data gathered were "true" as far as each participant interpreted his own experiences. Memories, even faulty ones, can define human realities. As Thomas and Thomas (1929) famously observed: situations that we define as real are real in their consequences.

For the author, there was no clear indication that any participant was intentionally fabricating or dissembling. Indeed, many participants willingly discussed youthful illegalities that had not come to the attention of the police, and some referred to news articles that corroborated their accounts of their cases. Importantly, as Presser (2009, p. 181) notes, "the suspicion that offenders' stories are strategically pitched and thus potentially inauthentic belies a view of stories as social artifacts for some, when they are social artifacts for all."

The extinguishment of the lives of the victims in these homicide cases is supremely tragic and immutable. There is no doubt that the youth involved in the killings merit criminal punishment. Now that the death penalty for juveniles is unconstitutional, it is impossible to achieve a *quid pro quo* in terms of these crimes and their punishment. Though JLWOP is presently the most severe sanction that can be imposed, the social, geographic, and legal parameters of its use raise difficult ethical questions. Those issues are exacerbated by the developmental immaturity of youth and by the extreme length of the sentence when applied to juveniles. The themes that resonate through the experiences of the participants in the present study would seem to counsel that it may be preferable to preserve at least a flicker of hope, acknowledging that every person is somehow better than the worst thing he has ever done.

NOTES

1. If persons sentenced to life-without-parole (LWOP) for crimes committed as adults are added to this number, in total there are nearly 41,100 persons serving LWOP. In aggregate, the number of LWOP prisoners tripled between 1992 and 2008 (Nellis & King, 2009).

2. While erroneous convictions in capital cases have received more attention (e.g., Prejean, 2005), such errors may be more common in LWOP cases, which do not entail the "super due process" protections and level of review mandated for capital cases (Fagan, 2007; Mauer, King, & Young, 2004).

3. Though it is not academic research, the documentary film *When Kids Get Life* (Bikel, 2007), provides an in-depth examination of the experiences of a set of "juvenile lifers" in Colorado, and it has appreciably impacted public policy in that state.

4. All participants are given pseudonyms to protect confidentiality.

5. In accord with the phenomenological nature of this study, statements about the psycho-social status of participants are based strictly on participants' own descriptions of their life experiences. No standardized assessment instruments were used as part of the present study.

REFERENCES

Appleton, C., & Grover, B. (2007). The pros and cons of life without parole. *British Journal of Criminology, 47*, 597–615.

Ashkar, P. J., & Kenny, D. T. (2008). Views from the inside: Young offenders' subjective experiences of incarceration. *International Journal of Offender Therapy & Comparative Criminology, 52*, 584–597.

Beckett, K., & Sasson, T. (2004). *The politics of injustice: Crime and punishment in America* (2nd ed.). Thousand Oaks, CA: Sage.

Bikel, O. (Producer). (2007). *When kids get life* [Motion picture]. United States: WGBH Educational Foundation (PBS Frontline).

Cohen, S. (1980). *Folk devils and moral panics: The creation of the Mods and the Rockers*. New York, NY: St. Martin's Press.

Creswell, J. W. (2007). *Qualitative inquiry and research design: Choosing among five approaches*. Thousand Oaks, CA: Sage.

Densmore, J., & Walhberg, M. (Producers). (2004). *Juvies* [Motion picture]. United States: Chance Films.

deYoung, M. (1998). Another look at moral panics: The case of Satanic day care centers. *Deviant Behavior, 19*, 257–278.

Equal Justice Initiative. (2007). *Cruel and unusual: Sentencing 13- and 14-year old children to die in prison*. Montgomery, AL: Equal Justice Initiative.

Fagan, J. (2007). End natural life sentences for juveniles. *Criminology & Public Policy, 6*, 735–746.

Feld, B. C. (2003). The politics of race and juvenile justice: The "due process revolution" and the conservative reaction. *Justice Quarterly, 20*, 765–800.

Feld, B. C. (2006). Police interrogation of juveniles: An empirical study of policy and practice. *Journal of Criminal Law & Criminology, 97*, 219–286.

Feld, B. C. (2007). Unmitigated punishment: Adolescent criminal responsibility and LWOP sentences. *Journal of Law & Family Studies, 10*, 11–82.

Fletcher, G. P. (1980/1981). Reflections on felony-murder. *Southwestern University Law Review, 12*, 413–429.

Flynn, E. H. (2008). Dismantling the felony-murder role: Juvenile deterrence and retribution post-*Roper v. Simmons. University of Pennsylvania Law Review, 156*, 1049–1076.

Forrester, D. B. (1997). *Christian justice and public policy*. New York, NY: Cambridge University Press.

Gibson, W. J., & Brown, A. (2009). *Working with qualitative data*. Thousand Oaks, CA: Sage.

Goode, E., & Ben-Yehuda, N. (1994). *Moral panics: The social construction of deviance*. Cambridge, MA: Blackwell.

Gorringe, T. (1996). *God's just vengeance: Crime, violence, and the rhetoric of salvation*. New York, NY: Cambridge University Press.

Hassine, V. (2009). *Life without parole: Living in prison today* (4th ed.). New York, NY: Oxford University Press.

Hesse-Biber, S. N., & Leavy, P. L. (2007). *Feminist research practice: A primer*. Thousand Oaks, CA: Sage.

Human Rights Watch. (2005). *The rest of their lives: Life without parole for child offenders in the United States*. New York, NY: Human Rights Watch.

International Covenant on Civil & Political Rights. (1966). Retrieved March 21, 2010, from http://www2.ohchr.org/english/law/ccpr.htm

Johnson, R., & McGunigall-Smith, S. (2008). Life without parole, America's other death penalty: Notes on life under sentence of death by incarceration. *Prison Journal, 88,* 328–346.

Kappeler, V. E., & Potter, G. W. (2005). *The mythology of crime and criminal justice* (4th ed.) Long Grove, IL: Waveland.

Leighton, M., & de la Vega, C. (2007). *Sentencing our children to die in prison: Global law and practice.* San Francisco, CA: Center for Law & Global Justice (University of San Francisco School of Law).

Liamputtong, P. (2007). *Researching the vulnerable.* Thousand Oaks, CA: Sage.

Logan, E. (1999). Furor over crack babies. *Social Justice, 26,* 115–137.

Logan, W. A. (1998). Proportionality and punishment: Imposing life without parole on juveniles. *Wake Forest Law Review, 33,* 681–725.

Marshall, C. D. (2001). *Beyond retribution: A New Testament vision for justice, crime, and punishment.* Grand Rapids, MI: William B. Eerdmans.

Mauer, M., King, R. S., & Young, M. C. (2004). *The meaning of "life": Long prison sentences in context.* Washington, DC: The Sentencing Project.

Morris Kent v. U.S., 383 U.S. 541 (1966).

National Institute of Justice. (2009). *The code of the street and African–American adolescent violence* (No. NCJ 223509). Washington, DC: National Institute of Justice.

Nellis, A., & King, R. S. (2009). *No exit: The expanding use of life sentences in America.* Washington, DC: The Sentencing Project.

Paluch, J. A. Jr. (2004). *Life for a life: Life imprisonment: America's other death penalty.* Los Angeles, CA: Roxbury.

Platt, A. M. (1977). *The child savers: The invention of delinquency* (2nd ed., Enlarged). Chicago, IL: University of Chicago Press.

Prejean, H. (2005). *The death of innocents: An eyewitness account of wrongful executions.* New York, NY: Random House.

Presser, L. (2009). The narratives of offenders. *Theoretical Criminology, 13,* 177–200.

Reiman, J., & Leighton, P. (2010). *The rich get richer and the poor get prison: Ideology, class, and criminal justice* (9th ed.) Boston, MA: Allyn & Bacon.

Reinarman, C. (1988). Social construction of an alcohol problem: The case of Mothers Against Drunk Drivers and social control in the 1980s. *Theory & Society, 17,* 91–120.

Rogers, R., Hazelwood, L. L., Sewell, K. W., Shuman, D. W., & Blackwood, H. L. (2008). The comprehensibility and content of juvenile *Miranda* warnings. *Psychology, Public Policy & Law, 14,* 63–86.

Roper v. Christopher Simmons, 543 U.S. 551 (2005).

Scott, E. S., & Steinberg, L. (2003). Blaming youth. *Texas Law Review, 81,* 799–840.

Scott-Hayward, C. S. (2007). Explaining juvenile false confessions: Adolescent development and police interrogation. *Law & Psychology Review, 31,* 53–76.

Sellers, B. G., & Arrigo, B. A. (2009). Adolescent transfer, developmental maturity, and adjudicative competency: An ethical and justice policy inquiry. *Journal of Criminal Law & Criminology, 99,* 435–487.

Schneider, E. C. (1992). *In the web of class: Delinquents and reformers in Boston, 1810s–1930s.* New York, NY: New York University Press.

Singleton, R. A. Jr., & Straits, B. C. (2005). *Approaches to social research* (4th ed.). New York, NY: Oxford University Press.

Steffen, L. (1998). *Executing justice: The moral meaning of the death penalty.* Cleveland, OH: Pilgrim Press.

Stimson, C. D., & Grossman, A. M. (2009). *Adult time for adult crimes: Life without parole for juvenile killers and violent teens.* Washington, DC: The Heritage Foundation.

Terrance Graham v. Florida, & Joe Sullivan v. Florida. (2009). *Brief amicus curiae of the Criminal Justice Legal Foundation.* Washington, DC: U.S. Supreme Court.

Thomas, W. I., & Thomas, D. (1929). *The child in America* (2nd ed.). New York, NY: Alfred Knopf.

UNICEF website. (2010). Retrieved March 21, 2010, from http://www.uni.org/crc/index_30229.html

United Nations Convention on the Rights of the Child. (1989). Retrieved March 21, 2010, from http://www2.ohchr.org/english/law/crc.htm

United Nations Treaty Collection website. (1992). Retrieved March 21, 2010, from http://treaties.un.org/Pages/ViewDetails.aspx?src=TREATY&mtdsg_no=IV-4&lang=en#EndDec

Villaume, A. C. (2005). "Life without parole" and "virtual life sentences": Death sentences by any other name. *Contemporary Justice Review, 8,* 265–277.

Zatz, M. S. (1987). Chicano youth gangs and crime: The creation of a moral panic. *Contemporary Crisis, 2,* 129–158.

***Frank Butler** is a professor of criminal justice at La Salle University, Philadelphia.

Butler, Frank. "Extinguishing All Hope: Life-Without-Parole for Juveniles." *Journal of Offender Rehabilitation* 49 (2010): 273–292.

Life Without Parole for Children

*by Victor Streib and Bernadette Schrempp**

What should we do with a child who commits a violent crime, particularly murder? Must our sentence be based on the crime and thus ignore the youthfulness of the offender? Or can we sentence the child and moderate our demands for retribution for violent crime? A related question is whether we should just lock them up and throw away the key. Can we accurately predict what today's violent adolescents will be like when they are middle-aged adults? Although some justifications may be found for sentencing career adult criminals to life in prison without parole (LWOP), what about youngsters under age 18 who are still works in progress?

In the sea of criminal sentencing, LWOP for mere children may be comparatively rare but still numbers in the thousands. The vast majority of LWOP sentences for children are for crimes of murder, and this ultimate crime is the primary focus of this article. Some cases catch the attention of the media, such as that of Cameron Kocher, a nine-year-old, fourth-grade Cub Scout, arraigned for a 1989 murder and facing LWOP. (*Commonwealth v. Kocher*, 602 A.2d 1308 (Pa. 1992).) At the same time on the West Coast, a Washington trial court sentenced 13-year-old Raymond Massey to LWOP for a robbery-murder. (*State v. Massey*, 803 P.2d 340 (Wash. Ct. Ap. 1990).) More recently in Florida, 12-year-old Lionel Tate was sentenced to LWOP for murder. (*Tate v. State*, 864 So. 2d 44 (Fla. App. 4 Dist. 2003).)

Very serious delinquent and criminal offenses of youthful offenders often result in visceral demands for the harshest punishments. But in situations such as those above, were the laws really meant to include this type of offender? These punitive demands may lead us to forget that, no matter how adult-like the offense may be, the youthful offender is not an adult. This article proposes that sentences for youthful offenders recognize that key fact and not simply impose an adult sanction upon a child. Two primary reasons exist for this principle. First, youthful offenders are less culpable than adult offenders, simply because of the innate characteristics of their youthfulness. This basic premise has been repeatedly recognized by the United States Supreme Court, most recently in *Roper v. Simmons*, 543 U.S. 551, 567 (2005). That Court also expressly approved of key mitigating considerations in sentencing youth offenders, all of which suggest the appropriateness of less harsh punishments. This article recommends, therefore, that juvenile and criminal sentences for youthful offenders be generally less punitive than they are for adult offenders convicted of committing the same offenses.

Second, a fundamental characteristic of youthful offenders, certainly as compared to adult offenders, is their potential for growth and maturation into nonthreatening, productive citizens. This growth potential counters the instinct to sentence youthful offenders to long terms of incarceration in order to ensure public safety. Whatever the appropriateness of parole eligibility for 40-year-old career criminals serving several life sentences, quite different issues are raised for 14-year-old, first-time offenders sentenced to prison. They may have committed essentially the same acts and have been convicted of the same offenses, but 14-year-olds, certainly as compared to 40-yearolds, are almost certain to undergo dramatic personality changes as they mature from adolescence to middle age. Sentences for such offenders should not conclude today what kind of adults these adolescents will be many years from now. As any parent knows, predicting what teenagers will become by next week, let alone when they are adults, is nearly impossible. That key decision should wait until adolescents have reached adulthood and can be assessed more accurately. If they have evolved into promising and nonthreatening adults, strong consideration should be given to various forms of release on parole.

CURRENT STATUS OF SENTENCING MITIGATION FACTORS

The very youthfulness of juvenile offenders is well established as grounds for imposing less severe punishments, even when juveniles commit the most serious crimes. Indeed, this principle of lesser culpability undergirds the earliest juvenile court systems. As juvenile rights and responsibilities have been adjudicated over the last century, this premise typically has been assumed.

The United States Supreme Court has long accepted the assumption of lesser culpability for juvenile offenders and the proposition that youth by itself mitigates even the most serious crimes. The Court confirmed this basic premise on March 1, 2005, in the landmark juvenile sentencing case, *Roper v. Simmons*, observing once again that there is "sufficient evidence that today our society views juveniles ... as 'categorically less culpable than the average criminal.'" (*Id.* at 567.) The *Simmons* Court identified three distinct reasons why juvenile offenders cannot be reliably classified as among the worst offenders:

First, as any parent knows and as the scientific and sociological studies respondent and his amici cite tend to confirm, "[a] lack of maturity and an underdeveloped sense of responsibility are found in youth more often than in adults and are more understandable among the young.

These qualities often result in impetuous and ill-considered actions and decisions."

It has been noted that "adolescents are overrepresented statistically in virtually every category of reckless behavior."

The second area of difference is that juveniles are more vulnerable or susceptible to negative influences and outside pressures including peer pressure. This is explained in part by the prevailing circumstance that juveniles have less control, or less experience with control, over their own environment.

The third broad difference is that the character of a juvenile is not as well formed as that of an adult.

The personality traits of juveniles are more transitory, less fixed.

These differences render suspect any conclusion that a juvenile falls among the worst offenders. The susceptibility of juveniles to immature and irresponsible behavior means "their irresponsible conduct is not as morally reprehensible as that of an adult." Their own vulnerability and comparative lack of control over their immediate surroundings mean juveniles have a greater claim than adults to be forgiven for failing to escape negative influences in their whole environment. (Id. at 569–70.) (Internal citations excluded.)

The Court's observations are supported by an increasingly large body of scientific research. Psychologists attribute the differences between adolescents and adults to both cognitive factors (children think differently than adults) and psychosocial factors (children lack developed social and emotional capabilities). (See Elizabeth Cauffman and Laurence Steinberg, (Im)maturity of Judgment in Adolescence: Why Adolescents May Be Less Culpable Than Adults, 18 BEHAV. SCI. & L. 742 (2000).) Research shows that adolescent thinking is oriented to the present and largely overlooks consequences or implications. Other research shows that children tend to make decisions based on emotions, such as anger or fear, to a much greater extent than do adults. (See Thomas Grisso, What We Know About Youth's Capacities, in YOUTH ON TRIAL: A DEVELOPMENTAL PERSPECTIVE ON JUVENILE JUSTICE 267 (Thomas Grisso and Robert G. Schwartz eds., 2000).) This is particularly true in stressful situations.

More recently, neuroscientists using magnetic resonance imaging have provided a physiological basis for these adolescent behaviors. There are dramatic differences between the brains of adolescents and those of adults. Studies show that the brain continues to develop into the twenties, and this is particularly true of physiological developmental processes relating to judgment and impulse-control. (*See, e.g.,* Elizabeth R. Sowell et al., *Mapping Continued Brain Growth and Gray Matter Density Reduction in Dorsal Frontal Cortex: Inverse Relation-ships During Postadolescent Brain Maturation,* 21 J. NEUROSCIENCE, 8,821 (2001).) Researchers have found that the parts of the brain in the frontal lobe associated with regulating aggression, long-range planning, abstract thinking, and, perhaps, even moral judgment are not sufficiently developed in adolescents to support these functions. These parts of the brain are not fully developed until adult-hood. (ELKHONON GOLDBERG, THE EXECUTIVE BRAIN: FRONTAL LOBES AND THE CIVILIZED MIND 434 (2001).) Because they lack frontal lobe functions, adoles-cents tend to make decisions using the amygdala, a part of the brain associated with impulsive and aggressive behavior. (*See* Jan Glascher and Ralph Adolphs, *Processing of the Arousal of Subliminal Emotional Stimuli by the Human Amygdala,* 23 J. NEUROSCIENCE 10,274 (2003).)

In *Simmons,* the Court took into account the diminished culpability of juve-niles under the age of 18 in concluding that the two penological justifications for the death penalty applied to them with lesser force than to adults. The Court reasoned that the reduced culpability of juvenile offenders requires a correspond-ingly lower severity of punishment to meet retributive aims. Similarly, it recog-nized that juvenile offenders are less likely to engage in any cost-benefit analysis weighing the possibility of such harsh sentences, thereby reducing the deterrent value of harsh sentences.

Moreover, as the *Simmons* Court also recognized, the relative importance of rehabilitative aims are increased when considering the treatment of juvenile offenders because the rehabilitative potential of youth is intrinsically greater:

> The reality that juveniles still struggle to define their identity means it
> is less supportable to conclude that even a heinous crime committed by
> a juvenile is evidence of irretrievably depraved character. From a moral
> standpoint it would be misguided to equate the failings of a minor with
> those of an adult, for a greater possibility exists that a minor's character
> deficiencies will be reformed. Indeed, "[t]he relevance of youth as a miti-
> gating factor derives from the fact that the signature qualities of youth
> are transient; as individuals mature, the impetuousness and recklessness
> that may dominate in younger years can subside." (*Simmons,* 543 U.S. at
> 570.)

This consideration applies with equal force to all sentences for juvenile offend-ers, from the death penalty and life in prison without parole to much less severe sentences.

CURRENT STATUS OF PAROLE ELIGIBILITY

All jurisdictions permit trying youthful offenders in adult criminal court where they can and do receive adult sentences. Although these adult sentences no longer include the death penalty, essentially every other criminal sentence is available. Indeed, one of the political arguments to abolish the death penalty for juveniles was that they would remain eligible for LWOP, a sufficiently harsh punishment even without the death penalty. This LWOP eligibility was expressly noted by the Court in *Roper v. Simmons*. Juvenile LWOP has been around for some time but grew substantially during the 1990s. (Wayne A. Logan, *Proportionality and Punishment: Imposing Life Without Parole on Juveniles*, 33 WAKE FORREST L. REV. 681 (1998).) As of 2002, an estimated 2,225 prison inmates were serving life in prison without parole for crimes they had committed when under age 18. (*The Rest of Their Lives: Life Without Parole for Child Offenders in the United States*, HUM. RTS. WATCH (Amnesty Int'l (2005).)

This growth in the use of LWOP for juvenile offenders has occurred during the time period in which violent juvenile crime rates are decreasing. The National Center for Juvenile Justice reports that juvenile crime levels have been falling since the 1980s, stating that "[i]n 2002, the number of murders by juveniles dropped to its lowest level since 1984." (*Juvenile Offenders and Victims: 2006 National Report* at 65). Further, in about 39 percent of murders involving juveniles, the juvenile offenders acted with an adult. (*Id.* at 66.) This fact supports the conclusion that in many instances, the child acts subject to outside influence when committing crimes.

Federal constitutionality issues. Last year marked the end of the practice of giving the death penalty to juvenile offenders. Such sentences had been rare and, according to a 1982 Supreme Court ruling, had to overcome strong considerations of youthfulness: "[T]he chronological age of a minor is itself a relevant mitigating factor of great weight." (*Eddings v. Oklahoma*, 455 U.S. 104, 116 (1982).) In 1988, the Court held in *Thompson v. Oklahoma*, 487 U.S. 815 (1988), that the death penalty for juvenile offenders under age 16 is cruel and unusual under the Eighth Amendment. However, the Court the next year declined to extend that minimum eligibility to age 18. (*Stanford v. Kentucky*, 492 U.S. 361 (1989).)

The Court overruled *Stanford* in 2005 when it raised this minimum age to 18 in *Simmons*. Noting that the death penalty for juveniles had been declining in jury sentences, in actual executions, and in state statutes, and that no other country in the world condoned it, the Court relied upon the well-established measure of "evolving standards of decency" to find that the death penalty for all juveniles had now become cruel and unusual punishment.

The *Simmons* analysis focuses on narrow death penalty considerations, but it may have opened the door to reconsideration of many other presumptions currently accepted by juvenile and criminal courts. If juveniles facing the death penalty have lesser culpability and are not to be punished with the same severity as we punish adults, in what other areas should we question the old maxim: "Old enough to do the crime, old enough to do the time?"

In contrast to this steady evolution away from the death penalty for juvenile offenders, no such evolution has occurred as to other severe sentences for juveniles. Generally, the leading federal cases apparently do not impose a constitutional requirement that sentences be proportional to the offender as well as to the crime, except under the most extraordinary circumstances. On the precise issue of LWOP for juvenile offenders, the robbery-murder case of 15-yearold Michael Harris is the most significant. (*Harris v. Wright*, 93 F.3d 581 (9th Cir. 1996).) When this case reached the appellate court, *Harris* raised the federal constitutional issue of cruel and unusual punishment: "[Harris] claims that a mandatory sentence of life imprisonment without parole is unconstitutionally cruel and unusual as applied to punish an offense committed when the perpetrator was less than sixteen years of age." The *Harris* court first used the evolving standards of decency analysis familiar to death penalty cases. However, the court found clear evidence of support for life without parole for 15-year-olds in contemporary statutes: "[T]here are at least twenty-one states that do impose mandatory life without parole on fifteen-year-old offenders."

The Ninth Circuit in *Harris* found that *Harmelin v. Michigan*, 501 U.S. 957 (1991), rejected any need to conduct a detailed proportionality analysis except possibly in the most extreme situations. Ultimately the *Harris* Court rejected the appellant's claim:

> Youth has no obvious bearing on this problem: If we can discern no clear line for adults, neither can we for youths. Accordingly, while capital punishment is unique and must be treated specially, mandatory life imprisonment without parole is, for young and old alike, only an outlying point on the continuum of prison sentences. Like any other prison sentence, it raises no inference of disproportionality when imposed on a murderer. (*Harris*, 93 F.3d at 585 (internal citation omitted).)

The current state of the law remains pretty much the same. The *Harris* case never went past the Ninth Circuit, cases like *Harmelin* have not been revisited by the Supreme Court, and a majority of state criminal codes continue to permit life imprisonment without parole for offenders as young as 10 to 12 years of age.

State constitutionality issues. Even if the federal Constitution is not currently interpreted to prohibit LWOP for youthful offenders, each state can nonetheless rely upon its own state constitution to test constitutionality. An oft-cited example is *Workman v. Commonwealth*, 429 S.W.2d 374 (Ky. 1968), reviewing LWOP sentences for two 14-year-olds who were convicted of raping and robbing a 71-year-old woman. Relying upon the due process provision of the Kentucky Constitution, the *Workman* court rejected life without parole for 14-year-old offenders: "Life imprisonment without benefit of parole for two fourteen-year-old youths under all the circumstances shocks the general conscience of society today and is intolerable to fundamental fairness."

Moving to the more modem era, the Nevada Supreme Court followed a state constitutional analysis in *Naovarath v. State*, 779 P.2d 944 (Nev. 1989). The trial court had sentenced the defendant to LWOP for an unspecified degree of murder, despite the fairly sympathetic fact that the 13-year-old offender killed the adult who had been sexually molesting him. *Naovarath* considered the applicability of deterrence and retribution to the 13-year-old who kills and concluded that a 13-year-old boy would not perceive any significant difference between life without parole and life reviewable by a parole board after a period of time in prison. On the other issue, the court simply thought that a 13-year-old does not deserve life without parole to the same degree that an adult offender might. Given this nowstandard Eighth Amendment analysis, the Nevada court concluded that life without parole for a 13-year-old convicted murderer was cruel and unusual under both the United States Constitution and the Nevada Constitution.

However, most state supreme courts have not followed the *Workman-Naovarath* line of reasoning. An example is the case of the codefendant in the crime reviewed in *Harris v. Wright*. *State v. Massey*, 803 P.2d 340 (Wash. Ct. App. 1990), involved the appeal of a 13-year-old (with an IQ of 77 and a mental age less than a 10-year-old) who—along with Harris, his 15-year-old accomplice—was sentenced to LWOP after being convicted of robbery and murder. In *Massey*, the Washington appellate court refused to place any special significance on the offender's age: "[T]here is no cause to create a distinction between a juvenile and an adult who is sentenced to life without parole for first degree aggravated murder."

Statutory issues. Among the states, the varying statutes typically allow LWOP as a sentence for youthful offenders, imposed either on a discretionary or a mandatory basis. Although many states do not currently differentiate between an adult and a juvenile for this particular sentence, there seems to be a growing trend among state laws toward modifying it as it applies to juveniles.

In two states LWOP for any offender is not an authorized sentencing disposition, and therefore no juveniles would be subject to a sentence of life without parole. (*See* ALASKA STAT. § 12.55.125 (2005); N.M. STAT. ANN. § 31-21-10 (2006).) These two states do, however, allow for lengthy punishments.

Table 1. States That Do Not Permit Juvenile LWOP

Alaska	ALASKA STAT. § 12.55.125 (2005)
Colorado	COLO. REV. STAT. § 18-1.3-401, as amended in May 2006 (parole availability after serving 40 years)
District of Columbia	D.C. CODE § 22-2104(a)
California	CAL. PENAL CODE § 190.5(b) (no LWOP for offenders under age 16)
Indiana	IND. CODE § 35-50-2-3(b)(2) (no LWOP for offenders under age 16)
Kansas	KAN. STAT. ANN. § 21-4622
Kentucky	*Workman v. Commonwealth*, 429 S.W.2d 374 (Ky. 1968)
New Mexico	N.M. STAT. ANN. § 31-21-10
New York	N.Y. PENAL LAW § 125.27(1)(b)
Texas	TEX. FAM. CODE ANN. § 54.04(d)(3)(A) (2006)

Several states have begun to treat juveniles differently than adults in sentencing, even for violent crimes, many recognizing the difficulties in sentencing children, while still considering the maturity and developmental differences that are unique to these offenders. Although these jurisdictions are a minority among the states, five states plus the District of Columbia specifically disallow LWOP for offenders under age 18 and two states specifically disallow LWOP for offenders under age 16. Therefore, eight jurisdictions expressly forbid sentencing a juvenile (either age 16 or 18) to life without parole. Taken with the two states where LWOP is not an authorized disposition for any offender, 10 jurisdictions forbid this sentence for juveniles. (*See* Table 1.)

A decade ago, when the Ninth Circuit decided *Harris v. Wright*, the court noted that there were at least "twenty-one states that do impose mandatory life without parole on fifteen-year-old offenders." (*Harris*, 93 F.3d at 584.) Today, this number stands at 22. Sixteen states authorize LWOP on a juvenile, as either a mandatory minimum or maximum punishment for enumerated crimes. (*See* Table 3.) Six more states generally sentence offenders to LWOP on a discretionary basis, but their laws authorize mandatory life without parole only after certain additional factors are proven, such as recidivism or sexual motivation. (*See* Table 4.) Additionally, in 18 states, life without parole is an authorized disposition imposed at the discretionary level, but it is not a mandatory sentence. (*See* Table 2.)

Table 2. States That Impose Juvenile LWOP on a Discretionary Basis

	Statute for sentencing	Age at which a juvenile may be transferred to adult court
Arizona	Ariz. Rev. Stat. Ann. § 13-703.01	Age 14: Ariz. Rev. Code Ann. §§ 13-501 (A), (B)
Hawaii	Haw. Rev. Stat. Ann. § 706-656; Haw. Rev. Stat. Ann. § 706-667	No age limit on transfer for murder charges. Haw. Rev. Stat. Ann. § 571-22(d)
Illinois	730 Ill. Comp. Stat. 5/5-8-1	Age 13: 705 Ill. Comp. Stat. Ann. 405/5-805(3)
Maine	Me. Rev. Stat. Ann. Tit. 17-A § 1251	No age limit for murder charges. Me. Rev. Stat. Ann. tit. 15 § 3101
Maryland	Md. Code Ann. Crim. Law § 2-202	No Age limit on transfer for murder charges. D. Code Ann. Cts. & Jud.Proc. § 3-8A-06(A)(2)
Mississippi	Miss. CODE ANN. § 97-3-21	Age 13: Miss. Code Ann. § 43-21-157(1)
Montana	Mont. Code Ann. § 46-18-219	Age 12: Mont. Code Ann. § 41-5-206
Nebraska	Neb. Rev. Stat. § 28-105	No age limit. Neb. Rev. Stat. 43-247
Nevada	Nev. Rev. Stat. Ann. § 193.130	No age limit on transfer for murder charges. Nev. Rev. Stat. Ann. § 62B.330(3) Children under age 8 are not liable to punishment. Nev. Rev. Stat. Ann. § 194.010
North Dakota	N.D. Cent. Code § 12.1-32-01	Age 14: N.D. Cent. Code § 12.1-04-01
Oklahoma	Okla. Stat. Tit. 21 § 701.9	Age 13: Okla. Stat. Ann. tit. 10 § 7306-1.1 (B) (mandatory transfer if charged with first degree murder)
Oregon	Or. Rev. Stat. § 163.105(1)	Age 15: Or. Rev. Stat. § 137.707
Rhode Island	R.I. Gen. Laws § 11-23-2	No age limit. R.I. GEN. LAWS § 14-1-7
Tennessee	Tenn. Code Ann. § 39-13-202	No age limit for enumerated offenses. Tenn. Code Ann. § 37-1-134
Utah	Utah Code Ann. § 76-3-206	Age 14: Utah Code Ann. § 78-3a-502(3)
Vermont	Vt. Stat. Ann. Tit. 13 § 2303	Age 10: Vt. Stat. Ann. tit. 33 § 5506

West Virginia	W. Va. Code Ann. § 61-2-2; W. Va. Code Ann. § 62-3-15	No age limit (mandatory at age 14 for certain crimes, discretionary below age 14). W. Va. Code § 49-5-10
Wisconsin	Wis. Stat. Ann. § 973.014	Age 10: Wis. Stat. Ann. § 938.183
Wyoming	Wyo. Stat. Ann. § 6-2-101	Age 13: Wyo. Stat. Ann. § 14-6-303

Although the majority of states permit LWOP for juveniles, in several of the states that generally impose mandatory or discretionary LWOP sentences on adults, the legislature affords special consideration for juvenile offenders. California law provides that offenders under age 16 will not be sentenced to mandatory life without parole. (See Cal. Penal Code § 190.5(b) (2006); see also Ind. Code § 35-50-2-3-(b)(2) (2006) (imposing similar punishment).) In Montana, a statutory mandatory minimum does not apply if the offender was under the age of 18 at the time of the crime. (See Mont. Code Ann. § 46-18-222 (2005).) Oregon also gives special consideration to juveniles, providing that there are no mandatory minimums when sentencing for juveniles waived from juvenile court, although LWOP does remain an authorized disposition. (See Or. Rev. Stat. § 161.620 2005) (providing no mandatory minimums for juveniles waived from juvenile court, except a mandatory 30-year minimum for aggravated murder).) Additionally, in Kentucky there are no restrictions on parole for juveniles. (See Ky. Rev. Stat. Ann. § 640.040 (Baldwin 2005).)

Of special notice is Colorado, whose legislature recently passed an amendment whereby if a person is convicted as an adult, parole is possible after serving 40 years. (2006 Colo. Legis. Serv. Ch. 228 (H.B. 06-1315) (West).) In this act, the legislature recognizes that LWOP for children results in an "irredeemable loss to society," and that children are developmentally different than adults and should be treated as such. (Id. at § (1)(2).) Although the legislation recognizes that persons younger than 18 commit serious crimes, it states:

> [B]ecause of their level of physical and psychological development, juveniles who are convicted as adults may, with appropriate counseling, treatment services, and education, be rehabilitated to a greater extent than may be possible for adults whose physical and psychological development is more complete when they commit the crimes that result in incarceration. (Id. at §§ (l)(b), (c).)

[T]he general assembly finds, therefore, that it is not in the best interests of the state to condemn juveniles who commit class 1 felony crimes to a lifetime of incarceration without the possibility of parole. Further,

Table 3. States That Impose LWOP as a Mandatory Sentence, Juveniles Included

	Statute for sentencing	Age at which a juvenile may be transferred to adult court
Arkansas	ARK. CODE ANN. § 5-4-104	Age 14: ARK. CODE ANN. § 9-27-318
Connecticut	CONN. GEN. STAT. § 53A-35A	Age 14: CONN. GEN. STAT. ANN. § 46b-127
Delaware	10 DEL. CODE ANN. TIT. 10 § 4209	No age limit for transfer. DEL. CODE ANN. tit. 10 § 1010
Florida	FLA. STAT. § 775.082	No age limit. FLA. STAT. § 985.225(1)
Iowa	IOWA CODE § 902.1	Age 14: IOWA CODE ANN. § 232.45(6)(a)
Louisiana	LA. CRIM. CODE ANN. ART. 14:30	Age 15: LA. CHILD. CODE ANN. art. 305
Massachusetts	MASS. GEN. LAWS ANN. CH. 265 § 2	Age 14: MASS. GEN. LAWS ANN. ch. 119 § 72(B)
Michigan	MICH. COMP. LAWS ANN. § 750.316	Age 14: MICH. COMP. LAWS ANN. § 712A.4
Minnesota	MINN. STAT. § 609.106	Age 14: MINN. STAT. ANN. § 260B.125
Missouri	MO. ANN. STAT. § 565.020	Age 12: MO. STAT. ANN. § 211.071
New Hampshire	N.H. REV. STAT. ANN. § 630:1-A	Age 13: N.H. REV. STAT. ANN. § 628:1
New Jersey	N.J. STAT. ANN. § 2c:1 1-3(B)(3)	Age 14: N.J. STAT. ANN. 2a:4A-26
North Carolina	N.C. GEN. STAT. § 14-17	Age 13: N.C. Gen. Stat. § 7B-2200
Pennsylvania	42 PA. CONS. STAT. ANN. § 9711; 18 PA. CONS. STAT. ANN. § 1102	No age limit if charge is murder. 42 PA. CON. STAT. ANN. § 6355
South Dakota	S.D. CODIFIED LAWS § 24-15-4; S.D. CODIFIED LAWS § 22-6-1	Age 10: S.D. CODIFIED LAWS § 22-3-1 S.D. CODIFIED LAWS § 26-11-3.1
Washington	WASH. REV. CODE ANN. § 10.95.030	Age 15: WASH. REV. CODE ANN. § 13.40.110

the general assembly finds that it is in the interest of justice to recognize the rehabilitation potential of juveniles who are convicted as adults of class 1 felonies by providing that they are eligible for parole after serving forty calendar years of their sentences. (*Id.* at § (2).)

Table 4. States That Impose Mandatory LWOP Only upon Finding of Additional Factors

	Statute for sentencing	Age at which a juvenile may be transferred to adult court
Alabama	ALA. CODE § 13A-5-2; ALA. CODE § 13A-5-9	Age 14: ALA. CODE § 12-15-34
Georgia	GA. CODE ANN. § 17-10-6.1 (a)(2); (mandating LWOP for recidivists)	No age limit for transfer. Minimum age for criminal liability is 13. GA. CODE ANN. § 16-3-1
Idaho	IDAHO CODE § 18-4004 (2006); (mandating a fixed life sentence for murder, after a finding of aggravating factors); IDAHO CODE § 18-4004	Discretionary at any age, mandatory at 14 for certain crimes. IDAHO CODE ANN. § 20-509
Ohio	OHIO REV. CODE ANN. § 2971.03 (mandatory if sexual motivation in aggravated murder); OHIO REV. CODE ANN. § 2929.03(E)(1)	Age 14: OHIO REV. CODE ANN. § 2152.10(b)
South Carolina	S.C. CODE ANN. § 17-25-45 (2005) (mandatory if there are prior convictions for enumerated crimes); S.C. CODE ANN. § 16-3-20	No age limit for murder. S.C. CODE ANN. § 20-7-7605(6)
Virginia	VA. CODE ANN. § 53.1-151, VA. CODE ANN. § 53.1-151 (E) (2006) ("A person convicted of an offense and sentenced to life imprisonment after being paroled from a previous life sentence shall not be eligible for parole.")	Age 14: VA. CODE ANN. § 16.1-269-1

Among state statutes, the age at which a juvenile can be sentenced to such adult punishment varies greatly, ranging from age 10 (*see* VT. STAT. ANN. tit. 33 § 5506 (2005), up to age 15. (*See* Wash. Rev. Code Ann. § 13.40.110 (West 2006).) Other states, such as Delaware and Florida, have no minimum age at which a child can be transferred to adult criminal court. (*See* DEL CODE ANN. tit. 10 §§ 1010, 1011 (Westlaw, current through 2006); FLA. STAT. § 985.225(1) (2005).) In these two jurisdictions, LWOP is also a mandatory sentence for crimes such as murder. This means that a very young child, if found guilty of murder in a jurisdiction such as these, would be sentenced to a life without parole.

Federal law also permits juveniles to be sentenced to LWOP, with it being the minimum sentence for first-degree murder. (18 U.S.C.A. § 1111 (West 2003) (providing, "[w]hoever is guilty of murder in the first degree shall be punished by death or by imprisonment for life."), *and see US. v. LaFleur*, 971 F.2d 200, 209 (9th Cir. 1991) (recognizing that parole is no longer a possibility in the federal system and stating "[t]he language of [§ 1111(b)] is clear—life imprisonment is the minimum sentence available for first degree murder under § 1111.").) Decided 10 years ago, the *Harris* case determined that a Washington court's sentencing a 15-year-old to LWOP was not cruel and unusual punishment. (*See Harris*, 93 F.3d 581.) The Supreme Court in *Simmons* also recognized the availability of this sentence for minors, stating, "[t]o the extent the juvenile death penalty might have residual deterrent effect, it is worth noting that the punishment of life imprisonment without the possibility of parole is itself a severe sanction, in particular for a young person." (*Simmons*, 543 U.S. at 572.)

International and comparative law issues. Although it was not a controlling factor, the *Simmons* Court took notice of the fact that the United States was the only country that continued to give official sanction to the juvenile death penalty:

> It is proper that we acknowledge the overwhelming weight of international opinion against the juvenile death penalty, resting in large part on the understanding that the instability and emotional imbalance of young people may often be a factor in the crime.... The opinion of the world community, while not controlling our outcome, does provide respected and significant confirmation for our own conclusions. (*Simmons*, 543 U.S. at 578.)

International treaty law against the juvenile life without parole penalty is no less overwhelming. The United Nations Convention on the Rights of the Child (CRC) includes an absolute prohibition on life without parole sentences for crimes committed by juveniles under the age of 18. In addition, United States treaty obligations under Article 14(4) of the International Covenant on Civil and Political Rights (ICCPR) require that "in the case of juvenile persons," criminal trials "shall be such as will take account of their age and the desirability of promoting their rehabilitation."

Other international standards, while not binding, are persuasive. U.N. standards have strong persuasive force because they reflect the collective policy of the 192 U.N. member states, generally having been negotiated by governments over many years and adopted by U.N. bodies by consensus. They have been taken into account by numerous U.S. courts in interpreting domestic and applicable international law.

The applicable international standards concerning juveniles stress the rehabilitative aims of juvenile justice systems. They emphasize the importance of discretion in treatment of juvenile offenders and that imprisonment should be imposed only as a last resort, for the minimum period necessary, and that sentences be reviewed periodically in order to take into account the rehabilitation of the young offender as he or she matures and develops. Above all, they require that the welfare and the best interests of the child be taken into account in determining treatment at all stages.

Most of America's closest allies, especially those who "share our Anglo-American heritage," do not subject juveniles to mandatory sentences of life imprisonment without the possibility of parole. For example, the European Court of Human Rights, which has authority over all European Union members, observed that a mandatory life sentence for a 16-year-old convicted of murder would raise problems under the Convention for the Protection of Human Rights and Fundamental Freedoms (European Convention). (*See Hussain v. United Kingdom*, 33 EHRR 1 (1996).) In sentencing juveniles, the European court concluded that the term of detention "must of necessity take into account...any development in the young offender's personality and attitude as he or she grows older," and that a sentence of life imprisonment with no possibility of parole would constitute "a failure to have regard of the changes which inevitably occur with maturation." (*Id.* at 53.) The court concluded that a sentence of life imprisonment without the possibility of parole imposed upon a juvenile would violate Article 3 of the European Convention, which prohibits inhuman or degrading treatment or punishment. The Convention has been signed and ratified by all European Union members and a total of 41 European nations.

CONCLUSIONS

All of these lines of analysis lead to the conclusion that sentences authorized and implemented for offenders under age 18 should incorporate several well-established mitigating considerations unique to the youthfulness of such offenders. Their crimes may be the same as those of adults, but these offenders simply are not adults and should not be sentenced as if they were. Sentences should take into consideration both the nature and circumstances of the offense and the character and background of the offenders. This approach leads naturally to unique mitigating circumstances for young offenders.

The other characteristic of young offenders is the understanding that they will change significantly as they grow into adulthood. A 14-year-old today will be a quite different person when he or she is 40. To decide today whether or not this adolescent offender should continue to be imprisoned into those adult years and even into old age is to assume extrahuman powers to predict human behavior generations into the future. The crucial decision to release or not release offenders on parole should be made at the time of such release and not decades earlier. This conclusion leads to the principle that youthful offenders should be eligible for parole consideration at reasonable points during their sentences, even in those jurisdictions that do not provide parole eligibility for adult offenders.

*Victor Streib is the Fisher Professor of Law at Ohio Northern University and has written extensively about sentencing juvenile offenders. He also is a thirty-year member and immediate past cochair of the .Juvenile Justice Committee.

Bernadette Schrempp was managing editor of the *Ohio Northern University Law Review* at the time that this article was written. She is currently a St. Claire County Assistant State Attorney.

Streib, Victor, and Bernadette Schrempp. "Life Without Parole for Children." *Criminal Justice* 21, no. 4 (Winter 2007): 4–12.

Part 5:

Should the Juvenile Justice System Be Reformed?

As we pointed out in the general introduction, the original goal of the juvenile justice system, which was to rehabilitate juvenile offenders and encourage them to develop their positive potentials, took a backseat to a more punitive policy in the latter part of the twentieth century. This punitive policy continues today. Most U.S. states make it relatively easy for juveniles to be transferred to adult courts, where they have little understanding of the proceedings, where judges and prosecutors often have too little sensitivity to their needs as juveniles, and where they are often sentenced to harsh time in adult prisons. However, even those who are sentenced to juvenile prisons most often find themselves in a fundamentally alienating, dehumanizing, stigmatizing, and traumatizing environment where they are isolated from their communities and experience what some sociologists call "social death," a feeling that they are no longer accepted as part of the human community. In addition, many young people who go through the juvenile justice system are not given the right to a jury trial and can be incarcerated for relatively trivial or nonviolent crimes.

These and other such problems have led some criminologists to argue that the *juvenile* justice system is broken beyond repair and that it should be abolished and replaced either with a "youth discount" in the *criminal* justice system that reduces the sentence according to the age of the defendant,[1] or with various forms of community programs, community and family supervision, and therapeutic intervention.[2] Ironically, these critics on the left are joined by conservative critics who also want to abolish the juvenile system but for very different reasons. For these critics, the goal would be to place most, if not all, juveniles in adult court, where their status as juveniles gives them no immunity from the most severe penalties under the law.[3]

In contrast to these abolitionists on both the left and the right, the authors of the articles in this section, while aware of the many problems and flaws in the juvenile justice system, argue not for abolition but for substantial reform. In his article "The Contradictions of Juvenile Crime and Punishment," Jeffrey Fagan argues that the juvenile justice system needs a significant overhaul that would downplay, if not eliminate, many of the existing punitive components and return it to its original goal of rehabilitation. He notes that while some juvenile facilities have the look of a boarding school, a therapeutic community, or even a small college campus, they are still essentially prisons that have as their "primary goals... security, control, discipline, and punishment." Those juveniles who are in these juvenile facilities have been incarcerated for any number of reasons: "because their homes are too dangerous or criminologenic; because they are both delinquent and mentally ill or addicted to intoxicants... because they need therapies that are unavailable elsewhere, even though they pose no security risks; because they are homeless; because they are sexually active at young ages; or because we think they may commit some crime in the near future." In other words, there is good reason to say that perhaps the majority of them should not be incarcerated.

Fagan's main thesis is that the problems of the juvenile justice system stem in large part from a set of contradictions within it—contradictions between wanting juveniles to receive harsh punishment *and* wanting to rehabilitate them; between wanting to have them in separate juvenile facilities *and* wanting them to be tried in criminal courts; between providing juvenile offenders with a good education, emotional support, and therapeutic intervention *and* a vision that is punitive and indifferent to those interventions; between protecting juvenile offenders from stigma and brutality *and* transferring them to adult courts and incarcerating them in both juvenile and adult prisons. Fagan insists that the punitive component of these contradictions has caused more harm than good—first, because neurobiological and psychological research supports the idea that children have poorer emotional regulation and decision-making skills than do adults, which means that they are less culpable than are adults; second, because the rate of recidivism is higher among juveniles who were sentenced to adult prisons than among those sentenced to juvenile prisons; and third, because there is no relation between longer sentences for juveniles and public safety. Fagan then proposes that in order to resolve the contradictions indicated above, we need "to return to the first principles of juvenile justice: avoiding harm and stigma and building the social capital and human capacity for the child."

In the second article in this section, titled "Adolescent Development and the Regulation of Youth Crime," Elizabeth S. Scott and Laurence Steinberg, who also argue for significant reform, call for a "developmental and mitigation" model for the juvenile justice system. This model stakes a middle ground between youth advocates and conservatives who support the punitive turn. Their model rejects the idea that the only options are either the juvenile offender be tried as an adult or given a "slap on the wrist," and instead proposes that juveniles are different from both children and adults, more responsible for their actions than children but less so than adults. Thus, their model would not treat adolescents as children whose crimes should be excused, but would place them "in an intermediate legal category of offenders who are less blameworthy and deserve less punishment."

Their argument for this position rests largely on recent studies in developmental psychology and neurobiology. Research in developmental psychology provides evidence that adolescents differ from adults in a number of ways that mitigate their culpability. They have diminished decision-making abilities, not so much because they cannot reason and process information but because they are "less capable than adults are in *using* these capacities in making real-world choices." They are more subject to peer pressure and group approval than are adults. They are more impulsive and are less capable of evaluating risks and benefits. They are more subject to emotional influences, and therefore they will often make bad choices. They lack "future orientation," which makes them less able to evaluate consequences and less likely to perceive the risks involved in their behavior. Juveniles are more prone to mood swings, and their characters are not fully formed.

These conclusions from developmental psychology are supported by recent studies of adolescent brain development, which show that the frontal lobes and especially the prefrontal cortex are still undergoing development. What this means is the areas of the brain that are most responsible for the "executive functions"—functions that regulate thinking, planning, emotions, control of impulses, and awareness of consequences—are less developed in adolescents than adults. From these developmental and neurobiological studies, Scott and Steinberg conclude that the "evidence indicates that the immaturity of adolescent offenders causes them to differ from their adult counterparts in ways that mitigate culpability." Thus, for these authors, most juvenile criminals should still be dealt with by the juvenile justice system. Punishment is still appropriate but with an orientation that takes youth as a mitigating factor. Also, while not returning completely to the original rehabilitative intent of the juvenile justice system, various kinds of rehabilitation programs and therapeutic interventions should be used in both institutional and community programs with the goal of helping young people acquire skills that would in the long run reduce crime.

In the last article in this section, "The Need for Cognitive Skills Educational Therapy in Juvenile Justice," Kimora, one of the coeditors of this book, emphasizes the need for a particular kind of rehabilitative reform in the juvenile justice system—cognitive skills education—the lack of which, she argues, is one of the main reasons that the juvenile justice system is ineffective. Kimora defines cognitive skills education as encompassing social skills, problem-solving skills, creative skills (learning to think "out of the box"), management of anger and other emotions, and critical thinking skills. While these are useful skills for anyone, they are especially needed by young people who break the law and who often suffer from cognitive dissonance, distorted cognitions, self-defeating and impulsive behaviors, a lack of ability to manage emotions and assess consequences, and a lack of problem-solving skills. Learning critical thinking skills is especially important, as it can teach young offenders to think before they act and can improve their social reasoning and social behavior.

Kimora discusses a number of cognitive skills educational programs, including therapeutic interventions, and explains and evaluates their usefulness in helping young offenders. Among these programs are cognitive therapy, which can identify and change distorted and irrational thought patterns; rational emotive behavioral therapy, which can identify forms of cognition that lead to self-defeating behaviors; and "Breaking Barriers," which emphasizes that young people can change as they transition from prison to the workforce and community. Through an examination of these cognitive skills education programs, she builds a case for her claim that enhanced cognitive skills education can prevent juveniles from entering the juvenile justice system in the first place, and that it can also provide the skills young offenders need for a productive and better life once they leaves the prison and reenter the community—in short that it can reduce the juvenile rate of recidivism. At the end of her article, Kimora makes clear that as someone who has been a cognitive skills educator for over twenty-five years, she is confident that these programs really do work.

As you read the excerpts in this section, consider some of the following questions:

- In your opinion, what needs to be the prime objective of juvenile corrections?

- Is it possible to reform the juvenile justice system? If so, how?

- Compare the punitive "adult time for adult crime" with one of the alternative models proposed in this section. With which model are you more sympathetic, and why?

- What should be done about those juveniles who many people might consider too dangerous to *ever* be allowed to return to society?

- Should the community be involved with the ongoing well-being of the juvenile offender, and, if so, what kinds of community involvement are necessary?

- Develop a cognitive skills program for a juvenile detention center. What aspects of cognitive skills education would you include? Why?

- Is it possible to prove that cognitive skills education changes the juvenile offender into a more productive and positive person? If so, how would you attempt to prove it?

NOTES

1. See Barry Feld, "Criminalizing the American Juvenile Court," in *Readings in Juvenile Justice Administration* (New York: Oxford University Press, 1999), 356–372.
2. See Nell Bernstein, "Against Reform: Beyond Juvenile Prison," in *Burning Down the House: The End of Juvenile Prison* (New York: New Press, 2014), chap. 6.
3. See Ernest van den Haag, "Thinking About Crime Again," reprinted in Part 3 of this book.

The Contradictions of Juvenile Crime and Punishment

by Jeffrey Fagan*

Juvenile incarceration in the United States is, at first glance, distinctly different from its adult counterpart. While some juvenile facilities retain the iconic aesthetic of adult incarceration[1]—orange jumpsuits, large cellblocks, uniformed guards, barbed wire, and similar heavy-security measures—others have trappings and atmospherics more reminiscent of boarding schools, therapeutic communities, or small college campuses. These compact, benign settings avoid the physical stigmata of institutional life and accord some autonomy of movement and intimacy in relations with staff. They also give primacy to developmentally appropriate and therapeutic interventions.

However, like its adult counterpart, juvenile corrections, whether located in a human warehouse or a therapeutic community, is designed mainly to control its residents and restrict their personal freedoms. Movement and association are intensively regulated; outside contact with family, friends, and intimate partners is attenuated and used as an incentive for good behavior; access to media and culture is restricted; privacy is nonexistent; and choice of clothing, language, and other modes of personal expression is off-limits. Whatever developmental importance these forms of self-expression and self-determination may have for adolescents, it is sacrificed to the primary goals of security, control, discipline, and punishment. Most important, at either end of the continuum of institutional climate, the options of solitary confinement, physical restraint, or other forms of extreme deprivation exist to control the defiant and unruly or to punish wrong-doing. Accordingly, the naming conventions for these juvenile facilities are deceptive: these are not "training schools" or "centers" or any other kind of school or academy, nor are they "homes." These are correctional facilities whose primary purpose is to punish.

One would expect such institutions to be reserved for those who are most deserving of punishment or those who pose a nontrivial risk to public safety. But under the enduring doctrine of *parens patriae*,[2] we incarcerate children for a mixed bag of rationales, ones that do not always comport with the punitive dimensions of juvenile incarceration. *Parens patriae* obligates the court to act beyond the need simply to protect children from the harms of noxious social circumstances or to avail them of developmental and material supports that their families have failed to provide. The doctrine allows—even mandates—juvenile courts to protect children from themselves: from their associations with antisocial peers, from poor decision-making with respect to crime, and from harms to their physical and mental health to which they expose themselves.[3] As a result, we incarcerate children because their homes are too dangerous or criminogenic; because they are both delinquent and mentally ill or addicted to intoxicants and there are no other appropriate placements; because they need therapies that are unavailable elsewhere, even though they pose no security risks; because they are homeless; because they are sexually active at young ages; or because we think they may commit some crime in the near future.[4]

The resulting landscape of juvenile incarceration has been, not surprisingly, complex and shifting since the 1970s, the decade when adult incarceration trends began their robust increase. Since that time, juvenile incarceration, and juvenile justice itself, has been situated in a space bounded by the transcendent nineteenth-century child-saving movement, the procedural rights movement of the 1960s, and the raw emotional politics of violent crime and punishment in the past three decades. Accordingly, we see contradictions everywhere in this terrain. Growth in the incarcerated population since the 1970s has been restrained, even in the face of a youth violence epidemic,[5] and even as rhetoric has grown harsher and statutes have been revised to express the language of retribution and incapacitation.[6] States, for the most part, have acknowledged the advantages of small facilities to advance the core rehabilitative and therapeutic projects that informed the creation of separate institutions for juveniles nearly two centuries ago, even if they have not necessarily acted on those ideas and instincts.[7] At the same time, the conditions in juvenile corrections often remain harsh, a sign of both cynicism about rehabilitation and institutional self-interest, as well as neglect.[8] States have quickened the pace of expulsions of juvenile offenders to the criminal courts and prisons as a way to "get tough,"[9] even as they refuse to lower the age of majority and fundamentally alter eligibility for the protections of juvenile institutions. Racial disparities remain durable and defy explicit legislative and policy efforts to reduce them.

These contradictions and puzzles inform this essay on juvenile incarceration. The patterns of growth in juvenile corrections suggest ambivalence about the reform and rehabilitation of juvenile offenders, notions that have been battered by three successive waves of high crime over the past thirty years. On the one hand, courts and legislatures want to be tough; on the other hand, there are strong preservationist instincts at play that have muted the growth in incarceration of minors. "Getting tough" on juvenile offenders has thus been assigned to the criminal courts and adult correctional institutions. But there are signs of ambivalence there, with relatively short sentences and a responsiveness to crime rates in new admissions (flow) and total population (stock) that is the opposite of what we see for adults. States have demonstrated their ambivalence by avoiding change to the age of majority, the last resort in increasing punitiveness for juveniles. Such a step would be a poison pill for the doctrine of *parens patriae* in which juvenile corrections is steeped. Racial disparity pervades juvenile incarceration, yet Congress attempted remedial steps never contemplated for adults, by engaging states in a collaborative project to reduce racial inequalities in juvenile detention and corrections. What this all adds up to is an institutional landscape that at once fears child criminals and wants to punish them harshly, but at the same time adheres to the transcendent philosophy of child-saving.

Beginning in the 1970s, the traditional discretion of juvenile court judges to place youths in correctional confinement was contested, as was the discretion of corrections officials to determine how long youths would remain in placement. On balance, discretion lost. The introduction of mandatory minimum sentences for juveniles in New York and elsewhere in the 1970s was followed in subsequent decades by new laws mandating waiver to adult court and mandatory placement in a secure facility.[10] In this hardening political atmosphere, fueled by rising juvenile arrest rates and a punitive drift toward more formal processing and less diversion, one might have predicted rapid and persistent growth in the rate of juvenile imprisonment starting in the 1970s. By the 1990s, when a moral panic over a new species of juvenile offenders known as "superpredators"[11] and the spread of violent youth gangs further animated legislatures to pass tougher sentencing laws for juveniles,[12] the conditions seemed ripe for the juvenile court to follow a trajectory of incarceration growth similar to the rise in adult rates.

But it didn't happen, at least not in juvenile corrections. Growth in juvenile incarceration in both public and private facilities was only a fraction of the growth in adult incarceration. Juvenile incarceration—both in short-term detention and longer-term correctional placements—rose from 73,023 youths in public institutions and private residential facilities in 1977 to 95,818 in 1992, the year preceding the modern peak in juvenile arrests for felony crimes.[13] Juvenile incarceration peaked in 2000 at 108,802, a rate of 356 per 100,000 youths ages ten to seventeen. The placement rate declined by more than 20 percent by 2008, to approximately 81,000 children living in either state-operated facilities or privately operated group homes, or 263 youths per 100,000 persons ages ten to seventeen.[14] This juvenile placement rate today pales in comparison to the adult incarceration rate of 762.[15]

Figure 1. Juvenile Placements in Public and Private Facilities and Juvenile Arrests for Violence, 1977–2006

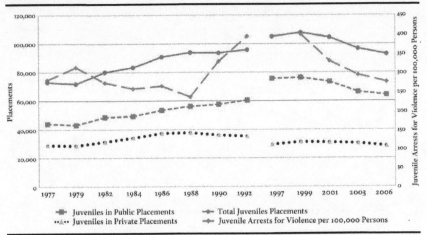

Juveniles in Public Placements
Juveniles in Private Placements
Total Juveniles Placements
Juvenile Arrests for Violence per 100,000 Persons

Source: Melissa Sickmund et al., *Easy Access to the Census of Juveniles in Residential Placement* (National Center for Juvenile Justice, 2008), http://ojjdp.ncjrs.gov/ojstatbb/ezacjrp; Steven D. Levitt, "Juvenile Crime and Punishment," *Journal of Political Economy* 106 (1998): 1156–1185.

Figure 1 shows that placements in public facilities accounted for most of the rise and fall in juvenile incarceration, and that these were somewhat responsive to the rise and subsequent fall in juvenile arrests. Between 1997 and 2008, juvenile arrests declined by 33 percent, while the overall correctional placement of youths declined by 26 percent.[16] Placement in private facilities rose more slowly and was fairly stable over time.

About 70 percent were committed following an adjudication of delinquency, and 28 percent were detained prior to the resolution of their case.[17] They were incarcerated on a variety of offenses, with the greatest number placed for person offenses (34 percent) followed by property offenses (25 percent). Drug offenses accounted for 9 percent of the incarcerated population, but more were placed for "public order" offenses such as alcohol or disorderly conduct (11 percent) than were placed for drugs. As with their adult counterparts, many (16 percent) were placed for technical violations of probation or juvenile parole. One in twenty was placed for any of several "status offenses": social behaviors that do not violate any criminal code but that capture the court's attention due to the risk of danger to the child's well-being.[18]

The area that grew most, however, was the number of juveniles below age eighteen in state prisons. The pattern in Figure 2 shows a rise in the number of

Figure 2. Inmates Under Eighteen in State Prisons, 1985–2004

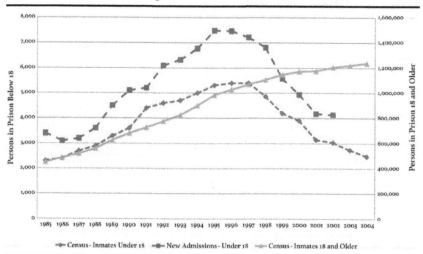

Source: Howard Snyder and Melissa Sickmund, *Juvenile Offenders and Victims: 2006 National Report* (Washington, D.C.: Office of Juvenile Justice and Delinquency Prevention, U.S. Department of Justice, 2006), 236–238, http://ojjdp.ncjrs.gov/ojstatbb/nr2006.

persons below age eighteen incarcerated in state prisons from 1985 to 2004, as well as new admissions for that same group. The patterns reflect broader trends in juvenile crime and arrest, especially the spike in juvenile violence from 1987 to 1996. The census population of minors in prison peaked at 5,400 in 1996 and declined by nearly half, to 2,477, in 2004.[19] The population remained stable through 2007, when 2,283 youths were in state prisons or privately operated correctional facilities programmed for adults.[20]

Two trends in Figure 2 are notable and suggest conflicting instincts.

One is the rapid growth in the number of youths sentenced as adults. This trend is responsive to crime trends and also reflects a growing punitiveness toward youth crime that was structured into sentencing statutes. (The "get tough" trend for juveniles is discussed later in this essay.) But the sentences seem to be attenuated, suggesting that the legislatures were tempered in setting tariffs for minors. Figure 2 shows that the number of new admissions of minors to adult prisons tracks the trend for the one-day census. There is no buildup of "stock" for this population, unlike the steady growth for adults.

The similar trend lines for the population census and the new admissions suggest that the sentences for this population were shorter and releases were quicker, reflecting a de facto youth discount that many states structure into sentencing statutes under "youthful offender" or "juvenile offender" provisions.[21] The responsiveness in the decline of juveniles in adult prisons beginning in 2000 shows a sensitivity to declining crime rates that is not evident for the adult population.

Nevertheless, even short-term exposure for youths to adult prisons has risks for youths and for public safety. To the extent that legislators ignored these risks, the wholesale transfer of minors to the criminal courts was a reckless experiment. A robust body of research shows that recidivism rates are in fact higher for youths sentenced as adults, after controlling for relevant offender and offense characteristics.[22] There appears to be no marginal deterrent effect from incarcerating minors as adults, which was a cornerstone of youth policy in the 1990s. One explanation for the elevated recidivism rates may be the effects of adolescents' exposure to prison life and adult convicts. While likely to be separated physically from older inmates, the institutional climate on the youth side may hardly differ from other blocks in the prison: the separation may be one of degree rather than kind. Indeed, it may even worsen the chaos and violence of correctional confinement by concentrating youths who are at their peak ages of criminality and diminished self-control.[23] Only a few studies have compared the correctional experiences of youths in prisons and juvenile incarceration, but all agree that placing youths in prisons comes at a cost: they are less likely to receive education and other essential services, they are more likely to be victims of physical violence, and they manifest a variety of psychological symptoms.[24]

The residual consequences of adolescents' exposure to violence in adult prisons are uncertain. But as a matter of principle, it is not easy to reconcile this particular harm with the diminished blameworthiness and culpability of adolescents. Social and behavioral science informed recent Supreme Court jurisprudence on youth crime and punishment,[25] but criminal court sentencing policies more generally are hostile to the new cognitive science of diminished culpability of adolescents.[26] Potentially disfiguring punishments seem disproportionate, if not cynical, in the context of this new evidence about the blameworthiness of adolescents, especially if criminal justice goals are not well served by transfer and subsequent incarceration.[27]

There are puzzles and contradictions behind these trends. While American lawmakers exponentially expanded prison capacities for adults starting in the 1980s, there was—with rare exceptions—no expansion of the capacities to incarcerate minors. This was one of two non-events in modern juvenile justice that illustrate the dissonance in thinking about responses to serious youth crime. Figure 1 shows that the rate of increase in juvenile confinement was a fraction of the rate of increase in juvenile arrests; as crime declined, juvenile courts responded quickly by decelerating the rate of placements.

Yet in the juvenile system, even as states made the choice not to build new juvenile space and not to dramatically increase youth confinement, every state toughened its juvenile delinquency codes rhetorically to deemphasize rehabilitation and focus on punishment, retribution, and incapacitation.[28] Thus, "getting tough" in the juvenile system was not an institutional project, but a statutory one. Programming was largely unaffected, as the locus of effects of these new measures was on court decisions. The changes took several forms, but all had the combined effect of marginally increasing the likelihood of juvenile correctional confinement or lengthening the time spent in placement.

The harder work of "getting tough" was outsourced to the criminal justice system, with states more often than not using "regular" criminal law for juveniles. Statutes were amended to ease and expand the number of youths transferred to the criminal courts for sentencing as an adult.[29] The results are evident in Figure 2, as the number of youths confined in adult prisons rose (and fell) sharply. The "get tough" measures took several forms. Between 1990 and 1997, every state in America modified both its juvenile and criminal codes to expand the number of youths eligible for transfer to the criminal courts.[30] In 1995 alone, nineteen states amended their criminal codes to facilitate the discretionary transfer of delinquents to the criminal court or the wholesale exclusion of youths from the juvenile court.[31] Each strategy was designed to increase punishment in numbers and in severity. Several states adopted mandatory minimum sentences for youths committed to state juvenile corrections authorities. Others adopted sentencing guidelines that fixed sentences in the juvenile system based on a grid of offense, offender characteristics, and victim characteristics. Still other states expanded eligibility for sentencing minors to life without parole, or death in prison, and made those sentences automatic upon conviction for enumerated crimes.[32] Prior to the 2010 U.S. Supreme Court ruling in *Graham v. Florida* that banned life-without-parole sentences for juveniles who did not commit murder,[33] approximately 2,484 youths were serving such sentences in 2008, many as young as thirteen, and many others for crimes other than murder or manslaughter.[34]

But these developments point to the second non-event in the toughening of juvenile justice and juvenile incarceration. Certainly, a state that truly wanted to crack down on juveniles and make incarceration harsher could simply have lowered its age of majority and sent all its older juvenile offenders to adult prisons. Only two did so: Wisconsin and New Hampshire lowered the age of majority from seventeen to sixteen in the 1990s.[35] In fact, one state, Connecticut, has begun a process to incrementally *raise* its age of majority from sixteen to eighteen.[36] New York and North Carolina maintain the age of majority at sixteen; in most states, it is still eighteen.

Stopping short of the more obvious and expedient step of lowering the age of majority, states have instead used an incremental and piecemeal legislative strategy to criminalize delinquency and thereby allow them to sentence adolescents to adult punishment for crimes committed as minors. But despite the wave of transfer legislation, the current statutory landscape is an elaborate game of chutes and ladders, with some youths automatically transferred to the criminal courts only to be "reverse waived" back to the juvenile courts. As a result, many adolescent offenders (though no one knows exactly how many) escape the reach of the criminal law and its harsher punishments. Nevertheless, a large number are removed from the juvenile to the criminal courts by statutory exclusion, judicial discretion, or the administrative practices and preferences of prosecutors.[37]

Viewed in this way, legislators appear ambivalent, refusing to abandon completely the principles of juvenile justice, yet seeking to divide delinquents into two categories: those worthy of the remedial and therapeutic interventions of the juvenile court and those who should be abandoned to the punitive regime of criminal justice in the name of retribution and public safety. The complexity of state laws, the piecemeal character of the statutory landscape, and the fact that most states have overlapping transfer mechanisms suggest a philosophical duality. The punitive and child-saver instincts for youth crime coexist uneasily in the current statutory environment, forcing a binary choice between criminal and juvenile court jurisdiction—a choice that is not well suited to reconcile these tensions.[38]

On balance, the business of getting tough on juvenile offenders was assigned to the criminal justice system, while the juvenile system remained relatively small and still wrapped, however thinly, in its rehabilitative and child-saver clothing. Why did juvenile corrections expand so little during a time of unprecedented and unrestrained growth in adult corrections? And why did it transform from warehousing to embracing smaller, more therapeutically grounded facilities?[39] The numbers reveal the tension between two features of American jurisprudence surrounding juvenile offenders. We believe deeply in child-saving, yet we are quick to expose violent children to the harshest punishments in service to the same punitive instincts that drive mass incarceration of adults. But even there, we pull our punches. We pull back from the brink of fully embracing punitiveness toward juveniles, reserving it instead for adults. Not only is the philosophy of child-saving an important normative modifier of these instincts, it is also deeply embedded in the institutions of juvenile justice and juvenile corrections.

One episode illustrates the connections between the visceral push for punitiveness and political culture. In 1996, former U.S. Secretary of Education William Bennett and two colleagues published *Body Count*.[40] The book offered a "moral poverty" theory of youth crime, rejecting social theories of juvenile crime causation that focused on economic poverty, discrimination, family dysfunction, or savage levels of inequality. Instead, for Bennett and his coauthors, it was moral poverty that characterized a coming wave of "superpredators" who would commit extremely violent crimes and be immune to rehabilitative interventions. They characterized this new breed of young offenders as impulsive and remorseless, fearing not "the stigma of arrest, the pains of imprisonment, [or]the pangs of conscience." These (predicted) young criminals were portrayed nearly as a separate species. The authors' predictions were based on data that were compiled through 1993, the peak year of juvenile crime and violence in the United States.[41] Their predictions turned out to be horribly wrong.[42]

But the damage was done. The book supplied strong and scary rhetoric to fuel the legislative panic that, in general, produced a wave of get-tough legislation across the country. So strong and persuasive was this rhetoric that it led one state (Pennsylvania) to build a youth prison in anticipation of a surge of superpredators, not a juvenile center that emphasized rehabilitation and other services. The State Correctional Institute at Pine Grove opened in 2000, its plan and design based on population projections from the superpredator era and with that profile of the young offender in mind. At its opening, the prison housed 178 young offenders, well below its capacity of 1,000.[43] By that time, youth crime had fallen in Pennsylvania, and the number of youths below eighteen in adult prisons had fallen to sixty-six.

To fill this new youth prison, the state moved young offenders from some traditional correctional settings to Pine Grove, and the state's juvenile court judges made good use of the new placement option. Pine Grove today is well occupied, housing approximately one thousand inmates below the age of twenty-one. Built to house the expected wave of superpredators, today it is filled with a heterogeneous group of adolescent offenders whose profiles are more typical of the variety of youth crimes that characterize contemporary youth dockets.

The character of juvenile incarceration has also changed dramatically over three decades. Beginning in the 1970s, as adult correctional populations surged, large juvenile corrections facilities in several states were replaced by smaller facilities housing fewer than thirty children per center, sometimes in community-based residential programs but other times in "campuses" that included cluster or residential "pods."[44] Jerome Miller, architect of the Massachusetts reforms, showed that scandals involving staff abuse of youth residents, as well as youth suicides and uncontrolled violence, often sparked these changes. Massachusetts, Pennsylvania, Utah, and Florida, among others, moved from large, toxic warehouses to these smaller, disaggregated dormitory-like units.[45] In effect, the capacities of these systems were capped, and any expansion required the participation of the private sector.[46]

Yet noxious conditions still prevail in many juvenile corrections facilities and systems, and litigation is not uncommon. In *Galloway v. Texas*,[47] for example, plaintiff Galloway was placed in detention at fourteen and held until he reached nineteen, the maximum age of juvenile jurisdiction, based on unreviewable administrative decisions by facility staff. The trial record showed that Galloway and many others had been physically and sexually abused, subjected to physical punishment, abused by other inmates (abuse that was often sanctioned by staff), and denied access to counsel. Essential services—medical care, education, psychiatric treatment—were found to be substandard. More than five hundred children were released from unlawful juvenile corrections confinement in Texas as a result of the ruling.

Conditions in New York State juvenile corrections facilities were investigated recently by the Civil Rights Division of the U.S. Department of Justice, which reported similar problems. As a result, there is now federal oversight of four of the state's largest youth corrections facilities.[48] And in California, the state was ordered back to court for failure to comply with the terms of a consent decree that committed the juvenile corrections authority, the Division of Juvenile Justice of the California Department of Corrections and Rehabilitation (formerly the Youth Authority), to conform to professional and legal standards for essential services and the safety of its wards.[49] These cases are not isolated instances; litigation to remedy violent, abusive, and other substandard conditions in juvenile incarceration and detention has been repeated across the country for decades.

Structurally, federal civil rights litigation in these instances is constrained in its force and reach by the Prison Litigation Reform Act (PLRA).[50] In *Galloway*, for instance, relief was limited by the PLRA's constraints on which conditions can be litigated, its short paths to termination of existing remedial decrees, and its restrictions on the authority of federal judges to order future remedies. The PLRA applies fully to juvenile corrections and detention facilities: Congress classified juvenile facilities as "prisons" and their occupants "prisoners." In doing so, it erected tall and robust barriers to children's assertion of their rights: in effect, they face the same hurdles that adult prisoners do. For children, the problem is compounded because they cannot sue in their own name, and also by the fact that Federal Rule of Civil Procedure 17 relegates the question of capacity and overcrowding to state law. Under these conditions, children cannot get to court without a guardian, and most lack the social capital and experience to activate those resources. Furthermore, there simply are no local enforcement mechanisms to ensure compliance with federal litigation. It is up to local district attorneys to enforce the law when abuses are revealed. The political complications are obvious.

Again, we see very different visions of juvenile justice and incarceration. One is represented by the development of new models and institutional designs for the rehabilitation of serious juvenile offenders. This vision includes attention not just to basics such as education, but to new models for working with children and their families to sustain therapeutic successes beyond the time of correctional confinement.[51] The other vision is typified by institutions that are violent, abusive, and indifferent to the essential developmental interventions for adolescent offenders. Attorney and legal scholar Michael Tigar characterizes these as places where juvenile punishment has taken on the distorted values of criminal law and correctional institutions, where intervention is secondary to security and punishment, and where indifference tolerates abuse and violence.[52] In these places, services are thin and differ little from ordinary jails, only that the residents are younger, smaller, and more easily exploited. Between these poles are the institutions that struggle to mount effective programs with a population of difficult children who pose security as well as therapeutic challenges.

Racial disparities in juvenile detention and incarceration closely resemble racial disparities in the imprisonment and jailing of adults. Considering the negative consequences of incarceration on crime and social well-being, these disparities unfortunately may multiply the effects of other forms of disadvantage and may become an endogenous form of inequality that is difficult to escape. Social scientists call this a "poverty trap."[53]

In the 2006 census of juveniles in residential placement, 40.2 percent of residents were African American and 20.5 percent were Hispanic, compared to 35 percent white.[54] These disparities were greater for person crimes and drug offenses (44 percent were African American in each category) and less for technical violations (37 percent were African American) and status offenses (33 percent were African American). In fact, 50 percent of incarcerated status offenders counted in the 2006 juvenile corrections census were white.

Racial disparities are far worse for pre-trial detention, compared to those who are incarcerated following a finding of delinquency. Nearly half (48 percent) of those detained for person crimes, 45 percent detained on drug offenses, and 46 percent detained for public order offenses were African Americans, compared to less than 30 percent whites in each of these categories.[55] (Public order offenses include weapons offenses as well as public drinking and a range of low level—and high police-discretion—misdemeanor offenses.)

These disparities are not well explained by differences in crime rates.[56] Studies using several designs and analytic strategies conclude that racial disparities in the decision to detain and incarcerate youths are influenced by race and risk factors such as family structure that are correlated with race more than criminal behavior.[57]

Other research implicates fundamental cognitive and unconscious processes in the production of disparities. Two studies based on observations of decisions by police or probation officers illustrate the role of race in the attribution of blame-worthiness, risk of future crime, and recommendations for punishment. Sociologists George Bridges and Sara Steen, analyzing narratives of presentence reports by probation officers in three counties in Washington State, showed that probation officers were more likely to attribute the causes of crime for African American youths to internal character and personality attributes rather than external factors such as family, neighborhood, or school. These internal attributions led to conclusions about "responsibility," whereas external attributions tended to reduce culpability by externalizing the origins of crime (and its severity) for white youths to the defendant's social surroundings. These internal attributions in turn led to racially disparate attributions of risk of future offending and harsher sentencing recommendations. Bridges and Steen also noted that a criminal history tends to multiply these effects.

Educational psychologist Sandra Graham and organizational behavior scholar Brian Lowery produced similar results using an experimental paradigm in which police and probation officers made judgments about culpability and predictions of future crime following exposure to race-specific or race-neutral subliminal primes. Compared to officers given a race-neutral prime, police and probation officers given race-specific primes rated a hypothetical offender with more negative traits such as hostility and immaturity, attributed greater culpability, had higher expectations of recidivism, and endorsed harsher punishment. These results were robust to controls for consciously expressed beliefs about African Americans.

Studies based on case-processing data also reach the same conclusions, as does a research summary prepared for the Department of Justice. This is true both in criminal court and for juveniles who are transferred to criminal court.[58]

The policy studies raise two difficult questions. First, are the effects of disparate outcomes at early stages predictive of outcomes—including the decision to detain or incarcerate a young offender—at later stages? Researchers disagree on this point. Some suggest that disadvantage at early decision points, such as the decision to detain or to treat a case formally instead of using a diversionary alternative, at a minimum carries forward and perhaps multiplies across decision points. Others suggest that disparities at each stage are unique to decisions at that stage, net of filtering at each stage. In either case, there is a unique additive component for race that seems to produce disparate outcomes overall, including correctional placements.[59]

Second, and more fundamentally, does the combined evidence from experimental and observational studies suggest that racial bias is present in the juvenile justice system with sufficient salience to produce disparities? It is always difficult to identify and control for all the counterfactuals that would have to be defeated in order to make such a claim. At the least, these would include a set of institutional preferences and norms that are difficult to measure and that are likely to vary widely across locales. But what is important to note is that the two most likely counterfactuals—differences in criminal behavior and differences in social risk indicia—are not significant producers of racial disparities.

Based on the research of Graham and Lowery, conscious bias is not a significant producer of racial disparity either, but subconscious bias may be, as well as racial differences in punitiveness and racial stereotypes. Sociologist Lawrence Bobo and Victor Thompson, for example, summarize public opinion research to show that negative racial stereotypes, antiblack affect, and collective racial resentments translate into increased punitiveness.[60] We have no reason to believe that this might not apply to probation workers and police officers who produce a supply of cases for the juvenile court. Research on "colorism" shows that both African Americans and white Americans associate skin tone with criminality and deserved punishment.[61] In a series of tests on implicit bias, every population group except African Americans unconsciously associates "African American" with crime or danger and reacts accordingly.[62] Tests include recognition of African American faces in crime situations (including possession of weapons)[63] and whether to shoot unarmed suspects when they are shown holding ambiguous objects other than guns.[64] Confirming what Bridges and Steen and Graham and Lowery reported, the Plant and Peruche tests given to police officers produced the same results.

The impacts of racially disparate decisions in juvenile detention and incarceration go beyond the loss of liberty and exposure to socially and emotionally disfiguring punishments. Juvenile incarceration attenuates the accumulation of social capital to access job networks and other supports; instead—at a developmentally sensitive and strategic period of transition from adolescence to adulthood—it leads to the accrual of criminal capital that sustains delinquency beyond the time of placement.[65] In this way, incarceration compounds social and racial disadvantage to sustain inequalities over the life course,[66] with crime itself only a partial explanation of the sources of that disadvantage. For minors, developmental trajectories following incarceration suggest that crime is less a factor than cascading social disadvantage. Studies of criminality over the life course show the unique and lasting disadvantage that accrues from an early incarceration experience, no matter the behavior that led to the period of incarceration.[67] Incarceration at a young age not only increases the risk of future incarceration, it mortgages the long-term prospects of young males for marriage, employment, and social stability over a lifetime. Even a short spell in detention adversely influences the outcomes of cases once they get to court, tipping the odds toward harsher punishment instead of diversion or probation.[68] Young offenders who are detained in jails or group homes while their cases work their way through court are more likely to be placed in a correctional institution at the conclusion of the case than those who return home or to school as their cases are resolved. Early correctional placement has a multiplier effect on the prospects of future imprisonment. To the extent that incarceration effects carry forward, we might ask whether the social harms of incarceration on young people are simply those of their parents revisited on them—and whether the harms to them will be revisited on their children.[69]

In the political economy of incarceration, it is remarkable that either a legislative or executive branch would acknowledge racial disparity much less seek remedies to it. Thus, the efforts of the Department of Justice and Congress to reduce racial disparities in juvenile confinement through public interventions are courageous and noteworthy. Because this step was reserved for minors, it again signals the special place child-saving holds as a normative imperative and policy preference in the culture of crime and punishment.

To regulate public sector practices that might lead to racial disparities, Congress took a rare step in 1992, passing legislation requiring states that receive federal juvenile-justice funds to implement strategies to reduce disparities (where those disparities exist) in the confinement rates of minority juveniles. This provision, known as the disproportionate minority contact statute (DMC),[70] seems modest in comparison to Title VII of the Civil Rights Act: it applies only to state-run juvenile justice programs receiving federal funds. Failure to comply can cost an agency at least 25 percent of its federal juvenile-justice support.

Legal scholar Olatunde Johnson[71] describes the DMC provision as unique in several ways. First, it calls on public actors to reduce disparities no matter what the cause, no matter whether intentional or reflective of the types of passive discrimination that characterize everyday institutional business, even if these practices advance the criminal justice interests of the public agency. Action requires only that there be a showing that the agency was complicit in producing disparity. Second, the statute requires states to gather analytic data to diagnose the institutional practices or public policies that produce racial disparities, and to identify appropriate steps to change those practices. In effect, the statute requires states to look beyond "invidious bias" to discover and remedy the sources of disparity. States were tasked with submitting intervention plans that reflected their analysis of the sources of disparity, developing interventions, and assessing the success of their efforts. In 2002, Congress broadened the mandate of DMC to look not just at confinement, but also at any type of contact. This expansion recognized the role that police and early-stage juvenile justice decisions play in producing disparities.

There are stories of both success and failure under DMC. Johnson notes that when DMC succeeds, it is because it leveraged the power of internal and external local advocates to design measures to reduce disparity. The data analytic component has also produced informational transparency that levels the playing field between advocates and government officials. It is a process of what legal scholar Heather Gerken calls "federalism all the way down," in part localizing solutions and also developing local expertise that competes with interior institutional logic and norms.[72]

Johnson suggests that failures under DMC reflect the weakness of local enforcement and ambivalence, if not resistance, that are, in turn, reflections of the local political structure. It requires internal change agents within agencies as well as external agents, especially advocacy groups. Localities could be exposed to lawsuits based on the information developed through the data analytic process, creating an untenable political tension. A set of political scripts that invokes public safety concerns in the face of systemic reform efforts is a blunt instrument to neutralize reform.[73] Thus, the recurring renewal of political support—based on research—is essential to sustain the reform. And this, as Johnson points out, is hardly a sure bet, since radically disparate treatment is not a strong motivation to expend political capital. The counterargument is that revelations of the connection between public policy and racially disparate treatment leading to incarceration make a strong normative argument that political actors ignore at their own risk. Perhaps the current low-crime era affords a moment to push ahead with this project.

The opposing, if not contradictory, trends in the philosophy and practice of juvenile incarceration can be observed empirically in states' variations in the practice and reach of juvenile incarceration. At the peak of juvenile incarceration, states varied in their incarceration populations from a low of 70 per 100,000 juveniles in Vermont to a high of 583 in Louisiana.[74] Explanations for variation are themselves varied: from racial threat and symbolic threats to public order, to violent crime rates, to loose couplings between juvenile and adult correctional systems, to variation in the political traction of "get tough" policies.[75] These diverse explanations matter because they speak to different strains in the political culture of crime and punishment—in particular about whether *juvenile* crime and punishment is itself a symbolic or substantive concern.

Symbolic threats are sociologically connected to structural conditions, including minority threat, inequality, and public manifestations of crime such as gangs. When professor of law Jonathan Simon speaks about "governing through crime," he portrays a discourse and subsequent political mobilization built on crime fears that translate into legislative action. These threats create emotions beyond the facts of crime itself by imparting social meaning to crime: gang violence signals the rise of an enemy, for example, and the trifecta of gangs, guns, and drugs signals a very particular and urgent threat to social order. Even property crime can translate into a threat through its spurious connection to violent crime. If crime itself is racially skewed, whether among juveniles or adults, then disconnecting symbolic threats from the real fears of crime becomes more difficult.

Sorting out these threats is a difficult empirical task. An analysis by criminologist Daniel Mears of state variation in juvenile incarceration suggests that it is not just the threat of violent crime that explains differences between states, but a combination of adult crime rates, adult incarceration rates, and juvenile property crime rates. What happened to the superpredator discourse about juvenile violence? Why was it not a more powerful predictor of juvenile incarceration? Quite likely, the discourse was already incorporated into other "get tough" measures, including adult incarceration rates and policies, as well as adult crime.

State variation may also conceal internal systemic and political factors that bear on institutional capacities. Consider the stories told earlier about Texas, California, and Pennsylvania (and add New York to the analysis). Texas made no changes in capacity in the face of litigation and a consent decree. California's Youth Authority reduced its capacity from ten thousand a decade ago to less than two thousand today in response to litigation. Pennsylvania built a juvenile prison that now houses nearly one thousand young offenders, but New York State is attempting to close several of its juvenile incarceration facilities, and may yet do so if the Civil Rights Division of the Justice Department proceeds from its investigation to pursue litigation. However, New York's efforts to downsize its system have been neutralized by the structure of union contracts and political constraints from local legislators fearing adverse economic impacts from the closing of institutions. There are 241 empty beds out of about 300 in the six nonsecure residential facilities targeted for closing, and 254 state employees will lose their jobs if the closings proceed.[76] The math suggests part of the reason why closing is so hard to achieve.

The number of minors locked up across the nation is a small fraction of the adolescents under the supervision of the juvenile and criminal justice systems, but it casts a long shadow over the principles and practice of juvenile and criminal justice. Separate institutions for juveniles, and later a separate court, served the twin goals of protecting adolescent offenders from the stigma and brutality of criminal justice and intervening in their lives to remedy the conditions that animated their antisocial behavior. Yet the punitive turn in juvenile justice increased the use of incarceration by juvenile courts and the expulsion of juvenile offenders to adult jails and prisons.[77] Not only are both forms of juvenile incarceration plagued by unconstitutionally cruel conditions and institutional neglect, but the emphasis on punitiveness, including the exile of juveniles to the criminal justice system, before adolescent development may do more harm than good.

Three facts suggest that the punitive turn in juvenile corrections is neither a socially productive nor a principled path. First, new behavioral and biological research about maturity and criminal culpability, largely focused on emotional regulation, impulsivity, decision-making, and other behavioral functioning closely linked to brain development and the social psychological skills that it controls, suggests that children remain immature and therefore less culpable well into late adolescence.[78] Second, adolescents who are tried and punished as adults are rearrested and incarcerated more often, more quickly, and for more serious crimes.[79] They are more likely to suffer mental health problems, including traumatic stress reactions, and are less likely to receive effective services to overcome their developmental or other behavioral deficits. And third, lengthened sentences for juvenile offenders, whether in juvenile or adult corrections placements, are of no apparent consequence to public safety.[80]

These facts argue for a return to the first principles of juvenile justice: avoiding harm and stigma and building the social capital and human capacity of the child. Declining crime rates, the pervasiveness of racial disparities in detention and incarceration, the intellectual and political exhaustion of the "toughness" paradigm in juvenile justice, and new gains in the science of adolescent development have converged to create an opportunity for principled reform. More careful regulation and deliberation of the use of incarceration can lay the foundation for more effective and fair policies. While the law has moved toward increasing the incarceration of younger teens, social and biological evidence suggests moving in the other direction. Perhaps it is time for the law to change course and follow the science and the principles it evokes.

ENDNOTES

1. Sharon Dolovich, "Incarceration: American Style," *Harvard Law & Policy Review* 3 (2009): 237.

2. *Parens patriae* is a doctrine commonly associated in both policy and law with the rights and obligations of the state and courts toward children and incapacitated adults. The diminished competence and autonomy of children is the court's justification for invoking *parens patriae* to supplant parental authority and assert control over children. See Julian Mack, "The Juvenile Court," *Annual Report of the 32nd Conference of the American Bar Association* (1909), 451.

3. In *Schall v. Martin* (467 U.S. 253, 1984), Justice Rehnquist argued that preventive detention is designed to protect the child and society from the potential consequences of the child's own "folly."

4. Ibid. The court said that the combined interest in protecting both the community and the juvenile himself from the consequences of future criminal conduct is sufficient to justify such detention. The court rejected claims about accuracy of such predictions, stating that "from a legal point of view, there is nothing inherently unattainable about a prediction of future criminal conduct" and that a prediction of future criminal conduct is "'an experienced prediction based on a host of variables' which cannot be readily codified" (citing *Greenholtz v. Nebraska Penal Inmates*, 442 U.S. 1, 16 [1979]).

5. Philip J. Cook and John H. Laub, "The Unprecedented Epidemic in Youth Violence," in *Crime and Justice: A Review of Research*, vol. 24, *Youth Violence*, ed. Michael Tonry and Mark H. Moore (Chicago: University of Chicago Press, 1998), 27.

6. Barry C. Feld, *Bad Kids: Race and the Transformation of the Juvenile Court* (New York: Oxford University Press, 1999); Franklin E. Zimring, *American Youth Violence* (New York: Oxford University Press, 1998).

7. Paul Lerman, "Twentieth-Century Developments in America's Institutional Systems for Youth in Trouble," in *A Century of Juvenile Justice*, ed. Margaret K. Rosenheim et al. (Chicago: University of Chicago Press, 2002).

8. See, for example, *Inside Out: Youth Experiences Inside New York's Juvenile Placement System* (Citizens' Committee for Children of New York, 2009), http://www.cccnewyork.org/publications/CCCjuvenilejusticereport2009.pdf.

9. Jeffrey Fagan, "Juvenile Crime and Criminal Justice: Resolving Border Disputes," *Future of Children* 8 (2008): 81.

10. Ibid.

11. William J. Bennett, John J. Dilulio, Jr., and John P. Walters, *Body Count: Moral Poverty—and How to Win America's War Against Crime and Drugs* (New York: Simon & Schuster, 1996).

12. Malcolm W. Klein, *The American Street Gang* (New York: Oxford University Press, 1995); Feld, *Bad Kids*.

13. Placement data for the years between 1993 and 1997 are not available. Prior to 1993, data were collected every three years as part of the Children in Custody (CIC) census, conducted by the Office of Juvenile Justice and Delinquency Prevention. It was based on a mail survey with response rates that varied by year. Starting in 1997, CIC was replaced by the Census of Juveniles in Residential Placement (CJRP), a one-day count conducted by the U.S. Bureau of the Census of all children placed in public and private facilities. The differences in the two

data sets reflect both the types of facilities included and whether residents are counted based on the state from which they were committed or, in the newer census, the state where they were placed. When aggregated to examine national trends, any biases resulting from these differences are minimized.

14. Melissa Sickmund, *Juveniles in Residential Placement, 1997–2008* (Office of Juvenile Justice and Delinquency Prevention, U.S. Department of Justice, 2010), http://www.ncjrs.gov/pdffiles1/ojjdp/229379.pdf.

15. The rate for adults is 509 per 100,000 persons in prisons and 762 per 100,000 in prisons or local jails. Heather C. West and William J. Sabol, *Prison Inmates at Mid-Year 2008—Statistical Tables* (Bureau of Justice Statistics, U.S. Department of Justice, 2009), Table 1, http://bjs.ojp.usdoj.gov/content/pub/pdf/pimo8st.pdf.

16. Sickmund, *Juveniles in Residential Placement*.

17. Melissa Sickmund et al., *Census of Juveniles in Residential Placement Databook* (National Center for Juvenile Justice, 2008), http://www.ojjdp.ncjrs.gov/ojstatbb/cjrp/.

18. These offenses include running away from home, incorrigibility, truancy, curfew violation, and underage drinking.

19. Howard N. Snyder and Melissa Sickmund, *Juvenile Offenders and Victims: 2006 National Report* (Office of Juvenile Justice and Delinquency Prevention, U.S. Department of Justice, 2006), http://www.ojjdp.ncjrs.gov/ojstatbb/nr2006/.

20. See West and Sabol, *Prison Inmates at Mid-Year 2008*, Table 21.

21. See, for example, Ruth D. Peterson, "Youthful Offenders Designations and Sentencing in the New York Criminal Courts," *Social Problems* 35 (1988): 111–130.

22. Andrea McGowan et al., "Effects on Violence of Laws and Policies Facilitating the Transfer of Juveniles from the Juvenile Justice System to the Adult Justice System: A Report on Recommendations of the Task Force on Community Preventive Services," *Morbidity and Mortality Weekly Report* 56 (RR-9) (November 30, 2007): 1–11; Donna Bishop, "Juvenile Offenders in the Adult Criminal System," *Crime and Justice* 27 (2000): 81–167; Fagan, "Juvenile Crime and Criminal Justice." But see Steven D. Levitt, "Juvenile Crime and Punishment," *Journal of Political Economy* 106 (1998): 1156.

23. This separation, however meaningful or substantively vague, was at the heart of the earliest forms of juvenile justice in the nineteenth century, when separate institutions for youths were created to shield them from the stigma and exploitation of older convicts. The motivations, though, were not entirely benevolent. The new youth-only institutions were also accommodations to the growing tendency among judges to avoid harsh punishments by dismissing criminal cases against older children, setting child offenders free without any form of social regulation or control. See John Sutton, *Stubborn Children: Controlling Delinquency in the United States, 1640–1981* (Berkeley: University of California Press, 1988); and David J. Rothman, *The Discovery of the Asylum: Social Order and Disorder in the New Republic* (Boston: Little, Brown, 1971). In 1851, in New York, the Children's Aid Society opened the House of Refuge for Delinquent Children under twelve, ostensibly to separate the "older" cohort of juvenile offenders from the very young ones. This division effectively created a disputed developmental territory between early and later adolescence; reformers used the territory to contest age-based linkages between vulnerability and culpability and the appropriate institutional responses.

24. Martin Forst, Jeffrey Fagan, and T. Scott Vivona, "Youth in Prisons and Training Schools: Perceptions and Consequences of the Treatment-Custody Dichotomy," *Juvenile & Family Court Journal* 40 (1989): 1; "The Changing Borders of Juvenile Justice: Transfer of Adolescents to the Adult Criminal Court," research brief no. 5 (MacArthur Research Network on Adolescent Development and Juvenile Justice), http://www.adjj.org/downloads/3582issue_brief_5.pdf.

25. Two recent Supreme Court opinions cited a body of robust social and behavioral science that demonstrates the diminished culpability of adolescents with respect to regulation of emotions and impulses, capacity to foresee consequences of their actions, and susceptibility to peer influences. See *Roper v. Simmons* (543 U.S. 551 [2005]) and *Graham v. Florida* (No. 08-7412, 982 So. 2d 43, reversed and remanded [2010]).

26. Elizabeth S. Scott and Laurence Steinberg, *Rethinking Juvenile Justice* (Cambridge, Mass.: Harvard University Press, 2008).

27. Fagan, "Juvenile Crime and Criminal Justice."

28. Feld, *Bad Kids*; Zimring, *American Youth Violence.*

29. See, for example, Patricia Torbet et al., *State Responses to Serious and Violent Juvenile Crime* (Office of Juvenile Justice and Delinquency Prevention, U.S. Department of Justice, 1996).

30. Fagan, "Juvenile Crime and Criminal Justice"; Donna Bishop, "Juvenile Offenders in the Adult Criminal System."

31. Torbet et al., *State Responses to Serious and Violent Juvenile Crime.*

32. See *State v. Standard*, 569 S.E.2d 325, 329 (2002). In general, see *The Rest of Their Lives* and *The Rest of Their Lives, 2008 Update* (Amnesty International and Human Rights Watch, 2005 and 2008), http://www.hrw.org/en/node/11578/section/1 and http://www.hrw.org/sites/default/files/reports/us1005execsum.pdf. The fact that mandatory life-without-parole sentences require a predicate of transfer, the cumulative disadvantage of poor counsel and early-stage detention compound the risks for a life-without-parole sentence through disadvantages at the early stages of charging and plea bargaining.

33. See *Graham v. Florida.*

34. See *The Rest of Their Lives, 2008 Update*; also *Cruel and Unusual: Sentencing 13- and 14-Year-Old Children to Die in Prison* (Equal Justice Initiative, 2008), http://eji.org/eji/files/Cruel%20and%20Unusual%202008_0.pdf.

35. Torbet et al., *State Responses to Serious and Violent Juvenile Crime.*

36. See *The Connecticut Juvenile Justice Strategic Plan: Building Toward a Better Future* (State of Connecticut Judicial Branch, 2006), http://www.jud.ct.gov/external/news/JuvenileJustPlan/CJJ_ExecutiveSummary.pdf.

37. Fagan, "Juvenile Crime and Criminal Justice."

38. A few states developed statutes to try juveniles as adults but sentence them to juvenile correctional institutions. The theory was that the determination of guilt or innocence should respond to an adult standard of culpability, and that the trial itself was a form of expressive condemnation for the minor's offense. However, the reach of these laws was narrow, affecting few youths in a small number of states. Moreover, although the laws did succeed in shielding juveniles from placements with adults, they were no more than half-measures with respect to avoiding the stigma of a criminal conviction. See Patricia Torbet et al., *Juveniles Facing Criminal Sanctions: Three States that Changed the Rules* (2000), http://www.ncjrs.gov/pdffiles1/ojjdp/181203.pdf.

39. Even California's controversial Youth Authority has conformed to this trend; for many years it was an exception. However, the total incarcerated juvenile population declined from approximately 10,000 in 1996 to 1,568 today. See *2008 Population Report* (Division of Juvenile Justice, California Department of Corrections and Rehabilitation, 2008), http://www.cdcr.ca.gov/reports_research/research_tips.html.

40. Bennett, Dilulio, and Walters, *Body Count.*

41. Cook and Laub, "The Unprecedented Epidemic of Youth Violence."

42. Zimring, *American Youth Violence.*

43. "Pennsylvania Opens Nation's First Youth Prison," *Corrections Digest*, December 15, 2000.

44. See, for example, Jerome G. Miller, *Last One Over the Wall: The Massachusetts Experiment in Closing Reform Schools* (Columbus: Ohio State University Press, 1991).

45. See, for example, Lloyd Ohlin et al., "Radical Correctional Reform: A Case Study of the Massachusetts Youth Correctional System," *Harvard Educational Review*, special issue on The Rights of Children, 120 (1974).

46. Edmund F. McGarrell, *Juvenile Correctional Reform: Two Decades of Policy and Procedural Change* (Albany: State University of New York Press, 1988).

47. Civ No. 1:07-CA-276 (W.D. Tex.). See also Sylvia Moreno, "In Texas, Scandals Rock Juvenile Justice System," *The Washington Post*, April 5, 2007.

48. Nicholas Confessore, "Federal Oversight for Troubled N.Y. Youth Prisons," *The New York Times*, July 14, 2010. Letter from Loretta King, Acting Assistant Attorney General, to Governor David A. Paterson, Re: Investigation of the Lansing Residential Center, Louis Gossett, Jr. Residential Center, Tryon Residential Center, and Tryon Girls Center, August 14, 2009, http://www.justice.gov/crt/split/documents/NY_juvenile_facilities_findlet_08-14-2009.pdf.

49. *Farrell v. Gate*, RG03-079344 (Cal. Super. Ct. 2004).

50. See 18 U.S.C. section 3626 (1995).

51. See Michelle Inderbitzin, "Reentry of Emerging Adults: Adolescent Inmates' Transition Back Into the Community," *Journal of Adolescent Research* 24 (2009): 453. Also see Scott Huey et al., "Mechanisms of Change in Multisystemic Therapy: Reducing Delinquent Behavior through Therapist Adherence and Improved Family and Peer Functioning," *Journal of Consulting and Clinical Psychology* 68 (2000): 451.

52. Michael E. Tigar, "What are We Doing to the Children?: An Essay on Juvenile (In)Justice," *Ohio State Journal of Criminal Law* 7 (2010): 849.

53. Robert J. Sampson and Jeffrey Morenoff, "Durable Inequality: Spatial Dynamics, Social Processes, and the Persistence of Poverty in Chicago Neighborhoods," in *Poverty Traps*, ed. Samuel Bowles, Steven Durlauf, and Karla Hoff (New York: Russell Sage Foundation, 2006), 176–203.

54. Sickmund et al., *Census of Juveniles in Residential Placement Databook*.

55. Juvenile arrest rates for drug offenses are strongly at odds with their involvement in drug use and drug selling. See, for example, Leonard Saxe et al., "The Visibility of Illicit Drugs: Implications for Community-Based Drug Control Strategies," *American Journal of Public Health* 91 (2001): 1987.

56. Ibid. See also, Donna M. Bishop, "The Role of Race and Ethnicity in Juvenile Justice Processing," in *Our Children, Their Children: Confronting Racial and Ethnic Differences in American Juvenile Justice*, ed. Darnell F. Hawkins and Kimberly Kempf-Leonard (Chicago: University of Chicago Press, 2005).

57. George S. Bridges and Sara Steen, "Racial Disparities in Official Assessments of Juvenile Offenders: Attributional Stereotypes as Mediating Mechanisms," *American Sociological Review* 63 (1998): 554; Sandra Graham and Brian S. Lowery, "Priming Unconscious Racial Stereotypes about Adolescent Offenders," *Law & Human Behavior* 28 (2004): 483.

58. Kareem L. Jordan and Tina L. Freiburger, "Examining the Impact of Race and Ethnicity on the Sentencing of Juveniles in the Adult Court," *Criminal Justice Policy Review* 21 (2010): 185.

59. Carl E. Pope, Rick Lovell, and Heidi M. Hsia, *Disproportionate Minority Confinement: A Review of the Research Literature From 1989 Through 2001* (Office of Juvenile Justice and Delinquency Prevention, U.S. Department of Justice, 2002), http://www.ojjdp.ncjrs.gov/dmc/pdf/dmc89_01.pdf; David Huizinga et al., *Disproportionate Minority Contact in the Juvenile Justice System: A Study of Differential Minority Arrest/Referral to Court in Three Cities* (U.S. Department of Justice, 2007), http://www.ncjrs.gov/pdffiles1/ojjdp/grants/219743.pdf.

60. Lawrence Bobo and Victor Thompson, "Unfair by Design: The War on Drugs, Race, and the Legitimacy of the Criminal Justice System," *Social Research* 73 (2006): 445.

61. See, for example, Jennifer L. Eberhardt et al., "Seeing Black: Race, Crime, and Visual Processing," *Journal of Personality and Social Psychology* 87 (2004): 876; Jennifer L. Eberhardt et al., "Looking Deathworthy: Perceived Stereotypicality of Black Defendants Predicts Capital-Sentencing Outcomes," *Psychological Science* 17 (2006): 383.

62. Anthony Greenwald and Linda Hamilton Krieger, "Implicit Bias: Scientific Foundations," *California Law Review* 94 (2006): 945.

63. Eberhardt et al., "Seeing Black."

64. E. Ashby Plant and B. Michelle Peruche, "The Consequences of Race for Police Officers' Responses to Criminal Suspects," *Psychological Science* 16 (2005): 180.

65. Patrick Bayer, Radi Hjalmarsson, and David Pozen, "Building Criminal Capital Behind Bars: Peer Effects in Juvenile Corrections," *Quarterly Journal of Economics* 124 (2009): 105. Bayer and colleagues show that adolescents placed in correctional institutions are more likely than those in smaller residential placements to form stronger peer networks with other delinquents that lead to higher rearrest rates within two years of release.

66. Bruce Western, *Punishment and Inequality in America* (New York: Russell Sage Foundation, 2006); Todd R. Clear, *Imprisoning Communities: How Mass Incarceration Makes Disadvantaged Neighborhoods Worse* (New York: Oxford University Press, 2007).

67. Robert J. Sampson and John H. Laub, *Crime in the Making: Pathways and Turning Points Through Life* (Cambridge, Mass.: Harvard University Press, 1993); Jeffrey Fagan and Richard B. Freeman, "Crime and Work," *Crime and Justice* 25 (1999): 113.

68. Fagan and Freeman, "Crime and Work." Also see Donna M. Bishop, "The Role of Race and Ethnicity in Juvenile Justice Processing"; Rodney L. Engen, Sara Steen, and George S. Bridges, "Racial Disparities in the Punishment of Youth: A Theoretical and Empirical Assessment of the Literature," *Social Problems* 49 (2002): 194; Donna M. Bishop and Charles E. Frazier, "Race Effects in Juvenile Justice Decision-Making: Findings of a Statewide Analysis," *Journal of Criminal Law and Criminology* 86 (1996): 415.

69. See, for example, Christopher Wildeman, "Parental Imprisonment, the Prison Boom, and the Concentration of Childhood Disadvantage," *Demography* 46 (2009): 265. Also see Bruce Western and Christopher Wildeman, "The Black Family and Mass Incarceration," *Annals of the American Academy of Political and Social Sciences* 621 (2009): 221.

70. See Act of Nov. 4, 1992, Pub. L. No. 102-586, section 2(f)(3)(A)(ii), 106 Stat. 4982, 4993–94 (codified as amended at 42 U.S.C. section 5633 [Supp. III 2005]).

71. Olatunde C.A. Johnson, "Disparity Rules," *Columbia Law Review* 107 (2005): 374.

72. Heather Gerken, "Federalism All the Way Down?" *Harvard Law Review* (forthcoming).

73. See Jonathan Simon, *Governing through Crime: How the War on Crime Transformed American Democracy and Created a Culture of Fear* (New York: Oxford University Press, 2007).

74. Sickmund, *Juveniles in Residential Placement.*

75. Daniel Mears, "Exploring State-Level Variation in Juvenile Incarceration Rates: Symbolic Threats and Competing Explanations," *The Prison Journal* 86 (2006): 470.

76. Matt Schwarzfeld, "Fewer Lock-Ups, Enough Money?" *City Limits Weekly*, February 25, 2008.

77. In addition to expanding the crime categories that triggered transfer to the criminal court, many states reduced the minimum age at which offenders could be sentenced by criminal courts to age ten or younger. In a few states, all barriers to criminal court were removed down to the age of infancy; Snyder and Sickmund, *Juvenile Offenders and Victims.*

78. For a discussion of this evidence, see *Roper v. Simmons* (543 U.S. 551 [2005]); and *Graham v. Florida* (560 U.S. 130 S. Ct. [2010]). See also Scott and Steinberg, *Rethinking Juvenile Justice.*

79. Andrea McGowan et al., "Effects on Violence of Laws and Policies."

80. Thomas A. Loughran et al., "Estimating a Dose-Response Relationship Between Length of Stay and Future Recidivism in Serious Juvenile Offenders," *Criminology* 47 (2009): 699; Daniel Nagin, Francis T. Cullen, and Cheryl Lero Johnson, "Imprisonment and Reoffending," *Crime and Justice* 38 (2009): 115; Anthony N. Doob and Cheryl Marie Webster, "Sentence Severity and Crime: Accepting the Null Hypothesis," *Crime and Justice* 30 (2003): 143; Emily G. Owens, "More Time, Less Crime? Estimating the Incapacitative Effect of Sentence Enhancements," *The Journal of Law and Economics* 52 (2009): 551.

*Jeffrey Fagan is the Isidor and Seville Sulzbacher Professor of Law at Columbia Law School. He is also director of the JSD program at Columbia Law School and chair of graduate legal studies. He has published extensively in the area of criminology and public policy.

Fagan, Jeffrey. "The Contradictions of Juvenile Crime and Punishment." *Daedalus* 139, no. 3 (Summer 2010): 43–61.

Adolescent Development and the Regulation of Youth Crime

by Elizabeth S. Scott and Laurence Steinberg*

SUMMARY

Elizabeth Scott and Laurence Steinberg explore the dramatic changes in the law's conception of young offenders between the end of the nineteenth century and the beginning of the twenty-first. At the dawn of the juvenile court era, they note, most youths were tried and punished as if they were adults. Early juvenile court reformers argued strongly against such a view, believing that the justice system should offer young offenders treatment that would cure them of their anti-social ways. That rehabilitative model of juvenile justice held sway until a sharp upswing in youth violence at the end of the twentieth century led both public opinion and public policy toward a view that youths should be held to the same standard of criminal accountability as adults. Lawmakers seemed to lose sight of developmental differences between adolescents and adults.

But Scott and Steinberg note that lawmakers and the public appear now to be rethinking their views once more. A justice system that operates on the principle of "adult time for adult crime" now seems to many to take too little note of age and immaturity in calculating criminal punishment. In 2005 the United States Supreme Court abolished the juvenile death penalty as cruel and unusual punishment, emphasizing that the immaturity of adolescents made them less culpable than adult criminals. In addition, state legislatures recently have repealed or moderated some of the punitive laws they recently enacted. Meanwhile, observe the authors, public anger has abated and attitudes toward young offenders have softened somewhat.

In response to these changes, Scott and Steinberg argue that it is appropriate to reexamine juvenile justice policy and to devise a new model for the twenty-first century. In this article, they propose what they call a developmental model. They observe that substantial new scientific evidence about adolescence and criminal activity by adolescents provides the building blocks for a new legal regime superior to today's policy. They put adolescent offenders into an intermediate legal category—neither children, as they were seen in the early juvenile court era, nor adults, as they often are seen today. They observe that such an approach is not only more compatible than the current regime with basic principles of fairness at the heart of the criminal law, but also more likely to promote social welfare by reducing the social cost of juvenile crime.

During the closing decades of the twentieth century, juvenile justice policy under-went major change. In less than a generation, a justice system that had viewed most young lawbreakers as youngsters whose crimes were the product of immaturity was transformed into one that stands ready to hold many youths to the same standard of criminal accountability it imposes on adults. These changes took place through far-reaching legal and policy reforms in almost every state that have facilitated adult prosecution and punishment of juveniles and expanded the use of incarceration in the juvenile system. As the reforms proceeded, often in a frenzy of public fear and anger about violent juvenile crime, law-makers appeared to assume that any differences between adolescents and adults were immaterial when it comes to devising youth crime policies.

Today, lawmakers and the public appear to be having second thoughts about a justice system in which age and immaturity often are ignored in calculating criminal punishment. In 2005, the United States Supreme Court, in *Roper v. Simmons*, abolished the juvenile death penalty as cruel and unusual punishment in an opinion that emphasized that the immaturity of adolescents made them less culpable than adult criminals.[1] Further, legislatures recently have repealed or moderated some of the punitive laws enacted with enthusiasm just a few years ago. Meanwhile, opinion polls show that public anger has abated and that more paternalistic attitudes toward young offenders have resurfaced.

At such a time, it seems appropriate to reexamine juvenile justice policy and, if the contemporary regime proves unsatisfactory, to devise a better model for the twenty-first century. In this article, we undertake this challenge, proposing what we call a developmental model of juvenile justice policy.[2] Our thesis is that a substantial body of new scientific knowledge about adolescence and about criminal activity during this important developmental period provides the building blocks for a new legal regime superior to today's policy. Under the developmental model, adolescent offenders constitute an intermediate legal category of persons who are neither children, as they were under the traditional rehabilitative model, nor adults, as they often are today. Not only is this approach more compatible than the current regime with basic principles of fairness at the heart of the criminal law, it is also more likely to promote social welfare by reducing the social costs of juvenile crime.

A BRIEF HISTORY OF JUVENILE JUSTICE IN AMERICA

The history of juvenile crime policy over the course of the twentieth century is a narrative about the transformation of the law's conception of young offenders.

At the dawn of the juvenile court era in the late nineteenth century, most youths were tried and punished as adults. Much had changed by 1909 when Judge Julian Mack famously proposed in a *Harvard Law Review* article that a juvenile offender should be treated "as a wise and merciful father handles his own child."[3] Like the other Progressive reformers who worked to establish the juvenile court, Judge Mack viewed youths involved in crime first and foremost as children; indeed, by his account, they were no different from children who were subject to parental abuse and neglect. The early reformers envisioned a regime in which young offenders would receive treatment that would cure them of their antisocial ways—a system in which criminal responsibility and punishment had no place. Because of the juvenile court's rehabilitative purpose, procedures were informal and dispositions were indeterminate.

The rehabilitative model of juvenile justice seemingly thrived during the first half of the twentieth century, but it began to unravel during the 1960s. Youth advocates challenged the constitutionality of informal delinquency proceedings, and, in 1967, the Supreme Court agreed, holding, in *In re Gault*, that youths in juvenile court have a right to an attorney and other protections that criminal defendants receive.[4] But the sharpest attacks on the juvenile court came from another direction. As youth crime rates rose during the 1980s, conservative politicians ridiculed the juvenile system and pointed to high recidivism rates as evidence that rehabilitation was a failure. According to some observers, the juvenile court may have met the needs of a simpler time when juveniles got into school yard fights, but it was not up to the task of dealing with savvy young criminals who use guns to commit serious crimes. Although in truth, the juvenile justice system had evolved considerably since the early days, its paternalistic rhetoric persisted, obscuring the changes; even to a sympathetic ear, descriptions of young criminals as wayward children who would respond to the caring treatment of the juvenile court seemed to bear little relation to the reality of youth crime during the late twentieth century.

Proponents of more punitive policies cast the available options as either adult punishment or a "slap on the wrist," suggesting that if teens are not held fully responsible for their crimes, they bear no criminal responsibility at all. Youth advocates often appeared to accept these constrained policy choices, so the debate pitted self-styled "child" advocates against those who favor "adult time for adult crime." Thus, both sides implicitly accepted that youths charged with serious crimes would either be treated as children in juvenile court or tried and punished as adults. The new generation of reformers went beyond rejecting the paternalistic characterization of young offenders; some advocates for tough policies seemed to view juveniles involved in crime as more culpable and dangerous than adult criminals. John Dilulio's description of "superpredators" in the mid-1990s captured the image of remorseless teenage criminals as a major threat to society and was invoked repeatedly in the media and in the political arena.[5]

As juvenile crime rates—particularly homicide—rose during the 1980s and early 1990s, politicians across the country rushed to enact tough policies through several legislative strategies.[6] First, the age of judicial transfer was lowered in many states to allow the criminal prosecution of teens aged fourteen and younger. Some legislatures expanded the range of transferrable offenses to include a long laundry list of crimes. But perhaps the most dramatic changes came in the form of automatic transfer statutes, under which many youths are categorically treated as adults when they are charged with crimes—either generally (all sixteen-year-olds) or for specific crimes (all thirteen-year-olds charged with murder).[7] These legal reforms resulted in the wholesale transfer of youths into the adult criminal system—more than 250,000 a year by most estimates. The new statutes avoid individualized transfer hearings, shifting discretion from juvenile court judges, who are seen as soft on crime, to prosecutors, who are assumed not to have this deficiency. At the same time, juvenile court dispositions today include more incarceration and for longer periods—extending well into adulthood under some statutes. Questions about whether juveniles should be subject to the same punishment as adults occasionally do get attention—usually when a very young juvenile commits a serious crime. Thus a national conversation was sparked by the case of Lionel Tate, the twelve-year-old Florida boy who was given a life sentence (later reversed) for killing a six-year-old neighbor girl.[8] But the new policies play out in many more mundane cases involving drug sales and property crimes, which make up about half of the criminal court cases involving juveniles.

The upshot of this reform movement is that the mantra "adult time for adult crime" has become a reality for many young offenders. Through a variety of initiatives, the boundary of childhood has shifted dramatically in a relatively short time, so that youths who are legal minors for every other purpose are adults when it comes to their criminal conduct.

Supporters defend the recent reforms as a rational policy response to a new generation of dangerous young criminals that the juvenile court was unable to control. There is some truth to this claim. Young offenders today do cause more harm than their predecessors, largely because, with the ready availability of firearms, the injuries they inflict are more likely to be fatal. Moreover, the juvenile system's failure to deter or incapacitate violent young criminals fueled outrage that sometimes was legitimate. But close inspection reveals that the process of legal reform has been deeply flawed and often has had the hallmarks of what sociologists call a moral panic, a form of irrational collective action in which politicians, the media, and the public reinforce each other in an escalating pattern of alarmed response to a perceived social threat.[9] Other features of a moral panic are evident in the response to juvenile crime that has led to the reforms—intense public hostility toward young offenders (often identified as members of minority groups), exaggerated perceptions about the magnitude of the threat, and the conviction that drastic measures in response are urgently needed. Reform initiatives often have been triggered by a high-profile crime that stirs public fears. In Arkansas, for example, legislative reforms lowering the minimum age of criminal adjudication for juveniles followed the Jonesboro school shootings in which two youths, aged eleven and thirteen, killed four schoolmates and a teacher. In some states, racial biases and fears appear to have played a role in reform initiatives. In California, for example, enthusiasm for Proposition 21, a sweeping referendum expanding criminal court jurisdiction over juveniles, was generated by sensational television ads in which African American gang members killed innocent bystanders in drive-by shootings.[10] But by the time that California voters approved Proposition 21, juvenile crime had been on the decline for several years.[11]

The politics of contemporary juvenile justice law reform leaves little reason to be confident about the soundness of the new regime—or even to believe that it reflects stable public desires for harsh policies. Although politicians claim that the public demands tough policies, moral panics tend to dissipate when the crisis passes. As we will show at the end of this article, the evidence suggests that the public may demand tough policies in the short term, but not support them in the long term.

The fact that the law reform process has been deeply flawed and that the policies themselves are anomalous as a form of legal regulation of minors does not answer the critical question of whether the criminalization of juvenile justice is *substantively* deficient as legal policy. We turn now to this question.

ADOLESCENCE AND CULPABILITY: THE CASE FOR MITIGATION

A substantive assessment of contemporary youth crime regulation begins by examining the punitive reforms in the framework of criminal law doctrine and principles. The heart of the analysis is the principle of proportionality, which, as first-year law students learn in their criminal law class, is the foundation of fair and legitimate state punishment. Proportionality holds that criminal sanctions should be based on the culpability of the actor as well as the harm he causes. It recognizes that two defendants who cause the same harm (killing another person, for example) can vary in their blameworthiness and in the punishment that society thinks they deserve.[12] Most criminals, of course, are held fully responsible for their crimes and receive whatever punishment the state deems appropriate for the harm they cause. But actors who are thought to be blameless (children, for example, or someone who kills in self-defense) deserve no punishment—and their crimes are excused. As we have seen, the history of youth crime policy during the twentieth century was an account of radical change in lawmakers' conception of young offenders—from innocent children under the rehabilitative model to (often) fully responsible adults today.

But the criminal law does not view culpability in such binary terms; the concept of *mitigation* plays an important role in the law's calculation of blame and punishment and should be at the heart of youth crime policy. Mitigation applies to persons engaging in harmful conduct who are blameworthy enough to meet the minimum threshold of criminal responsibility, but who deserve less punishment than a typical offender would receive. Developmental research clarifies that adolescents, because of their immaturity, should not be deemed as culpable as adults. But they also are not innocent children whose crimes should be excused. The distinction between excuse and mitigation seems straightforward, but it is often misunderstood. In the political arena, as we have suggested, it is often assumed that unless young offenders are subject to adult punishment, they are off the hook—escaping all responsibility. Instead, under the developmental model, youths are held accountable for their crimes but presumptively are subject to more lenient punishment than adults. A justice system grounded in mitigation corresponds to the developmental reality of adolescence and is compatible with the law's commitment to fair punishment.

Research in developmental psychology supports the view that several characteristics of adolescence distinguish young offenders from adults in ways that mitigate culpability. These adolescent traits include deficiencies in decision-making ability, greater vulnerability to external coercion, and the relatively unformed nature of adolescent character. As we will show, each of these attributes of adolescence corresponds to a conventional source of mitigation in criminal law. Together they offer strong evidence that young offenders are not as culpable as adults.

DIMINISHED DECISION-MAKING CAPACITY

Under standard criminal law doctrine, actors whose decision-making capacities are impaired—by mental illness or retardation, for example—are deemed less blameworthy than typical offenders. If the impairment is severe, their crimes are excused. Considerable evidence supports the conclusion that children and adolescents are less capable decision makers than adults in ways that are relevant to their criminal choices.

Although few would question this claim as applied to children, the picture is more complicated for sixteen- or seventeen-year-olds. The capacities for reasoning and understanding improve significantly from late childhood into adolescence, and by mid-adolescence, most teens are close to adults in their ability to reason and to process information (what might be called "pure" cognitive capacities)—at least in the abstract.[13] The reality, however, is that adolescents are likely less capable than adults are in *using* these capacities in making real-world choices, partly because of lack of experience and partly because teens are less efficient than adults in processing information. In life, and particularly on the street, the ability to quickly marshal information may be essential to optimal decision making.

Other aspects of psychological maturation that affect decision making lag behind cognitive development and undermine adolescent competence. Research documents what most parents of adolescents already know—teenagers are subject to psychosocial and emotional influences that contribute to immature judgment that can lead them to make bad choices. Thus, even at ages sixteen and seventeen, adolescents' developmental immaturity likely affects their decisions about involvement in crime in ways that distinguish them from adults.

First, teens tend to lack what developmentalists call "future orientation." That is, compared with adults, adolescents are more likely to focus on the here-and-now and less likely to think about the long-term consequences of their choices or actions—and when they do, they are inclined to assign less weight to future consequences than to immediate risks and benefits. Over a period of years between mid-adolescence and early adulthood, individuals become more future oriented.[14]

Substantial research evidence also supports the conventional wisdom that teens are more oriented toward peers and responsive to peer influence than are adults. Several studies show that susceptibility to peer influence, especially in situations involving pressure to engage in antisocial behavior, increases between childhood and mid-adolescence, peaks around age fourteen, and declines slowly during the late adolescent years.[15] Increased susceptibility to peer pressure in early adolescence may reflect changes in individuals' capacity for self-direction (as parental influence declines) as well as changes in the intensity of pressure that adolescents exert on each other. Some research evidence suggests that teens who engage in certain types of antisocial behavior may enjoy higher status among their peers as a consequence, perhaps because they appear to be independent of adult authority.[16] The result is that adolescents are more likely than *either* children or adults to change their decisions and alter their behavior in response to peer pressure.

Peer influence affects adolescent judgment both directly and indirectly. In some contexts, adolescents might make choices in response to direct peer pressure, as when they are coerced to take risks that they might otherwise avoid. But desire for peer approval (and fear of rejection) affects adolescent choices indirectly as well. Teens appear to seek peer approval especially in group situations. Thus, perhaps it is not surprising that young offenders are far more likely than adults to commit crimes in groups.[17]

Consider the case of Timothy Kane, a fourteen-year-old junior high school student who never had any contact with the justice system until one Sunday afternoon in January 1992. Tim was hanging out with a group of friends when a couple of older youths suggested that they break into a neighbor's house; Tim agreed to go along. On entering the house, the boys were surprised to find the elderly neighbor and her son at home—whereupon the two older boys killed them while Tim watched from under the dining room table. Interviewed years later as he served a life sentence under Florida's draconian felony murder law, Tim explained that he went along because he didn't want to stay behind alone—and he didn't want to be called a "fraidy-cat." Tim's fatal decision to get involved in the break-in appears to be, more than anything else, the conduct of a fourteen-year-old worried about peer approval.[18]

Another psychosocial factor contributes to immature judgment: adolescents are both less likely to perceive risks and less risk-averse than adults. Thus, it is not surprising, perhaps, that they enjoy engaging in activities like speeding, unsafe sex, excessive drinking, and committing crimes more than adults do. The story is actually a bit more complicated. In the abstract, on paper and pencil tests, adolescents are capable of perceiving risks almost as well as adults. In the real world however, risk preference and other dimensions of psychosocial immaturity interact to encourage risky choices.[19] Thus, a youth who might be able to identify the risks of stealing a car if presented with a hypothetical case in a psychology lab may simply never consider these risks when he is on the street with his friends planning the theft.

Another (compatible) account of why adolescents take more risks than adults is that they may *evaluate* the risks and benefits of risky activity differently. Psychologists refer to the outcome of weighing risks and rewards as the "risk-reward ratio." The higher the ratio, the less likely an individual is to engage in the behavior in question. Studies suggest that in calculating the risk-reward ratio that guides decision making, adolescents may discount risks and calculate rewards differently from adults. In studies involving gambling games, teens tend to focus more on potential gains relative to losses than do adults.[20] So, for example, in deciding whether to speed while driving a car, adolescents may weigh the potential rewards of the behavior (for example, the thrill of driving fast, peer approval, or getting to one's destination quickly) more heavily than adults would. Indeed, sometimes adults may view as a risk—fast driving, for example—what adolescents see as a reward. What distinguishes adolescents from adults in this regard, then, is not the fact that teens are less knowledgeable about risks, but, rather, that they attach different value to the rewards that risk-taking provides.[21]

In addition to age differences in susceptibility to peer influence, future orientation, and risk assessment, adolescents and adults also differ with respect to their ability to control impulsive behavior and choices. Thus, the conventional wisdom that adolescents are more reckless than adults is supported by research on developmental changes in impulsivity and self-management. In general, studies show gradual but steady increases in the capacity for self-direction through adolescence, with gains continuing through the high school years. Research also indicates that adolescents are subject to more rapid and extreme mood swings, both positive and negative, than are adults.[22] Although the connection between moodiness and impulsivity is not clear, it is likely that extreme levels of emotional arousal, either anger or elation, are associated with difficulties in self-control. More research is needed, but the available evidence indicates that adolescents may have more difficulty regulating their moods, impulses, and behaviors than do adults.

These psychosocial and emotional factors contribute to immature judgment in adolescence and probably play a role in decisions by teens to engage in criminal activity. It is easy to imagine how an individual whose choices are subject to these developmental influences—susceptibility to peer influence, poor risk assessment, sensation seeking, a tendency to give more weight to the short-term consequences of choices, and poor impulse control—might decide to engage in criminal conduct.

The following scenario is illustrative. A teen is hanging out with his buddies on the street, when, on the spur of the moment, someone suggests holding up a nearby convenience store. The youth does not go through a formal decision-making process, but he "chooses" to go along, even if he has mixed feelings. Why? First and most important, like Tim Kane, he may assume that his friends will reject him if he declines to participate—a negative consequence to which he attaches considerable weight in considering alternatives. He does not think of ways to extricate himself, as a more mature person might do. He may fail to consider possible options because he lacks experience, because the choice is made so quickly, or because he has difficulty projecting the course of events into the future. Also, the "adventure" of the holdup and the possibility of getting some money are exciting. These immediate rewards, together with peer approval, weigh more heavily in his decision than the (remote) possibility of apprehension by the police. He never even considers the long- term costs of conviction of a serious crime.

This account is consistent with the general developmental research on peer influence, risk preference, impulsivity, and future orientation, and it suggests how factors that are known to affect adolescent decision making in general are likely to operate in this setting. As a general proposition, it is uncontroversial that teens are inclined to engage in risky behaviors that reflect their immaturity of judgment. Although it is not possible to study directly the decisions of teens to get involved in criminal activity, it seems very likely that the psychosocial influences that shape adolescents' decision making in other settings contribute to their choices about criminal activity as well. Not every teen gets involved in crime, of course. That depends on a lot of things, including social context. But these psychosocial and emotional influences on decision making are *normative*— as psychologists use this term—that is, typical of adolescents as a group and developmental in nature.

Research over the past few years has increased our understanding of the biological underpinnings of psychological development in adolescence. Very recent studies of adolescent brain development show that the frontal lobes undergo important structural change during this stage, especially in the prefrontal cortex.[23] This region is central to what psychologists call "executive functions"— advanced thinking processes used in planning ahead, regulating emotions, controlling impulses, and weighing the costs and benefits of decisions before acting. Thus, the immature judgment of teens may to some extent be a function of hard wiring.

MITIGATION ON THE BASIS OF EXTRAORDINARY CIRCUMSTANCES

Another source of mitigation in the criminal law also applies to adolescents—and reinforces the conclusion that young offenders are less blameworthy than their adult counterparts. This form of mitigation involves situations in which a person offends in response to extreme external pressures. For example, a person who robs a bank in response to a credible threat that otherwise he will be physically injured may qualify for the defense of duress. The criminal law does not require exceptional forbearance or bravery—a defense (or a reduced sentence) may be available if an ordinary (that is, "reasonable") person might have responded to the unusual situation in the same way the defendant did. Because of the coercive circumstances, the actor is deemed less blameworthy than other offenders.

Ordinary adolescents are subject to peer pressure, including pressure to commit crimes, to a far greater extent than adults. As we have suggested, most juvenile crimes are committed in groups, while most adult criminals act alone. In some high-crime neighborhoods, peer pressure to commit crimes is so powerful that only exceptional youths escape. As Jeffrey Fagan and others have explained, in such settings, resisting this pressure can result in loss of status, ostracism, and even vulnerability to physical assault.[24] The circumstances many teens face in these social contexts are similar to those involved in adult claims of mitigation due to duress, provocation, necessity, or domination by co-defendants— and appropriately are deemed mitigating of culpability. As the Supreme Court recognized in *Roper v. Simmons*, in holding that imposing the death penalty on juveniles was unconstitutional, the case for mitigation on this ground is all the more compelling because, unlike adults, teens as legal minors are not free to leave their schools, homes, and neighborhoods.[25] When teens cross the line to legal adulthood, of course, the formal disabilities of youth are lifted. Young adults can avoid the pressure by removing themselves from social settings that make it difficult to avoid involvement in crime. Thus, adults have no claim to this kind of situational mitigation.

UNFORMED CHARACTER AS MITIGATION

A third source of mitigation in the criminal law is evidence that a criminal act was out-of-character. At sentencing, offenders often can introduce evidence of their general good character to demonstrate that the offense was an aberrant act and not the product of bad character. Here mitigation applies to the crimes of young offenders as well—not because of their good character *per se*—but because their characters are unformed.

Beginning with Erik Erikson, psychologists have explained that a key developmental task of adolescence is the formation of personal identity—a process linked to psychosocial development, which for most teens extends over several years until a coherent "self" emerges in late adolescence or early adulthood.[26] During adolescence, identity is fluid—values, plans, attitudes, and beliefs are likely to be tentative as teens struggle to figure out who they are. This process involves a lot of experimentation, which for many adolescents means engaging in the risky activities we have described, including involvement in crime. Self-report studies have found that 80–90 percent of teenage boys admit to committing crimes for which they could be incarcerated.[27]

But the typical teenage delinquent does not grow up to be an adult criminal. The statistics consistently show that seventeen-year-olds commit more crimes than any other age group—thereafter, the crime rate declines steeply.[28] Most adolescents literally grow out of their antisocial tendencies as individual identity becomes settled. How many adults look back on their risky adventures or mishaps as teenagers with chagrin and amazement—and often with gratitude that they emerged relatively unscathed?

Researchers find that much juvenile crime stems from experimentation typical of this developmental stage rather than from moral deficiencies reflecting bad character. It is fair to assume that most adults who commit crimes act on subjectively defined values and preferences—and that their choices can be charged to deficient moral character. Thus an impulsive adult whose "adolescent" traits lead him to get involved in crime is quite different from a risk-taking teen. Adolescent traits are not typical of adulthood. The values and preferences that motivate the adult criminal are not transitory, but fixed elements of personal identity. This cannot be said of the crimes of typical juvenile offenders, whose choices, while unfortunate, are shaped by developmental factors that are constitutive of adolescence. Like the adult who offers evidence of good character, most adolescent offenders lack a key component of culpability—the connection between the bad act and the offender's bad character. In *Roper v. Simmons,* the Supreme Court recognized that adolescents' unformed character mitigates culpability. The court observed that it is not possible to be confident that "even a heinous crime by an adolescent is the product of an irretrievably depraved character."[29]

The reality, of course, is that not all young offenders grow up to be persons of good character. Some grow up to be criminals. Psychologist Terrie Moffitt, in a major longitudinal study, has placed adolescent offenders into two rough categories: a large group of what she calls "adolescence-limited" offenders—typical delinquents whose involvement in crime begins and ends in adolescence—and a much smaller group of youths that she labels "life-course-persistent offenders." Many youths in this latter group are in the early stages of criminal careers: their antisocial conduct often begins in childhood and continues through adolescence into adulthood. In adolescence, the criminal conduct of youths in these two groups looks pretty similar, but the underlying causes and the prognosis are different.[30]

This insight raises an important issue. Even if adolescents generally are less mature than adults, should immaturity not be considered on an individualized basis, as is typical of most mitigating conditions? Not all juvenile offenders are unformed youths. Adolescents vary in the pace of psychological development and character formation, and some may not deserve lenient treatment on the basis of immaturity.

The problem with individualized assessments of immaturity is that practitioners lack diagnostic tools to evaluate psychosocial maturity and identity formation on an individualized basis. Recently, courts in some areas have begun to use a psychopathy checklist, a variation of an instrument developed for adults, in an effort to identify adolescent psychopaths for transfer or sentencing purposes. This practice, however, is fraught with the potential for error; it is simply not yet possible to distinguish incipient psychopaths from youths whose crimes reflect transient immaturity. For this reason, the American Psychiatric Association restricts the diagnosis of psychopathy to individuals aged eighteen and older. Evaluating antisocial traits and conduct in adolescence is just too uncertain.[31]

Other problems may arise if maturity is litigated on a case-by-case basis. Research evidence suggests that racial and ethnic biases influence attitudes about the punishment of young offenders; thus decision makers may be particularly inclined to discount the mitigating impact of immaturity in minority youths. The integrity of any individualized decision-making process is vulnerable to contamination from racist attitudes or from unconscious racial stereotyping that operates even among those who may lack overt prejudice.[32]

In sum, the developmental evidence indicates that the immaturity of adolescent offenders causes them to differ from their adult counterparts in ways that mitigate culpability. Scientific knowledge also supports recognizing this difference through categorical classification of young offenders. The presumption underlying the punitive reforms—that no substantial differences exist between adolescents and adults that are relevant to criminal responsibility—offends proportionality, a core principle of criminal law. The developmental psychology evidence does not support a justice system that treats young offenders as children whose crimes are excused, but it does support a mitigation-based model that places adolescents in an intermediate legal category of offenders who are less blameworthy and deserve less punishment than typical adult offenders. Under our developmental model, adolescence is a separate legal category for purposes of responding to youthful criminal conduct.[33]

SOCIAL WELFARE AND THE REGULATION OF YOUTH CRIME

In reality, although the scientific evidence of adolescent immaturity is substantial, principle alone will not dictate juvenile crime policy. Ultimately, the most compelling argument for a separate, less punitive, system for dealing with young criminals is utilitarian. An important lesson of the research on juvenile crime by Moffitt and others is that most delinquent youths, even those who commit serious crimes, are "adolescence-limited" offenders who are likely to mature out of their antisocial tendencies. These youths are not headed for careers in crime—unless correctional interventions push them in that direction. This lesson is reinforced by developmental research showing that social context is critically important to the successful completion of developmental tasks essential to the transition to conventional adult roles associated with desistance from crime.[34] For youths in the justice system, the correctional setting is their social context. Youth crime policy should not lose sight of the impact of sanctions on the future life prospects of young offenders. Sanctions that effectively invest in the human capital of young offenders and facilitate their transition to adulthood are likely to promote the interests of society as well as those of young offenders—as long as they do not unduly compromise public safety.

Supporters of tough sanctions argue that contemporary policies promote society's interest and point to the declining juvenile crime rates in the past decade as evidence of the effectiveness of the reforms. There is no question that reducing crime is a critical justification for more punitive sanctions, but evaluating the impact of the reforms on the recent crime-rate trend is an uncertain business, with studies giving mixed reports. A few researchers have studied the effect of automatic transfer statutes, either by comparing two similar states with different laws, or by examining crime rates in a single state before and after a legislative reform. Their studies have found that punitive reforms have little effect on youth crime.[35] Only one substantial study has found that crime rates appear to decline under harsh statutes, and the methodology of that study has been sharply criticized.[36] Interview studies of incarcerated youths find that many express intentions to avoid harsh penalties in the future, but the extent to which these intentions affect behavior is unclear. Studies comparing recidivism rates of similar juveniles sentenced to adult and juvenile facilities have found higher rates of re-offending for youths sentenced to prison.[37] In short, little evidence supports the claim that adolescents are deterred from criminal activity by the threat of harsh sanctions, either generally or because their experience in prison "taught them a lesson."

If the recent reforms have reduced juvenile crime at all, it is mostly through incapacitation. Long periods of incarceration (or incarceration rather than community sanctions) keep youths off the streets where they might be committing crimes and do indeed reduce crime, at least in the short run—but the costs are high in several respects. The economic costs of the recent law reforms have been substantial, as many states have begun to realize. According to a careful analysis of the costs and benefits associated with one state's policy reforms increasing juvenile sanctions, serious youth crime declined 50 percent between 1994 and 2001, while spending in the juvenile justice system increased 43 percent.[38] The increased spending has opportunity costs as well; resources spent to build and staff correctional facilities to incarcerate more juveniles for longer periods are not available for other social uses. Economists explain that some amount of incarceration yields substantial benefits in terms of reducing crime, but that the benefits decrease (that is, fewer crimes are avoided) for each unit of increased incarceration.[39] Thus, incarceration may be justified on social welfare grounds for youths who are at high risk of re-offending. But no social benefit is gained, in terms of crime reduction, when youths are confined who would *not* otherwise be on the streets committing crimes. Moreover, if less costly correctional dispositions effectively reduce recidivism in some juvenile offenders, incarcerating those youths may not be justified on utilitarian grounds.

Harsh policies carry other social costs as well—particularly if incarceration itself contributes to re-offending or diminishes youths' future prospects. Almost all young offenders *will* be released at some point to rejoin society. Thus the impact of incarceration on re-offending and generally on their future lives must be considered in calculating its costs and benefits. The research on the impact of adult incarceration on normative adolescent offenders is not yet extensive, but the available evidence suggests that imprisonment undermines social maturation and educational progress and likely contributes to recidivism. This finding is not surprising: adolescence is a critical developmental stage during which youths acquire competencies, skills, and experiences essential to success in adult roles. If a youth's experience in the correctional system disrupts educational and social development severely, it may irreversibly undermine prospects for gainful employment, successful family formation, and engaged citizenship—and directly or indirectly contribute to re-offending.

The differences between the juvenile and adult systems have blurred a bit in recent years, but, even today, juvenile facilities and programs are far more likely to provide an adequate context for development than adult prison. Prisons are aversive developmental settings. They are generally large institutions, with staff whose function is custodial and who generally relate to prisoners as adversaries; programs are sparse, and older prisoners are often mentors in crime or abusive to incarcerated youths.[40] The juvenile system, although far from optimal, operates in many states on the basis of policies that recognize that offenders are adolescents with developmental needs. Facilities are less institutional than prisons, staff-offender ratio is higher, staff attitudes are more therapeutic, and more programs are available.[41]

The effectiveness of juvenile correctional programs has been subject to debate for decades. Until the 1990s, most researchers concluded that the system had little to offer in the way of effective rehabilitative interventions; the dominant view of social scientists during the 1970s and 1980s was captured by the slogan "nothing works" to reduce recidivism with young offenders.[42] Today the picture is considerably brighter. A substantial body of research over the past fifteen years has showed that many juvenile programs, in both community and institutional settings, can substantially reduce crime; the most promising programs cut crime by 20–30 percent.[43] In general, successful programs are those that heed the lessons of developmental psychology. These programs seek to provide young offenders with supportive social contexts and authoritative adult figures and to help them acquire the skills necessary to change problem behavior and attain psychosocial maturity. Some effective programs focus directly on developing skills to avoid antisocial behavior, often through cognitive-behavioral therapy, a therapeutic approach with substantial empirical support.[44] Other interventions that have been shown to reduce crime focus on strengthening family support. One of the most effective treatment programs with violent and aggressive youths is Multisystemic Therapy, the dual focus of which is to empower parents with skills and resources to help their children avoid problem behaviors and to give youths the tools to cope with family, peer, and school problems that can contribute to reinvolvement in criminal activity.[45] Effective juvenile programs offer good value for taxpayers' dollars, and the benefits in terms of crime reduction far exceed the costs.[46]

The success of rehabilitative programs does not mean that we should return to the traditional rehabilitative model of juvenile justice; punishment is an appropriate purpose when society responds to juvenile crime. Both adult prisons and juvenile correctional programs impose punishment, however, and the juvenile system is better situated to invest in the human capital of young offenders and facilitate the transition to conventional adult roles—a realistic goal for youths who are adolescence-limited offenders. To be sure, the future prospects of juveniles in the justice system are not as bright as those of other adolescents. But developmental knowledge reinforces a growing body of empirical research indicating that juvenile offenders are more likely to desist from criminal activity and to make a successful transition to adulthood if they are sanctioned as juveniles in a separate system.

Under a mitigation model, most young criminals would be dealt with in the juvenile system. From a developmental perspective, punishing a sixteen-year-old car thief or small-time drug dealer as an adult is likely to be short-sighted—because these are typical adolescent crimes. But a justice policy that takes mitigation seriously is viable only to the extent that it does not seriously compromise public protection. In our view, older violent recidivists *should* be tried and punished as adults. These youths cause a great deal of harm and are close to adults in their culpability. They are also less likely to be normative adolescents and more likely to be young career criminals than most young offenders.[47] The authority to punish violent recidivists as adults constitutes a safety valve that is essential to the stability of the juvenile justice system. An important lesson learned from the collapse of the rehabilitative model is that juvenile justice policy must pay serious attention to the public's legitimate concerns about safety.

LOOKING TO THE FUTURE

This is a good time to reflect on youth crime policy. The alarm that fueled the punitive juvenile justice reforms of the past generation has subsided as juvenile crime rates have fallen for several years. Even supporters of tough policies have had second thoughts. John Dilulio recently expressed regret about characterizing young offenders as "superpredators" and acknowledged that his predictions about the threat of juvenile crime had not been realized.[48]

The public too may be less enthusiastic about punitive policies than politicians seem to believe. In 2006, with colleagues, we conducted what is called a "contingent valuation survey," probing how much 1,500 Pennsylvania residents were willing to pay (from their tax dollars) for either an additional year of incarceration or a rehabilitation program for juveniles. The alternatives were described (accurately, according to the research) as offering a similar prospect for reducing crime. We found that participants were willing to pay more for rehabilitation than for punishment—a mean of $98.00 as against $81.00. Of course, this kind of survey is somewhat artificial, since the willingness-to-pay question is hypothetical. Nonetheless, these findings should be interesting to policymakers, particularly in light of a fact that we did *not* disclose to our participants—that a year of juvenile incarceration actually costs five times as much as a year-long rehabilitation program.[49]

Our study, together with other recent survey evidence, suggests that the public cares about safety but is quite open to rehabilitative programs as a way of reducing juvenile crime.[50] Politicians claim that the public has demanded "get-tough" policies, but this demand may often be a transitory response to a highly publicized juvenile crime. The research suggests that the political risk that policymakers face in responding cautiously to public pressure in the wake of these incidents may not be as great as they might surmise.

Legislatures also appear to be having second thoughts about the punitive laws that they have enacted—partly because the juvenile crime rate has fallen and partly because adult prosecution and punishment of juveniles carry a high cost. In several states, punitive laws have been repealed or scaled back. For example, in 2005, Illinois repealed a statute mandating adult prosecution of fifteen-year-olds charged with selling drugs near schools or public housing projects, acknowledging that the statute had a substantial budgetary impact and was enforced disproportionately against minority youths.[51] Other states have also changed course. Colorado abolished the sentence of life without parole for juveniles, and Connecticut recently raised the age of adult court jurisdiction from sixteen to eighteen.[52] Lawmakers may be ready to approach juvenile justice policy more thoughtfully today than they have in a generation. If so, a large body of recent research that was not available twenty years ago offers insights about adolescence and about young offenders. Using this scientific knowledge to shape the direction of juvenile justice policy will promote both social welfare and fairness.

ENDNOTES

1. *Roper v. Simmons*, 543 U.S. 541 (2005).

2. This article is based on Elizabeth S. Scott and Laurence Steinberg, *Rethinking Juvenile Justice* (Harvard University Press, 2008).

3. Julian Mack, "The Juvenile Court," *Harvard Law Review* 23, no. 104 (1909).

4. *In re Gault*, 387 U.S. 1 (1967).

5. John Dilulio, "The Coming of the Super-predators," *Weekly Standard*, 27 November 1995, p. 23. On June 28, 2007, the term "super-predator" generated 30,300 Google hits, suggesting its salience.

6. See the article by Jeffrey Fagan in this volume.

7. Ibid. During the three years between 1992 and 1995, eleven states lowered the age for transfer, twenty-four states added crimes to automatic/legislative waiver statutes, and ten states added crimes to judicial waiver statutes. See Patricia Torbet and others, *State Responses to Serious and Violent Juvenile Crime*, vol. 6 (Washington: Office of Juvenile Justice and Delinquency Prevention, 1996).

8. William Claiborne, "13-Year-Old Convicted in Shooting: Decision to Try Youth as Adult Sparked Juvenile Justice Debate," *Washington Post*, 17 November 2001.

9. Erich Goode and Nachman Ben-Yehuda, *Moral Panics: The Social Construction of Deviance* (Malden, Mass.: Wiley-Blackwell, 1994), p. 1.

10. Lori Dorfman and Vincent Schiraldi, *Off Balance: Youth, Race, and Crime in the News* (Washington: Building Blocks for Youth, 2001).

11. Anna Gorman, "State Juvenile Court Still Struggles to Find Balance; Participants in the System Gather in L.A. for Its 100th Anniversary and Discuss How Best to Blend Punishment and Rehabilitation," *Los Angeles Times*, 26 December 2003, B2.

12. For a discussion of proportionality see Richard Bonnie and others, *Criminal Law* (New York: Foundation Press, 2004). Proportionality has been addressed by the Supreme Court in the context of the death penalty, including the application of the death penalty to juveniles. Ibid., pp. 901–62; *Roper v. Simmons*, 543 U.S. 541 (2005).

13. Robert Siegler and Martha Alibali, *Children's Thinking* (Englewood Cliffs, N.J.: Prentice Hall, 2005), pp. 55–64.

14. Anita Greene, "Future-Time Perspective in Adolescence: The Present of Things Future Revisited," *Journal of Youth and Adolescence* 15 (1986): 99–113.

15. See Laurence Steinberg and Susan Silverberg, "The Vicissitudes of Autonomy in Early Adolescence," *Child Development* 57 (1986): 841–51. See research summarized in Elizabeth Scott and others, "Evaluating Adolescent Decision-Making in Legal Contexts," *Law and Human Behavior* 19 (1995): 221–44.

16. Terrie Moffitt, "Adolescence-Limited and Life-Course-Persistent Antisocial Behavior: A Developmental Taxonomy," *Psychological Review* 100 (1993): 674–701.

17. Albert Reiss Jr. and David Farrington, "Advancing Knowledge about Co-Offending: Results from a Prospective Longitudinal Survey of London Males," *Journal of Criminal Law and Criminology* 82 (1991): 360–95.

18. Adam Liptak, "Jailed for Life after Crimes as Teenagers," *New York Times*, 3 October 2005, A1.

19. See Lita Furby and Ruth Beyth-Marom, "Risk Taking in Adolescence: A Decision-making Perspective," *Developmental Review* 12 (1992): 1–44.

20. Leonard Green, Joel Myerson, and Pawel Ostaszewski, "Discounting of Delayed Rewards across the Life Span: Age Differences in Individual Discounting Functions," *Behavioural Processes* 46 (1999).

21. Laurence Steinberg, "Risk-Taking in Adolescence: New Perspectives from Brain and Behavioral Science," *Current Directions in Psychological Science* 16 (2007): 55–59.

22. Ellen Greenberger, "Education and the Acquisition of Psycho-Social Maturity," in *The Development of Social Maturity*, edited by D. McClelland (New York: Irvington, 1982), pp. 155–89.

23. See Elkhonon Goldberg, *The Executive Brain: Frontal Lobes and the Civilized Mind* (Oxford University Press, 2001), p. 35; Linda P. Spear, "The Adolescent Brain and Age-Related Behavioral Manifestations," *Neuroscience and Biobehavioral Reviews* 24 (2000): 417–63.

24. Jeffrey Fagan, "Contexts of Choice by Adolescents in Criminal Events," in *Youth on Trial*, edited by Thomas Grisso and Robert Schwartz (University of Chicago Press, 2000).

25. *Roper v. Simmons*, 543 U.S. 541 (2005). In its proportionality analysis, the Court drew on Elizabeth S. Scott and Laurence Steinberg, "Less Guilty by Reason of Adolescence: Developmental Immaturity, Diminished Responsibility, and the Juvenile Death Penalty," *American Psychologist* 58 (2003): 1009–18.

26. Erik Erikson, *Identity: Youth and Crisis* (New York: W. W. Norton & Co., 1968).

27. Moffitt, "Adolescence-Limited and Life-Course-Persistent Antisocial Behavior" (see note 16).

28. Alex Piquero, David Farrington, and Alfred Blumstein, "The Criminal Career Paradigm," in *Crime and Justice: An Annual Review of Research* 30, edited by Michael Tonry and Norval Morris (University of Chicago Press, 2003).

29. *Roper v. Simmons*, 543 U.S. 541(2005).

30. Moffitt, "Adolescence-Limited and Life-Course-Persistent Antisocial Behavior" (see note 16).

31. American Psychiatric Association, *Diagnostic and Statistical Manual of Mental Disorders* (4th ed. 1994). See Daniel Seagrave and Thomas Grisso, "Adolescent Development and the Measurement of Juvenile Psychopathy," *Law and Human Behavior* 26 (2000): 219–39.

32. George S. Bridges and Sara Steen, "Racial Disparities in Official Assessments of Juvenile Offenders: Attributional Stereotypes as Mediating Mechanisms," *American Sociological Review* 63 (1998): 554–70; Sandra Graham and Brian Lowry, "Priming Unconscious Racial Stereotypes about Adolescent Offenders," *Law and Human Behavior* 28, no. 5 (2004): 483–504.

33. Franklin Zimring contemplated a similar construction of adolescence in describing adolescents as having a "learners' permit" for the purpose of developing adult competency in certain legal activities. Franklin Zimring, *The Changing Legal World of Adolescence* (New York: Free Press, 1982).

34. Laurence Steinberg, Hen Len Chung, and Michelle Little, "Reentry of Young Offenders from the Justice System: A Developmental Perspective," *Youth Violence and Juvenile Justice* 1 (2004): 21–38.

35. Simon Singer and David McDowell, "Criminalizing Delinquency: The Deterrent Effects of the New York Juvenile Offender Law," *Law & Society Review* 22 (1988): 521–35; Eric Jensen and Linda Metsger, "A Test of the Deterrent Effect of Legislative Waiver on Violent Juvenile Crime," *Crime & Delinquency* 40 (1994): 96–104.

36. Steven Levitt, "Juvenile Crime and Punishment," *Journal of Political Economy* 106, no. 6 (1998): 1158–85. This study has been criticized in Anthony Doob and Cheryl Webster, "Sentencing

Severity and Crime: Accepting the Null Hypothesis," in *Crime and Justice* 30, edited by Michael Tonry (University of Chicago Press, 2003): 143–95.

37. Donna Bishop and Charles Frazier, "Consequences of Transfer," in *The Changing Borders of Juvenile Justice*, edited by Jeffrey Fagan and Franklin Zimring (University of Chicago Press, 2000), pp. 227–77. See also Martin Forst, Jeffrey Fagan, and T. Scott Vivona, "Youths in Prisons and Training Schools: Perceptions and Consequences of the Treatment-Custody Dichotomy," *Juvenile and Family Court Journal* 40 (1989): 1–14.

38. Steve Aos, "The Criminal Justice System in Washington State: Incarceration Rates, Taxpayer Costs, Crime Rates and Prison Economics," Washington State Institute for Public Policy, January 2003, available at wsipp.wa.gov.

39. Economists find that policies increasing incarceration rates have diminishing marginal returns. Ibid.

40. Bishop and Frazier, "Consequences of Transfer" (see note 37).

41. Forst, Fagan, and Vivona, "Youths in Prisons and Training Schools" (see note 37); Bishop and Frazier, "Consequences of Transfer" (see note 37).

42. Douglas Lipton and others, *The Effectiveness of Correctional Treatment: A Survey of Treatment Evaluation Studies* (New York: Praeger, 1975); Robert Martinson, "What Works? Questions and Answers about Prison Reform," *Public Interest* 35 (1975): 22–54; Susan Martin, Lee B. Sechrest, and Robin Redner, eds., Panel on Research on Rehabilitative Techniques, National Research Council, *New Directions in the Rehabilitation of Criminal Offenders* (Washington: National Academy Press, 1981).

43. Mark Lipsey, "Can Rehabilitative Programs Reduce the Recidivism of Young Offenders? An Inquiry into the Effectiveness of Practical Programs," *Virginia Journal of Social Policy & Law* 6 (1999): 611–41. See also Steve Aos and others, "The Comparative Costs and Benefits of Programs to Reduce Crime," Washington State Institute for Public Policy, 2001; available at wsipp. wa.gov.

44. Judith Beck, *Cognitive Therapy: Basics and Beyond* (New York: Guilford, 1995); Mark Lipsey, Gabrielle Chapman, and Nana Landenberger, "Research Findings from Prevention and Intervention Studies: Cognitive-Behavioral Programs for Offenders," *Annals of the American Academy of Political and Social Science* 578 (2001): 144–57.

45. See Multi-systemic Therapy, *Office of Juvenile Justice and Delinquency Prevention Model Programs Guide*, www.dsgonline.com/mpg2.5/.

46. Aos and others, "The Comparative Costs and Benefits of Programs to Reduce Crime" (see note 43).

47. See Moffitt, "Adolescence-Limited and Life-Course-Persistent Antisocial Behavior" (see note 16).

48. Elizabeth Becker, "As Ex-Theorist on Young 'Superpredators,' Bush Aide Has Regrets," *New York Times*, 9 February 2001, A19.

49. Daniel Nagin and others, "Public Preferences for Rehabilitation Versus Incarceration of Young Offenders: Evidence from a Contingent Valuation Survey," *Journal of Criminology and Public Policy* 5 (2006): 627–51.

50. Julian Roberts, "Public Opinion and Youth Justice," *Crime and Justice* 31 (2004): 495–542; Elizabeth Scott and others, "Public Attitudes About the Culpability and Punishment of Young Offenders," *Behavioral Sciences and the Law* 24 (2006): 815–32.

51. The statute repealed was *Ill. Comp. Stat. Ann.* Ch. 705, Sect. 405/5–7(a). See Illinois Juvenile Justice Commission, "Disproportionate Minority Contact in the Illinois Juvenile Justice System," Annual Report to the Governor and General Assembly, 2005.

52. "Back Where They Belong," Editorial, *New York Times*, 5 July 2007; "Connecticut Raises Age of Juvenile Court Jurisdiction," State Action Blog, stateaction.org/blog.

*Elizabeth S. Scott is the Harold R. Medina Professor of Law at Columbia Law School.

Laurence Steinberg is Distinguished University Professor and Laura H. Carnell Professor of Psychology at Temple University.

Scott, Elizabeth S., and Laurence Steinberg. "Adolescent Development and the Regulation of Youth Crime." *Future of Children* 18, no. 2 (Fall 2008): 15–33.

The Need for Cognitive Skills Educational Therapy in Juvenile Justice

*by Kimora**

The juvenile justice system in the United States exists to "treat" youths who have engaged in illegal activity. It was developed with the primary goal of rehabilitating young offenders. Yet studies have shown that existing correctional treatment programs have failed to prevent subsequent delinquency.[1] Most current programs are ineffective because they do not help young people develop the skills that they will need to transform their lives and keep them from returning to prison or jail.

If we are to help young offenders, we must look at corrections programs through a developmental lens, utilizing programs based on a cognitive-behavioral approach.[2] Teaching young offenders cognitive skills improves their lives and gives them more positive options in life that do not include criminal behavior. In this chapter, the author will outline theories of cognitive development and describe several cognitive behavioral therapies to build a case for the use of cognitive skills education in juvenile correctional settings.

WHAT IS COGNITION?

Cognition is the way in which individuals process information. It is the mental processes—perception, memories, expectations, abstract reasoning, judgment, intelligence—that mediate between a stimulus and a response. It relates and connects events.

Although psychologists such as Wilhelm Maximilian Wundt and William James introduced the concept in the early twentieth century, cognitive psychology did not gain popularity in the United States until mid-century, with the advent of computers.[3] In what became known as the "cognitive revolution," American psychologists abandoned the dominant behaviorist school of psychology, which emphasized the study of observable behaviors rather than internal states, and adopted a cognitive model of the mind based on the computer, which seemed to mimic the way the brain receives and processes information.

What Is Cognitive Development?

The behavioral school was never prominent in Europe, and over the course of the early twentieth century, European psychologists, led by Swiss psychologist Jean Piaget, began exploring cognitive development—the development of a child's ability to think and understand. Cognitive development looks at the construction of thought processes—remembering, symbolizing, problem solving, categorizing, reasoning, judging, creating, and decision making—as well as learning structures and brain development.

Piaget, who developed the most influential and widely used theory in the field, proposed a theory of genetic epistemology, in which a combination of gradual biological maturation and environmental experience contributes to the development of a child's ability to think. He asserted that humans went through four stages of cognitive development, and that we think and understand the world differently in each stage, based on the *schemas* we develop.[4] A schema is the mental process humans use to understand and remember an object, idea, or event. Piaget's stages are as follows:

1. *Sensory-motor period (years 0–2)*: Infants learn to "think" by interacting with the world through their five senses. They begin to develop essential spatial abilities and an understanding of the world by enacting goal-directed behavior, appreciating physical causality, anticipating events, internally representing absent objects and past events, imitating, and playing make-believe.

2. *Preoperational period (years 2–7)*: This is a period of rapid development of representational or symbolic activity. Children learn to represent objects by using images and words, are able to classify objects according to simple criteria (all blue pegs), and are able to understand spatial symbols (for example, simple maps). However, thought is generally not logical and includes animism and elements of egocentrism.

3. *Concrete operational period (years 7–11)*: Children demonstrate the beginnings of thought that is logical, flexible, and organized when applied to concrete information and experience (for example, hierarchical classification and seriation). However, there is a lack of capacity for abstract thinking.

4. *Formal operational period (years 11 and older)*: This signals the development of abstract scientific thinking and the ability to reason logically and draw conclusions from the information available.

In each of these stages, our understanding becomes more mature because we gain more information, more experiences, and more efficient ways to perceive or organize the experiences we have. Piaget further believed that errors are vital in this process, so that in each stage we improve our cognition by correcting errors or misinformation from previous stages.

What Is Cognitive Learning Theory?

Cognitive learning theory uses cognitive development theory to explain how children learn. It emphasizes the brain and its functioning in learning, through processing, memory, thinking, and mental executive functions such as planning, organizing, and categorizing. The cognitive-learning process begins with attention and recognition. As we process information, we categorize it and organize it based on prior experience, memory, and logic. Then when we want to retrieve the information, we use the same memory, categories, and plan of organization to "find" it and use it later.

Building on Piaget's theories, psychologist Jerome Bruner and others suggest that an important part of cognitive learning is constructivism, or the development of individual schema, resulting in the unique way each individual perceives (and, therefore, processes and remembers) an event or experience.[5] Each person's perception is based on experience, both with the content at hand and with the process of learning and remembering.

Cognitive Dissonance and Its Role in Breaking the Law

When our various cognitions and beliefs about others, the world, and ourselves collide, they create a tension known as cognitive dissonance.[6] For example, young people who break the law may dismiss or avoid information that in the end can actually help them. They convince themselves that the actual conflict between their understanding of right and wrong and committing a crime does not exist. Rather, they can rationalize that they *had* to break the law because they had to survive. One way to address this state of tension is to educate juvenile offenders so as to change their attitudes and consequently their behavior. One successful way of doing so is through the use of cognitive behavior therapy.

What Is Cognitive Behavior Therapy?

The term "cognitive behavioral therapy" (CBT) encompasses a group of treatment techniques that emerged from the cognitive revolution. These techniques aim to change disordered behaviors, cognitions, and feelings through goal-oriented procedures designed to modify patterns of thinking. CBT is based on the cognitive understanding of learning: the way an individual perceives situations influences his emotions and behaviors. CBT assumes that maladaptive behaviors are learned through reinforcement, and the aim of therapy is thus to unlearn those behaviors. CBT is not concerned with the patient's past or the roots of the problem but rather with the present symptoms. Its objective is to identify problematic behaviors, establish concrete behavioral goals, and change the dysfunctional behaviors through a focused and short-term period of therapy.[7] CBT encompasses a range of therapeutic approaches including rational emotive behavior therapy and cognitive therapy.

WHAT IS RATIONAL EMOTIVE BEHAVIOR THERAPY?

Rational emotive behavior therapy (REBT) was developed by American psychologist Albert Ellis, the father of cognitive behavior therapies, in the 1950s. Ellis's model assumes that an individual's understanding of the world contains beliefs that contribute to his emotional problems. Rational emotive behavior therapy focuses on identifying and addressing these maladaptive cognitions that result in self-defeating behaviors and/or feelings. It uses the "ABC" structure underlying the cognitive model wherein relationships between (A) activating events, (B) beliefs about them, and (C) the emotional or behavioral consequences of the beliefs are explored. The REBT model is based on three principles:

1. Although external circumstances have recognized psychological effects, psychological troubles are predominantly viewed as a matter of choice, the result of the unconscious or conscious selection of rational or irrational beliefs when a negative event occurs.

2. Past and present life experiences affect individuals, but it is their responses to such situations that cause disturbances.

3. Restructuring one's cognition is possible but requires perseverance and hard work. Individuals undergoing REBT are encouraged to recognize the rationality of their thoughts, and, when thoughts are deemed irrational, substitute them with more adaptive ones.

Therapeutic techniques used in REBT are similar to those used in other cognitive therapies, such as homework assignments and role playing. Also, the therapist plays an active role, often seeking to dispute the client's irrational beliefs and taking a more aggressive approach than in most therapeutic models.[8]

What Is Cognitive Therapy?

Cognitive therapy was developed by American psychiatrist Aaron T. Beck in the 1960s. Beck's theoretical assumption is that a person's emotions and behaviors are determined by her perceptions, which structure her experience.[9] The purpose of cognitive therapy is for people to identify distorted and maladaptive cognitions and change them into more rational and positive thought patterns. Beck believes that people can be active participants in modifying their disruptive cognitions and then be relieved from a range of psychological conditions.

Beck asserts that most of the thoughts that a person has in any given situation are automatic. These thoughts, based on beliefs a person has about herself and the world, lead to an emotional response. Automatic thoughts can lead to logical errors, cognitive distortions that do not allow for objective reality but usually go in the direction of self-deprecation.

According to Beck, these cognitive distortions need to be reconstructed. To do so, an individual must first identify the emotions underlying the distortions and the positive and negative consequences of them. Next, she must identify situations and stimuli that initiate the sequence of events that lead to certain feelings and behavior. Unproductive behaviors need to be identified; then the automatic thoughts that precede the behavior must be recognized. These thoughts are researched to find the underlying maladaptive behaviors or cognitive biases that produce them. With the therapist's help, the individual begins to question the objectivity and rationality of the thoughts. Finally, the individual develops new, constructive cognitions to be used in similar situations in the future.[10]

Why Is a Cognitive Approach So Important in Educational Correctional Programs in the Juvenile Criminal Justice System?

Programs based on cognitive behavioral therapies should have an important role in the juvenile criminal justice system because they can help young offenders identify self-defeating behaviors and change distorted and irrational thought patterns. These therapies can change lives, redirecting behaviors and offering troubled young people positive options for their future.

One of the most essential elements of the cognitive approach in correctional programs is cognitive skills education, which improves social skills, creativity, problem-solving skills, management of emotions (especially anger), negotiation skills, and values enhancement. If you have ever talked to a young incarcerated individual, you will discover that in most cases, the person lacks these skills. Without them young people may make illogical and unethical decisions that can lead to criminal activity.

A central component of cognitive skills education is teaching critical thinking, the particular quality of thinking carefully, logically, and rationally. Many juvenile offenders think emotionally rather than rationally. They stubbornly and rigidly cling to erroneous beliefs and unreasonable attitudes, impervious to new information (or advice or counseling) because they are unable to critically evaluate their own opinions. Ironically, the same lack of critical reasoning may make them easily misled by others because they are unable to adequately judge the reasonableness of information and suggestions presented to them.[11]

Young offenders must be able to evaluate their thinking and the thinking of others to ensure that it is logical and rational, that the conclusions they draw or that are presented to them have been arrived at without flaws in logic and are based on sufficient and correct information, rather than on biases, unwarranted assumptions, distortions of facts, or untested opinions.[12]

Training in critical thinking has been incorporated into a variety of other programs, including multi-systemic approaches for juvenile offenders, with very positive follow-up outcomes.[13] As participants become skilled at critical thinking, they are in a better position to evaluate their own and others' ideas, attitudes, and actions. They also tend to withhold judgments and consider all the evidence in a careful and orderly manner. Training in critical reasoning also fosters

- intellectual curiosity;
- objectivity;
- flexibility (avoiding dogma, rigidity, and thinking that one has all the answers);
- sound judgment;
- open-mindedness;
- relevance (avoiding irrelevancies);
- persistence (in seeking evidence);
- decisiveness (accepting conclusions only when evidence warrants it); and
- respect for other points of view (humility and accurate considerations of contradictory views).[14]

Finally, training in critical thinking also improves social behavior as young people learn tolerance. They react to the statements of others (even contrary statements) rationally rather than emotionally, and *reason* with others rather than argue with them.[15]

COGNITIVE-SKILLS-BASED PROGRAMS

Cognitive-skills-based programs are now being tested and used in a variety of correctional settings. One such program is "A Framework for Breaking Barriers: A Cognitive Reality Model" (Breaking Barriers). Written by Gordon Graham, it is a rehabilitative program designed to address the attitudes, thinking, and behaviors that contribute to criminality and which, if changed, reduce the likelihood of recidivism.[16]

Graham's main goal is to convince parolees and probationers that they can change their behavior. His highly effective, nonthreatening approach takes into account the fact that many offenders reject the idea that they may be basing their life decisions on incomplete or inaccurate information about themselves.

From his own prison experience, Graham realized that self-image controls performance. Furthermore, controlling how we think is a learnable process. For example, Graham's program shows how trust can be learned. Talk to almost any offender and you will discover that he or she does not trust you. That is because these offenders do not trust *themselves*. Graham teaches that "the foundation of good mental health is a sense of trust, both in ourselves, and in being trustworthy to others."[17]

Based on cognitive psychology, Graham's program guides offenders toward an understanding and acceptance of four educational values:

1. Change is possible.
2. The current reality is the result of beliefs, habits, and attitudes that we have adopted in the past.
3. Our future is determined by the beliefs, habits, and attitudes that we adopt today.
4. It is possible to *choose* our beliefs, habits, and attitudes in order to reach our visions.[18]

The program can be used in any correctional setting but is particularly useful for offenders transitioning from prison or jail.

EVALUATION OF "BREAKING BARRIERS"

Breaking Barriers has been assessed using the Correctional Program Assessment Inventory (CPAI), developed to measure how closely correctional rehabilitation programs meet the principles of effective correctional treatment.[19] The program's overall composite score on the CPAI was 50.8 percent, which corresponds to "satisfactory but needs improvement." Program implementation and other characteristics each scored "very satisfactory." Staff characteristics scored "satisfactory," and client assessment, program characteristics, and evaluation each scored "unsatisfactory."[20] Breaking Barriers needs improvement, but it is the best program we have and is far better than programs such as boot camps, which have not reduced recidivism.

RECOMMENDATIONS REGARDING COGNITIVE SKILLS PROGRAMS

More research needs to be done to determine whether cognitive skills programs such as Breaking Barriers are effective. Did the juvenile finally change and become more productive and positive *because* of a cognitive skills program? This research is vital not only from an academic perspective but also because of the political climate in which we live. Currently, more and more state legislatures—and taxpayers—are insisting on evidence-based research that indicates that recidivism rates will be lower as a direct result of education, such as cognitive skills education. Nonprofit alternative-to-incarceration programs are faced with proving that their cognitive skills programs actually do lower recidivism rates, or they may not be funded in the future.

At present, there is a lack of research on theory, program implementation, and evaluation methodology. No practitioner or researcher can ever really prove that the particular cognitive skills program made *all* the difference. Yet, as a cognitive skills educator in prisons and jails for over twenty-five years, the author can personally attest to this fact. It is also clear to me that if a staff member understands cognitive skills programming and teaches it well and with integrity, the juvenile clients will benefit. More research is needed to prove the effectiveness of *any* cognitive skills program for juvenile offenders.

CONCLUSION

We must rethink corrections in the juvenile criminal justice system. If we persist in using the ineffective programs now in place, the system will remain training grounds for criminals. We need to prepare those young people who have had or continue to have issues with the criminal justice system with cognitive skills so they can become productive and fulfilled individuals to serve our country and the world, now, and in the future.

In 1964, Malcolm X, in a speech in New York City, stated: "Education is our passport to the future, for tomorrow belongs to the people who prepare for it today.... We must establish all over the country schools of our own to train our own children to become scientists, to become mathematicians. We must realize the need for adult education and for job retraining programs that will emphasize a changing society in which automation plays the key role. We intend to use the tools of education to help raise our people to an unprecedented level of excellence and self-respect through their own efforts."[21]

That level of excellence and self-respect Malcolm X talked about is possible for all juveniles caught in the web of the criminal justice system. Cognitive skills education needs to play an integral part throughout the educational process to ensure the proper cognitive restructuring.

NOTES

1. John Whitehead and Steven Lab, "A Meta-Analysis of Juvenile Correctional Treatment, *Journal of Research in Crime and Delinquency* 26 (1989): 276–295.
2. Carol J. Garrett, "Effects of Residential Treatment on Adjudicated Delinquent: A Meta-Analysis," *Journal of Research in Crime and Delinquency* 22 (1985): 287–308.
3. "Cognition," in *The Sage Glossary of the Social and Behavioral Sciences*, ed. Larry Sullivan (Los Angeles: Sage Publications, 2009), 84.
4. Jean Piaget, *The Child's Conception of the World* (London: Routledge & Kegan Paul, 1928).
5. Jerome S. Bruner, "The Act of Discovery," *Harvard Educational Review* 31, no. 1 (1961): 21–32.
6. Leon A. Festinger, *A Theory of Cognitive Dissonance* (Evanston, IL: Row, Peterson, 1957).
7. "Cognitive Behavior Therapy," in Sullivan, *Sage Glossary*, 81.
8. "Rational Emotive Behavior Therapy," in Sullivan, *Sage Glossary*, 434.
9. Aaron T. Beck and Gary Emery with Ruth L. Greenberg, *Anxiety Disorders and Phobias: A Cognitive Perspective* (New York: Basic Books, 1985).
10. "Cognitive Therapy," in Sullivan, *Sage Glossary*, 84.
11. Kimora, "The Need for Cognitive Skills Training in Correctional Vocational Educational Programming at Minnesota Correctional Facility–Lino Lakes at Lino Lakes, Minnesota" (PhD diss., Center for Correctional Education and the University of Minnesota, 1999).
12. Ibid.
13. Scott W. Henggeler, Sonja K. Schoenwald, Charles M. Borduin, Melisa D. Rowland, and Phillippe B. Cunningham, *Multisystemic Treatment of Antisocial Behavior in Children and Adolescents* (New York: Guilford Press, 1998).
14. Edward D'Angelo, *The Teaching of Critical Thinking* (Amsterdam: Gruner, 1971).
15. Robert R. Ross, Elizabeth Fabiano, and Roslynn D. Ross, *Reasoning and Rehabilitation: A Handbook for Teaching Cognitive Skills* (Ottawa: University of Ottawa, 1991).
16. Gordon Graham, *A Framework for Breaking Barriers: A Cognitive Reality Model* (Bellevue, WA: Gordon Graham and Co., 1998). In order to teach this particular cognitive skills program, the facilitator must be certified by Graham and his team of associates. Contact Graham at www.instarperformance.com for updated information, including a schedule of trainings.
17. Gordon Graham, interview by Kimora, December 6, 2004.
18. Graham, *Framework for Breaking Barriers*, iii.
19. Vicki Verdeyen, "Changing the Criminal Mind," *Corrections Today* 61 (1999): 52.
20. Nicolle Parsons-Pollard, "A Framework for Breaking Barriers: A Program Process and Outcomes Evaluation of a Correctional Intervention Program" (PhD diss., Virginia Commonwealth University, 2004).

21. Malcolm X, speech at the founding rally of the Organization of Afro-American Unity, Audubon Ballroom, New York City, June 28, 1964.

*Kimora is associate adjunct professor at John Jay College of Criminal Justice. Her research expertise includes cognitive skills education. She is also education director for prevention and treatment services, El Rio, the Osborne Association, in New York City.

Written for this book and used by permission of the author.

Part 6:

Are There Reasonable Alternatives to Punishment?

The United States is the most punitive society in the world today, incarcerating significantly more young people than does any other nation. But what if the emphasis on punishment cannot be justified, either practically or philosophically? What if none of the philosophical attempts to justify punishment (see Part 2) work? What if our criminal justice system does not deter crime? What if prisons are more likely to be breeding grounds for future crimes than a means to prevent crime? What if our punitive attitude toward criminals promotes more criminality? Are there any reasonable alternatives to punishing the criminal offender?

It is not enough to notice the problems created by our current system. We need to consider possible alternatives that speak directly to the problems. The solution to the problems needs to begin with a vision of what an alternative to punishment would be like and how it would address the concerns that motivate the punishment aspects of the criminal justice system. This is what the two articles in this section attempt to do.

In the first article, "What If Punishment Is Not Justified?," Deirdre Golash argues that the alternative to our punishment system needs to address the underlying economic, social, cultural, and psychological causes of crime. This could be done through redistributive taxation that would reduce inequality, through specific social policies that would reduce poverty and unemployment, through policy changes that would focus on the problems of social disintegration in certain communities, and through cultural and economic support for the family unit.

At the same time, such an alternative does not preclude police intervention to prevent imminent harm. What it does preclude is the widespread incarceration system that we now have. In its place, Golash advocates using jury trials and decisions by a judge not to imprison the criminal offender but to send a public message of symbolic condemnation. She also advocates creating a victim-offender reconciliation program and a "reintegrative shaming" program. However, the criminal offender would still have to *pay* for her crime in a material sense. As a substitute for incarceration, the state would mandate that the offender pay compensation directly to the victim. Assets and wages could be attached. For victims of offenders who are unwilling or unable to provide compensation, the state could establish a common fund to which the convicted offender is required to contribute. In effect, this last proposal entails that the criminal justice system establish a system of reparations as an alternative to punishment. Is such an alternative fair and reasonable?

In the last article in this section, "Criminal Justice and Legal Reparations As an Alternative to Punishment," Geoffrey Sayre-McCord argues that a system of reparations speaks more effectively to the concerns that motivate the retributive, the utilitarian, and the moral educative justifications of punishment. With respect to the retributive theory, a system of reparations still treats the offender as responsible for her wrongdoing. However, in contrast to the retributive theory, which would inflict suffering or other kinds of harm on the offender, a system of reparations would insist that the offender has both a duty and a right to make amends. Furthermore, he argues that while the suffering imposed by retribution cannot annul the crime and restore the criminal's standing in the community, the offender's attempt to make amends can do so.

With respect to the utilitarian justification, Sayre-McCord argues that punishment is generally ineffective as a deterrent, especially in regard to the future action of the offender, but, in contrast, there are reasons to think that the attempt to make amends can serve as a deterrent. Finally, with respect to the moral educative (rehabilitative) justification, it is generally agreed that punishment does not work to positively change the character of the offender and that it is often, in fact, counterproductive with regard to that goal; whereas, he argues, a system of reparations could work effectively to convey a powerful moral message. The implication of these comparisons is that the main attempts to justify punishment point instead to reparations as a fair, reasonable, and more effective alternative to punishment.

As you read the excerpts in this section, consider some of the following questions:

- Are there reasonable alternatives to punishment? If so, what kinds of alternatives to punishment would you advocate?

- Examine models of punishment throughout the world. Can you find alternatives to punishment in any other juvenile justice system?

- Does a system of reparations more effectively address the concerns that motivate different attempts to justify punishment? Would you prefer a system of reparations to the punishment system that now exists? Why or why not?

- To what extent do you think it is possible to reduce crime by addressing the economic, social, cultural, and psychological causes of crime? Do you think that, without the threat of prison, such techniques as symbolic condemnation (with judge and jury), victim-offender reconciliation programs, and reintegrative shaming could be effective in reducing crime and rehabilitating the criminal offender?

What If Punishment Is Not Justified?

by Deirdre Golash*

I. INTRODUCTION

We have seen that punishment as a social institution, and particularly as currently practiced in our society, is deeply problematic. The question naturally arises whether it is an institution that we can, in practical terms, do without. Is the price of a morally defensible approach to crime complete social disintegration? I think we need not become moral martyrs; that the criminal justice system is not in fact serving the functions we intend it to serve; and that measures short of punishment can serve many of these functions as well as or better than current punishment practices. Rather than seeking to prevent crime by deterring or incapacitating offenders, we can address the structural, cultural, and psychological causes of crime at the level of social policy while using defensive measures to discourage crime and force to prevent imminent harm. For crimes we cannot prevent, we can continue to try and convict offenders, communicating censure through symbolic condemnation and requiring offenders to compensate victims, as well as offering victims appropriate emotional support. Keeping a public record of convictions will expose offenders to a range of social sanctions that may lead them to seek reconciliation. For those offenders who are open to change or seek expiation, we can offer the opportunity for voluntary redress through reconciliation hearings, apology, and a level of social contribution commensurate with the seriousness of the crime.

The kinds of measures that might be used to replace punishment are implicit in the arguments I have given against the various justifications of punishment. With respect to prevention, I [have] argued . . . that using punishment to prevent crime probably causes more harm than good; there are other ways to prevent crime without doing harm; and punishment uses offenders as mere means to social ends. Thus, we must seek out non-harmful methods of preventing crime to avoid these criticisms. . . . I [have] argued that punishment is not properly characterized as fair reciprocity where, as a result of other social choices, some are much more likely than others to incur punishment, and social policies could be changed to reduce crime without imposing risks comparable to the risk of being punished. The obvious step here, as well, is to change the structural and cultural conditions known to increase crime before considering punishment.

We may not use punishment in self-defense because the past offenders we punish are not the cause of the future harms we seek to shift on to them, and punishment does not meet the necessity constraint on self-defense .... What we may do is to shift harms from victims to the offenders who caused them, and to take self-defensive measures meeting necessity (and proportionality) constraints in situations where such measures can prevent imminent harm.

Because punishment is closely parallel to crime, it cannot annul crime or vindicate victims, and the anger of victims or others does not provide a separate justification for punishment [...]. Crime can never be literally annulled, but, by requiring compensation, we can mitigate the harms that it does; and by offering emotional support to victims we can assuage their anger without using measures analogous to crime.

We may not punish offenders in order to promote their moral good because moral development as a sole purpose of punishment is unacceptably paternalistic, and state punishment cannot communicate the wrongness of the offense to offenders or promote their moral good [...]. But we can communicate censure through symbolic condemnation, and we can seek to promote voluntary moral reform through the personal attachments of the offender.

I begin with changing conditions conducive to crime as an alternative to deterrent and incapacitative punishment. These conditions range from the broad social level, through the community and the family, to the individual psychological level. I suggest that change in these conditions holds out much greater promise of constructive change than punishment. Such changes are to be supplemented with more direct interventions to prevent imminent crime. Both sets of preventive measures are discussed in part II. Responses to unprevented crime are considered in part III.

II. Crime Prevention

At present, our main strategy for crime prevention is to try to reduce the motivation of potential offenders through the general threat of apprehension and punishment, and to isolate those who have already committed crimes. This strategy, I have argued, is not morally defensible. But it has other weaknesses as well. It does not address the sources of deep social alienation. Instead, by taking an aggressive stance, it encourages marginalized individuals to see themselves as locked in battle with the forces of order, so that getting away with behavior that harms others becomes the goal and refraining from such behavior becomes capitulation.

This is a battle we should not fight. We should instead turn our attention to the underlying causes of crime and to the constructive measures that can be taken to respond to it.

We can assume that punishment exerts some downward pressure on the crime rate, although I have argued that this effect is likely insufficient to outweigh its negative effects. But punishment is not the only way to reduce crime, and I have argued that the possibility of achieving crime reduction in other ways undercuts both utilitarian and reciprocity arguments for punishment. Crime is not solely a function of the bad moral decisions of individuals. There is broad (though not universal) agreement among criminologists that social factors such as income inequality, poverty, unemployment, and local social disorganization contribute to crime. In addition, some individuals are at higher risk of committing crimes because of physical or sexual abuse, drug dependence, lack of job skills, and mental illness. The mechanisms by which these various factors affect the crime rate, and the extent to which they do so, are disputed,[1] and I do not pretend to resolve that dispute here. Instead, I shall discuss how, in an effort to prevent crime without punishment, we might address the causes of crime most commonly cited by criminologists today.

A. Reduce Income Inequality

Income inequality in the United States rose almost 25 percent on the Gini scale in the 1980's and is significantly greater than in other stable industrial democracies.[2] The connection between income inequality at the national level and violent crime is well documented worldwide.[3] Yet such inequality can easily be reduced by redistributive taxation, which requires much less in the way of resources than a prison system. Messner and Rosenfeld suggest that income inequality is not an aberration, but rather represents a necessary backdrop to the culture of economic competition, providing significant stakes for players of the game.[4] If they are right, change in the income structure may have to be preceded by cultural change. Moving money away from the wealthy is also made more difficult by the political power that money can buy, while spending tax money on more prison space is politically easy. Thus, the social choice to date has been for income inequality, and for the costs that it imposes in the form of a higher rate of violent crime. It is open to us to continue to make that choice, recognizing that when we do so we are choosing a higher risk of victimization. Alternatively, we can wage a fight on both political and cultural fronts for greater equality and lower rates of crime.

B. Reduce Poverty and Provide Job Training

Since the Kerner Commission concluded in 1967 that "crime flourishes where the conditions of life are the worst," it has been a commonplace that poverty breeds crime. Poverty (absolute deprivation) is a separate issue from income inequality (relative deprivation). Poor countries do not always have higher rates of crime than wealthier ones, and the poor of the United States are better off in absolute terms than the poor of most nations. It is nevertheless true that higher rates of crime are found in severely impoverished communities and among the unemployed. Recent work suggests that it is not the temporarily unemployed, but the chronically unemployed young man who is likely to turn to crime.[5] Such individuals often face multiple obstacles to decent employment: poor literacy, lack of skills, learning disabilities, lack of role models or sources of effective counseling, drug dependency, and so on. If these problems could be effectively addressed, the burden of unemployment caused by economic fluctuations could be spread more widely across the population and would cease to be a crushing chronic burden on particular individuals and communities. These are not easy problems, but it would be relatively easy to put within reach of all families the resources that middle-class families now call upon when their children face school and other life difficulties. Not every middle-class family is able to rescue a troubled child from lifelong problems, but they have a much better chance of doing so than poor families. Services such as individual counseling, drug treatment, and help with finding a job are now sometimes offered to youths who have run afoul of the law; there is no reason, except lack of funds, not to offer those and other services to all. Doing so would, again, reduce the dramatic differences between rich and poor, lowering the stakes in the economic competition and probably decreasing economic efficiency. Again, we can choose: maximum efficiency, or lower crime rates?

C. Foster Social Organization in Crime-Prone Communities

Some communities, as Robert Sampson and William Julius Wilson have shown, have particularly high rates of crime even when compared to demographically similar communities. What these particularly crime-prone communities seem to have in common is a high level of local social disorganization, caused, in their view, by the interaction of larger social forces (such as housing discrimination and the transformation of the economy from an industrial to a service economy) with community-level factors (such as residential turnover and concentrated poverty). For example, the flight of more stable middle-class black families to the suburbs results in a higher local concentration of poverty, while high residential turnover contributes to the loss of community networks that aid supervision and accountability. At the same time, concentrated unemployment resulting from loss of nearby industrial jobs both reduces opportunities and decreases the availability of marriageable partners, so that single motherhood becomes the norm. In this environment, youths increasingly lack positive role models, and groups of unsupervised teens become more prevalent.[6]

These problems, many of which are attributable to poor public policy in the first place, can also be addressed by policy changes. More broadly distributed public housing can reduce concentrations of poverty. Since Wilson's 1987 work first highlighted this issue,[7] some efforts have been made in this direction. In recent years, however, the focus has been on denying priority to the poorest eligible families to achieve a more mixed population in public housing, and demolishing large public housing complexes.[8] The residents of demolished units have been offered vouchers, but the reduction in total housing stock has in turn increased the likelihood that more people will become homeless. Such policies may in fact decrease residential concentrations of poverty, but doing so at the expense of increasing the desperation of the poor simply trades one factor in high crime rates for another. These policies—and more globally, the sheer unwillingness of governments and taxpayers to spend money on housing for the poor—must change if residential concentrations of poverty are to be addressed in a meaningful way.

Key to the social disintegration of the communities Sampson and Wilson studied was the exodus of middle-class blacks to the suburbs. These residents had been the backbone of local organizations such as churches and community centers, as well as providing a local network of longtime residents who knew each other, knew each other's children, and were therefore a source of continuing support and supervision.[9] This kind of network, once disrupted, is not easily put back into place. But measures can be taken to encourage stability of residence, by preventing the development of the conditions that make neighborhoods unlivable. For example, when there is a sudden loss of jobs because a large employer closes down, assistance should be provided to jobless workers before their lack of income further reduces their available choices. They may need help in the form of retraining, resume preparation, or transportation to job sites, for example. What is likely to make the biggest difference, over all, would be acting on the understanding that job loss is not simply an individual misfortune, for the individual to deal with as best he can, but rather a community-level problem to which resources must be devoted. The current approach, at its best (a best it has not seen in recent decades) is to provide a fixed level of assistance to those individuals who have the initiative to seek it out; when that assistance is exhausted, the community in effect shrugs its shoulders and gives up on the problem. Many are thus left with nowhere to turn, or do not know where to turn in the first place. Again, these are frustrations unknown to the middle-class person, for whom there is always another (if a less desirable) option: unable to get a job at his former level, he accepts one at a lower level; unable to find work in his field, he retrains in a new one; unable to find work at all, he calls upon family and friends for aid until things improve; they, in turn, make sure that he is directed to appropriate medical or counseling resources. The gap left when these alternatives are lacking for an individual, and especially for a large number of individuals in a particular community, has to be filled if the blight of local social disorganization is to be halted.

D. Support Families to Reduce Stress and Increase Supervision

Both social disorganization and institutional-anomie theories of crime identify the tremendous strains on working families as significant contributors to crime. Lack of broad cultural support for the family as an important institution and for the nurturing of children as important work combines with economic strain to produce troubled, often dismembered, families unable to provide effective nurturing or supervision for their children.[10] Such children are easily recruited by rudderless peer groups that are fertile breeding grounds for criminal activity. Culture cannot be changed by fiat, but governmental agencies do not have to participate in spreading the message that the economic sphere is the only one that counts. Schools can support the idea that family life is as important as work life; community centers can offer classes on parenting as well as counseling and support for overburdened parents. Instead of viewing children as consumer luxuries for their parents, we must learn to see them as everyone's responsibility. Parents must be provided with the resources to give their children the attention they need for healthy development. From a broader point of view, this makes sense because without children, society will die. From the narrow point of view of crime prevention, it makes sense because if we refuse to help struggling parents, some predictable number of their children will turn to crime.

I am no expert on social policy, and no doubt my policy suggestions are unsophisticated, if not entirely wrongheaded. But the point is that there is a body of knowledge about the social factors associated with crime, and there is also a body of knowledge about how to address those issues most effectively. It is obvious that in many respects we have simply chosen not to address them, or to do so in suboptimal ways. My point at bottom is that we can and should draw on these bodies of knowledge to derive policies that will reduce crime without raising the serious moral issues associated with punishment, and that indeed have a much greater potential for long-term crime reduction than any penal policy.

It is worth noting that most of the social factors associated with reduced crime are also independently desirable as ways to foster individual development and flourishing. Some, however, will find many of them objectionable as interferences with economic efficiency, as contrary to the spirit of rugged individualism, or even (in some instances) as unconstitutional. Such critics must yet accept that the enforcement of a social preference for these values comes—insofar as we can tell from current research—at the price of a higher rate of crime. Punishment, I have argued, is ruled out as an approach to crime prevention. The question, then, becomes one of choosing between the alternatives of preventing crime through social measures such as those I have suggested above, on the one hand, and accepting the higher rates of crime caused by their opposites, on the other. What is not acceptable, I have argued, is choosing the set of policies that tend to increase crime, and relying on punishment to reduce the rate of crime thus produced.

E. Intervene to Prevent Imminent Harm

The approach I have suggested so far would not bring immediate dividends in the form of lower crime rates, even if it was wildly successful in the long term. But measures aimed more immediately at crime prevention need not be dispensed with entirely. As we have seen, the objections to using punishment as a method of crime prevention do not apply to direct intervention to prevent crime. When the police intervene to prevent burglaries or assaults in progress, for example, we don't need to strain the analogy of self-defense to justify such direct defensive action, taken before the harm is done.

We do not, of course, wish to restrict our crime-preventive efforts to the last ditch, nor do we need to do so. My objections to punishment and preventive detention do not apply to surveillance of those reasonably suspected of criminal activity or to disruption of criminal conspiracies or operations. The use of passive defenses—or what criminologists call "target-hardening"—raises none of the issues posed by punishment. We may use locks, bars, fences, alarms, and even barbed wire or tire-damaging spikes to prevent people from entering places from which they are legitimately excluded without exceeding our right to self-defense, assuming that any harm done by such measures is both proportional to the harm threatened by trespassers and necessary to prevent that harm. (We may not, for example, defend our right to collect entrance fees to parking lots through the use of land mines, or defend our homes from burglars with spring guns, because the force used is disproportionate to the property rights defended.) Those who ignore or circumvent these measures may be arrested and removed before they do further damage. The detention of an individual until the opportunity or motive for commission of a specific crime that he clearly intends has passed may well pass muster as defensible direct intervention (again depending on proportionality and necessity constraints). For example, participants in a barroom brawl might be detained until sober; members of feuding gangs might have their activities curtailed until they are able to resolve their differences. Such specific interventions raise far fewer problems than detention for inchoate "dangerousness."

III. Responding to Unprevented Crimes

Even full implementation of the measures I have suggested so far would not prevent all crimes, and might not prevent as many as punishment. Clearly, it will not do simply to ignore those that are committed. The harms—and the wrongs— done by crime cannot be undone, and for many victims of serious crime life will never be the same. It is important for victims, and for the community, that these wrongs be acknowledged and condemned in a meaningful way. For those harms that can be redressed, some means of redress must be provided. How can we do these things without punishment? I shall argue that they can be done through formal condemnation, requiring compensation, and providing an opportunity for voluntary reconciliation and the making of amends.

A. Communicate Wrongness Through Trial and Symbolic Condemnation

The formal processes that we now use as a prelude to criminal punishment themselves serve many of the purposes ascribed to punishment, without raising the same serious moral issues. Even the preliminary public events of arrest and formal charging have been shown to have some deterrent effect for those most likely to care about their reputations as solid citizens. The trial provides an occasion for the victim to be heard and assures that blame is not improperly placed. Conviction by judge or jury in itself carries a measure of condemnation of the defendant's conduct and corresponding vindication of the victim. The cognitive communication that the defendant's conduct was wrong and is condemned by his community is well begun by the verdict and can be elaborated upon by the judge as she sees fit; it might be appropriate for the judge to announce some formal measure of just how wrong the defendant's conduct was, perhaps by comparing it to well-known earlier cases. Finally, the entry of the judgment against the defendant's name in public records will provide an appropriate caution to anyone who cares to inquire.

We may well fear that the offender will be untouched by the judge's words of condemnation, that he and others will be undeterred from similar behavior in the future, and that the court proceedings will not change his character for the better. We should remember, though, that the same objections apply with similar force to punishment. Those who don't care for the opinions of their fellows can rather seldom be made to do so through harshness; those who do care may well find the solemn public condemnation reason enough to repent.

B. Vindicate Victims and Reverse Some Effects of Crime by Requiring Compensation

Current victim-offender reconciliation programs are premised on the idea that the needs of victims are given insufficient attention by the criminal justice system, which may relegate them to the role of witness or exclude them entirely from the process. The victim-offender reconciliation proceeding or victim-offender mediation, in which the offender hears the victim's account of the crime and the harm that it did, can benefit victims in several ways. It provides an outlet for the victim's emotions, often leading to a reduction in fear and anger. The offender may offer an apology, backed up by willingness to make appropriate reparations. Victims may be skeptical of the sincerity of the apology,[11] but often find partial or symbolic restitution on the part of the offender more meaningful than compensation that comes from the state.[12] Although most studies show that the majority of victims feel they had an opportunity to be heard and are satisfied with the outcome, a significant minority report feeling worse after the hearing than before.[13] A great deal depends upon the sensitivity with which the hearing is conducted, and the skill of the leader in bringing it to a successful conclusion. Making such programs routine, rather than exceptional, would likely raise significant challenges in maintaining and improving the quality of the hearing and the outcome for victims. At minimum, victim participation must be voluntary and victims should be informed in advance of the possibility of an undesired outcome.

That said, the reconciliation proceeding, or something similar, has potential for addressing the anger of victims in a way that is much more appropriate than providing vindictive satisfaction through harsh penalties. I [have] argued ... that justified anger does not provide an independent basis for punishment. Anger in response to undeserved harm is justified anger, but the resulting demand for action in the form of punishment of the wrongdoer depends on the separate judgment that it is good to make wrongdoers suffer—a judgment that I have argued is unsupported. What we can offer to victims is, first, a clear recognition that they have been wronged; second, an opportunity to express their anger and to have it validated; third, the meeting of the demand for action by requiring compensation; and finally, the possibility that the offender will offer a face-to-face apology.

Currently, recognition that the victim has been wronged is bound up with punishment of the offender. Reconciliation hearings that are offered as an alternative to court adjudication bypass judgment and sentencing, thus potentially leaving victims feeling that the wrong done has not been recognized, to the extent that the reconciliation proceeding does not result in the offender's accepting responsibility. The nature of such proceedings may inhibit the facilitator from expressing any opinion at all. In addition, many offenders are not caught, and the victims of those crimes typically receive no recognition beyond the taking of their report by the police. Dispensing with punishment entirely, as I have argued we should, would remove one of the ways in which victims can obtain recognition that they have been subjected to undeserved harm.

It is important to remember, however, that the use of punishment as recognition of wrong done is largely conventional, and conventions can be changed—not overnight, but eventually. The process of trial and formal judgment can itself offer official recognition of the wrong. Appropriate compensation for all victims—including victims of crimes whose perpetrator is never apprehended—would provide further evidence that the victim's rights are valued.

In shifting the costs of the harm done to the wrongdoer, insofar as that is possible, we act on a principle similar to that underlying self-defense: where the offender's culpable actions have resulted in costs that would not otherwise have to be paid, we are justified in choosing that the person to bear those costs will be the offender. He incurs these costs in much the same way as he incurs other debts, for example, ordering food in a restaurant or destroying his own property. In shifting the harm from the victim to the offender, we do not impermissibly use the offender as a means to social ends; instead, we make him bear the consequences of his own choices. Importantly, in shifting harms in this way, we do not increase the total harm done, but only reallocate it to the person responsible for its existence.

Compensation is not subject to the same objections as retributive punishment. It is a question of the shifting of harm from the victim to the offender who brought it about, rather than a question of imposing an additional, gratuitous harm over and above that caused by the offense. The metaphors often used in defense of retribution ("paying one's debt to society," "restoring the balance," "removing unfair advantage," "annulling the crime") apply much more obviously and literally to compensation. The principle underlying self-defense—that harms may be shifted from the innocent to those responsible for them—does not support punishment, but does support making offenders pay the costs of their crimes. For the state to require offenders to undo, insofar as possible, the harm they have done is also unequivocally to affirm and vindicate the rights of victims—a function I have argued retributive punishment does not serve.

It will not have escaped the reader's notice that the shifting of harm from wrongdoer to innocent is exactly the principle that underlies civil liability. Many criminal defendants, of course, are unable to pay damages; some have thought that this is the primary reason we have the criminal law as well as the civil law. Nietzsche presents a darker version of this view: where the offender cannot pay with money, he must pay with suffering; punishment is compensatory because we revel in the suffering of others.[14] Rather than indulge such notions, we might do better to ask how else compensation can be assured.

Under the current civil law, tortfeasors who have no significant assets or income are considered "judgment-proof" and are rarely sued. Moreover, smaller judgments entered against individuals are seldom collected because collection, and the payment of its costs, are left in the hands of the successful plaintiff. In turn, plaintiffs who are aware of this state of affairs seldom pursue civil suits in which the stakes are low or the prospective defendant is not wealthy. As a result, a large proportion of the civil damages to which crime victims are even now theoretically entitled remains uncollected. Putting collection of civil judgments (and collection costs) in the hands of the government could significantly improve this situation. Assets and wages could be attached, or the amount of compensation could be added to the offender's tax bill and be subject to withholding. It may go further: the wealthy offender may move her assets out of the jurisdiction or find ways to hide them; the wage worker may quit his job and change his name rather than continue to see compensation subtracted from his wages. It seems that at this juncture we either have to shrug our shoulders and give up on obtaining compensation for the victim or resort to the threat of punishment to force the offender to pay. Note, however, that similar moves on the part of prospective criminal defendants are not unknown, and that it is open to the state to pursue the evasive offender and to charge him for the additional costs so incurred.

Compensation rates could be increased significantly over current civil collections through the use of measures short of the threat of punishment—even though there will be some instances in which we have to give up on the possibility of collection. Credit card companies, for example, continue to thrive even though their only legal recourse against nonpayment is the civil law (imprisonment for debt was abolished in the mid-nineteenth century). There are plenty of nonpayers who have been able to get away with it, but there are many more individuals sufficiently concerned with their reputations among lenders to keep the business of extending credit going. Failure to pay compensation for crimes might become part of one's credit history as well as part of one's criminal record; both would be of interest to potential employers, and it would be difficult for nonpaying offenders to escape a range of collateral consequences.

The victims of particularly stubborn nonpayers (or of the truly destitute) need not be left out in the cold. Victims could be compensated from a common fund to which convicted offenders would be required to contribute, rather than being compensated directly by the offender; the costs of administering the fund would be considered part of the costs of the offense, to be borne by offenders. The shortfall caused by nonpaying offenders could then either be distributed over all victims through less than full compensation, or made up by tax revenues (thus distributed over all taxpayers).

C. Provide Opportunities for Reconciliation with Victim and Community

Proposals to replace punishment with restitution often meet with the objection that to do so would be to trivialize the intentional harm done to victims through crime, and to allow the wealthy to purchase the right to commit crimes whenever they choose. But it is unlikely that a person once convicted of a crime would leave the courtroom to resume her life as before, whether or not he is required to make compensation. As Roger Wertheimer points out:

> Wrongdoing can justify denying the wrongdoer claims and
> entitlements—to protection against injury during the wrongdoing, to
> the profits of wrongdoing, to goods needed to compensate victims of
> the wrongdoing. Further, we may properly deny loyalty to the disloyal,
> deny equal opportunity to the treacherous, and deny to the disaffecting
> any claim on our affections. We may justly deny a wrongdoer any claim
> to our generosity, benevolence, esteem, trust, and virtually any of our
> goods. We may desert those who desert us, abandon them to a desert of
> their own making, a lifeless, desolate wasteland bereft of the benefits of
> our community and society.[15]

Although Wertheimer makes these observations in support of retributive punishment, most of the consequences of wrongdoing he notes here have little to do with criminal punishment: they are either social consequences imposed by private individuals repelled by the offender's behavior or civil sanctions imposed by the state for the purpose of compensating the victim. The social consequences, by themselves, can contribute not only to retributive ends but also to crime prevention. The person convicted of theft could expect to find it more difficult to find employment, for example. Rapists and murderers could expect virtual ostracism and constant surveillance. The social stigma created by conviction would have a much greater impact without the intervening prison sentence; offenders who did have a stake in community acceptance might find themselves seeking ways to restore themselves to the good graces of the community.

In such instances the offender might agree to some specific restoration project, which might include apology, payment of compensation, and ongoing work to resolve underlying conflicts. The reconciliation proceeding might substitute for trial (if the victim decided not to press charges after an early reconciliation hearing), or might be undertaken after conviction—perhaps initiated by an offender seeking to restore her good standing.

D. Promote Moral Change Through Personal Attachments

Is this enough? Retributivists and advocates of moral reform press the point that the offender must be made to feel the weight of his wrongdoing, and that he can only be made to do so through hard treatment. But, because of the lack of an emotional bond between the offender and the state, there is little hope that punishment will accomplish this, even supposing that other objections to these theories could be met. It may be that we simply are not in a position to make him see what we want him to see. In those cases where the offender is not so deeply alienated as to be unreachable, however, our best hope of making the communication effective will be through those to whom he does have some emotional attachment. This is the premise of "reintegrative shaming" programs, which, while not unproblematic, hold out some promise of genuine change.

Police in Wagga Wagga, Australia, developed a diversion program for young offenders, based on family group conferences initiated in New Zealand. These programs, though initiated for pragmatic reasons, turned out to mesh well with John Braithwaite's idea of reintegrative shaming and are now explicitly informed by that model.[16] The program is designed for young offenders arrested for less serious offenses who have admitted to their offense. The conference is held at the police station and facilitated by a police officer, whose role is limited to resolving difficulties that arise during the conference and acting as a witness to the agreement. The offender is accompanied by his family and other supporters, and the victim by his or her supporters. The outcome of the conference is determined by the participants. A follow-up conference with the offender and family is held after four to six weeks.[17]

Braithwaite has argued that, when done appropriately, shaming can result in constructive change, as offenders are forced to drop the various rationalizations that they use to convince themselves that their behavior is permissible. One theory identifies five such rationalizations: "They can afford it," "I didn't really hurt anyone," "They're crooks themselves," and "I had to stick by my mates."[18] The conference is designed to break down these rationalizations, primarily by having the victim recount the effects of the offense in the presence of the offender and people close to him. If things unfold according to plan, the offender will find his own supporters chagrined by his behavior, and will accordingly realize the extent of its wrongfulness, show remorse, and seek to make amends. The literature is replete with touching stories of offenders who break down and cry, victims who decide he is not such a bad fellow after all, and families that vigorously support the offender's new efforts to make amends and turn his life around. This is a lot to ask from a brief hearing, and, unsurprisingly, it happens in only a minority of cases.[19] Critics argue that, contrary to the claims of its proponents, reintegrative shaming is less effective in changing offender behavior than the traditional criminal justice approach.

Preliminary results from a large experimental group in Australia show that those randomly assigned to a Family Group Conference on the reintegrative shaming model have resulting attitudes and outcomes generally comparable to those assigned to court, but notably with a large (38 percent) reduction in recidivism for youthful violent offenders.[20] This is a strength of restorative justice programs, which have overall shown a modest reduction in recidivism as compared to the traditional criminal justice approach.[21] The typical outcome of a conference was more likely to include reparations to the victim or community service and less likely to include a fine. Imprisonment was not an option for the conference group, but only a very small percentage of court-assigned offenders were sentenced to imprisonment. Significantly more conference-assigned offenders than court-assigned controls in the Australian study considered their outcome to be "severe."[22]

There are also a few disturbing stories of "shaming" gone wrong. Braithwaite stresses the distinction between "disintegrative" shaming that stigmatizes the offender and drives a wedge between him and the community, and "reintegrative" shaming that causes him to accept the view that his behavior was wrong while conveying the strong message that he is a worthwhile person who can be welcomed back into the community. But where the shaming process is left up to untrained (or poorly trained) individuals, or where the result of conferencing is heavily influenced by the desires of a vengeful victim, the result can be a horror story such as that of a shoplifter required to parade in front of the store wearing a placard: "I stole from this store" or a sex offender required to post a sign on their house and car, "Dangerous Sex Offender—No Children Allowed."[23] These stories provide a caution to those who seek to leave the conference outcome strictly up to the participants, or worse yet, strictly up to the wishes of possibly vengeful victims.

Importantly for present purposes, offender participation in these conferences is usually coerced, in that the offender who declines to participate or fails to carry out the resulting agreement will be sent to court. Thus, the shaming model is dependent upon the punitive model. Insofar as punishment is ruled out by moral considerations, obtaining cooperation through the threat of punishment is similarly ruled out. Some advocates of restorative justice consider voluntary participation a prerequisite.[24] On a practical level, voluntary participants are likely to provide more fertile soil for desired outcomes than those who are coerced. However, expansion of these programs beyond their current clientele of primarily youthful offenders would also mean that participating offenders would be more likely to be entrenched in their behavior and disinclined to repentance.

E. Protect the Community Through Circles of Support

In the Ojibway community of Hollow Water, Manitoba, a widespread pattern of incest and sexual abuse (75 percent of the community of six hundred had been victimized, and 35 percent had offended) was addressed through the traditional method of the Healing Circle. This circle involves everyone who has been or will be touched by the crime or its disclosure.

> They evolved a detailed protocol of 13 steps, from initial disclosure to the Healing Contract to the Cleansing Ceremony. The Healing Contract, designed by people involved in or personally touched by the offence, requires each person to "sign on" to bring certain changes or additions to their relationships with the others. Such contracts are expected to last more than 2 years, given the challenges in bringing true healing. One is still being adhered to 5 years after its creation. If and when the Healing Contract is successfully completed, the Cleansing Ceremony is held to "mark a new beginning for all involved" and to "honour the victimizer for completing the healing contract/process."[25]

Abusers were formally charged with their crimes, and those who pleaded guilty were offered the support of the team. Team members include survivors of abuse and also past victimizers who have completed their "healing work." The team would then request a delay in sentencing as they began their work with the offender and victim(s). They work with the victim to help him or her become strong enough to confront the abuser, as well as with all those who will be affected by disclosure. After the confrontation and initial team efforts to gain the cooperation of the abuser in the healing process, the team prepares a presentence report indicating the sincerity of the offender's participation and the amount of work that remains to be done. Although at the start of the project the team members held the view that a prison term must be imposed in "serious" cases, they have concluded after long involvement in healing work, first, that there is little correlation between the offender's degree of culpability and the severity of its effects on victims; and second, that the threat of incarceration only serves to impede the healing process:

> In order to break the cycle, we believe that victimizer accountability must be to, and support must come from, those most affected by the victimization: the victim, the family/ies, and the community. Removal of the victimizer from those who must, and are best able to, hold him/her accountable, and to offer him/her support, adds complexity to already existing dynamics of denial, guilt and shame. The healing process of all parties is therefore at best delayed, and most often actually deterred.[26]

The Healing Circle approach requires the ongoing involvement of all those affected, as well as of medical professionals and team members. Its ultimate goal is to repair the relationships destroyed or impaired by abuse. Holding the offender accountable is an essential part of this process. Team members, informed by their own experience of abuse, work closely with offenders to overcome the psychological barriers to acknowledging responsibility. The Hollow Water approach recognizes the complexity and breadth of the effects of serious crimes, and in turn addresses them in a way that is similarly complex and far reaching.

Use of the Healing Circle is not limited to cases of endemic offending such as that found at Hollow Water, but is used in cases involving individual offenders as well. One published example is the use of a Healing Circle in a case of rape in the Innu community of Sheshahit, Labrador. As in Hollow Water, the process began between conviction and sentencing in a criminal court. After extensive preparatory work, a Healing Circle was held with friends and family of both parties to allow the offender an opportunity to take responsibility for his actions and to allow the victim to present "what needed to happen for her to feel that the situation was being made more right." After the release of much emotion by the participants and the expression of recommendations for sentencing, victim and offender (who had been previously acquainted) were sufficiently reconciled to embrace one another.[27]

The most striking feature of the Healing Circle approach is that, despite rejection of punishment, it is clearly an approach that takes crime seriously— more seriously, indeed, than the typical punitive approach. The emphasis is on restoring damaged relationships—between offender and victim, and between offender and community—rather than on the moral badness of the offender. Offenders are nonetheless made to face the harm done by their behavior and to try to make amends. Their accountability is assured by close monitoring. As with most programs, this one operates in the shadow of the criminal justice system, in that the alternative to participation in the healing circle is traditional sentencing by the court. Moreover, the influence of the group's eventual sentencing recommendation is undoubtedly a factor for many offenders. The desire for restoration would have to replace coercion as a motivation for offenders to participate, which might make it more difficult to secure their participation. It would also mean, however, that the efforts of those who did participate would be more likely to be genuine, and that there would be continued pressure on organizers to assure the meaningfulness of the program.

The approach of the healing circle is similar to that of the reintegrative shaming model, but with the important difference of ongoing participation rather than one or two brief conferences. If the shaming conference is more likely than the traditional formal trial to precipitate moral change, the ongoing involvement of team members, importantly including past offenders, in the life of the offender is more likely yet to make a real difference. The contract that persists over time and the ongoing participation of the team in the life of the offender are the key factors that make it plausible that real change and real healing can occur, even for the repeat sexual offenders in these cases.

The Ojibway approach is, of course, much more suited to a small, closed community than to the typical modern setting. But a somewhat similar approach has been taken by "circle of support" programs in Canada and the United Kingdom. These circles, formed after the offender's release from prison, consist of a group of four to six people who befriend the offender, offering both practical and emotional support for the process of reintegrating with the community. They also help to reassure the community by taking on the responsibility for confronting the offender over any risky behavior. The idea behind these groups is to help even these despised offenders live safely in the community, while also keeping the community safe.[28] Such programs may succeed where the threat of punishment fails, and offenders anxious to soften the social effects of their conviction might readily volunteer to participate.

Whether there has been a reconciliation proceeding or a formal conviction, the offender who finds himself reviled and excluded in various ways may (immediately or eventually) wish to take the steps necessary to restore himself to good standing. The steps required for a particular instance of wrongdoing could be specified at sentencing or at a reconciliation hearing, but if not, it is likely that a common understanding on what kinds of behavior, and how much of it, would count as expiation for a particular type of crime would soon develop. A formal apology and acceptance of responsibility is a likely first step. Property offenses might be considered fully expiated when the victim has been compensated in full—or some further step, such as volunteer service, might be needed as well. Offenders who have done physical harm to others might be more readily forgiven if they volunteered to risk their own physical safety to save others through rescue work, or performed services for the physically disabled. Those who have harmed the community at large through uncivil conduct might restore themselves to general respect by volunteering for cleanup or beautification projects. And many offenders would be able to smooth the path to reacceptance by seeking to remedy any personal failings (impulsiveness, irascibility, avarice, drug dependence, lack of marketable skills) that led them to offend. There might be a place, as well, for a formal restoration proceeding, like the Ojibway Cleansing Ceremony, at which the offender's efforts to redeem herself would be recognized and his restoration to the good graces of the community noted on her public record.

Those guilty of the most serious crimes, such as murder, would appropriately find expiation a lifelong effort. The point, however, is not that the offender should suffer. He should not subject himself to deprivation for its own sake; instead, he should seek to do good, and in that way to change, little by little, the moral quality of his own life. We are all, in moral terms, only the sum of our actions, and some wrongs are so grave that they threaten to define us. Yet it is also true that some exceptional individuals have been able to redefine themselves through later actions and so to escape the shadow of their crimes. Some will never be able to restore themselves fully, no matter what they do; but, because everyone is capable of some good actions, there is no one who cannot at least mitigate the community's judgment of his moral worth.

IV. Conclusion

Looking back at the arguments against punishment, we can see that, while they indicate that radical change is needed, they do not entail surrender to crime or even the abandonment of our entire current approach to criminal justice. There are many other things we can do to secure our safety, and many more appropriate ways to respond to wrongdoing than to impose harm on the wrongdoer. It is time for us to take these alternatives seriously, and to begin as soon as we can to reduce our reliance on punishment to serve purposes which, insofar as they are worthwhile, are better served by measures that do not require us to do wrong ourselves.

NOTES

1. Bruce Western et al., "Crime, Punishment, and American Inequality," unpublished manuscript, June 2003. Available online at http://www.princeton.edu/~western/ineq2.pdf; Internet; accessed November 4, 2003.

2. Income inequality in a population can be measured by the Lorenz curve, which maps the percentage of households, from lowest to highest income, against the percentage of total income they have. On this curve, perfect equality would be represented by a 45-degree line. A sag in the Lorenz curve below the 45-degree line represents inequality. The Gini coefficient captures this sag numerically by comparing the area under the Lorenz curve for a population to the total area under the line of perfect equality. A Gini coefficient of 0 thus represents perfect equality, while a Gini coefficient of 1 would be perfect inequality (top 1 percent have all the income). The Gini coefficient for the United States in 1998 was .456. U.S. Census, *The Changing Shape of the Nation's Income Distribution, 1947–1998*, June 2000, fig. 2. Available online at http://www.census.gov/prod/2000pubs/p60-204.pdf; Internet; accessed January 5, 2004. Worldwide, the most unequal countries (e.g., Sierra Leone, Brazil, South Africa) have coefficients of around .6 and the most equal (e.g., Slovak Republic, Sweden, Norway) around .25. Data from Luxembourg Income Study, available online at http://www.lisproject.org/; Internet; accessed January 11, 2004.

3. See, e.g., C. Hsieh and M. D. Pugh, "Poverty, Income Inequality, and Violent Crime: A Meta-Analysis of Recent Aggregate Data Studies," *Criminal Justice Review* 18(2): 182–202 (1993), concluding that both poverty and income inequality were associated with violent crime; B. P. Kennedy, I. Kawachi, D. Prothrow-Stisth, K. Lochner, and B. Gibbs, "Social Capital, Income Inequality, and Firearm Violent Crime," *Social Science and Medicine* 47, no. 1 (1998): 7–17, concluding that both income inequality and lack of social capital were highly correlated with firearm violent crime rates in the United States. Western et al. found that correlations were weaker at the county level. "Inequality," 31.

4. S. Messner and R. Rosenfeld, *Crime and the American Dream*, 3rd ed. (Belmont, CA: Wadsworth, 2000), 7–10.

5. Western et al., "Inequality," 36.

6. Robert J. Sampson and William Julius Wilson, "Toward a Theory of Race, Crime, and Urban Inequality," in *Crime and Inequality*, ed. John Hagan and Ruth D. Peterson (Stanford, CA: Stanford University Press, 1995).

7. William Julius Wilson, *The Truly Disadvantaged: The Inner City, the Underclass, and Public Policy* (Chicago: University of Chicago Press, 1987).

8. National Low Income Housing Coalition, *2003 Advocates' Guide to Housing and Community Development Policy*, 87–90. Available online at http://www.nlihc.org/advocates/2003ag.pdf; Internet; accessed December 18, 2003.

9. Sampson and Wilson, "Race, Crime, and Inequality," 42–43.

10. Messner and Rosenfeld, *Crime and the American Dream*, 7–8, 101–104.

11. Kathleen Daly, "Restorative Justice: The Real Story," *Punishment and Society* 4, no. 1 (2002): 55–79. Available online at http://www.gu.edu.au/school/ccj/kdaly_docs/kdpaper12.pdf; Internet; accessed January 11, 2004. Page references are to Web version.

12. Gerry Johnstone, *Restorative Justice* (Cullompton, Devon, U.K.: Willan 2002), 80.

13. Daly, "Real Story," 26.

14. Friedrich Nietzsche, "'Guilt,' 'Bad Conscience,' and the Like," second essay in *On the Genealogy of Morals* in *On the Genealogy of Morals and Ecce Homo*, trans. Walter Kaufman (New York: Vintage Books, 1967).

15. Roger Wertheimer, "Understanding Retribution," *Criminal Justice Ethics* 3 (Summer/Fall 1983): 22–23.

16. Terry O'Connell, "From Wagga Wagga to Minnesota," paper presented at the First North American Conference on Conferencing, Minneapolis, August 6–8, 1998. Available online at http://www.restorativepractices.org/Pages/nacc/nacc_oco.html; Internet; accessed November 15, 2003; John Braithwaite, *Crime, Shame and Reintegration* (Cambridge: Cambridge University Press, 1989).

17. New South Wales Law Reform Commission, "Community Based Sentences," chap. 9 in *Discussion Paper 33: Sentencing* (April 1996). Available online at http://www.austlii.edu.au/au/other/nswlrc/dp33/9_78.html; Internet; accessed January 10, 2004.

18. Johnstone, *Restorative Justice*, 97, citing John Braithwaite, "Restorative Justice: Assessing Optimistic and Pessimistic Accounts," in *Crime and Justice: A Review of Research*, vol. 25, ed. Michael Tonry (Chicago: University of Chicago Press, 1999), 47.

19. Daly, "Real Story," 24–25.

20. Heather Strang, Geoffrey C. Barnes, John Braithwaite, and Lawrence W. Sherman, *Experiments in Restorative Policing: A Progress Report on the Canberra Reintegrative Shaming Experiments (RISE) July 1999.* Available online at http://www.aic.gov.au/rjustice/rise/progress/1999-6.pdf; Internet; accessed January 5, 2004. The leader of the Wagga Wagga effort, Terry O'Connell, reports that recently the police coordinators have been replaced by outside facilitators. O'Connell, "From Wagga Wagga to Minnesota."

21. John Braithwaite, *Restorative Justice and Responsive Regulation* (Oxford: Oxford University Press, 2002), 54–66. Braithwaite reviews the results of a large number of empirical studies, most of which showed some improvement over traditional practices, and some of which showed dramatic improvement.

22. Strang et al., *Experiments in Restorative Policing.*

23. Johnstone, *Restorative Justice*, 124.

24. Jeff Latimer, Craig Dowden, and Danielle Muise, *The Effectiveness of Restorative Justice Practices: A Meta-Analysis* (Ottawa: Department of Justice, Canada, 2001), 5.

25. Rupert Ross, "Duelling Paradigms? Western Criminal Justice versus Aboriginal Community Healing," in *Justice as Healing: A Newsletter on Aboriginal Concepts of Justice.* Native Law Centre of Canada, Spring 1995. Excerpt available online at http://www.usask.ca/nativelaw/jah_ross.html; Internet; accessed October 20, 2003. See also Berma Bushie, "Community Holistic Circle Healing: A Community Approach," available online at http://www.iirp.org/Pages/vt/vt_bushie.html; accessed November 15, 2003.

26. Ross, "Duelling Paradigms?"

27. "A Healing Circle in the Innu Community of Sheshashit," *Justice as Healing* 2, no. 2 (Spring 1997). Also available online at http://www.usask.ca/nativelaw/jah_sellon.html; Internet; accessed October 20, 2003.

28. Johnstone, *Restorative Justice*, 106.

*Deirdre Golash is associate professor emerita in the department of justice, law and society at American University, Washington, D.C. In addition to being the author of *The Case Against Punishment*, from which this selection is taken, she is the editor of *Freedom of Expression in a Diverse World*.

Golash, Deirdre. "What If Punishment Is Not Justified?" In *The Case Against Punishment*. New York: New York University Press, 2005, pp. 153–172, 193–195.

Criminal Justice and Legal Reparations as an Alternative to Punishment[1]

by Geoffrey Sayre-McCord*

[...]

III. THE FAMILIAR JUSTIFICATIONS FOR PUNISHMENT

The familiar justifications of punishment fall into three groups, according to whether they appeal primarily to considerations of justice and desert,[18] or to utility and the prevention of crime,[19] or to the role of punishment in expressing moral condemnation and contributing to moral education.[20] The division is, of course, more than a little artificial; members of society might deserve to have institutions that work to prevent crime, and respecting constraints of justice might contribute significantly to overall utility, and both justice and utility might require mechanisms that forcefully condemn certain behavior and work effectively towards the moral education of actual and potential offenders.[21] Nonetheless, I will discuss them as if they were separate and independent.

A. Appeals to Justice and Desert

Often, arguments offered in defense of punishment take the proper focus of considerations of justice to be the criminal and what he deserves for having committed the crime. Sometimes, the thought is that in committing a crime the criminal has acted immorally and, because the immoral deserve to suffer, criminals deserve to suffer. Punishment is justified, then, because it involves giving the criminal what he deserves. As H.L.A. Hart puts the view, "the justification for punishing ... is that the return of suffering for moral evil voluntarily done, is itself just or morally good."[22] If this is the argument , one might of course question the claim that those who commit crimes have *ipso facto* done something evil, or the claim that those who do something evil deserve to suffer, or the claim that those who deserve to suffer (because they have done evil) are rightly made to suffer *by the state*. I have my doubts on all three fronts, but here will simply assume that even if criminals are morally defective and therefore deserve to suffer, it is not the state's role to make them suffer for that reason.[23] I am not saying that a state never rightly makes someone suffer. Assuming the state's coercive power is sometimes justified it will almost surely sometimes justifiably coerce in circumstances where someone is thereby made to suffer. What seems mistaken is the suggestion that the justification of such coercion rests directly on the state's determination of moral defect. Making people suffer *because of their immoral acts* is not legitimately within the state's purview.[24] Moreover, to the extent one holds that those who act immorally deserve to suffer and that the state is properly involved in distributing that suffering in proportion to the immorality, such a distribution of suffering would it seems have to take into account not just how immoral the criminal is, but also how much he has already suffered.[25]

Other times, the thought is that punishing a criminal is a way of acknowledging him as a responsible agent and he deserves this acknowledgment (whatever he has done).[26] This line of thought does not depend on holding that the criminal is evil or immoral at all, but instead sees treating him a certain way, within a public system of justice, as part and parcel of recognizing his standing as a responsible agent. Here a system of reparations and a system of punishment can agree that a criminal actually deserves to be treated as a responsible agent—to do otherwise is to commit an offense against him. But agreeing on this is not yet to find grounds for punishing the criminal as opposed to responding to his crime in some other way, as long as the alternative constitutes a way of acknowledging his standing as a responsible agent. Indeed, it is a bit puzzling why anyone would think punishment *per se* is important to this acknowledgment, except incidentally as its legitimacy is seen as presupposing a finding to the effect that the criminal is responsible for the crime for which he is being punished. Of course this link to responsibility is maintained within a system of reparations that demands efforts toward making amends only from those who have been found to be responsible for the crime in question.

Still other times, a system of punishment is seen as justified to the extent, and on the grounds, that it would (under the appropriate circumstances) secure the consent of those subjected to it. Here the idea is often that people have a right to have their standing as moral agents recognized and that this is done properly only when one's treatment of them is such that they themselves would (under the appropriate circumstances) give their consent to it. Yet if a system of punishment might secure such consent, it seems pretty clear that a system that demanded reparations in place of punishment would likewise secure the relevant consent (and, likely, more easily). So, to the extent properly recognizing the moral standing of others involves subjecting them only to institutions that could, under the appropriate circumstances, secure their consent, reparations looks as if it would stand at least no worse than would punishment in giving the due recognition.

In any case, reparations, unlike punishment, finds a place for the thought that criminals—in addition to having a right to be treated as responsible agents—might also deserve the opportunity to make amends (a right that runs in parallel with the duty to make amends that reparations recognizes, which is in turn a duty that reflects the rights of those suffering the offense). A new injustice comes in (except perhaps in the most extreme cases) if a person who commits a crime is denied the opportunity to make amends. There are limits here—some crimes are so heinous that , in committing them, a person has forfeited this right—but most crimes surely don't fall into this category. And even those that do fall in this category might so fall more because the criminal has established himself as beyond the pale than because he would not have a right to make amends if he could take advantage of it. While I am somewhat ambivalent about seeing this as a right the criminal has, I think there is a point to the idea that people should be given the opportunity to "pay their debt to society" and to be free, as a result, of further recriminations. This idea is sometimes in play when people see undergoing punishment as a way of earning back one's place in society. There is, on this picture, a kind of rehabilitation to be sought, not a rehabilitation that depends on a reformation in the character of the criminal (as I noted above), but instead one that is accomplished by bringing the criminal back into society—by reinstating him.

So far the justifications discussed have concentrated on the idea that the criminal, for one reason or another, deserves to be punished. Other attempts to justify punishment by appeal to considerations of desert, however, see the proper focus as being on the victim and what he deserves as a victim. The general idea is that the victim has a right to have the criminal punished—perhaps as a way for the state to annul the crime, or as a way to right the wrong, or as a reaffirmation of the victim's standing. In each case, there is a serious question as to how punishment in particular is supposed to be crucial to meeting these aims. Why does making the criminal suffer annul his crime? How does the punishment right the wrong? In what way does it reaffirm the victim's standing? I ask not because I think punishment cannot possibly do these things, but because an explanation of how and why punishment might do them will reveal, I believe, that the difference between punishment (with its intentional infliction of pain) and reparations, is irrelevant to the explanation. This is because punishment, so far as I can see, serves these purposes only by taking on a conventionally established symbolic role. Punishment works to "annul a crime" or "right a wrong" or reaffirm a victim's standing not naturally, so to speak, but only in a context within which suffering the intentional infliction of pain or harm of the sort in question is accepted as having achieved these aims. Within the bounds set by general considerations of justice, precisely what can achieve these aims reflects a shared understanding of what to accept. What might serve as proper payment for offense, like what might serve as legal tender, is largely a matter of what people collectively are willing to recognize and treat as such.

If this is right, then to the extent punishment can reasonably be seen as annulling the crime, righting the wrong, or reaffirming the victim's standing, reparations can as well, as long as it can take on the crucial symbolic role. At the same time, I think, reparations can more effectively speak to the demand that the crime really be annulled (i.e., wiped out) and the wrong righted and the victim's rights reaffirmed, since it involves demanding of the criminal that he make efforts directly designed at accomplishing these ends. Here the system of reparations and a system of punishment can agree that a victim deserves to have the state enforce his rights where this might involve instituting efficient protections of it and reasserting them in contexts where they have been challenged or breached. But a system of reparations goes on to hold that he also deserves from the perpetrator of the crime effort to repair the situation and make amends for the offense.

It is reasonable, though, to see crime as an offense against not only particular victims (when there are victims) but also as an offense against society at large. As a result, some attempts to justify punishment give pride of place, in appealing to considerations of justice, either (i) to the idea that society as a whole has a right (say of self-protection) to punish the criminal for the violation of its rules[27] or (ii) to the idea that members of society deserve a fair distribution of social burdens which has been upset by the criminal (who, in committing a crime, shirks the burden of restraint that the law places on all).[28] Either way, punishment is justified on the grounds that law-abiding citizens have a certain claim of justice that requires allocating certain burdens (of suffering a threat or of self-restraint) to those who voluntarily break the law. Punishment is supposed to speak to burdens unjustly imposed or shirked by criminals by imposing new burdens on them and thereby establishing the balance of burdens demanded by fairness. Reparations too, though, can countenance shifting burdens in the name of justice. Yet it would do the shifting not by introducing a brand new burden—the pain of punishment—but by demanding that criminals (who have either imposed or shirked burdens) compensate others for the burdens even as it also acknowledges, and focuses on, the fact that in committing the crime they have done more and worse than simply imposing or dodging a burden—they have failed to treat others with the respect they are due. This aspect of their crimes calls not for the imposition of pain or some new burden, but rather an effort at reparations on the part of the criminals.

Putting aside the—I think indefensible—claim that punishment by the state is justified and demanded directly and simply by the immorality a criminal's acts exhibit, the various arguments for punishment that appeal to what the criminal, or the victim, or society at large, deserve all capture something important. Yet they all, also, mobilize considerations that are not essentially tied to punishment. In fact, it seems to me that a system of reparations clearly speaks to these considerations more directly and effectively than does punishment.

B. Appeals to Utility and the Prevention of Crime

Of course appeals to justice and desert are often not the primary justifications offered for punishment, even if such considerations are often seen as constraining what sort of punishment might be justified by other considerations. Long ago, Protagoras argued that "he who desires to inflict rational punishment does not punish for the sake of a past wrong which cannot be undone; he has regard to the future and is desirous that the man who is punished, and he who sees him punished, may be deterred from doing wrong again."[29] Ever since, one of the main justifications for punishment has been found in its serving as an effective deterrent—thanks either to punishment effectively reducing recidivism or to the prospect of punishment working as a disincentive. This justification plays right to the core of punishment by claiming that the pain punishment intentionally inflicts keeps people from committing crimes they otherwise would commit.

There are of course familiar moral worries about this sort of justification that arise unless it is combined in some way with effective constraints on who might be liable to punishment and on just how much punishment might be administered.[30] Absent such constraints a direct appeal to the benefits one might secure by intentionally inflicting pain on people risks countenancing the 'punishment' of innocent people and the torturing of people, innocent or not, for minor as well as major crimes.

Yet even with appropriate constraints in place, the plausibility of a deterrence justification of punishment is seriously undermined by the evidence available— evidence that seems to show that the prospect of pain (and punishment in general) is an ineffective deterrent (at least as long as the punishment is not draconian), especially among those disposed to be criminals in the first place.[31] Witness the high recidivism rates among offenders who have been punished and the extraordinary failure of programs like Scared Straight that are aimed at making vivid the prospect of pain as a consequence of crime.[32]

Any justification of punishment that speaks to what motivates criminals needs to recognize that a great deal other than the prospect of pain is in play—including impulsiveness, perceived injustice, desire for excitement, apparent lack of better options, the need to establish one's standing, honor...[33] Threatening pain, as a system of punishment does, speaks to none of these, nor does it seem likely to have much impact on what, down the road, might come to motivate those who have been subjected to punishment. All it does is try to shift the balance of considerations by introducing one—the prospect of pain—that evidently does not figure very heavily when it comes to criminal behavior. Of course punishment can, under the rubric of inflicting harm, impose costs on criminals other than the costs of pain. Presumably a system of punishment that takes into account the extent to which criminals seem not to give significant weight to the prospect of pain would devise punishments that speak to depriving criminals of what they do value. Even then, though, evidence suggests that, to a large extent, long term and uncertain prospects of the imposition of a cost do not figure prominently in deterring crime.[34] Rather, the near term perceived certainty of some penalty or other—pretty much regardless of severity—appears to have a significantly greater deterrent effect. Indeed there is some evidence that increasing the severity of penalties actually increases crime rates.[35] The very fact that the severity of the penalty (given equal certainty) has at most little effect suggests that the importance of certainty of penalty is found not in its providing a cost (the imposition of which is central to punishment) but in something else. Plausibly, the relevant something else is, at least in part, its providing a clear message that the behavior is forbidden. This, however, is a message easily—and well—conveyed by a system of reparations.[36]

There is at least some additional evidence that what matters to deterrence is the message that the violation of the law is to be taken seriously. A number of studies suggest that police "cautions" as opposed to court appearances,[37] probation as opposed to conviction and fine,[38] and being discharged as opposed to being charged and fined,[39] all showed significant increases in subsequent criminality. When the authorities do not take the crime seriously, neither do the criminals. Yet there was no decrease in criminality when the serious responses were augmented by more severe penalties. It seems that once it is clear that the crime is being taken seriously, increasing the severity of the penalty has no positive impact on recidivism.[40] A reasonable hypothesis is that what is crucial, when it comes to an institutional response to crime, is that the significance of the offense be unambiguously conveyed. In any case, however much people think it a matter of common sense that punishment deters, the evidence shows fairly convincingly that the relationship between crime and the prospect of punishment is neither as simple nor as reliable as many would suppose.

C. Appeals to the Expressive and Educative Role of Punishment

That society must convey the significance of criminal offenses is one of the main ideas behind the suggestion that punishment is justified by its expressive or educative role. The thought is that a society can effectively mark its condemnation of certain behaviors, and thus conveys that they are wrong, only by backing prohibitions with threats of punishment. At the same time, society's willingness to follow through on the punishments and enforce citizens rights is a way of affirming both that the violation of the rights will not be tolerated and that the person whose rights were violated has standing in the community. To let violations go by, to offer only cautions or merely sentence someone to probation is to send the message that the violation, and by implication the person violated, is not to be taken very seriously. Punishment, so the argument goes, is society's way of not letting such things go by.[41]

I do think there is substantial evidence (cited above) that a light touch of the law will engender disregard both for it and for what it claims to protect. However, the evidence does not show that punishment is the best, let alone the only, way for society to indicate the significance it attaches to respecting the law. The expressive function of punishment, as important as it is, is pretty clearly a function that can be played by something other than punishment—and to better effect, I suspect. Indeed, to the extent there are grounds for thinking increasing the severity of penalties has no deterrent effect there is reason to think the important and effective message is not centrally conveyed by the punishment itself even when punishments are in place, but rather by society palpably taking the offense seriously. And conveying that the offense is to be taken seriously is something enforcing efforts at reparations would seemingly do effectively.

In addition to thinking punishment can play a crucial expressive role, when it comes to conveying condemnation, many have thought punishment works (either via the expressive role, or in some other way) to reform the criminal morally, to make him a better person. On this view, as Jean Hampton presents it, "there is a concrete moral *goal* which punishment should be designed to accomplish, and that goal includes the benefiting of the criminal himself. The state, as it punishes the lawbreaker, is trying to promote his moral personality . . . "[42] To the extent this goal is legitimately adopted by the state, the question remains as to whether punishment is the best way of achieving it. Hampton appeals to punishment's capacity to communicate a moral message in defending its educative role. And surely to the extent punishment does actually advance the cause, it is partly by being a means of effective communication. But, as I have already suggested, there is every reason to think that a system of reparations could play the same communicative role. Of course, punishment might also serve the goal of moral improvement in some other way. It might be, for instance, that by altering incentives for available actions, punishment works to change what people choose to do, and thus what habits (and so, character) they develop. Again, though, the evidence suggests that whatever impact punishment might have on incentives, it works poorly as a deterrent (and therefore cannot be working positively to change character by leading people away from crime). Most strikingly, it seems that increasing severity (which presumably increases disincentives) is often counter-productive. Still, if punishment does work to promote a criminal's "moral personality" either by getting him to act in certain ways or by forcing him to take responsibility for his actions, a system of reparations could justifiably claim the same advantages.

This has been, I realize, a whirlwind tour through what are, in point of fact, highly complex and subtle arguments. I have not even come close to doing them justice. My purpose, though, has not been to evaluate the arguments or to refine them to the point where I might fully endorse one or the other. The strategy has been, instead, to convey the extent to which arguments that are offered in defense of punishment regularly leave unexplored an important and attractive possibility—legal reparations. The quick discussion of the various familiar justifications of punishment are thus offered primarily as an invitation to those who find one or another attractive to ask whether reparations might actually speak to the morally legitimate purposes of the criminal law more effectively than does punishment.

[…]

V. CONCLUSION

I have tried, in this paper, to describe and defend a system of legal reparations that might serve as a genuine, and genuinely attractive, alternative to the current practice of subjecting criminals to punishment.

I have not addressed the practical problems that might come with changing over from a system of punishment to one of reparations. I suspect, though, that the change might be effected without drama by gradually introducing alternative sentencing programs that embrace reparations (rather than punishment or treatment) as their underlying aim. Nor have I explored the practical complexities involved in the actual workings of a system of reparations. Most significantly, I have pretty much passed over the question of how appropriate reparations for specific offenses might be determined. There are, undeniably, serious issues here. Yet these problems have identical twins that stand as problems for any justifiable system of punishment. So they do not represent distinctive problems for a system of reparations. Moreover, by and large whatever solutions work in one system can (I believe) be fairly easily adapted to the other.

What I have done is argue that the most plausible justifications for punishment—whether they appeal to justice and desert, or to utility and deterrence, or to moral expression and education—all actually recommend a system of legal reparations. If this is right, then the best justifications of punishment are not justifications of punishment at all but are instead elements in a justification for an important alternative. This alternative, I maintain, has the signal advantage that, by enforcing efforts at making amends, it steers clear of the morally problematic practice of intentionally inflicting harm while publicly, clearly, and productively acknowledging crimes as offenses that call for redress.

NOTES

[...]

18. See, for example, Immanuel Kant's *The Metaphysical Elements of Justice* (Indianapolis: Bobbs-Merrill, 1965); Jeffrie Murphy's "Marxism and Retribution," in *Retribution, Justice, and Therapy* (Dordrecht: D. Reidel, 1979); and David E. Cooper's "Hegel's Theory of Punishment," in *Hegel's Political Philosophy*, edited by Z.A. Pelczynski (Cambridge: Cambridge University Press, 1971).

19. See, for a classic example, Jeremy Bentham's *An Introduction to the Principles of Morals and Legislation*, edited by J.H. Burns and H.L.A. Hart (London: Athlone Press, 1970).

20. See, for example, Joel Feinberg's "The Expressive Function of Punishment" in *Doing and Deserving* (Princeton: Princeton University Press, 1970), pp. 95–118; Herbert Morris's "A Paternalistic Theory of Punishment," *American Philosophical Quarterly* 18 (1981), pp. 263–71; and Jean Hampton's "The Moral Education Theory of Punishment," *Philosophy and Public Affairs* 13 (1984), pp. 208–38.

21. Most attempts to justify punishment mix these various considerations in some way or other, which seems only reasonable in that they all appear to capture something both relevant and important. John Rawls' "Two Concepts of Rules," *Philosophical Review* 64 (1955), pp. 3–32, is especially concerned with sorting out the mix, as are H.L.A. Hart's "Prolegomenon to the Principles of Punishment," *op. cit.* and Thomas Hill's "Kant on Punishment: A Coherent Mix of Deterrence and Retribution?" in *Respect, Pluralism, and Justice* (Oxford: Oxford University Press, 2000), pp. 173–199.

22. *Punishment and Responsibility*, p. 231.

23. There are all sorts of reasons for rejecting this as the state's role, not least being that the state is in no position to determine how immoral people are over-all, and such a determination would presumably be necessary in order to settle how much punishment a particular person deserves. See Gertrude Ezorsky, "The Ethics of Punishment," in Gertrude Ezorsky (ed.), *Philosophical Perspectives on Punishment* (Albany: State University of New York Press, 1972), in which she argues that an appeal to a criminal's deserving punishment because of his moral defects would require balancing "all of his moral wrongs against the sufferings of his entire life" (p. xxvi) in order to determine whether, for instance, he has already suffered enough.

24. See Jeffrie Murphy, "Retributivism and the State's Interest in Punishment," in *NOMOS XXVII: Criminal Justice*, edited by J.R. Pennock and J. Chapman (New York: New York University Press, 1985), pp. 156–64.

25. At the same time, this view seems also to encourage the idea that the law should expand to cover all immorality or at least that all such immorality is properly within the domain of the state as it exercises its power to distribute suffering. See Gertrude Ezorsky's "The Ethics of Punishment," in *Philosophical Perspectives on Punishment, op. cit.*, pp. xxiv–xxvi.

26. See Herbert Morris's "Persons and Punishment," in *Punishment and Rehabilitation*, edited by Jeffrie Murphy (Belmont: Wadsworth Publishing Company, 1973), pp. 40–64.

27. See Phillip Montague's "Punishment and Societal Defense," *Criminal Justice Ethics*, 2 (1983), pp. 30–36.

28. See Herbert Morris's "Punishment and Fairness," *The Monist*, 52 (1968), pp. 476–79.

29. Plato. *Protagoras*, 324b, translated by B. Jowett, revised by Martin Ostwald, 1956 (Indianapolis: Bobbs-Merrill, 1956), p. 22.

30. See H. L. A. Hart's "Prolegomenon to the Principles of Punishment," *op. cit.*

31. See David Farrington, "Social, Psychological and Biological Influences on Juvenile Delinquency and Adult Crime," in *Explaining Criminal Behaviour*, edited by W. Buikhuisen and S.A. Mednick (New York: E.J. Brill, 1988), pp. 68–89; J.H. Satterfield, "Childhood Diagnostic and Neurophysiological Predictors of Teenage Arrest Rates: An Eight-year Prospective Study," in *The Causes of Crime: New Biological Approaches* edited by S.A. Mednick, T.E. Moffitt, and S.A. Stack (Cambridge: Cambridge University Press, 1987), pp. 146–167; J. Hinton, M. O'Neill, S. Hamilton, and M. Burke, "Psychophysiological Differentiation Between Psychopathic and Schizophrenic Abnormal Offenders," *British Journal of Social and Clinical Psychology*, 19 (1980), pp. 257–269; and *Deterrence and Incapacitation: Estimating the Effects of Criminal Sanctions on Crime Rates* edited by Alfred Blumstein, Jacqueline Cohen, and Daniel Nagin (Washington, D.C.: National Academy of Sciences, 1978).

32. See A.C. Petrosino, C. Turpin-Petrosino, and J.O. Finckenauer "Wellmeaning programs can have harmful effects! Lessons from experiments of programs such as Scared Straight." *Crime & Delinquency* 46 (2000), pp. 354–379; J.C. Buchner and M. Chesney-Lind, "Dramatic Cures for Juvenile Crime: An Evaluation of a Prisoner-run Delinquency Prevention Program," *Criminal Justice and Behavior*, 10 (1983), pp. 227–247; and R.V. Lewis, "Scared Straight-California Style," *Criminal Justice and Behavior*, 10 (1983), pp. 284–289.

33. See Joan McCord, "He Did It Because He Wanted To . . . ," W. Osgood (ed.) *Nebraska Symposium on Motivation: Motivation and Delinquency* (Lincoln: University of Nebraska Press, 1997), pp. 1–43.

34. See T. E. Moffitt, "The Learning Theory Model of Punishment: Implications for Delinquency Deterrence," *Criminal Justice and Behavior*, 10 (1983), pp. 131–158.

35. See G. Antunes and A.L. Hunt, "The Impact of Certainty and Severity of Punishment on Levels of Crime in American States: An Extended Analysis," *Journal of Criminal Law and Criminology*, 64 (1973), pp. 489–493.

36. There are, of course, other possibilities. It may be, for instance, that certainty offsets an otherwise dramatic discount criminals might place on future costs.

37. David P. Farrington and T. Bennett, "Police Cautioning of Juveniles in London," *British Journal of Criminology*, 21 (1981), pp. 123–135.

38. D. Glaser and M.A. Gordon, "Profitable Penalties for Lower Level Courts," *Judicature*, 73 (1990), pp. 248–252.

39. David P. Farrington, S.G. Osborn, and D.J. West, "The Persistence of Labeling Effects," *British Journal of Criminology*, 18 (1978), pp. 277–284.

40. This fits nicely with the research concerning the impact of certainty to the extent low certainty is due to lack of enforcement or casual or inconsistent treatment of offenders that would convey the message that the offenses in question are not being taken very seriously.

41. For an account of punishment that emphasizes its expressive role, see Joel Feinberg's "The Expressive Function of Punishment," in his *Doing and Deserving* (Princeton: Princeton

University Press, 1970), pp. 95–118; and Robert Nozick's *Philosophical Explanations* (Cambridge: Harvard University Press, 1981), pp. 363–397.

42. "The Moral Education Theory of Punishment," in *Punishment*, edited by A.J. Simmons, M. Cohen, J. Cohen, and C. Beitz (Princeton: Princeton University Press, 1995), pp. 112–142, p. 119. See also Herbert Morris' "A Paternalistic Theory of Punishment," *American Philosophical Quarterly*, 18 (1981), pp. 263–271; and R.A. Duff's *Trials and Punishments* (Cambridge: Cambridge University Press, 1986).

*Geoffrey **Sayre-McCord** is the Morehead Alumni Distinguished Professor in the Department of Philosophy at the University of North Carolina, Chapel Hill. He is director of UNC's *Philosophy, Politics, and Economics Program* and a Professorial Fellow in Philosophy at the University of Edinburgh. He has published extensively on moral theory, epistemology, and modern philosophy and edited *Essays on Moral Realism* and *Hume: Moral Philosophy*.

Sayre-McCord, Geoffrey. "Criminal Justice and Legal Reparations as an Alternative to Punishment." *Philosophical Issues* 11, no. 1 (October 2001): 510–518, 525–529.